FLYING THE
CANYONS
OF THE SKY

FLYING THE

CANYONS OF THE SKY:

Navigations of an Aviator's Soul

MEMOIR BY
Neal Schupbach

Carl,

Thanks for your help!
Always the Best for
you AND yours.

Neal Schupbach

Some names, places and events throughout this book have been altered to protect confidentiality and security.

Schupbach, Neal, 1957-
Flying the Canyons of the Sky: Navigations of an Aviator's Soul Memoirs.
Neal Schupbach.

Printed in the United States of America.
ISBN: 978-1-4243-0786-9
       1-4243-0786-4

ROOFHANSA LLC.
3125 Bayshore Oaks Dr.
Tampa, FL 33611-4475

ACKNOWLEDGEMENTS

My father, Paul Schupbach told me over the years to write about my flying stories. *"There we were at twenty thousand feet when..."* he coached. He admired pilots and thought this book was a very good idea. Little did he know how the twists and turns of my travels turned this book around, creating a humanitarian effort on my part.

I remember the day I sat in front of him in a nursing home, reading to him my initial Navy flight training stories, sharing several high flying adventures about how his youngest son nearly died. Weakened from a previous stroke and now a heart attack, Paul Schupbach was still one very tough customer. His only comment was that *"it was well written but not commercial."* The consummate television professional was right, just when I thought I had it together. I am grateful for his encouragement and high standards.

I would like to thank my copyeditors Gaylen Andrews and Katheryn Freeberg, for their excellent contributions to my book. I thank Dr. Daphne Brown and Annice Ernst for their contributing edits. I am indebted to Rodger Johnson, John Ora, Peter Dolle, Mrs. Ihms and the Parenteau family for their endless patience, guidance and inspiration through countless conversations during the creation of this work. Finally, special thanks goes out to Senator "Smiling Bob" Kerrey for encouraging my twenty-five years of aviation, exploration and education.

DEDICATION

I would like to dedicate this book to my mother, Phyllis Schupbach, for her decades of giving selfless service and education to the weak, the hungry and the disabled, to the elderly and to the children of America. Thanks Mom, you touched my heart and I hope through this work, your kind spirit will touch others as well.

FOREWORD

Neal balances the humanity of mankind with its ugly alter ego—inhumanity. He illuminates the dichotomy of the proverbial "haves" and "have-nots," and how interchangeable they really are—a divide separated by mere opportunity. I identify with Neal's story because it is my story, too. I am a female aviator, provided with the opportunity to soar and explore in the same manner that Neal has shared with his readers. I fall into that category of "haves." I have been blessed with the chances to see many parts of the world. And Neal illustrates how cruel the vast part of that world can be. He strikes at the core of our souls—we know better than to assume that the "have-nots" must have done something wrong to deserve their lot in life. Or that the "haves," like myself, have done something right to deserve our apparently elevated position. It is the human condition to deny that misfortune is only a step away from each of us, and only befalls someone else. Neal reminds us that our compassion must be delivered to those less fortunate. It is this understanding that each of us, regardless of our position in life, can reach out in some small manner and have a positive effect. We just need to care enough to make it happen.

Kate Malone, Airline Pilot

INTRODUCTION

Flying the Canyons of the Sky: Navigations of an Aviator's Soul is a provocative travel/adventure memoir written as testimony for those I met throughout my twenty-four years of flying the globe. As I wrote these words, I contrasted my highly technical and impersonal military training against the empathetic chambers of my heart. At times, I was haunted by the images I revealed; and I was compelled to deliver powerful, firsthand accounts of the 20th century hells I have seen on earth.

Military history, politics and poverty dominate my work. I share many lifelong experiences, including the trials and tribulations of Naval flight school, prosecuting submarines during the cold war, the fall of the Berlin Wall, witnessing war torn Africa, the Soviet Union, and flying the Muslim pilgrims during the Hajj.

Flight school taught me survival mode. Emotions were forbidden and seen as weakness. It was important and necessary to suppress them. Otherwise, chances were good I'd never get through preliminary flight school—a scenario even more likely in advanced training. Under extreme pressure, the only emotions I allowed myself were fear of failure, miniscule doses of elation and…the effervescence from beer.

Anyone who couldn't hack getting kicked around wasn't built for flight school. We were there to learn to fly and become able-bodied killers. In order to do so, we were dehumanized in many respects. *Hard targets* and *soft targets* was the language describing buildings and people. Killing five thousand was the average for the A-7 Corsair pilot during the first Gulf War—it's the job you signed up for. Without such dehumanization, such killing would never take place.

Navy pilots learned to shut down emotions, not examine them. Although I woke sooner from this realization than many of my colleagues, it's still hard for me to comprehend the ongoing years of it all. If I hadn't roused from it eventually, this story would never be told. This reality is one of the overall, subtle contrasts I write without considering the 21st century's media overload. With this in mind, I quietly question the current corporate mentality, take no survivors and dog-eat-dog for mere scraps, so many Americans experience. How great we have it, yet, we want only more.

It is said behavior is learned from impressions and imprinting from others. Looking back, I see myself as one who worked very hard traveling around the world and seeing the billions of people that life left behind. Why did I observe those that so many simply ignore? Where did I learn that trait? *Why me* I ask? Ironically, it was only after others recommended that I explain myself as the protagonist that I sat down and wrote about my life and discovered the answers to these questions.

I hope this book challenges your perspective to no longer look through your own eyes, nor through my traveled eyes; but rather to observe yourself through the eyes of the less fortunate looking back at you. This was a high hurdle I set for myself and I am no athlete. However, I climbed this ladder—one wrenching rung at a time. I reached for my goal, driven by the sound of my heart, whenever I chose to listen.

Look up and never look down. This ladder is the secret to climbing to new heights, I said to myself.

The view from over the top will be our just reward.

Neal Schupbach
Tampa, Florida
October 17, 2005

Nebraska

CHAPTER ONE

I was born in 1957, the youngest of four boys, growing up in the safety of the heartland of America. We lived on Plymouth Avenue, near Winthrop Road, in Lincoln, Nebraska. A block to the west stood Sheridan, a brick elementary school. A half-block to our east rambled the three-mile-long Antelope Park with its adjacent Rock Island Railroad line. Like any red-blooded American boy, I grew to adore the park and railroad more than the grade school. I was a junior hobo in the making.

Adventure and exploration, from chasing freight trains to climbing in boxcars, were all mine in Antelope Park. From my earliest memory, travel gripped the very nature of my spirit. As my mother and I walked or drove to various locations within the park, she pointed out landmarks and explained their purposes to my inquisitive three-year-old mind. At one end of the park, a World War II Sherman tank stood proudly on static display. A vintage blue airplane stood next to it—but this was not just any old airplane. It was a *Navy* airplane. Little did I know that my first sight of that plane would foreshadow a significant portion of the rest of my life.

A slender woman with chestnut hair pulled neatly behind each ear, I remember my mother saying, "Neal, during World War II, I served in the Navy along with my Cousin Ruth." Mother continued, "We were in the WAVES. Ruth worked in the control tower and I delivered the mail. We freed up men so that they were able to serve on the ships and fight in the war."

As a precocious three-year-old, I thought that to be a pretty good idea, delivering the mail.

She went on to explain, "In the Navy, the airplane's wings fold. Neal, do you see how they hinge the wing and move it above the cockpit?"

At that tender age, I had my first issues with aviation. I remember taking one look at what my mother described and thinking it was a bad idea. *Why do they fold the wings? What happens if they fold in flight? Can they stop that from happening?*

Seeing my perplexed expression, she continued, "They fold the wings so that many more airplanes can land on the ships, which are large aircraft carriers. When they want the wings to remain down, the men put large pins in the wings so they can't fold in flight."

All I could think of was the World War II movies on television and images of potential disaster immediately flooded my young brain. I recalled the dog-fighting films and imagined having a bullet hit a pin, causing it to come out and the wings folding. It was a scary proposition for anyone, let alone a three-year-old, and it was hard to shake that image. Being blunt the way children often are, I told my mother that I much preferred the four-engine, B-17 from the television show, *Twelve O'Clock High*. At least its wings didn't fold!

We walked along to another nearby point of interest. A large, split-stone drinking fountain provided welcome relief during that warm summer's day. After our water break, we journeyed back to the car and followed a meandering path under large elm trees, crossing the railroad tracks before we drove the short distance home.

As I look back on that day, although the airplane was tops, the railroad track took on a new meaning for me. It was something more than just the sights and sounds of a passing train. The tracks spelled navigation and that became important. As young as I was, I realized that I could now find my way across town and back just by following the tracks. This gave birth to a newfound freedom to roam through the park and return home, putting one foot in front of the other, balancing on the silver rails. The drinking fountain gave me the currency I needed to ensure my return—a big drink of cold water. In turn, the blue Navy airplane gave me sufficient reason for hiking a couple of miles—the need to look inside the cockpit of the plane, even if its wings folded. I knew they would not fold on me!

Before my mother realized the extent of my wandering spirit, her youngest son thoroughly alarmed and embarrassed her. On more than one occasion, the police and fire departments joined up in searches for me.

"I just left him alone in the back yard to play for a few minutes and now he's gone!" became her familiar litany, as half the south end of town looked for me. Meanwhile, I waited several blocks away at my usual hangout, Antelope Park at South Street, waiting for traffic to pause so I could cross and continue my trek to the plane. But it wasn't until the tender age of four that I developed enough courage to cross that busy street on my way to adventure.

Shortly after our first outing to the airplane and my first roundtrip solo hike, I found my father's former U.S. Army uniforms pressed and hung in his closet. Playing army in Antelope Park was a great adventure; the army movies I watched were my source of inspiration. My mother saw my interests and allowed me to play in my father's green Korean War army shirts—complete with sergeant stripes. Far too big for me, she rolled up the sleeves and safety-pinned them in place above my elbows. We walked about the small neighborhood and I saluted the neighbors and the postman. They responded with broad smiles. I had given them something else to talk about other than my disappearing acts. I am sure many reasoned that the sleeves could double as a restraining straitjacket if needed.

A very old man, Mr. Whitcome, lived several houses away. He and my mother were friends and she walked me down the block to his small stone house for a visit. I always thought him to be a very nice person. He seemed to like me and he especially enjoyed it when I visited him while "in uniform." I could tell it brightened his day, although I never understood why. He always returned the favor with a cinnamon fireball candy that kept me coming back for more.

I grew to like Mr. Whitcome very much. However, as time passed, he no longer came out to play in the warm sunshine on his front steps. For reasons I didn't understand, he began to stay indoors and kept more of a distance in the back of his living room. This puzzled me.

As most four-year-old children would, I wanted to visit this grandfather figure as often as possible. Of course, I wanted the cinnamon balls as well. I even gathered up the courage to visit my old friend by myself a few times. Only then, he rarely moved from a sitting position and a woman attended him. On my last visit, she answered the door and I conned my way into seeing him. She spoke quietly to me before my visit.

"Mr. Whitcome is sick, but you won't catch his illness. He's very weak; he might catch *your* germs, so you can't be near him."

I stood near the door next to the closed curtains that covered a beautiful picture window. I remember him turning his head to smile at me, his face illumined only by the light of the lamp on one side of the room. He couldn't get up, but he said he wanted me to have all of the cinnamon balls. I thought he didn't want me coming over anymore and felt that I had done something wrong. Nevertheless, I took a handful of candy anyway.

Shortly afterwards, I stood with my mother on our street corner up the small hill as we watched an ambulance arrive at Mr. Whitcome's house. A few hours later, my mother explained that he had died.

"Do you know what that means Neal?"

At such a young age, at least for my relationship with Mr. Whitcome, I said, "Yes."

I never suspected that my mother had a reason for introducing me to Mr. Whitcome until my own father's passing. During the latter years of his life, my dad grew listless in the afternoons and slept more and more. But during visits from my three-year-old niece, Meg, he was entertained and remained fully awake in his easy chair. In short, Meg did the things young children do best—bringing smiles to the faces of the old and the ill. I finally saw the parallel and understood why my mother had introduced me to Mr. Whitcome. I realized it wasn't for my fondness of his fireball candies.

By the time I was five, Antelope Park held my attention like nothing else could. Often I hiked in the opposite direction of the airplane, all the way to the bridges on Sheridan Boulevard. Underneath those bridges was a great place to play and the adventure of exploring kept me focused on getting out of the house. Lincoln, Nebraska was an extremely safe environment for children then. I met many other children doing much the same. They were a bit older than my spirited five-years, perhaps seven or eight.

One day at the bridge, we entertained ourselves by filling paper grocery bags full of soil and rock and dropping them from the bridge to the rail bed below. We were children caught up in the drama of our games, pretending the clouds of dust generated were smoke bombs directed against German soldiers lurking beneath us.

Looking up, as I was retrieving and refilling my bags on the tracks, I saw death hurtling toward me—not from above, nor from a hostile German soldier, but from a high-speed freight train coming from around the bend just down the tracks. There was neither a whistle nor engine noise to warn me. I froze in my shoes for a brief moment, standing firm between the rails as the train plummeted toward me.

The steep terrain on my left posed a formidable barrier to climb and on my right stood a wet creek bed and an overgrown swamp. Running down the length of the track to a better exit would have been suicide. So at the grand old age of five, while the other children watched horrified from above, I took off running straight for the oncoming train. At the last moment, I darted off the tracks to my left, jumped across the small ditch and scrambled up the steep ravine of soft, dusty dirt under the bridges.

I will never know if the engineer saw me, or even believed what he saw, as the train raced under the bridges close enough to blow wind in my face as I climbed that slippery slope. A deafening train whistle screamed above the roar of the four diesel locomotives in full gallop, echoing under the overpass, piercing through my entire body and passing by in one terrifying instant.

I knew I was safe, but the scare turned me white as a ghost, so the other children said when I returned to the top of the bridge. All danger aside, they laughed at my near death experience while I waited for a bit of sympathy or at least "Are you alright?" Although their reaction hurt my feelings and made me feel lower than the dirt we dropped on the tracks, I had to suck it up around those *big* kids, hiding my fear and need of comfort.

It all made for a long walk home alone as I vowed the next time would be different. The next time, I waited for the unsuspecting train at the top of the bridge where it was safe. From that vantage point, I took revenge on the afternoon train, timing my smoke bomb drops for the exhaust ducts and cooling fans located on top of the locomotive engines. After considerable practice, I actually managed to score a few bulls-eyes even on some of the faster moving freight trains. Revenge!

I was saved from possible premature death when I was six—we moved several blocks away from those railroad tracks. Our new home was a large old house on a beautiful street called Stratford Avenue. Stratford was a special neighborhood with plenty to distract me from my previous obsession of playing "chicken" with freight trains.

This new neighborhood had old cast iron streetlights, tall canopies of elm, oak and maple trees, and an island dividing the street into a miniature boulevard. Locusts filled the trees with their soft songs and dogs were everywhere, as every house was home to at least one canine companion. Like most kids, I played baseball, attended cub scouts and went off to summer camp once or twice. All of this should have made for a blissful childhood except for one thing. It was the 1960s.

Two years before, I grieved with the rest of the nation at the assassination of President Kennedy, and I thought that was enough public violence and sorrow for my lifetime. But I was wrong about that. Unfortunately, events were just beginning to heat up in America and I was the perfect age for all of it to impact me.

The Beatles, with their long hair, divided American opinion and their revolutionary music quickly rose to the top of the charts, pushing aside the folk singers of the day. Electric guitars were the new rage and the Fab Four were alternately worshipped, or vilified, depending on the listening generation. By today's standards, they were clean-cut, ambitious kids welcomed in any household, but certainly not back then. Their rise gave birth to a new term "the generation gap."

During the same time period, I became aware of the potential nuclear conflict of the Cuban Missile Crisis. I learned that, with a brief thirty-minute exchange, the communists' arsenal of nuclear weapons could destroy all life in America. Radiation, whatever that was, would snuff out whatever the blasts and fires left living. Living just fifty miles from the big ground zero—Strategic Air Command in Omaha, perhaps gave us more of a sense of urgency than many in the rest of the farm belt. People built bomb shelters in their basements and we played in them, pretending they were special concrete caves. The city even built civil defense shelters that calmed our nerves with false reassurances.

Shortly thereafter, a made-for-television movie came out and my mother wanted all of her children to watch it with her. She thought we needed to see the film as an educational experience. The movie dealt with a far-off city called Berlin. It documented the construction of the Berlin Wall, and with it, the failed escape attempts, the checkpoints and death under the spotlights. I saw the perspective of one family who tunneled their way under the nearby inner wall, past the death strip and outer wall to freedom in West Berlin. The family covered the noise of chiseling through their concrete basement walls with the sound of their father practicing the tuba. Their escape nearly collapsed because their route took them directly under a power pole that oscillated during a heavy rainstorm. A neighbor pointed that out and blackmailed them in order to take part in the escape. Whether the part about the pole was truth or fiction, the Berlin Wall and the family's escape were frightening and very real to my siblings and me. Little did I know that my life's journeys would take me to Berlin where I'd personally witness the horrors of that Wall, and ironically, its eventual fall.

Because of the missile crisis and the Berlin Wall, by age seven or eight I was a devout anticommunist. There were two major problems with my political views. The first was that I was the only kid on the block to have knowledge of such concerns. While other parents intentionally shielded their children from international politics, I was the one who saw the Berlin Wall program and watched the evening news. Those programs made a profound emotional impression upon me. I learned awareness of the Vietnam War from Walter Cronkite. In 1965, President Johnson committed American combat forces to South Vietnam and bombed communistic North Vietnam because North Vietnam allegedly fired torpedoes at one of our Navy ships. Every night for seven years, television news served up the latest from the distant land, including actual war footage and daily, weekly totaled body counts to our living room.

The war protests also began, but they seemed choreographed to me and I was confused by it all. Whom did I trust and what did I believe to be true? Teachers and police were part of "the establishment," yet hippies and draft-dodgers provided obvious bad impressions. Talking about the American presence in Vietnam generated arguments that led to fistfights after school. My oldest brother was eligible for the draft and hid from service in junior colleges that sprung up like weeds. Attending these colleges gave financially able students deferments from serving in the military, although no one spoke of them in those terms.

In the classrooms, the subject of the war was strictly off-limits. Teachers tried to shelter the students from this new television war. When I was in the fourth grade, I entered into a language arts program for English class. The teacher's big push for us was the events at the United Nations as well as other current events except, of course, the Vietnam War. She encouraged us to read periodicals such as *Time* and *Newsweek* and to stay current by watching the news. But the news and current events only contained the news of the 60s. Much of that was exactly what young children needed protection from in the first place: collateral damage, a multitude of generation gap conflicts, the threat of nuclear obliteration and a hot war against the communist forces in Southeast Asia.

Additionally, a rapid progression of events paraded through the streets of America including: the Civil Rights Movement, riots that consumed entire urban districts, two more political assassinations—Dr. Martin Luther King and Senator Robert Kennedy, LBJ weekly war protests, the Tet Offensive, sit-ins, retaliation by the establishment with college campus closings, free love, Nixon and Rock-n-Roll music. By the time Neil Armstrong had taken "one giant leap for mankind," America had turned on itself, taking a different leap right into the proverbial lake. The space race—impressive as all hell, with the Mercury, Gemini and Apollo adventures, seemed like an expensive diversion from the problems confronting America's citizens on a daily basis. Life for me oscillated between living in some dark storm to being an innocent kid, then back into the ominous dark again, with no end in sight. But oddly enough, even with all of these negative events and the possibility of nuclear annihilation bombarding me from every source of current events, I learned a bit of good about life from the very large heart of my mother. At the time, I did my best to ignore those lessons.

When I was in grade school, my mother taught half-days of kindergarten. She then became interested in the heartfelt world of educating both the physically and mentally handicapped children of Lincoln. Except for one mentally handicapped sister of a buddy from elementary school, neither my friends nor I ever dealt with any of these challenges. As a matter of fact, due to public policy and prejudice, most of the handicapped were kept away from the mainstream of our society. The community reflected state policy, and at my age, who was I to argue?

Yet, in spite of these policies, my mother quietly reached out to these Americans for many years and taught children with cerebral palsy, spina bifida, cystic fibrosis, and those incapacitated by mental illnesses. She also taught the *mentally retarded*, as they once were labeled. Meanwhile, on the playgrounds, we kids called each other "a retard," "rejects," or "retarded." As inaccurate and cruel as these insults may seem today, we thought nothing of them then. It didn't even occur to me that my mother worked with such handicapped children until she once told me details about them.

Every so often mom came home and simply wanted to "let off steam" from her short but emotionally trying days at work. Being home at the time, I became her sounding board of choice. She told me how lucky I was and compared her stories of the children she taught to my playing football or swimming at the neighborhood pool. On her really tough days, her stories made me cry—crying out to her, asking her to stop telling me these things, as they were too sad for me. On one or two occasions, she took me to her school when my classes were cancelled for administration days. Seeing those children personally impacted me much more than just hearing their stories, especially the stories about the children condemned to die prematurely.

My mother also volunteered to drive once a week for a charity program called "Meals on Wheels." In this program, utilizing church kitchens, volunteers provided hot lunches to elderly shut-ins, the handicapped and people who could not face the icy cold of a Nebraska winter. During a few of my days off from school, my mother asked me to join her and I escorted her to the apartments of the less fortunate residents of Lincoln.

We delivered those hot meals in Styrofoam trays with folding lids, sometimes carrying three meals at a time. Mom always left the car running to keep the heater working so the meals remained as warm as possible. We walked across the icy sidewalks, up snow-laden stairs to the front doors of large, run-down, clapboard houses that were divided into small apartments. The front doors to the buildings were unlocked, as was every front door in Lincoln in those days. We traipsed down cold and dank, rundown hallways, sometimes climbing a few additional flights of stairs to deliver our small packages of nutritious good will.

At first I thought it would be easy. What was so hard about dropping off a dozen meals or so? I presumed we would simply knock on the door and hand the food to the recipient of the program. I imagined it to be similar to delivering newspapers. Was I wrong!

For those who were too feeble to come to the door, mother knocked and the recipient would call out "come in." Those old doors would creak open and reveal living conditions like I had never imagined. In one place, a long, narrow hallway led back to the main living area, roughly twelve feet by fifteen feet. The cold gray of the north sky did little to augment the poorly lit apartment. Wooden floors peeked through worn-out carpet, and the small confines of this cold living room smelled of urine. At the far end sat an elderly man confined to a loveseat with blankets draped over his legs and shoulders.

Naively, I stood by the door with the other meals in hand and thought my purpose was to help carry the food and play security guard for my mother in case one of these awful, creepy people attacked her. Little did I remember that she did this with or without me looking after her. Nor did I think of all the other kind-hearted souls who participated in the program through the churches and organized charities, from the cooks to the sponsors to the other drivers.

As I stood in the doorway, supposedly watching over my mother, she carried out her routine in this rundown old rattrap. She delivered not only the food, but also her time to this elderly man, picking up litter strewn across his living room, taking his open meal from yesterday, gathering and straightening as she went around the room, adjusting the drapes for better lighting, adjusting his blankets for warmth, and holding a cheery ten-minute conversation with someone who could answer with just a few words, mostly "yes" and "no."

At such a young age, I didn't understand the significance of her work beyond the delivery of the meals. I only thought how I wished to be back home and watching daytime television. When we left that apartment and were safely back in the warm car, I asked why she did all of those things for that man in his apartment.

"The man has no one," she replied, "no living relatives to come and take care of him."

She felt that having someone to talk to and someone to help with his needs was important to him and other shut-ins. I didn't understand. All I understood were the awful conditions she worked in, and as a volunteer no less! Once I returned through the doors of our own warm home, I quickly buried those thoughts and feelings with hours of television.

Television provided countless hours of mindless, video spam that was about as exciting as the cornfields that surrounded us. But during the late 1960s in Lincoln, a new form of entertainment evolved—Nebraska football. As the *Big Red* machine got into high gear, football fever set in and it has yet to leave the state. For years I ate, drank and slept the game. The neighborhood even had its sandlot football league. Every fall we took a perfectly green, soft, beautiful yard of some unknown owner and ruined it playing tackle football. Later in the season we progressed to harder, more ragged, public school playgrounds to play. The crushed rock surface caused scrapes, cuts and plenty of bruises, but we played on until December's snow ended the season.

I played center in the midget football league when I was twelve. We won every game that season. I liked the feeling of winning. The next year, I had to sit out the season after breaking my hand while attending a Friday night high school football game. Whether my hand was in a cast or not, we teenagers climbed the fence at the Nebraska games, and once inside, ran like hell from the police. Sometimes we even went back out, just for the fun of having the police chase us a second time! That year the University of Nebraska achieved its first national title and the town painted itself red!

The following summer, when I was fourteen, I couldn't resist the call of my innate wanderlust and the romantic call to adventure of the open road. In 1971, the thought of looking for America, traveling alone and sleeping under the open sky, was too great for my wandering spirit to ignore. In August, when my parents traveled to Albuquerque to visit Uncle Fred and Aunt Imagene, I spied the perfect opportunity to escape and explore the nation. Nanny, my strong-willed but frail grandmother of eighty years who was suffering the beginnings of Parkinson's disease, would be a pushover for my kind. While my parents left me alone with Nanny, with a grand total of twenty dollars in my pocket, I packed my duffle bag, fed her a cover story of *being invited by the Anderson's to their cabin in Iowa* and left town, hitchhiking my way across the country.

I slept in a dormitory common room of the University of Iowa the first night out. The campus police came in and nearly arrested me, but I lied my way out of what would have been a thoroughly embarrassing situation to come home to. What would my friends think of me? The next day, I found myself on Interstate 80, overlooking the mighty Mississippi River. Mesmerized, I lost track of time, marveling at the river as highway traffic rushed by. After two more days and nights, I found someone willing to take me into New York City—or at least that was the plan. But the next morning, the stranger wisely convinced me to turn around. From mid-Pennsylvania, I hitchhiked back toward Lincoln. Looking back, I realize how lucky our chance meeting was. He was right. New York City was no place for a young teenager alone with just eight dollars in his pocket.

People were very nice to me on that last day of unobstructed freedom. One lady gave me a brown-bag lunch and a piece of apple pie, while another person handed me three dollars and wished me the best of luck. My good luck ran out, however, when the Ohio State Police pulled over. I stood on the freeway interchange of Interstate 70 and 75. Pedestrians are illegal on the interstate highways and I found myself being questioned, searched, and placed in the back end of a black and white. I was busted at fourteen. The Ohio State Detention Center in Dayton was home for the next four, long days.

Most people argued that I was safer locked up there than being on the open road with only eleven dollars to my name. But they never met my cellmates and I disagreed. For starters, the guards were fresh from fighting in Vietnam and tolerated very little from anyone. The older kids were there for good reasons, such as assault, robbery and possession of heroin. They had the rabbit tracks to prove it. A couple of guys were in my same boat, just passing through town. One was with his girlfriend on their way to a concert. It was a hell of a mix of people with little to do but eat, read magazines, go to the gym and watch television. By far, the most popular program on TV was *Mighty Mouse*. The guards even got into that one, something of a social statement that I never fully comprehended.

My father flew out to liberate me from captivity and quietly chewed me a new position in life.

"Neal, what in God's creation got into you? Do you realize the chance you took?"

He grounded me—it felt like forever—and left me with restricted activities after that. I did manage to play ninth grade football, starting as middle guard. Daily practice was scheduled after school at a high school across town. Between cycling to practice, warm-up exercises, running the hill, scrimmaging through plays, the seven-man sled and wind sprints, football squashed the wanderlust right out of me. I couldn't dream of going anywhere else. I was too tired.

We had a good season and I enjoyed the games that year to the fullest. Tragedy struck the following year; our quarterback lost his father during midseason. He immediately quit the team and we lost four of our five games. Despite that losing season, I knew we could play better and I worked harder, taking it out on every play, hitting and blocking as hard as I possibly could. I knew what it meant to win. I wanted the team to catch my fever, to just drive over the opposition with or without a quarterback. I guess that's why I received recognition and encouragement from my fellow players. Uncoiling on other people felt good, especially when the chips were down.

My junior year was the last year of my involvement in football. I came back to school determined to inspire the team with spirit, bust heads and win it all. The bitter taste of a 1 and 4 season the year before left me with something to prove. I knew we were better than that and I was right. We won five games and lost two, once beating ourselves with a two-point safety and losing by a score of 2 to 0.

Our record in midseason stood at 3 and 0; we were on a roll. I had just played my best game ever. Everyone could feel the excitement in the team during practice. Every drill had the players competing, every blocker kicked it up a notch, maybe two. Even driving the seven-man sled held appeal, although not for everyone, especially Ted Bluff.

Ted Bluff came from the privileged-kid crowd and acted like it. He began to arrive later and later for practice, long after warm-ups and agility drills. After a week of this irresponsible behavior, Coach McDouglas initiated an all-new, never-before-seen latecomer drill.

"Line up, line up, form a single line, all of you, starting right where I'm standing. Ted, you back up and stand right over there," he barked.

Thirty-nine of us formed a line. I stood around number thirty-five in the squad. Coach McDouglas then handed out a few footballs and started yelling the rules of this new drill.

"I want each of you to run full-speed at Ted."

Coach McDouglas turned to Ted, "You must tackle each and every one of your teammates, one at a time, in rapid succession. You must defend your position."

What kind of crazy drill is this? I wondered, thinking the drill would last just over a dozen or so players. I was wrong and the team cheered wildly with each successive hit of Ted Bluff.

At player twenty, Ted was having trouble finding his balance but the coach kept yelling, "Get on your feet! Up with you, on your feet! Here comes another man. Tackle him! Tackle him! On your feet, on your feet! Hit him harder. Bluff, don't dodge anybody, tackle 'em, tackle 'em, Ted."

Although I didn't care much for the guy, I felt this was too much for anyone to handle. And I knew I would be expected to lay down a very hard hit on this guy, who was exhausted and wobbly from all of the hard, physical contact. I would be a weapon instead of a player. This went against my values and all Christian teachings. The other players, in front of three coaches, not only kept hitting Bluff, but kept hitting him full-steam, without regard for his physical condition or possibility of injury.

Time was running out. Soon I would be first in line. *Wait a minute*, I thought. *Coach McDouglas is a leader in the Fellowship of Christian Athletes group that I attend. He'll listen to reason and put an early stop to this out-of-bounds punishment.* Because I realized that's what it was. I looked over at Coach McDouglas. "Coach, don't you think he's had enough?"

Coach McDouglas looked at me with eyes wrapped tighter than a rattlesnake's skin.

"Schupbach, you do what you think is right."

He seemed exhilarated, enjoying the power of turning his team of 16-year-old boys into a street gang, beating and beating and beating up on Ted Bluff.

By this time, Ted attempted to tackle people, but he only went down with them, gripping them to his body and hoping they would fall to the ground with him. I looked at his powerless rag-doll body, being helped up by the previous player. As the pressure of my approaching turn in line mounted, so did my confusion and bewilderment. This moment questioned my faith, testing my Christian values. I had reached an impasse. I could either bend to peer pressure and lay a legal, bone breaking hit on a rich kid I didn't like, or I could put a stop to things. I knew it would be wrong to use my body as a weapon against a defenseless teammate.

I had to make a major call. While my teammates cheered on, the coach sent me slamming against the pitiful Ted Bluff. It was decision time. My emotions ran high. Feeling alone on the field of forty, I wondered that no one had yet stepped out and questioned this action.

When Ted Bluff recognized me as the next runner, the tired, empty glaze in his eyes disappeared. Fear replaced all else in his stare, fear of my ability to uncoil on contact. Normally, I would have been complimented; but this time I, too, was scared. I was scared of crossing my faith, scared of injuring or maiming Bluff, and scared of the wrongness of it all.

I took my first step towards Bluff and listened to my heart. In spite of any consequence, I had to go against the coach and show disrespect to the entire football team. I ran at half speed, delivering him a mild, glancing blow. This infuriated Coach McDouglas. It may have been 1973, but that was just too much civil disobedience for the man to handle.

I heard about it, the coach mumbling, "...doesn't hit during latecomer drill." By the very next day, he had turned the entire team against me. The previous week, I had played my very best game. I was stripped of team captaincy and demoted to playing on the downgraded squad, running defenses for the varsity. The next afternoon, I severely sprained my ankle and was benched for three weeks. During films the following afternoon, all three coaches wanted to know who led the blocking during a broken play, when the other guard picked up a fumble. I cleared out the vast majority of the opposing team on an improvised end around, including blocking three guys into each other while the ball carrier made it to the goal line. I couldn't say "It was me, Coach" and no one else did because of Bluff's latecomer drill and my subsequent ostracism.

We finished the season as self-proclaimed city champs and each of us received a plaque that quoted a New Orleans Saints' football player. It read, "Never accept losing. When you accept losing, it comes more often." It was quite appropriate for our team. But for me, the price paid for listening to my heart instead of the cheering crowd, left me isolated through my senior year.

I began my college days in 1975, living at home while attending the University of Nebraska. I took organic chemistry and a few other courses to bring me up to full-time status. During my second semester, I lived in the dormitories with a roommate from Nigeria. Checkers was a great guy with many talents. Most of the enjoyment of my four months on campus was due, in large part, to him.

After that freshman year, I decided to try working full-time and applied for a permanent position with the State Department of Roads. It was my first real job, but not for long. The Department of Roads only paid two or three dollars hourly with straight time for overtime. There was plenty of overtime. I worked on survey crews, inspected various concrete works, and in the fall, analyzed asphalt for oil content and specific aggregate. Asphalt analysis quickly became the most interesting of my work. It was also the most dangerous and potentially lethal job assignment during my brief five-month career working for the State of Nebraska.

I worked out of a temporary trailer at an equally temporary asphalt mixing facility near Fremont. Each day my partner and I drove to the site from the North Lincoln main offices. Twelve-hour workdays became routine. Eventually the chief engineer lodged us in Fremont and paid us full per diem. A second, temporary asphalt plant started up directly across the road from the one we worked. The state needed analysis oversight there as well.

The state failed to increase manpower for the oversight of two plants and this increased our workload so problems resulted. Even our office secretaries complained about how we didn't claim lunches on our expense report because we weren't able to stop and eat lunch at the double plant site. Still there was no relief in sight.

Everyone involved with the operation knew of the potential danger our poorly ventilated, cramped workspaces imposed upon us at the job site. We encountered the chemical solvent Trichloroethylene, which is used in dissolving asphalt into its basic components. "Triclor" worked great but it is carcinogenic and damages the liver as well as the brain. We took precautions in handling the material by wearing rubber gloves; nevertheless, at least twice a day, one of us had to walk away from the trailer operations to come down from the cheap drunk it produced.

When evaporating the remaining solvent from the aggregate—essentially drying the rock in a cooking pan over a propane flame, if the exhaust fans did not keep up with the process, the heavier-than-air Trichloroethylene rose from the heat only to sink back into the flames. Should that happen, it would oxidize into Phosgene, a potent and deadly nerve gas used in World War I.

"Keep a careful eye on the color of the propane flames," the chief engineer warned. "Any changes require immediate attention and evacuation of the trailer."

It happened. These impromptu evacuations slowed down our overworked inspection process even more. We were unable to keep up with the paper bags full of asphalt arriving from various roadwork sites. They stacked up all over the trailer from lack of hands to process them. Since the samples could not be confirmed before roadway completion, the new roads turned dark black and soft from excessive oil. Finally, the state required one of the companies to provide us with a larger trailer, one with better ventilation, and sent a man to get his fingernails dirty by supervising us. It turned out that we had no more assistance than before.

The straw that broke the camel's back in my newly found career came from this extra "helping" hand who was sent to assist us with the asphalt analysis. In an oblique manner, he helped me all right. As a matter of fact, I credit him for saving my health, and quite possibly my life. Instead of rolling up his sleeves and solving the lack of adequate staffing, this man stepped into our new, well-ventilated facility, took a pan of rinsed aggregate away from me and poured the excess solvent into a holding container. He then proceeded to lecture me on the proper way to do things. It may have been that I was a bit loopy from the morning vapors, or maybe I was thinking straight for the first time since I arrived at the farm site. But for whatever reason, I walked out of that trailer without saying a word.

"Here is my expense report, my travel log and my resignation," I said, returning a few minutes later. "I quit!"

My project engineer was waiting for me when I drove the state truck back to Lincoln.

"They were poisoning me," was all that I could tell him. Back in 1976, EPA regulations and OSHA were viewed both as unnecessary and as undue interference from the Federal Government and I received little sympathy from him. The same was true for my father, who was disappointed with me.

Once again, I felt cut off and isolated, disillusioned by "the system." With time on my hands, I further distanced myself from all that was familiar and allowed the wanderlust of old to take over. Hitchhiking to California was just the ticket to get some fresh air and new ideas, and to clear my head from the hours standing next to pans of hot steaming Trichloroethylene and Phosgene.

The trip was beneficial. I rediscovered my former childhood romance of travel despite the inconveniences of no lodging or bathing and few, if any, hot meals. I had water and a sleeping bag so as long it didn't rain, I remained content. Next summer's trip plans were already formulating in my mind as I returned to Nebraska.

Another cold winter fell on the Cornhusker state that year, and worse yet, the economy slipped further into recession. Gripped within a drought cycle the past several years, there was little expendable income floating around. Our agrarian economy now relied on the U. S. Government for survival. Only irrigated crops produced a yield those years. Even wildlife, such as deer, pheasant and duck, retreated in numbers. It was tough all over.

By the next fall, I preferred living away from home and that meant having a job. To satisfy my strong desire for independence, I worked with a friend cleaning various restaurants and offices at night. To economize, and for the price of one month's salary, I bought a nice bicycle and cycled everywhere through all seasons. Approximately three hundred dollars a month got me by, whether it was enough or not. Winters in the late 1970s were especially harsh with plenty of snow and ice, strong winds and mind-numbing temperatures. Our inside work was appealing for obvious reasons.

For actual time spent on the job, I averaged eight dollars per hour, a decent wage considering the decade, the place and the farm belt recession. Since I cycled everywhere, the oil crisis that tripled the price of crude oil left me unaffected. I couldn't have cared less about the so-called magnitude of economic calamity those prices inflicted on America. How shortsighted I proved to be. Inflation took off and the price of oil affected every detail of our lives.

Nebraska had a couple of good harvests around that same time, reinforced by high demand from the Soviet Union's large grain purchase. This sent the price of farm commodities and subsequent profits higher. Unfortunately, this created an unforeseen and sinister consequence. The value of an average acre of land increased with the value of the grain it could produce. Naïve farmers bought each other out at these higher, historically unsustainable prices, thereby amassing large amounts of debt to be serviced with the sale of grain.

Those good times proved to be short-lived with events on the far side of the globe directly affecting all of us in Nebraska. The Soviet Union invaded Afghanistan and President Carter retaliated by shutting off our grain sales to the wrongful invaders. This policy could not have come at a worse time for the farmers who, straddled new debt, had *counted their chickens before they hatched*. President Carter used food as a weapon and it backfired. Thousands upon thousands of farms failed. Ironically, the Soviets simply bought the grain they needed from other world market countries.

In record time, the trickle-down effect of President Carter's foreign policy evaporated the money supply in Nebraska. On top of that, near hyperinflation from the price of oil raised interest rates and kept everyone from even whispering "expansion." The big squeeze on the money supply hit students in a very large way. For most, there were no summer jobs; there were no spring, fall or winter jobs. I kept alive by working two or three different job sites at one time, while eating popcorn purchased with student loans. I hated borrowing. I saw it as losing independence and believed it would lead to a vicious cycle, causing me to slowly sink deeper and deeper into debt.

For my precious independence and basic survival, I worked late nights, cleaning up on the western side of town, cycling across the railroad yard viaduct adjacent to a slaughterhouse. There were several accounts to work out there, the most interesting and difficult being a restaurant called Grandmother's Skillet. On a good night, the job required four hours of my time and on a bad night it took five. There were days that I slept through physics class because of the hours I kept.

I met an important contact in Grandmother's kitchen. Although unaware at the time, it was a trade-off I'd make any day of the week. One summer morning toward the end of my shift, I backed through the swinging doors that separated the bar from the large kitchen area, mop and dirty water trailing behind me. I wore a pair of soiled jeans and a smelly tee shirt, saturated with the sweat of a hard night's work. Over my left shoulder I noticed a thin man with brown hair standing at the employee coffee maker. The sight of him startled me because I worked alone. No one else came in at those hours, but here stood a man who I first thought might be a cop. *Had I left the back door open and was he searching the place for burglars?*

He turned towards me, stuck out his hand and said with a big smile, "Good morning. My name is Bob. I just brewed a fresh pot. How about joining me for a hot cup of coffee?"

His great handshake set me at ease. "Bob, I'm Neal. Sure, I would love a cup of coffee."

With that introduction, we stood around for fifteen or twenty minutes, chewing the fat, discussing the local news, and of course, the prospects for this year's Cornhusker Football Team. From that day on, I knew this kind man as "Smiling Bob," nothing more. I sensed from this first encounter, our first introduction, that there was a whole lot more to Smiling Bob, yet couldn't put my finger on it.

Smiling Bob had an ease of personality and the humility to disarm and befriend me in a heartbeat—the night clean-up guy. Soon we talked about each other's hobbies, mine being cycling. My bike stood out in full view in the back storage room. I took the time to promote riding as a sport, telling him of my trip through the Canadian Rockies. Smiling Bob just kept smiling and enthusiastically mentioned that his was swimming, that he swam laps at the YMCA in downtown Lincoln.

I detected something in that comment, something that said he wouldn't go near a bicycle no matter how persuasive or romantic my cycling stories might be. Curious, I kept asking myself, *Who is this guy in slacks and a tie, pouring me coffee to my heart's content; who spends his time finding out about a janitor and enjoys our time together at 6 A.M. out on West O Street?*

A few weeks later, I spoke with my boss, and casually mentioned my encounters with Smiling Bob.

"Neal, your Smiling Bob is Bob Kerrey, the owner of Grandmother's."

I could only think, *Oops, the owner is pouring me coffee at 6 A.M. and I'm calling him Smiling Bob?* That's when I learned of his disability and understood his preference for swimming to my cycling and running. Bob Kerrey lost a leg while fighting in Vietnam; rumor had it in North Vietnam.

I kept that information to myself, respecting his right to privacy, not wanting to tread on or risk the friendship we had established over coffee. From other Vets, I learned their combat experience in Vietnam was excruciating to talk about, not only for them but also for everyone else. So why bring up the past? But Bob Kerrey amazed me. This guy seemed special, so hard working, so focused, so driven in everything he touched. I often thought, *What's up with this guy? Shouldn't he be crippled? How much of a leg did he lose and which one was it?* But the most provocative question I had was, *How could he evoke so many powerful feelings in me just by walking into the back kitchen, in the early mornings, and pouring me a cup of coffee?*

21

Later that same summer I learned these feelings were just the tip of the iceberg when I came to understand how special this individual was. My Smiling Bob was Lieutenant Junior Grade Kerrey, who served America as a naval officer in an elite commando unit called the Navy SEALS. For his role in doing so, President Nixon awarded Bob Kerrey the nation's highest award, nothing less than the Congressional Medal of Honor. *Holy shit!*

The following winter, on one particularly cold and windy Nebraska morning, I finished my duties late, around 7:30 A.M. Physics class started at 8 A.M. and I rushed into my three layers of outer garments only to be greeted by Bob. He stood with his morning help in between the stainless steel sinks and the prep tables. As I wheeled my bicycle toward the back entrance, I became the center of attention. Everyone knew that it was a real bear of a morning outside.

"Good morning," I said to the three of them, while my thoughts centered on the weather.

They replied in kind, Bob curling his palm around a hot cup of coffee, added sympathetically, "Its cold outside."

"Yes, but its not all that bad. Besides, the cold makes you focus."

The ladies in the kitchen chuckled and laughed at me, but as I looked Bob Kerrey straight in the eye, a peculiar change took place: a change in his pupil, a change from somewhere inside that I touched just by standing there dressed in piles of old clothes, bicycle in hand, ready to take on the Arctic blast of yet another bad winter morning and saying "The cold makes you focus."

My last encounter with Smiling Bob Kerrey came less than a year later in the late fall of 1980. It happened quite by chance at a restaurant where I cleaned at night and worked as kitchen help during the afternoons, The Glass Onion, earning minimum wage but maximum lunch. As usual, I was dressed in blue jeans and a white tee shirt, sporting a wet kitchen apron for the occasion. It was a very important time in my life. Once again I was isolated from my peers. I had a decision to make and just the fact that I was considering this move made them shake their collective heads. They thought I was crazy.

Just prior to our chance meeting in the Glass Onion Restaurant, I had answered an ad and cautiously applied to the Navy for entrance to Aviation Officer Candidate School or AOCS. At AOCS, candidates earned commissions, completed water survival and progressed towards flight school to earn the coveted "Wings of Gold." At the time, my immediate future looked dismal after college. Nebraska's economy had the triple kick of bankruptcies, high inflation and rising interest rates. Jobs were extremely scarce and, even as I pondered leaving town to enter the service, people stood three deep in line, asking me for my night clean-up work.

Nebraskans, unfortunately, still fought each other over Vietnam, although it was a full seven years after the United States withdrew from the war. We also stood divided over the Nixon Administration, his use of the federal government to spy on citizens of America, Watergate, President Ford's pardon of Richard Nixon, the hostage crisis in Iran, and an upcoming Presidential election that featured right-wing Republican candidate, Governor Ronald Reagan.

In my colleagues eyes, for me to choose to join the military meant trusting a government that appeared to represent bitterness and corruption, international weakness and malaise. But the little boy in me remembered the past. In my eyes, becoming a navy pilot—"one of the best"—appeared as a career path in aviation, something no one else offered. As Governor Reagan campaigned on the "misery index," when referring to America's economy, he was right on the money. The term actually stood for so much more in Nebraska. I was hungry; I was at a crossroads and I knew it all too well.

"I can either make a living pushing the dirt, staring up at me from the floor, or become a pilot and travel the world, looking at the blue sky from above the clouds," I confided to a girlfriend.

Looking back, it seems the right decision should have been obvious, but my many stressful, conflicting emotions were difficult to resolve. To enter the Navy went directly against the antiestablishment sentiment my peer group harbored from growing up when we did. This group of friends did not support my interests, to say the least, in flight school of all things! I felt the weight of the world on my shoulders.

Steve, the owner of the Glass Onion Restaurant also knew of my flight school ambitions and of my acquaintance with Bob Kerrey. As I worked over an ever-increasing pile of dishes, Steve said to me, "Neal, Bob Kerrey is in the restaurant."

I shrugged this off.

"So, I have this pile of dishes to go through." I didn't want to go out to visit with him, embarrassed by my attire and wet hands.

But Steve was persistent. "Neal, I really think you should go out and talk with him about going into the Navy. In fact, I insist on it. Put down the dishes and go talk with him. After all, I am your boss, you know."

Convinced he was right, I complied with my boss' insistence and found Kerrey sitting against a red brick wall at a small, oak-trimmed and white-laminated table, entertaining a very pretty lady. Walking up, I stood a few feet from the couple, waiting to be recognized. The truth was the woman was so pretty that I could not imagine why Bob Kerrey would look away from her and recognize me. But he did, bestowing me with another one of his great smiles.

Knowing my time with them was limited; I courteously greeted him and got right to the point.

"Bob, I'm interested in joining the Navy, going to AOCS and learning to fly. I've taken their tests and so far so good. But now they want five recommendations from various people and...well, I was wondering what you thought of my idea. If it would be all right to use you for a reference...if you would fill out their questionnaire for me?" I nervously wiped my hands on my apron.

Smiling Bob's face lit up like the whoosh of a gas stove.

"Neal, I think that's a great idea! Yes, sure I would."

My indecisive argument vanished with that short conversation. The pressure I felt from my peers, the confusion and tension over this option instantly dissipated. *Hell, if Bob Kerrey thinks it's a great idea, the rest just have to be wrong*, I said to myself, walking back to the dish pile.

Sixteen years later, I wrote a letter to the then senior senator from the State of Nebraska, explaining how much difference his word made in my life, how far his generosity took me, and thanking him for his recommendation. His words ended my wavering and made me act on what

I knew to be right in my heart. I had a long, overdue debt to pay because a man doesn't get many chances like the one I was afforded.
I wrote:

Dear Senator Kerrey,

We haven't spoken in sixteen years. The last time I talked with you was at the Glass Onion Restaurant in Lincoln, Nebraska. At that time you were entertaining a pretty lady and I was sporting a white kitchen apron. I stepped away from my dish pile for a moment to ask you for a special favor.

I was the classic poor, starving college student. Late nights, I swept up at Grandmother's Skillet. During the day, I held down kitchen help as I went to school. For several years I cycled everywhere, frequently wearing my entire wardrobe, during many a Nebraska winter month. And, through all of that, I always enjoyed six A.M., when you would make a pot of coffee and pour me a cup.

I knew you to be a successful person and a hard driver. At twenty-two, I found that to be so impressive. Later I learned that you won the Medal of Honor for duty in North Vietnam and that you were a member of the elite group, the Navy SEALS. I put two and two together.

When we last spoke, I asked you for a recommendation to the Navy's Aviation Officer Candidate School. I asked if it would be all right to use you for a reference and if you would fill out their questionnaire. I remember so well how your face lit up with a large smile. You thought that to be a terrific idea and said, "Yes!"

Well, my peer group thought differently and I felt the world was on my shoulders. In 1980, our divisions as a nation ran deep. Everyone still argued over Vietnam and the military was out of favor. But with that short, two-minute conversation, Senator Kerrey, you influenced me and my life changed for the better, forever. I remember saying to myself, "Hell, if Bob Kerrey thinks it's a great idea, the rest just have to be wrong." Senator Kerrey, you and I were <u>right</u>. I never bothered you for the paperwork because your word was enough.

My military flying career took me to Pensacola, then to the west coast at Moffett for two deployments to Japan, a detachment in Diego Garcia and Adak, Alaska. My final eighteen months were in Key West, Florida. (Throw me in that briar patch.)

I spent the next four years flying as a civilian in Berlin, Germany. I witnessed the collapse of communism and the fall of the Berlin Wall, right in my backyard! For three years, following the Pan Am bankruptcy, I worked out of the JFK airport. Then I hired on at a small firm, Conditioned Airways Inc.

This week I arrived home from my first month of flying as Captain for Conditioned Airways. As Captain on the MD-11, my first landing was in Hong Kong. Later this month I will go back to Honolulu, fly to the Philippines, and then return home via Vancouver. Not bad, for a kid with dishpan hands!

Senator Kerrey, I never will forget 6 A.M. at Grandmother's. You made an impression and a difference in my life. For that, I know this is long overdue but it's all I can say. Thank you.

Neal Schupbach

I forgot all about my letter after a few days and went back out on a trip that took me, once again, on an extended stay in the Far East. When I returned, there was a small, handwritten letter waiting in a large stack of my mail. It was from Senator Robert Kerrey.

He wrote:

Dear Neal,

Thank you for your very kind letter, which gave me a boost. Strangers too often presume they have nothing to give or learn from each other. Heads down, hearts closed, minds steeled to our work, we forget to stay awake to our greatest gift: a dose of kindness. You are good to remember.

Best wishes to you always,

Bob Kerrey

Four years after receiving that letter, a full twenty years after the last conversation I had with Senator Kerrey, I sat down and wrote out what happened to me next in AOCS, flight school and beyond. The challenges of breaking free from my peer group, learning to fly, and serving my country against the Soviet Union, gave me the education of a lifetime. After working so hard cramming in the technical, I found, in Somalia of all places, that I had lost my humanity. But I was not alone on that one, which frightened me.

The mental conditioning of the Navy prepared me for the twists and turns of aviation. But the harsh realities of the world shocked my heart, pierced the "get it behind you" compartmental teachings of military service, and inspired me to write—in a large sense to pay off another very special debt.

These are the stories of what I found and of the people along the way. May they lift us all out from our safely enclosed environments and place us within the challenge of the slipstream beyond. May we listen to the whisper of the winds.

Aviation Officer Candidate School

CHAPTER TWO

They say that you can never go back. I have always believed otherwise, but time does leave its imprints. New and young walk hand-in-hand, but there comes a time to let go and press on with life. I came to this revelation after revisiting three very significant places in my time on this planet: my hometown of Lincoln, Nebraska; Berlin, Germany; and Navy Pensacola, Florida.

Life and its destiny are matters of choice in this free land of America. When I got a break in simulator training, I chose to go back to where I first learned to fly in the Navy. My return visit to "Hotel Pensacola" supported the argument that you can go back. I first attended AOCS there, and as the song says: "You can checkout any time you want, but you can never leave."

From Interstate 10, I drove through the back gate, thereby entering the base from the west. My first stop was the Naval Air Museum. No tour of the Pensacola base is complete without visiting this magnificent display of American Naval Aviation. I wish I could revisit it every day.

My impressions now, however, were not of the exhibit, but rather of my memories as an Aviation Officer Candidate visiting the museum for the first time. My buddy, Picket, first told me about the museum. Over the course of the AOCS program, I visited the national treasure twice: once with most of my classmates and another time with my parents when they attended my commissioning ceremonies.

I walked towards the museum entrance and thought of those good times with my mother and father. Once again, I viewed the magnificent engine cutaways, read the tales of the NC-4—the first aircraft to fly across the Atlantic Ocean, and marveled at the World War II fighter aircraft. Most impressive are the fundamental design changes that rapidly came about during the war effort. At that time, my mother served in the Navy as a WAVE in San Francisco, while my father served overseas in the Army. Being escorted by a son in a white, naval uniform and seeing him commissioned; well—especially for my mother, it was a very proud day, indeed.

Walking in front of the museum, I yearned to have my parents with me at Pensacola once again. They were part of my original journey and so pleased when I became a Naval Aviator. The times changed this visit to just a trip down memory lane. The Naval Air Museum had grown in size and complexity, and in some respects, so had I. With my Navy flying long behind me, the museum brought back the good times and I remembered the efforts required to succeed. At that moment in my minds eye, time painted a bittersweet, statuary masterpiece, as if the display was time itself gone by: time relived, time captured, through the sights and sounds of aviation. Momentarily, standing there on the front sidewalk, I forgot the currency, the cost of being part of the unusual business of aviation flight. Only thoughts of good times, not the bad, held me in thrall.

You actually grew to love the guys in green, the Marines. AOCS, Aviation Officer Candidate School, was boot camp for future officers: those who desired to become Navy pilots and naval flight officers. The Marines transformed men and women into officers, not privates. Eventually, you grew to love your drill instructor, the infamous DI. Each DI was the Marines' best, the top two percent of the Marine Corps drill instructor group. They were good—very, very good at everything and every detail. "Attention to detail" became a candidate's words to live and die by.

I remember meeting my DI after the first week of indoctrination, when the medicals were over and the paperwork had all been taken care of. It was time to get down to business. Promptly at five in the morning, we woke to the clean, crisp sound of a thirty-five-gallon trashcan being bounced down the hall. This was our alarm clock. Bullhorn sirens were followed by the sound of Staff Sergeant Black's amplified voice. Life couldn't get any better—a rack, a roof, three squares a day and push-up counts at the top of your lungs. Five in the morning became all too familiar.

One had to keep one's sense of humor or else leave the program on request—with a shaved head. The days were long, with seven hours of shut-eye in between and, whether or not a DI or Student Officer was on hand, the very thought of their presence kept the pressure-cooker boiling. But, I wasn't there to fail; I took the attitude that I would pull the floor tile up with my fingernails as they dragged me out before going back to Lincoln a defeated man. Besides, in Nebraska, a depression ravaged the state. I had nothing to go home to and fear of failure ran first place, several strides ahead of my fears of the DI.

The Pensacola Pressure Cooker quickly became nasty, in your face, and on you like white on rice for very good reasons. As a candidate, you were there to earn a commission, to become an officer in the United States Navy, to attend the finest flight school the world has to offer—or be weeded out. Typically, the weeding process eliminated fifty percent of those recruited. Many didn't even show up, while others "Dropped on Request" (DOR). To DOR was all too encouraged by the drill instructor as he often shouted, "If you can't hack it, why should we trust you with a thirty million-dollar airplane? NUT!"

Everyone thinks about dropping out, but you learn to compartmentalize. You learn that such moments come and go and in the morning, it's a brand-new day. The experience of the previous day is so far behind you that it doesn't matter anymore. *Compartmentalization* is a big word for one of the big lessons of the fourteen weeks spent earning a commission. *Never quitting* was another maxim for survival. Besides, there would come a day when others would be in flight school and you might not be able to look at the man in the mirror without being there yourself.

As the newest class, we were called "Poopies." Our daily routine began by doing push-ups and jumping jacks in our skivvies, followed by marshaling on the sidewalk, posthaste. We tried our very best to fall into three lines, shortest to tallest in rapid fashion. Staff Sergeant Black yelled at each and every one of us for our constant foul-ups, lack of military courtesy, discipline, desire and general unworthiness to be in his very presence. He was always present. He had eyes in the back of his head, ears in every room, and an attitude to let you know it. However, he was the easygoing DI of the battalion and wasn't always appreciated by his peer group because of it. At first, I wasn't convinced of this; but then we were introduced to Sergeant Dixon who liked very small classes.

We marched down to the chow hall, one that didn't contain enough seats for all of the classes at one sitting. Accordingly, meal times were staggered and limited to a certain number of people. When your time came to eat, you ate. When it was time to leave, you fell back as a class into formation in front of the mess. While dining, there were no privileges, no coffee, no talking, and no looking at your neighbor—not until the class passed inspection and was "secured."

Candidates and the Chow Hall

Moreover, during that first week, three other colleagues assisted the ever-present DI in patrolling the Poopies. That's where we met Gunnery Sergeant Fletcher, who made a point of getting to you any way he possibly could. That morning was the first any of us ever experienced someone walking on a dining table while eating. In full uniform, complete with a Smoky-the-Bear hat, he stepped between the trays, shouting "Keep your head down...drink your milk...don't look up...salt your food and eat everything on your plate! There's an inspection at the door."

The inspection consisted of push-ups and side-straddle hops for those who failed to ingest the government-issued nutrition. Up and down, back and forth, the DIs swarmed around the new classes, circling like sharks and making enough noise to wake the dead. It was quite an experience.

While going through the chow line, there were rituals each candidate performed with silverware and tray, carefully hiding one's face behind the tray until returning the class leader's greeting. We then lowered our trays and kept moving along the cafeteria line with bowed head, accepting the scrambled eggs and oatmeal without any gesture or common courtesy. At the end of the line, each Poopie went over to the table directed by the drill instructor and stood until the entire table was present. This seemed fine at first, but Pensacola early morning weather during February was quite cool. The open windows on both ends of the long tables frosted your meal by the time your class assembled. For the next fourteen weeks, everyone learned to force down cold eggs, cold toast, cold hamburgers and cold everything else in the name of nutrition and simultaneously pass inspection at the end of the dining experience. Many candidates didn't pass and come rain or shine, they paid for this transgression on the mess deck or lawn. "Just begin" was the command. "One-two, one-two, one-two, one-two...!"

Next came the issuance of the green Poopie-clothing, silver painted "chrome domes" followed by our new stylish haircut right down to the nubs. It hurt your hand to touch the top of your head. The women's hair was simply butchered, in line with indoctrination. A blur of 5 A.M. wake-up calls, inspections and drilling filled the rest of the week.

To help prepare for the first Friday inspection, the senior class of candidate officers intentionally wasted our time. They pretended to show us how to fold our clothing in a square. A half-hour later, they couldn't recall the small procedure. Much to my amazement, there was method to their madness that worked quite well as a process.

Three classmates dropped on request the evening before inspection. They prowled the hall, shouting, "This is a bunch of bullshit; they're just wasting our time!" Frustration completely overshadowed their goal of wearing the wings of gold—all over how to properly fold underwear and tee shirts. The system quickly weeded out undesirable candidates, while motivating those who could hack it and retain information at the highest possible rate.

People are as different as the day is long and their ability to deal with frustration is an important factor in Navy training. Psychologists demonstrated that those who easily frustrate are most likely to exhibit anxiety, worry and alcoholism than those who can manage stress. The programmed hazing also finds those who, as we used to scream in unison, are "highly motivated." Self-selection built a team from a group of individual college graduates and effectively eliminated many with undesirable personality characteristics. Those who deal with frustration well tend to put large amounts of effort into their work. Scared into pleasing from the hazing, Hotel Pensacola provided the candidate with the motivation to absorb material at twice the rate of their college days. In short, people began to focus.

On the next afternoon of what became the first of many inspections, each of the forty guys occupying each room within the battalion called "Poopieville" traded their Poopie greens for khaki uniforms, standing at attention alongside each locker. The sound the inspection made came close to what people say they hear for approaching tornadoes—a ferocious freight train. One DI broke the neck off of a small bottle of Listerine, chugged it and then began tearing apart all of the candidates, piece by piece.

Sergeant Black, a seriously proud, African American marine, led his group of Marines down the hall, up, over, around and through each room, locker and over each person; thus demonstrating the term RLP inspection for room, locker, personnel. We all failed, but still graduated as part of the program. We didn't yet measure up, but we didn't quit and thereby earned another chance to get squared away. You simply had to keep laughing or you had to DOR.

Right after the event, we were ordered downstairs to pick up a large box. We placed all of our possessions inside, hustled back downstairs and marched around the block. We surveyed the campus while carrying everything we either brought or purchased at NAS Pensacola. My recruiter warned me to take "a razor in one pocket and a toothbrush in the other." His sage advice to pack light was providential that day because it was a very heavy box.

Several people quit during the forced hike to the new battalion. Clothing, hats, personal items and people were strewn along the path leading from Poopieville. Quitters, in their new uniforms, just sat in the dirt or on the lawn, unable to go on. Yet another weed-out with very little money spent, especially on flight training. To be blunt, they would have quit during flight training or worse. In the not-so-distant future, lives would be at stake. A quitter is not the person you want flying on your wing or in a rescue helicopter at night over open water hovering directly above you. Quitters went to X-Company with shaved heads and civilian clothes. Every candidate learned to never look back. That day we learned the expression, "The breaks of Naval Air."

Once in the battalion with our possessions secured in lockers, they ordered us out in our physical training gear for what would become a ritual. The long run that followed every inspection served as a release for the pent-up energy, adrenalin, and fear of the thousand ways of failing. Each time we went out on such excursions, the course inevitably increased in length, proportional to our expectations that we were near the end of the exercise.

We ran in formation—left-left-lefty-riiighta-left—up and around the major roads of the Navy's largest base. Then we'd come back to the battalion for a few laps in the courtyard, only to be led out again down the street. We were frustrated, but we kept laughing; otherwise it could be *you* sitting in the dirt.

Just the disappointment and agitation of not knowing the length of a run broke more than one candidate's will to become a navy pilot. This easy and inexpensive "instruction" in the practice of patience claimed victims in its own way, not from physical exertion but from the psychological stress of not knowing the location of the finish line. AOCS repeated these lessons over and over and over again in every class. I survived by enjoying singing our first *joedies* along the way.

That night someone played the song *Hotel California* over the battalion loudspeakers: "You can check out anytime you like but you can never leave!" I thought it was a super-cool thing to do for the incoming class. For that reason, I always remember battalion life not as AOCS, but rather as Hotel Pensacola. No other hotel came with such "fun." Then, from out of nowhere came our big brother class, shouting and screaming orders and interrogating each candidate in the hallway. We pressed our backs firmly up against the bulkhead, shouting out answers or the all too familiar, "Sir, this candidate does not know but will find out, Sir!"

As the traditional hazing continued, we ran between the rooms, all forty of us crammed into one little room and then the next. The surprise party started in the fourth room. The guys had purchased cokes and candy bars for all of us and stored them in coolers under a bed. They ordered our group to discover the coolers and then open and inspect the contents. Each of us was uncertain as to the meaning of the last five minutes of terror. *This place just never gives up.* We didn't have anything to do with these forbidden "gee-dunk items." The surprise was on us. Led by a loud shout from the upper classmen, we all broke out in hysterical laughter. The surprise was the traditional Poopie-party and all of us had been had by the indoctrination chop. On Friday night, just two weeks into the fourteen, it felt just damn good to be alive.

The infamous rifle run started week three. Nine-pound rifles, M1A1 assault carbines were heavy enough locked away in their storage racks, but after a three mile run to the armory, these antiques became a real challenge. The trick to the next four miles of sweat and pleasure was keeping the rifle tight against your chest at all times. Forty guys and about five DIs started out in a formation run. When the pavement ended, the trail picked up at the cross-country circuit. It then went over to the beach for several hundred yards and finally onto the open road again. People launched two at a time with a marine at their side barking orders. By mid-course, everyone wondered about their decision to join the Navy.

My running partner fell on a sandy incline and I, like everyone else, just kept going. Out of the corner of my eye, I saw him close his eyes and pancake the dune. Immediately, two instructors were on the guy yelling, "Die candidate, just die!" But a few steps later, the most interesting resurrection came about. He magically appeared next to me, running with his rifle tucked neatly against his chest. The voices of the marines had transformed him from a horizontal stiff back into my running mate.

I could hardly believe my eyes. I thought he would never get up or, at least, be at the end of the line, not running next to me as if nothing occurred. Only the sand on his forehead gave testimony to his stumble. Others who failed had their rifles taken from them and tossed into the bay waters, suffusing them with salt and mud. Once we made it back to the barracks the exercising continued, but now with rifles for our conditioning. It was a bitch, but no one quit.

The one-mile swim, completed in a flight suit, helmet, and leather steel-toed boots was another week three hurdle each of us faced. To swim a mile is hard enough, but the Navy had us weighted down in all this gear. I realized that swimming on my back would be the easiest thing, sculling with my arms and frog kicking. *Never mind the boots kicking your face and the helmets colliding, simply cruise through the pool like enjoying a day on the beach.* This worked and I rapidly floated my bloated way into an early finish. If only everyone else could have seen me, I would have made good on the glory. But as I struggled out of the pool, I received a "Good job," verbal commendation from the instructor Lieutenant. This was enough to boost my spirits. I passed the check ride on the first attempt and didn't have to come back.

Yet life as I knew it became quite unbearable. I left a lifestyle filled with music and art. Hotel Pensacola denied even the simplest of pleasures. Besides class work and survival training, our other focus was water skills. Later that week, however, after drown-proofing in the deep end of the pool, a reprieve arrived by way of a request for volunteers to play in the AOCS parade band. Even if we couldn't play well, they used anyone interested. A large ceremonial piece, the band played at weekly graduations and only recently had received adequate funding from Uncle Sam. Unable to read music, I at least volunteered to listen to the music every day.

After just one practice parade, the band instructor understood I was not to be trusted with so much as a wooden block. "I can still use you," he said, "Stay put." So I hung tight and listened for what my lowly hairball self could do for him. Thus began my ten-week career as the AOCS band librarian. It wasn't a glorious job, but I listened to music and avoided rifle drill and marching in the parade on Thursdays and Fridays.

I organized and distributed the band's sheet music all week. On Fridays, I typed up the participant listing of everyone who played in the band. From this list, the drill instructors awarded points that were traded for demerits and extra military instruction. My newfound responsibilities were a good deal because I hated watching a long procession of public gatherings, week after week, only to wonder when it would be my turn to cross the stage. I dreaded the long march and ceremonial rifle drill every

Friday morning, having no escape from the routine of the Pensacola Pressure Cooker.

Taking all of this into consideration, I leapt at the opportunity to serve my country as the AOCS band librarian and delivered a filing system from complete chaos. After a few clowns ahead of me stepped aside, things came together nicely. In fact, I later heard how the band conductor thought highly of my assistance and organization. He was better able to find everything and conduct far more effective practice sessions because of my efforts.

I began to understand how my extra effort paid rewards. I saved up my brownie points in advance—the DI's never really gave them to me. I demonstrated self-motivation and Marines like motivation, as well as they like the Marine Hymn: both of which I aided. Unfortunately, my rifle drilling skills were not as adequate as the others. I didn't practice two days a week in the parade and everyone knew that. I wish someone had told my classmates. My tactics had their drawbacks.

My recruiter, "The Weasel," instructed me in my survival strategy. With knowledge of the Midwest, Weasel came across as a truthful, vibrant individual. He gave me a few ideas that quickly became near and dear to my heart. "To survive," he said, "be sure to hide so well that your Drill Instructor doesn't even learn your name."

This worked up until the last week of class. We were to raise the flag for the next graduation when Staff Sergeant Black called me *Williams*. I kept on responding. We readied the flag to be hoisted up the pole when he noticed that the flag would be upside down, a sign of surrender. After much to do about all of our careers, Staff Sergeant Black looked up at me and said, "You're not Williams." The Weasel's strategy worked.

The Weasel offered another piece of wisdom: "Always remember that they are all trying to kill you." But except for a few occasions in Deep Water Survival Training or DWEST as it's called, this dealt with flight school more than AOCS. Everything there was carefully orchestrated for realistic scenarios: the parachute disentanglement drill, the Dilbert Dunker (featured in the movie, *An Officer and a Gentleman*), the Helo-Dunker that brought sheer terror to many a grown man's soul, and trolling for sharks—you are the bait.

His immortal words, "They are all trying to kill you," stuck out in my mind. He said, "That's the hard way to earn your wings...to die trying. Unfortunately, there will be more."

Those early words taught me to take "The breaks of Naval Air" seriously. I knew there would be more. The Weasel's main complaint was that he was tired of going to funerals, especially those of the kids he recruited.

Water survival and qualifications seemed an every day occurrence. It's easy to forget classroom instruction on Naval history and the like. But no one forgets the hours spent jumping off towers and swimming the length of the pool underwater, or drown-proofing, where buoyancy must be maintained without using arms or legs *and* without touching pool bottom. Then, there was the mile swim. This turned into a ten-mile swim for some, because they failed at the last moment, always having to come back for another round.

We were coached to relax every time we entered the pool environment. Relax—while you have class examinations coming and an RLP inspection that afternoon, followed by an hour of close-order rifle drill. *Relax*, our mantra for the day, while surrounded by water deep enough to float a fifty-foot sail boat. Somehow I did learn to relax and I actually began to like the water environment.

I tried to gain as much from every water experience as I could because of two things: the Weasel and the "Breaks of Naval Air." In the very bottom of my heart, I knew "They were all trying to kill me," so I paid attention. I quickly learned that I needed to make every mistake possible during the work-ups to pass a check ride. Although the course work instilled what you were to do, I also learned exactly what not to do. It's sort of like having to drive in a strange city. You get lost a couple of times before you learn your way around. I took this to the extreme.

Our water indoctrination began with using survival life-preserver apparatus or "LPA." We stood beside the pool next to the parachute disentanglement device. Those issuing the gear told us to try it on for fit. I noticed two sets of inflatable devices on each side of this body harness. Obviously, I wanted my head floating above the waterline, so I concluded that the large bladders would be on top around my neck and the small ones around my waist. That's how I retrofitted myself within the LPA, only to be congratulated for being the first person to wear the LPA completely upside down.

After a brief bout of embarrassment, I began to understand my need to make every mistake possible beforehand in order to pass the check ride. Behaving in this manner afforded me more bang for my buck. Not only did I learn what to do, but also what not to do and why. It's the square of distance rule. The farther away from my goal, the larger the box I tend to operate in.

With that being said, my experience in the Dilbert Dunker became one of my most difficult and complex lessons in confidence-building and situational training. There are no escapes from the jaws of this "simulator device," a trainer that simulates an aircraft ditching in the ocean. From a height of fifteen feet, rails guided the cockpit as it slid down and slammed into the water with jarring force.

We first understood the great need for spatial orientation and situational awareness during this "E-ticket" ride. Initially, the ride made you nervous, startled you with the impact, and then rotated you 180 degrees upside down and left you hanging in your straps underwater. To begin the ride, we were fitted in our helmets, flight boots, and flight suits. Our hands were occupied with the simulated flight controls.

Our instructions were, "After the airplane comes to a complete stop, pull your canopy release handle, release your five-way seat restraint straps from their common fitting, press your body through the opening below your head, and swim away without kicking."

Even the slightest kicking motion might snare and entangle you in the sinking aircraft. Two divers with extra regulators were present in the water as safety observers and rescue swimmers. I found out that they get pretty bent out of shape when things go wrong ten feet under water.

For me, this "E-ticket ride" looked simple enough, so I took the ladder with great confidence. After all, everyone else came out of the pool alive and there were those two safety instructors, each of whom had an air lifeline should things go wrong. And did they ever go wrong!

I remember the anticipation, the slide, the crash, being flipped upside down, and actuating the canopy release handle. Next, I found the quick release for my belt, but I was unable to move away from the aircraft. I worked at it continually, still unable to free myself from the aircraft. Had I been in the real situation, the Weasel would have made yet another mournful trip, dressed respectfully in his service, dress-blue uniform into the heartland of America. Fortunately, this was a pool and the safety divers were in on me immediately. One stood by with the emergency regulator while the other reached in, pushed my hands out of his way and released my five-way harness. Finally free, I pushed out, pulled myself through the water and returned to the surface.

It was there that the diver informed me that I had released the parachute harness instead of the seat straps. Confused and embarrassed, I went back into the waiting line for a second ride, the check ride. I knew I needed to overcome my emotions and remember the diver's instructions as well as the others. My recruiter's words echoed in my mind, "They are all trying to kill you!" Once again, AOCS became personal.

The Dilbert Dunker shook my confidence. I spoke with my buddies and gathered my thoughts. All the while, I acted out my procedures for the trainer, moving my hands about the imaginary cockpit, as did others standing poolside watching our classmates go through the drill. Others made mistakes; no one came through water survival unscathed. It wasn't meant for that.

In all honesty, my second run through the Dunker came up too fast. I cautiously crept back into the trainer, strapped in and double-checked which fittings unbuckled the separate straps, and reminded myself to take a few deep breaths. I felt confident my previous conditioning would allow me a few extra moments to slow down, think and succeed. Then they said, "Wait for the bubbles to clear."

Slide, jolt, crash, flip, splash. Before I knew what hit me, I hung upside down, waiting for the bubbles to clear. *Shit,* I thought, *I forgot to hold my breath.* Now underwater, I remembered that I didn't catch a quick last breath. I had simply busied myself with a head full of instructions. While hanging upside down underwater, I cursed at myself. *You idiot, Schupbach!.* But then the training began to pay off. I kept calm, jettisoned the simulated canopy, let the bubbles pass while finding both releases, chose the correct one and climbed out of the craft in a slow and deliberate manner. I didn't die this time. But once I surfaced, the divers complained that I took too much time. Because they had contemplated giving me an air line, I had to go through yet another ride.

I didn't like their decision. *But*, I thought, *If I make every mistake before the authentic experience, I'll have a better chance of surviving.* Embarrassed, but not giving up, I went back in line for a third, hopefully final, try. There were few, if any, jeers while we rode this ride from hell. Everyone knew, but would not confess, that in the grips of this machine we were all equal. Pecking order, conceit, or rank, there were no favors given in water survival, which is as it should be. There were no drill instructors present during this training phase. We weathered enough stress without them and I never saw anyone DOR solely from water survival.

The water drills gave me a great appreciation and understanding of the need for spatial orientation and situational awareness. These trainers led up to the master ride of the Navy's underwater theme park, the dreaded and much feared Helo-Dunker. The Dilbert Dunker simply prepared you for the worst. The Helo-Dunker truly was the worst. Preparation or not, participant or spectator, everyone involved respected this machine. If you cheated on the warm-ups, may the Good Lord help you when you're in the real deal, blindfolded eight feet under water, fifteen feet from the only way out.

During the 1970s, there were numerous helicopter crashes at sea, and the fatality rate (although it could have been better) never drew much attention until one night over the Adriatic. An H-3 helicopter, with approximately six admirals on board, went into the drink. As all good helicopters do during a ditch, the machine rolled over because of the high center of mass. Into the ink-black sea they went, enlisted men and officers, E-3 to O-8, but the airmen showed an enormous advantage. The entire aircrew, from pilots to sonar operators survived. They oriented themselves and maintained reference points with their hands, found the escape doors and pulled their way out of the inverted bird, while submerged under the cold water at night. Fortunately, they were all rescued and their story became legendary.

The admirals were not so lucky. All of them died. The inquiry board feverishly raked through the details of the accident. Too much attention was focused on this event for it to quietly go away. At Flag level, everyone knows everyone else. The high brass wanted to know why their friends perished in the middle of the night while the aircrew survived. These leaders also realized their vulnerability. The investigation uncovered one important fact after another. The most important factor in crew survival was training. Lack of up-to-date practice in water-survival training came up as the most important factor in the loss of each and every one of the Admirals on board. Their training records documented this over and over again.

The Chief of Naval Operations (CNO) promulgated a new training program regarding all water-survival skills training and documentation. Now you are required to complete water-survival training every three years before going onboard a naval aircraft. After thirty-six months, your documentation expires and you are grounded, not even allowed to be a passenger. (It is interesting to note that rock star Jimmy Buffet played morale concerts on board ships for the price of an F-14 ride. He, too, went through the qualifications and he claimed that those same skills saved his life when his own amphibious aircraft crashed during takeoff one foggy morning. The training works.)

Undoubtedly, the helicopter dunker stood in everyone's way to commissioning. The enlisted men that ran the program had their fiefdom handed to them directly from the CNO. If you wanted to fly, fine. But you had to get through their program to do it and they played no favorites. Their kingdom consisted of a large, barrel-shaped object made of green fiberglass. Inside, fiberglass seats were molded right into the external frame. The shape of the object resembled the body of a CH-46 helicopter, a utility bird that could break into three pieces during flight if conditions were right. The Helo-Dunker would not break apart, but it well simulated water entry of this vehicle.

As with the Dilbert Dunker, there were at least two divers in the water with extra regulators at all times. They could communicate with each other and the surface instructors, who participated in grading each student as well as elevating the level of safety. The ride, or more specifically, rides (at least four were required to graduate) were designed to disorient the students and force them to work their way out of the sinking helicopter through the hand-to-fixed-object orientation method; all of this while dangling upside down in twenty-foot-deep water.

The simulator sat on cables that supported the barrel as well as controlled its rolling motion. From a height of eight or ten feet, the barrel and participants dropped to the surface, simulating the impact of a crash at sea. It rolled back and forth once or twice and finally sank upside down into the artificial abyss. The students were left to climb out of designated exits, some located behind them, others over and through the cockpit, simulating a jammed-door scenario. Understandably, it became a mess in a real hurry, which is probably what killed those Admirals.

After the poolside lectures, participants went up the ladder and into one of four varied positions. Each run through the beast became progressively harder. The four students traded seats and were given different exits to complete the maneuver. On the third and fourth ride, each student was blindfolded with goggles that were painted black, making things a little more interesting. One student candidate swam out of the bottom of the sinking bird. The door just happened to be facing straight down at the time. He kicked and pulled his way twenty feet straight down, hit the bottom of the pool with his head, and then swam straight up, reentering the dying chopper. Fortunately, a rescue diver was there to greet him with a bottle of air. Those who survived the first two rides by finding their way out with their eyes instead of their hands were now in a real bind. Their ass was grass and the Helo was the mower. And mow them down it did.

Many students repeated this maneuver a fifth time, a sixth time, and some came back for a full work-up on another day. There in the Helo-Dunker, terror was for sale to far too many buyers. My own floundering in the Dilbert Dunker and other places taught me to pay attention, learn from all of the mistakes and then not duplicate them during the check ride. My last position, the left front, came with two escape procedures. Ride three required me to go out the back hatch, while the final check ride had me exiting my copilot's emergency escape hatch to my immediate right. Blindfolded, each scenario was a terrific challenge, but I survived and made it through on the first try. I was quite proud of that, after my less-than-stellar showing on the Dilbert Dunker.

On that sunny afternoon of my return to Pensacola, I woke from my reverie beneath the F-14 Tomcat static display and entered the museum where I met an interesting British pilot. We talked for sometime about his experiences. Retired from flying the DC-10 in Great Britain, he told of picking up brand new aircraft at the factory, pilot training in the actual airplane, and spending great amounts of time with the factory test pilots and engineers. He could go on for hours about the details, right down to the millimeter. While we stood in front of a large-scale model of the U.S.S. Lexington, I shared the story of how the city of Chicago named an airfield after a man who flew from the U.S.S. Lexington in World War II. He won the Congressional Medal of Honor for his flying.

"Actually it's a story about a father and a son," I said. "The father felt shame for living the good life. He and his family occupied a large house and grounds that encompassed a full city block—compensatory reward for defending Al Capone, keeping the gangster out of jail. But he so much wanted to be someone his son could look up to and be proud of. So the father turned state's evidence, only to be gunned down in a dark alley a year later."

The British pilot was properly impressed.

"Al Capone, you say? How did this figure into the U.S.S. Lexington?"

"The young man exemplified his father's self-sacrifice by joining the Navy during the war. As a fighter pilot on an aborted mission, he single-handedly attacked two squadrons of Japanese planes before they closed on the defenseless carrier, the Lady Lexington. After depleting his ammunition, the young man rammed the enemy's fuselage, cloth and wooden Zeros, mid-flight and scattered their formation in the process. This single man saved the Lady Lexington and her crew to fight another day, earning nothing less than the Congressional Medal of Honor. The city of Chicago named Chicago's O'Hare Field after this recipient of the nation's highest honor. It's quite the father and son flying story."

My new acquaintance nodded and smiled, looking up at the Lady Lexington and no doubt remembering many such stories of his land. On his recommendation, I purchased an IMAX theater ticket featuring the Blue Angels before departing for lunch. *If I time it just right*, I thought, *my return will enable me to view the film and take the self-guided tour.* I drove to the nearby Chief's Club on the water. Over lunch, I peered out the window and noted the helicopter operating near an old amphibious assault boat. The boat appeared to be dropping men overboard from the stern of the vessel.

I've been there, I thought, *the drop, the splash, the roll onto the back, releasing the koak fittings, escaping the parachute drag, climbing into a life raft.* Coincidentally, I observed the open-water survival training classes in Pensacola Bay that I had been reminiscing about. *They are trolling for sharks and you're the bait,* I said to myself, remembering Weasel's words. *It must be chilly in those waters. Thank God I went through in May, not February.*

While I ate lunch, my attention was focused instead on the scene beyond the plate glass window. Water survival could be compared to how my elders told me they went to school: uphill, in the snow, both ways. If you wanted to proceed, you were the only one holding you back. If you wanted to give up or fail, why were you there in the first place? Repeating the maneuver wasn't a failure. Just get it done so that you can press on to the next obstacle. If you showed a good attitude, you wouldn't wash out of any water survival qualification program. Your attitude had to be "Just get it done" because you didn't graduate or attend flight training without the qualifications of water survival signed off in your NATOPS' jacket.

After lunch I took in the museum tour and the mighty display of four, blue–with yellow striped "Blue Angel" aircraft. They hung in the sky in their famous diamond formation, impressing everyone, myself included. On top of that, there was the movie. Watching the amazing, most dangerous flying scenes captured on film, I soared with those aircraft—absolutely exhilarating. The afternoon wore on. Priorities, compartmentalization, and time management were ever present to draw me away.

I drove toward the battalions, only stopping for a glimpse of the obstacle course. Nothing much had changed there. The walls were still high; the rat maze appeared to be the same long length and the main obstacle—the sand, as deep as ever. My back ached just looking at the course; but, my heart longed for the spirit the class demonstrated there, psyching each other up for better and better times, qualifying everyone in the end through cheering and willpower.

I parked near the sea wall, across from the battalions. These classic, red brick buildings are still in remarkable condition, just as beautiful that day as they were twenty years before. The two-story buildings were trimmed with wide verandas on each floor, faced by four white columns that supported a triangular, single peak over the entryway and quarterdeck. Blue stairs led to a lower veranda with broad, yellow borders, welcoming visitors and family alike. The wide lawns were in rough shape from mornings at five-fifteen sharp, and just about any other time anyone cared to complete fifty pushups and jumping jacks after eating.

In front of the chow hall stood the large tree Hackman marched into, taking the entire column of men with him as if it were scripted. Many others did just the same. That tree was quite the training aid. I found my old room, at least from the outside. I slept next to the window on the quiet north side. The trees there had a soft touch and I gained comfort and escape from AOCS through their whispers at night.

I walked down the block, around the corner, and past the instructional sand pit. Across the street was the classroom hall. The yard grew some grass but a drill instructor currently worked on that oversight. I remembered how one of my drill instructors actually trained his classes there during black flag days, even though soaring temperatures made outdoor physical exertion dangerous. Because the lawn sprinklers blazed hotter than the hot Florida sunshine, he could exercise his class on the muddy yard under the watchful eyes of the Commanding Officer's F-4 Phantom aircraft. I even saw Captain Raddison smiling at the creativity of the ordeal. Only the F-4 had changed; an A-6 Intruder now stood in its place.

I walked a few more blocks and recalled all of the mischief I shoveled out to Craytor, a fellow candidate who marched directly in front of me during class movement and formation. On occasions we were commanded "nuts to butts"—a maneuver in which no one felt comfortable. I remembered counting aloud the pimples and blemishes on Craytor's neck, just shy of earshot from the nearest instructor. On the sidewalk, I turned up the intensity and harassed poor Craytor about his legs, rear end, manly shoulders, membership in the man-boy love society, and every other gay or bisexual reference imaginable, all the while remaining at attention. Most of the class could hear the score, hardly containing their laughter. Even the Drill Sergeant at the front of the class caught a few laughing. I carefully suppressed my smiles.

A most interesting coincidence occurred during my original stay at Hotel Pensacola. We heard rumors that Hollywood wanted to produce a movie on campus about the AOCS program. Instead of a documentary, it was to be a full-length movie about the rigors of training and the beginnings of Naval Aviators. This made for interesting speculation, but the Commanding Officer read the script and thought it uncomplimentary to the Navy. Additionally, he felt the film crews would distract from the real training at NAS Pensacola. Not to be kept out of the limelight, however, was Gunnery Sergeant Fletcher.

Hollywood selected Fletcher for their technical advisor in the famous movie, *An Officer and a Gentleman.* To all who knew him, it became obvious who wrote much of the language found in the script. During inspections, Fletcher routinely made such comments and the candidates believed every word.

In reality, Fletcher didn't have to open his mouth to influence anyone. His gift of command presence came across to everyone within a fifty-yard radius. One evening he stood abreast of my doorway in his Marine, dress-blue uniform, complete with enough medals to sink a freighter.

"Oh, you just keep it up, candidate," he said in reaction to my feet being on the table in front of me while I talked with my roommates with a book in my lap. I straightened up in a hurry and my grades improved overnight.

Fletcher left the battalion to assist in the film and standards began to relax as a result. Classes started passing the RLP inspections on the first try. This granted them privileges such as talking in the chow hall, coffee, walking unescorted on campus and, of course, being allowed to visit momma. When Gunny Fletcher returned, my class had our first RLP, trying to become secured and regain privileges. We failed, not badly, but failed just the same. With our failure, a rumor arose that the base had become too loose and now it was time to crack the whip. Most likely this wasn't true, but it was rumored nonetheless. The next week we failed our second inspection as well. On our third, we failed again

During inspection, one of my mistakes became a joke for just about everyone. I was so involved with the goings-on of the band that I missed an item on my own rifle inspection. The rifle itself was clean and looked good throughout. The thing was perfect except for the butt plate, a small storage locker located in the rear of the stock. The butt plate contained a ring of rust inside the steel lip and face. In a very loud voice, the DI awarded me a zero on my rifle. Craytor, who resided across the hall from my room, laughed and laughed: "Schupbach, even if you just have a rifle, that's worth at least three points and you got a zero."

At the time of laying my infamous goose egg, my roommate, Picket, engaged Fletcher, lip-to-lip, in a yelling festival. The Gunny pushed his lips into Picket's and Picket, in perfect attention, bent backwards over his bed and touched the wall with the back of his head. These two went lip-to-lip in a resounding, high-volume question and answer period. I couldn't believe it but I saw it with my own eyes. The two returned to attention without flexing or falling, yelling back and forth. I was impressed.

Other classes made major mistakes during their RLP attempts, so we didn't feel alone in Battalion One. In one instance, the entire class had their clean laundry in their neighbors' classrooms. Why they didn't leave the items on the pick-up counter downstairs was beyond all of us. When the call came to produce their items, the next hallway was filled with every imaginable, unnecessary, inspection demerit. It truly became the classic, well out-of-bounds. They paid for their lack of planning. Bye-bye, Momma!

I walked back toward my car where I had parked between the battalion and the sea wall. As I turned east, I paused for a moment, standing near the same spot where a candidate got disciplined for laughing at my joking with Craytor. Some things stay with you and on that spot, I knew there were two of them: the Craytor incident and my first experience at command.

Every candidate took on the responsibility of being the class leader. We were placed in charge of the class for two days during our stay at Hotel Pensacola. Each of the candidates' turns came under different circumstances and different times during the class' progression toward commissioning. The selection of each candidate came in alphabetical order so my turn came later on in the game, toward the initial flight-training classes.

The challenge was two-fold for me. Our class had become too loose over time. Staff Sergeant Black's philosophy allowed for the self-motivation of candidates because he didn't preside over our every move. This was a two-edged sword. Certainly, if candidates are locked down and forced to perform, the class scores would rise. But what lessons would you take through life? Comply or die would be the simple explanation. Under Staff Sergeant Black, self-starting and self-motivation became the key ingredients for success. As future pilots, success would require internal discipline, focused concentration, and high levels of motivation without being strung out as tight as piano wire.

Enter Candidate Schupbach. Although I never paid much attention to who's up and who's on deck, I quite unexpectedly became the class leader. I simply hid from my DI and survived. "Never let him know my name" became my litany. My only introduction came with my mother's addressed care packages, chock-full of lemon squares and seven-layer cookies. On the evening one of my packages arrived, the class leader came up to me and told me that I would be class leader in the morning. I couldn't resist smiling.

The Good Lord gave me a deep voice. I can't sing more than an octave, but I can bark a hard line and with that talent came a rise in my class standing. I remember that first morning so well. The class formed up on the south sidewalk and waited for the ritual march to the chow hall. Candidate Painter came late to formation, as usual. This didn't go unnoticed. Not only did I think this extremely rude, I also knew it showed a serious lack of discipline. Not only that, this infraction was from a class that hadn't passed an inspection! Besides, getting your butt downstairs on time, just like the other 39 guys, was standard operating procedure. Without realizing it, I stumbled upon the one thing that held our class back, the lack of self-discipline.

Having some time on my hands, waiting for Painter and being the class leader, I figured the least I could do was drill the troops. I hoped peers would pressure Painter into improving his punctuality. Drilling the troops seemed like a good idea, but how? Physical training was left for the DI. I didn't dare go there. But marching was different altogether. After all, we already marched together and knew the commands. It also occurred to me as I waited, that we needed more pride in our class.

My command was born at 5:20 in the morning on the south side of the battalion, across from the sea wall. With my deep, booming voice, I called the class to attention. I wanted to hear a crisp pop, but nothing short of a sloppy shuffle came to pass. The sound of their boots was miserable, utterly miserable! The devil himself could not pull me away from my next idea.

I decided we were going to sharpen, drill and pop in place, at every seam and at every juncture, even after Painter arrived.

"IN PLACE, MARCH!" I boomed to the class.

"Left, left, left, come on, sharpen it up, tighten it up, one pop! I want to hear one pop when you stop. CLASS HALT!"

They clumped their feet onto the sidewalk with little precision. But this was just the beginning. There was opportunity to excel.

"Good morning, Candidate Painter. It's good to have you with us this morning, Candidate Painter," I taunted.

"Good morning, sir," came the reply. He slipped into his formation position.

Drilling from hell was my plan. I started the class off marching to chow, but with a twist. I capitalized on the fact that the group could follow commands.

"TO THE REAR, MARCH!" I bellowed.

The class took one more step forward, pivoted around and began their march away from the chow hall.

"TO THE REAR, MARCH!" I sounded out again.

The process was repeated and the class began their march toward the chow hall. *This is getting fun,* I thought.

Once in front of the blue and yellow stairs of the chow hall, I brought the class to a halt.

"Right face, forward march!"

The class proceeded to the grass to the immediate right of the stairs. Here I began the most rudimentary opening and closing of the ranks.

"Dress right, dress!" I kept it up.

I wondered why no one complained or interfered. Officers, drill instructors, class officers, even the Captain never stopped to take notice of the extra drill and the loudest candidate of them all. That is, none except Gunnery Sergeant Fletcher.

It happened early in the chow hall, the routine march into the line-up: stomp, stomp, stomp.

"Class Halt!"

I situated myself at the front of the line, facing the candidates. Between us were the fiberglass trays, condiments and an occasional DI. I forgot one thing and the unexpected occurred when, as if mechanical robots, they picked up their silverware, their napkin and then their tray in the prescribed manner. They were hidden behind those trays that covered their chests, including nametags, all the way to just beneath their eyes.

Every candidate unknowingly challenged my survival as class leader. Because I didn't spend free hours with the other candidates, my recollection of their names was poor. I had not the slightest notion of who half these candidates were, least by last name.

When it came my turn to greet each candidate in full volume with the appropriate "Good morning, Candidate Umpty-Bump," I froze, not knowing what to do. Then the answer came like a drink of cold water. *Lie about the situation. Just start making up names. No one can see the nametags in the first place.* Which is what I did at the top of my lungs, first thing in the morning. It worked!

Lying worked well until the following lunch program. There the simple routine of shouting out names of those I knew and lying about those I didn't came under the pinnacle of scrutiny. Sergeant Fletcher and two other DIs walked over and surrounded me while I greeted the candidates "by name." Fletcher was on my right side, and I could feel the presence of the other two DI's on my left and directly behind me. I couldn't stop. I had to continue with the big lie or my career would be dead in the water. To this day, I imagine that I would not be flying an airplane had my incompetence been discovered. Boldly, under the noses of the three drill instructors, I stood at attention and barked out the greeting of the day to each candidate, known or unknown. "Good afternoon, Candidate Smith, good afternoon, Candidate Jones, good afternoon, Candidate Smith, good afternoon, Candidate Benkelman." Then came my roommate, Candidate Hackman.

Hackman was extremely bright. He would later join the intelligence community, as he did not have the eyes for aviation, but that day his eyes gleamed with laughter at my predicament.

"Good afternoon, Candidate Hackman," I said with great confidence. Finally—I knew someone. Most others hid their laughter behind their trays, but not Hackman. As luck would have it, his eyes caught the eye of none other than Gunny Fletcher.

"What the hell is so funny, candidate?"

Fletcher came at Hackman, singling him out of the crowd and raising cane from behind his back. My roommate couldn't help himself at this juncture. The fact that I actually knew his name, that he became the victim and received the wrath of the twice- feared, three tours in Vietnam Marine instead of me, overcame Hackman. Even with food on his tray and Fletcher on his back, Hackman couldn't hold back the laughter and his body shook from the effort. Before you could say "Fletcher", the Gunny had Hackman out of the line, PT'ing him right there in the chow hall. It wasn't a pretty sight.

At the same time, the drill instructor on my left walked up to the front of the line and took a long hard look at the guys, shutting them down as if they needed any more encouragement to maintain strict order and discipline. After all, they had a leader who was trying to do just that. They were double-down serious about this matter and that made it all the more hilarious. But there would be no more laughing.

Gunny Fletcher returned to his former position at my immediate right, touched my ear with his lips and said, "Good job, candidate. Now just hold it down, turn down the volume and carry on."

"Sir, yes sir," came my reply. I then returned to making up candidate's names with the greeting of the day. I got away with the entire ordeal until we were back in our battalion.

I marched the choked-up group, including one very pissed-off Hackman, back to our battalion. Each command came as loud as the last; each stop and start became a bit sharper than the last. After lunch, the class followed their marching orders with newly found vigor and timing.

It's beginning to pay off. I didn't let up but rather had everyone march up the stairs and brace against the hallway's bulkheads before giving the command to "FALL OUT!" They did just that. To the man, each candidate buckled over, slapped the walls and fell onto their racks in uncontrollable laughter.

A variation on "That was the funniest thing I have ever seen, Schupbach" was their collective response, except, of course, for unfortunate Hackman. His face was beet red.

"Schupbach, I'm going to kill you! I'm going to kill you!" For a minute there, I thought he just might.

After the afternoon classes, I ordered up a new round of drilling—the old-fashioned way. I began my next round of snap, crackle and pop with the order, "Class 0881, with your rifles, FALL OUT ON LINE!"

We made it out to the veranda, facing east, and began yet another round of rifle drill. We were not "secured" and I was pissed. I didn't like being locked down for our countless mistakes, many of which were my own. I didn't care for losing, and I had only two days to do something about it.

I didn't have a bullhorn, nor did I have a trashcan, but I could drill my fellow class mates and drill them I did, until I liked what I heard—"just one pop." For the better part of an hour we practiced until the sound of our movements came as one. By the end of the day it sounded pretty good.

The routine was similar the next day, but I remembered many more names. That afternoon, our three-time loser class came back from our afternoon instruction and I had an idea. It would be my last chance to make an impression on these guys, my last chance to give voice to my hope for excellence, and as one of their leaders, to raise the bar. I decided to march the class past the Drill Instructor's offices as well as the Class Officer's offices, past their open windows and all within earshot of the sidewalk. I swear the devil made me do it.

I held the class at the corner and told them, "Listen Up!"

I gave instructions on how we would place our signature squarely in the face of our tormentors.

"Class, we will shout a four count, spelling out 0, two, three, four, 8, two, three, four, 8, two, three, four, 1, two, three, four—then a two count of the same and finally, a single count, 0–8–8–1 twice. We will make it on our left step and we will be loud about it. On my command, is this perfectly clear?"

"Sir, yes sir."

"I can't hear you!"

"SIR, YES SIR!"

And the stage was set. It was time to have the low-ball class, the kids who couldn't shoot straight, the gang who couldn't walk by themselves unescorted, visit momma, look up or even talk during meals, raise the bar and speak for their pride and commitment. And they did.

Off we marched down the cross street, past the sand pit and the rifle drill arena. The buildings blocked the breeze, but I wasn't just sweating from the heat. Once in front of the Class Officer's open windows, while still approaching the Drill Instructor's offices, I issued the command, "Just begin."

With our steel-toed boots coming down in distinctly disciplined manner, the class chant rang out from the hearts of the men. It must have surprised everyone who heard and I was amazed at how well the men performed. Their cadence was flawless; their understanding of the change in verse with cycle was complete to the man, and the silence following was broken only by the sound of two boots marching. I still savor that moment.

It sounded so good. When I later asked the senior class if anyone heard it, they replied, "Oh yes, they all heard it, heard it loud and clear." Then I became nervous. Now we really had signed up for the program just as I had intended. I had raised the bar in everyone's mind, and no one complained.

While we weren't ever as free as depicted in the movie, *An Officer and a Gentleman*, we did have a whole lot of fun when we finally secured. The first order of business came shortly afterwards. Whether decked out in uniform or our Navy-issued apparel, the girls on the beach didn't seem to care. Pensacola beach loved our dollars, too. My roommate, Picket, came from Slidell, Louisiana and was just nuts about Cajun culinary delights. Oysters on the half shell were first in his playbook and he was determined that this Nebraska native would have his first oyster, shucked and sucked in his very presence. I had no choice in the matter. But, with oysters at three dollars a dozen (13 there), peel and eat shrimp by the pound, and pitchers of ice cold beer delivered faster than you could order, it made no sense to complain.

Picket also knew of my need to visit the *Big Easy*, that is, New Orleans. He put three of us, all dressed up in our whites, in his car and drove to his mother's house just outside the city. From there we went to Lake Pontchartrain and visited his local, favorite bars and restaurants, all built on stilts over the water.

After the fall of South Vietnam, Watergate, oil embargos, and Iran holding our people hostage for 444 days, Americans were fed up. Our wounded pride resulted from many factors beginning with the disastrous leadership of the Nixon years. Americans needed someone to stand up for America. In 1981 President Ronald Reagan did just that. He made pride in the military his top priority. President Reagan generously supported the armed forces of the United States and publicly decreed the honor of military service and sacrifice. Coincidentally, timing for all of this jelled just as we stepped through the doorway of Fat City, Louisiana.

Traditionally, the southern region of the United States has ardently supported the military, and Reagan's words did not slip the minds of those we met on Lake Pontchartrain. We were in fashion there, decked in our whites, and literally in *Fat City*. It doesn't get better than that night. The food was superb. As for the drinks—we couldn't buy a drink. I distinctly remember one Chivas Regal that defied imagination. Served in a large tumbler, the ice cubes fell from off the top of the glasses. "On the rocks" meant the rocks never floated away until my white uniform collided with Fat City. People treated us like kings and we loved them for it. But this special welcome and terrific validation of being in the service was surpassed the following evening.

We toured Bourbon Street the next night. Far be it for me to know that the shrimp at Houlihan's would burn my lips off. There, too, was my first experience with oysters Rockefeller and other "must have" Creole culinary delights. Blackened red fish spices (hell, they blackened anything that didn't move in that restaurant) and good times were the order of the day. As for Picket, well, you just had to love the guy. We went through so much together in AOCS. Now I walked in his element, *The Big Easy of New Orleans.*

The grand finale came at a famous outdoor courtyard establishment named Pat O'Brien's, complete with their famous "Hurricane" drink. Unfamiliar with many mixed drinks, I was helpless as a baby and at the mercy of Picket and another candidate appropriately nicknamed "Wildman." The evening progressed nicely under the radiant propane heaters while groups of people came by and mingled with the men in white. We were young men trying to do well, serve our country in the military, earn a commission and attend flight school. What made it even better was that "The Big Easy" has always been a Navy town.

We basked under the glow of the heaters sitting squarely on the coattails of President Reagan. The crowd went wild. All night long, pretty women sat on our laps and wore our hats while their husbands and boy friends ordered the libations. A photographer came by selling his wares and I purchased three large photographs over the course of the evening. As they came out, I could only think the appropriate titles were *"The Good, The Bad and The Ugly."* The "ugly" was taken with a Hurricane Magnum situated directly in front of everyone. One of the gentlemen in the picture bought this sixty-dollar monstrosity for our vivacious enjoyment. Everyone should share at least one.

This sweet memory faded as I drove to the Mustin Beach O'Club for a drink at the Navy bar. As quickly as that memory faded, it was replaced by that bar, dredging up memories of my first visit there as a candidate officer. What impressed me most wasn't the memorabilia but rather the ballroom with its darkened stage. *I've been there; I've been on that stage.*

During AOCS, I was the "One M.C." or Master of Ceremonies at our Dining Out. In choker whites, I improvised audience one-liners, tossed zingers to the Captain's daughter who joined me on stage, and introduced the Naval School's Command Choir as "What-Nots" always having a laugh under the lights. Sometimes you can do no wrong. Until now, twenty years later, I never understood that it was a once-in-a-lifetime opportunity. That realization struck me, however, as I stood within the darkened room for those few short moments.

Later that day, I walked from my room at the Bachelor's Officer Quarters to the parade grounds, hoping to view a good bit of the daily activities Hotel Pensacola offered its guests. I crossed Admirals' Row, walked under tall cypress trees covered with Spanish moss, and heard the distinct sound of drums beating in the distance. *I'm in luck. I can review the parade practice and the band.*

Nostalgia changed my attitude from twenty years ago in Officer Candidate School, when I took my band experience lightly. But I was in for a shock. Instead of a full-fledged military marching band, I saw seven drums and three horns trying their best to keep time with "The Colors"—the Star Spangled Banner. Marching to that music would be an effort.

At NAS Pensacola, few things interrupted the business at hand, except for the playing of the colors. Even discipline and physical training came second. Now, as then, everyone on base stopped, faced either the flag or the music and rendered a salute to the United States of America, as long a salute as the music played. Not in uniform, I faced the flag in silence. Others pulled their automobiles over along the roadside and stopped, which is the appropriate response. This simple ceremony occurs twice a day on every United States military base throughout the world. Ask any soldier or sailor. Once in your spirit, the respect for the flag and the salute becomes ingrained, a part of your very nature.

I wondered at the small class sizes and the vastly reduced number of classes. "Times have changed," a Navy Commander said to me when I asked about what I had seen that day. I understand better now why my bandleader was so happy to have so many volunteers, even librarians who couldn't play a note. We constituted a full ceremonial band that played at commissioning ceremonies. That meant more now than I could ever have imagined back then. *Coming through Hotel Pensacola without a band? What the hell was it all about, anyhow?* The only constant was the Drill

Instructors because they were still Marines. Saddened after parade practice, I returned to my quarters at the Bayshores, NAS Pensacola.

I stopped by a few offices the next morning looking for memorabilia. A road map, a patch or brochure would suffice, but few were found. I drove around the campus and pulled into the parking lot across from the entrance of the AOCS Chapel.

Commissioning Photograph

May 29, 1981*

A white steeple rose above the chapel, a point of navigation for the fly-over salute during the parade. In some ways, to see it still standing after our fly-over was a miracle in itself. Under the steeple stood the chapel where we accepted our commissions and pledged to defend the Constitution of the United States of America. Our class graduation photographs were taken on the chapel steps, where drill instructor Staff Sergeant Robert Black gave us our first salute as officers. We returned that salute with pride.

According to tradition, after an officer returns his first salute, the officer presents the enlisted man or woman with a silver dollar. Drill Instructors have deep pockets for such occasions.

After a final few minutes of gazing at the chapel, I returned to my rental car and drove a last time around the campus. I exited through the new enlisted training facilities, a massive complex of barracks and schools. Several locations lent themselves to a photograph or two, the last within a wooded area near the golf course. Returning to the car, I turned on the radio. Goose bumps erupted at the station music being played, a live version of the Eagles' "Hotel California."

*U.S. Navy imagery used in illustration without endorsement expressed or implied. Photographer Unknown.

"Livin' it up at the Hotel California...you can checkout any time you like, but you can never leave!"

Listening to the guitar sounds that only Joe and the boys can make, I agreed with the verses wholeheartedly. Living it up at the Hotel Pensacola, I could check out any time I liked but a part of me would never leave! With that song on my lips, I passed through the front gate, drove over the bridge and realized that just like back then, I now had a date with my flight school.

Primary Flight Training
The Devil is in the Details

CHAPTER THREE

The first three weeks of flight school started at 5:30 A.M. I often showered, not remembering how I got there, but I well remembered what lay ahead on those mornings. A red Florida sunrise greeted me every day during my first June in aviation. With the warm sun at my back, I faced forward, placing one foot in front of the other and walked across the street to the Whiting Field Officer's Club. Although I ordered the same meal from the same short-order chef every morning, each day I was presented with a differently tabulated bill. I grew to like the women who greeted me with the same eggs, grits and sausage, in spite of their accounting methods.

My hometown Nebraska experiences taught me to enjoy their company. These were happy and caring folk who understood each student by reading the lines on their faces. They treated you well if you let them. Their companionship reminded me friendship still mattered above competition between the ranks.

I returned to my room in the Bachelor Officer Quarters or *BOQ*, for a quick review of the previous day and a glide over the upcoming work ahead. Nothing compared to this opportunity and I was highly motivated to succeed. Attitude was my most important guide to success in the flight program; motivational advantage from Aviation Officer Candidate School was my strongest resource.

Senior classmen in the program gave two pieces of advice: "Know your procedures" and "You're behind." You had to know your procedures cold because you're swimming up one powerful stream. If you aren't careful, you'll be washed out to sea along with the scrap heap of failed student naval aviators.

"The classroom scores are important, but knowing your procedures for flying and the emergency procedures for the aircraft are so much more important that you cannot start memorizing them soon enough." It proved to be good advice.

I decided early on that failure was too high a price to pay. It would hurt badly to return to a town that I last saw while pushing a broom and washing dishes. No, by grace the Good Lord afforded me, this opportunity to fly would not be lost. I was determined to look up from the dirt on the floor I cleaned and reach to the sky beyond. Besides, Uncle Sam was paying me to go to this school. Yes, motivated to succeed, I worked hard to get to this juncture and I knew this was a once in a lifetime opportunity.

The first of the flight orientations loomed ahead, the infamous meeting of the instructor at familiarization zero (FAM 0). The afternoon of truth, the moment of introduction to the instructor grew on the horizon. Late that day, I sat in the circle of student naval aviators (SNAs) in the briefing shack, a small room full of gloomy-faced men dressed in green flight suits and black boots. All of them were too scared to keep up with the conversation of the raucous instructors. They kept to themselves or hid in another room commonly referred to as "the morgue." Not me.

That afternoon, I sat facing the door, anxious to meet this instructor, to gain a first glimpse of the person who undoubtedly held my livelihood in the balance of his pen. Lt. Breed punched through the double doors, entering the hallway, and swaggered towards the Duty Officer. Unanticipated by all present, I stood up sharply with courtesy and respect. Such treatment was reserved for the Commanding Officer, but my instincts kicked in. Something told me it was the best way to introduce myself to my primary flight instructor. My spontaneous action surprised the wardroom and people remembered me for it.

Lt. Harry Breed was a tall man, thin but strong, regulated but cavalier in his grooming. His curly brown hair and overgrown moustache struck me as a sign of a rebellious streak. I grew to like this guy from the first day. Always happy the sun shone in his life, he surprisingly went by the call sign "Shadow Flight."

"Good afternoon, sir. Ensign Schupbach reporting for duty."

"Good afternoon. So you're one of my new students. Welcome aboard VT-6, the stick with the greatest. Let's hope you can measure up."

"Yes sir, I think I can, sir."

We took a short walk to the hangar and flight line where aircraft stood by the hundreds. Breed made small talk while crossing the parking lot, discussing the hometown where I went to school and, of course, what airplane I dreamed of flying someday in the fleet.

"We normally don't discuss the fleet with students. Their selection of which aircraft they would like to fly is entirely up to them. But what interests you, Schupbach?"

"Helicopters, sir. I think they offer a unique opportunity in life. To experience hovering, working in close quarters on small ships, flying rescue missions on the high seas, somehow all of that appeals to me."

Little did I know Lt. Breed flew the twin rotor H-46, enjoying his career immensely. My words quickly found an audience.

We entered the hangar and traversed the floor towards the flight line. Several engines sat on check stands, awaiting maintenance and propellers. *Just how much maintenance does this engine require that supports my life?* I wondered as I surveyed the collection. I suppressed that foolish question, simply observing and listening to the Lt.'s introductory snippets of Naval Aviation. My mind absorbed his words as if he were Orville or Wilbur Wright.

June 1981, Student Naval Aviator Neal Schupbach*
*U.S. Navy imagery used in illustration without endorsement expressed or implied. Photographer Unknown.   67

"Now is the time to begin looking over the aircraft. They said it was parked on the south lot, second row; so let's walk out to that location, find the plane by bureau number and begin our pre-flight before we even arrive at the airplane."

Lt. Breed spoke in rhythm with his fast-paced walk.

"Actually, our preflight began with a review of the logbook. Now is the opportune time for us to get much farther ahead of the airplane and view it from a distance. I look at the overall big picture from here, checking how the plane is sitting on its landing gear, checking the condition of the tires and what is going on around the plane. Is maintenance working on the plane or the one behind it? Do I want to start up with the surrounding circumstances? Is there a power cart in front of my airplane? Will this be a battery start? Schupbach, are you with me?"

"Sir, yes sir, Lt. Breed, sir."

"Good. Now, *this* is an airplane!"

So began the first preflight walk-around of my career. As soon as I touched the airplane, I relaxed a bit. I knew I could learn from this man. Soon my cautious demeanor faded in his presence. It made FAM 0 much easier, a good way to break the ice.

Walking on the left wing, I unlocked and slid open the canopy. After preflighting the parachute, I climbed into the cockpit, demonstrated the wearing of the chute and strapped into the bird with the five-way restraint harness.

"Schupbach, don the helmet and I'll show you the intercom system or ICS."

Lt. Breed used a show-and-tell system of teaching that made me feel more comfortable. He then instructed me on adjusting the rudder pedals, the proper seat height and the pneumatic canopy emergency release system. Yet, in spite of all this, I was somehow disappointed that I couldn't use the opportunity to demonstrate my knowledge and T-34 prowess. I wanted to score some points early in the program.

Just shut up and learn, Neal, I told myself. *The less time you spend with your mouth open, the fewer topics you can foul up.* This tactic was widely known as avoiding "digging yourself into a hole." Survival meant utilizing the KISS (keep-it-simple-stupid) principle, preferred when engaging in a brief and debrief.

But all of that changed when it was my turn to talk about the cockpit. I didn't realize how little I knew but I was about to find out. Unless I overlooked an important point, there would be no more show-and-tell for the rest of the afternoon. Fortunately, my homework paid off.

"Now, Schupbach, tell me about these round wheels you see stationed around the cockpit," Lt. Breed commanded.

"Lt. Breed, those are for controlling the trim tabs of the airplane."

"What exactly are trim tabs and what do they do for us, Schupbach?"

"Well, sir, the trim tabs use the airflow over the plane to relieve the aerodynamic pressures on the stick and rudder pedals. They are on each control surface and look like miniature control surfaces."

"Very good, Schupbach."

I revealed my rudimentary knowledge of the other switches in the cockpit and that completed the cockpit check of FAM 0. After removing my helmet, I placed it on the canopy slide rail, twisted the quick release and popped the three release snaps of my parachute. As I straddled the port side of the cockpit, I grabbed my helmet and climbed down to the ground from the backside of the wing.

Whew, I thought. *That was a whole lot of going over for a guy like me.* That was just the interior.

"All right, Schupbach, you're doing OK so far. Now let's go for the exterior walk-around. Tell me all about it, starting right here."

At the root of the left wing, where the flap joined the fuselage, I began my first official Navy walk-around of an aircraft.

Lt. Breed interrupted, "Schupbach, what is that hole doing in the landing gear support?"

"Where?"

"Right there, Schupbach." He pointed to the gear pin insertion hole. "Pray tell what that might be for. To save weight or what?"

"Sir, I do not know as I've never seen it before. But if I were to hazard a guess, I would say for the landing gear safety pins."

"Good, now let's continue with the walk-around."

We came out from beneath the airplane and continued down the left wing. I spoke about the aileron much the same as I did the adjacent flap. But this time Lt. Breed asked about the two-inch-wide control tab on the trailing edge of the aileron.

"That would be the trim tab, sir."

"Does Schupbach know how the trim tab works?"

"Sir, I do not know, but anything is possible, sir."

"Well, we'll find out."

"Sir, yes sir, sir."

"Yes, sir, sir?" With that came the first of many "Schooeebaaaach"s from Lt. Breed. He could make my ears ring when I screwed up bad enough.

"Ooooh-kay Schupbach. Now, which way does the trim tab move in order to move the control surface down?"

"To tell you the truth sir, I never gave it much thought."

To avoid showing my ignorance, I didn't hazard so much as a guess. The truth was better than my guesswork any day. After all, I never flew an aircraft, never had a lesson, and now I worked as a professional. My paycheck and career were on the line every day of the week. Just faking it didn't fly around NAS Whiting Field.

"All right, that's fair enough. No one else does, at least not yet; so pay attention to this. Are you with me?"

"Sir, yes sir!"

"To make the aileron descend, we must make this trim tab rise or move in the opposite direction to the desired movement of the control surface. The airflow follows the wing and control surface. As it reaches the tab, the curve or camber, created by the tab and aileron around the tab's hinge point acts in a dynamic manner. This exerts pressure on the control surface that varies by the amount of airflow over the surface or airspeed, whichever you prefer, Schupbach. Any questions?"

It was a lot to take in. By then I was pretty confused by it all, but I replied, "No Sir."

"Now, what might this metal tab be, sticking straight out of the wing tip, Schupbach?"

"Gosh sir, I don't have any great explanation for that one, sir."

"This multimillion dollar charge to the military came as an afterthought. The strobe lights were blinding the pilots; a vertical slice of metal was the solution. Blocking the reflection of the lights enabled the pilot to fly at night without inducing vertigo. When the strobe was thus blocked, there was no way for the pilot to tell if the strobe light worked or not. So, what did they do to solve such a problem, Schupbach?"

At this point I thought my instructor was joking so I replied in a lighthearted military manner, "This candidate doesn't know but will find out, sir."

"Well, they spent a truckload of money researching the problem and then decided to drill this one-sixteenth inch hole in the strobe deflector panel to enable the pilot to observe the strobe light on each wing tip. I'm sure you can impress someone with that tidbit of knowledge."

We turned the corner and inspected the leading edge of the wing, including the triangular-shaped angle of attack probe and the ram air pitot probe. We spoke of its inherent danger afterwards.

"Schupbach, the tube should be clear of obstructions, in good mechanical condition and under any circumstance, it should never be touched by the pilot. Do you know why?"

"No, not really sir."

"It's heated and if someone left the pitot heat switch in the on position, or if it failed in the on position, and if the battery switch was left on during a hangar check or preflight, the pitot tube would be heated. That isn't the real problem. Carelessness is the problem. However, having said all of that, the pitot tube doesn't give off heat and certainly doesn't glow like a stove, but for our discussion today, it should be considered just as hot. Words to live by, Schupbach."

"Yes, sir!"

We continued our inspection of the wing on our way to the engine cowling and the propeller area, an area that came with special precautions. Aircraft propellers caused many a man loss of life or limb. To combat this tragedy, the Navy taught everyone how to walk and where to walk around a prop, whether it was turning or not. It seemed rather simple but they drilled it into a habit pattern because a spinning propeller disappears, especially at night. They made up a poster that I always will remember. It said, "If you NEVER, NEVER, NEVER walk through a prop arc, then you will NEVER, NEVER, NEVER be hit by a prop!" It made sense to me.

We stood next to the prop and discussed all of this in a meaningful manner. Lt. Breed's sincerity emphasized the points of safety to me. He opened the engine cowling and discussed the items found underneath "the hood." We covered the individual parts. To me they were simply parts within a well-organized maze but I grew to appreciate them in a few short weeks. That day, I paid close attention to my instructor's lesson.

After closing the engine cowling, we continued around to the other side of the airplane and preflighted it in much the same manner, all the way back to the *empennage* or tail section. My head was spinning.

We departed the aircraft line and during the walk back, Lt. Breed said something unusual.

"Schupbach, there is a tie-cutting ceremony for those who solo, and you will solo, won't you Schupbach?"

"Sir, yes sir."

"If you solo, there are stories told on stage. Now I always show up without much to say. But, this time, I'm going to write things down. So if you find yourself on stage with me, then you may hear what happened on occasion. You got that Schupbach?"

"Ohhh, yes sir, loud and clear, sir."

"Good. Now let's see what we can do about your first flight, FAM 1."

On June 30, 1981, I went up on my first flight as a student naval aviator. Familiarization flight one was known as a show-and-tell ride. I did little flying, other than a flail at the controls. Discussion items included headwork, basic air work, procedures and bailout. The flight instructor demonstrated a take-off, a departure, the course rules, use and effect of the flight controls, use and effect of the flaps and landing gear, aircraft stability (which there was very little of), basic transitions, communications and identification friend-or-foe procedures. FAM 1 introduced: checklists, the engine start, taxi, the engine run up, visual scan patterns, use and effect of the trim tabs, straight and level, and a constant angle of bank turns. FAM 1 practiced the preflight.

The flight itself took us to working Area One, an area west of the city of Pensacola. As far as I was concerned, I came along for the ride and expected to be taught something. What happened next came as a shock to me. I actually flew the aircraft on my very first flight. There I was, flying in the open blue sky, admiring the beauty the bubble canopy provided, listening to my heart pounding, oblivious to everything else. For once I looked at my life from above the clouds, in a sky so blue I could taste the color. I couldn't keep the smile off my face as a distant dream from early childhood came to life. The dream of a little boy who had played under a World War II Navy fighter in the park, who watched *Twelve O'clock High* and was truant from school to witness America's John Glen orbit the earth, just came true. The dream of being a Navy pilot may have been conceived as a child, but that dream was birthed on June 30, 1981, or so it seemed in that moment.

A flying career—the words echoed in my mind. I took time-out to pause for the simple thrill and exhilaration of it all.

Lt. Breed brought me back to reality with a few demonstrations of the required maneuvers. After each instruction, he asked me to fly the plane and try one for myself. I couldn't fly for the life of me, but few things compared to the heady sensations I felt in the moment. The feel of new leather flight gloves, the motion of the prop, the pull of the straps, the feel of the airplane itself and the colors in the sky—they all came together that afternoon during my first experience with flight. I explored speed changes, turns, climbs and descents, and the color of the clear blue sky. I flew the airplane out of trim, couldn't find the flap handle or gear lever, and had difficulty in adjusting the power—but I knew I loved it. Whatever the cost, whatever the job required, I knew I needed to be in this cockpit, in this flight program and in the sky. Little did I know the price.

We flew through the requirements before departing the working area for our return to Whiting Field. Then, when I least expected it, Lt. Breed performed an aileron roll for the full 360 degrees. The total inversion of my world was surreal. This wasn't part of the program; it was my first flight. I asked my instructor about it.

"That's all right, Schupbach. I just wanted to see what you would do under the circumstance."

At the time I thought he meant that he wanted to see if I got airsick. But it felt good to be held in firmly by the straps, upside down, looking at the forested landscape below.

After we landed and taxied to parking, our walk back to aircraft issue was a slow one. I was slow in getting my gear together, slow to un-strap. I tried to stand up with my parachute still on my back and I almost fell from the aircraft wing. I struggled behind my instructor across the flight line, listening to his every word as if my life depended upon it.

We worked our way into the aircraft issuing office where I received more instruction on the yellow sheet and the Navy's aircraft gripe sheet, one for each mechanical irregularity. Fortunately, we had no irregularities for that particular flight and after the seasoned instructors socialized, we departed through the hangar, crossed the parking lot and entered the squadron's brief/debrief building for the flight review and grade sheet. Nothing much was said about my first hop.

FAM 2 came just two days later. This flight introduced the great challenge of aviation to the student naval aviator. During the briefing, we discussed abnormal engine starts, the hot start, the hung start, and when the engine just didn't start at all. Each had its limitations, procedures, and required write-ups in the logbook. We spoke of aborted take-offs, their causes, the stopping considerations, the requirements for hard braking and the possibility of departing the end of the runway. I didn't know enough to be scared of our runways. However, the T-34C typically worked from three-thousand-foot strips, short fields by any stretch of the imagination.

During the entire brief, I thought we would discuss the inevitable, my first take-off. But this was not the case. Somehow, Breed left that out of our briefing. I wanted my career to flourish, so I didn't bring up the subject. This was a tactical error on my part because I only thought of "my first take off" all the way out to the flight line.

It was a hot July day. When I finally started the motor. Lt. Breed's first response was to ask for the air conditioner. We shut both canopies and he encouraged me to move on through the checklists. I read aloud each item on the Navy checklist and then verified or moved the switch into position. This "do list" philosophy slowed everything to a crawl, especially with my being a new student.

After starting the engine I called Whiting Ground Control.

"Whiting Ground, six–echo–zero–five–three taxi, VFR, round robin with information whiskey."

"Six–echo–zero–five–three, taxi from parking to run up. Call the tower when ready for take-off," came the reply.

With this clearance, I gave the lineman the hand signal for brake release, both fists together, palms forward and a quick spread of the fingers. He returned the signal and checked each direction for oncoming traffic. Lt. Breed and I both checked for traffic in either direction: "Clear left, clear right." With concurrence of our lineman, we each said to one another, "Clear to taxi." I pumped the brakes to release the parking brake and added power, feeling the instructor's presence on the throttle lever. As we rolled forward, I tapped the left brake as I pushed forward on the rudder pedal. I then pressed the brake pedal again in a pumping motion and we lurched to the left, slowly making the left turn out to the taxi line.

Each time I changed direction, I invariably used differential braking to control the direction of the aircraft. While effective, so was the rudder, and for reasons known only to the Lieutenant, he allowed for this jerky technique. I brought us to the run-up area, centered the aircraft and set the parking brake. Once there, I initiated the propeller feather check by pulling back on the condition lever. The propeller's pitch changed, causing an audible frequency shift, the RPM gauge indicated a decrease and the torque gauge registered an increase. We completed several other engine checks and then checked for the correct flight control response. The aileron would rise when I moved the stick in its direction and fall when I moved it away from it. The elevators moved up when the stick moved backwards and down when the stick was pushed forward. The rudder moved toward the push of each rudder pedal. I then ensured the flaps were in the take-off position, checked the three trim tabs, completed the required checklist, and changed radio frequencies to the tower.

"Tower, six–echo–zero–five–three, run-up complete, ready for take off."

"Zero–five–three, taxi into position and hold," came the response.

At the center of the field was the main turn-off for entering and exiting the runway environment. With the clearance, we crossed the runway and took a position on the far centerline. The runways at Whiting Field were long enough and wide enough to accommodate four T-34C aircraft at one time. The Navy allowed two aircraft to use the first half of the runway for landing, while two other aircraft utilized the second half of the runway for take-off. I never knew any different procedure or any better.

"Six–echo–zero–five–three, cleared for take-off," barked the radio operator.

"Cleared for take-off," was my scared, weak, little response. My hands were in a death grip, one on the throttle and the other on the stick.

"Lt. Breed, this is FAM 2, and in the syllabus it says that for FAM 2, this is my take-off," I said over the intercom.

"That's right, Schupbach, SO GET MOVING!" rang through my ears.

The throttles in the forward and rear cockpits are interconnected and Lt. Breed jammed it forward. My whole body lunged forward as my iron grip on the power lever transferred motion from the top of my helmet to the soles of my boots. I was completely gripped with fear. We now moved forward, rapidly accelerating. My technique for steering with the brake pedals twisted and turned our airplane down the runway. At eighty knots, I pulled back on the stick and we jumped into the air. The next thing I saw was the blue sky covering my entire windscreen.

I realized that I had over controlled the airplane and reacted by pushing the stick forward. My windscreen then filled with the end of the runway. Terrified of the approaching concrete, I pulled back on the stick again and then tried to level off, but found us traveling slightly downward into the tree line. Once again I pulled back on the stick, only to find Lt. Breed now on the controls. His presence stopped the aircraft's oscillations.

"This is a yee-haw," I said, choking on my own words. I meant, seesaw or teeter-totter ride. During my first take-off I choked on everything. He wrote that one down, verbatim.

I only knew that I was fighting for my life at that time. The aircraft responded to my every touch, as would a high-strung Ferrari. After all, it was a two-seated vehicle with five hundred fifty horsepower and it flew!

We climbed out of the field area using the proper course rules and then the good Lt. contacted ATC for radar identification and separation. I tried my best to trim the nose, but each input demanded the corresponding control movement and disruption of the previous feel of the aircraft. Little did I know that was supposed to happen!

I completely forgot about the rudder trim, and the plane flew wing-low and sideways.

"Look at the ball, step on the ball and trim out the corresponding pressure," Lt. Breed politely encouraged me.

I did as he instructed. But my first handful of rudder trim mistakenly twisted the aileron trim wheel and the aircraft fought me in a rolling motion, coupled with the slip of the rudder. The slip indicator ball, as they say, banged on the fuselage trying to get back inside the airplane. It all became too much for me and Lt. Breed came to the rescue.

"I've got the aircraft," he said, rapidly placing all of the trim corrections into the flight controls.

"You've got it back."

"I've got it back," I echoed.

Miraculously, the airplane became my friend again, changing from the fighting, feuding alley cat to a pussycat with personality. *Will I ever know what he did to persuade this beast into behaving?*

We departed for the seven thousand foot level, choosing the five hundred foot increments of 7,500 feet to maintain visual flight rules or VFR. Once in level flight and after I thrashed at the trim tabs to control the aircraft, Lt. Breed took control of the airplane and re-trimmed and demonstrated a turn pattern. The turn pattern consisted of two turns of fifteen degrees angle of bank: one to the left and then a reversal to the right, stopping at the original cardinal heading. Two turns of thirty degrees of bank for ninety degrees of heading change followed. Finally, he initiated two at forty-five degrees angle of bank, each for one hundred eighty degrees of heading change, and he then terminated the maneuver.

Then Lt. Breed said the ever-dreaded words, "Now you try one."

My recall of the maneuver went immediately into the drink. It hit absolute bottom, as it would for every maneuver over the next two flights. The use and effect of the trim tabs became a distraction. Power was the invisible but life-giving quantity. Each froze and shattered my midnight oil into little pieces of memory without distinct function or purpose. The love of the blue sky came with an ever- increasing price. The level of forgetfulness was inversely proportional to the level of forgiveness demonstrated by the United States Navy.

On my second flight, I discovered something was different about the learning process in Naval Aviation. I knew then what people meant when they said "You're behind." While still airborne, I looked back on the days of June that preceded my first flight as a walk in the sunshine, a regular boondoggle, even though I asked the right questions of my seniors and studied my procedures almost every night.

The debriefing went well enough, but Lt. Breed said something I always remembered.

"No one ever said this wouldn't be semi-tough."

He said that a couple of times and when I heard it the first time, I could not have agreed more.

FAM 3 came four days later. Before all others, knowing procedures became my FAM 3 priority. I worked late for three nights preparing for its challenges, knowing I had to improve my level of recall while flying. FAM 3 meant discussions of the electrical system, its malfunctions, and the NATOPS (Naval Air Training and Operating Procedures Standardization) emergency procedures covering the event of an electrical fire during flight and ground handling operations. FAM 3 meant the business of a power-off stall, a turn pattern, outlying field entry, full flap approaches and landings, outlying field departure, student landings with two touch-and-goes and a level speed-change maneuver. FAM 3 meant frustration.

I recited the procedures during the briefing. But while at the controls of the airplane, my mind was so preoccupied with just controlling the Mentor that doing something useful with it became an impossibility. Instead of remembering my procedures, I recalled "No one ever said this wouldn't be semi-tough" over and over again.

However, it seemed more than semi-tough. On my third flight I had to land the airplane several times. These early landings challenged and frightened me so much that I generated the ultimate denial. I convinced myself that it was only a movie. I don't recall where my first landings took place, but I do remember the concrete announcing its presence to the undercarriage. *Bang!* I added power and the torque of the prop, coupled with the increase in velocity of the air swirling about the tail, and pushed the aircraft's nose to the left. I fought back with a push of the right rudder and tapped on the right brake pedal to position over to the centerline. My instructor pushed the power lever beyond my timid movement and I pitched us back into the sky with the over control of a new student. We oscillated between all of the shades of blue and green Mother Nature provided.

It's only a movie. It's only a movie, was the mental litany I recited, as I tried to calm my nerves. Four more landings to go!

Debriefing went south at Whiting Field. I received a below average grade for one of the flight's events. While I was just glad to have it behind me, taking home a below average check mark for an overall grade of "one below" was more than a disappointment; it was heart wrenching. I wanted to be a natural stick so badly. Now I knew better. Flying required a lot of work.

One of the guys in front office saw my long face and gave me some valuable advice.

"Tomorrow is another day," he told me, "so get it behind you. Remember. You're behind."

After that, I gave myself no more sympathy, only more studies. I thought again of what Lt. Breed had said: "No one ever said this wouldn't be semi-tough" and the fear of failure motivated me to study well into the night.

I learned that same night that I would fly my fourth hop the very next day. Naval Aviation is unforgiving, so I tried something new. I hit the books without a break, tapping out flight procedures with my hands against my desk. I recited them as if they were chants. Each procedure came on top of the next procedure, hour after hour, back and forth without any breaks. I tried to utilize my time more efficiently and effectively.

Before I knew it, my bed was calling. I hadn't seen the beach in four weeks, no television in three weeks, no alcohol during the week, no girlfriend; and, for all of this, I received a below average. It didn't make any sense, but "nobody ever said this wouldn't be semi-tough." The only thing I knew was that in the morning, five-thirty would come with the grace and pleasantry of a drill instructor.

As it turned out, my chants were useless. Neither the extra time spent concentrating instead of relaxing, nor the midnight oil, adequately prepared me for the following day's high altitude work. During the high work session, the distraction of flying took all my concentration. I didn't remember my procedures. I wasn't able to recall procedures while flying an airplane. My airmanship, confidence and self-esteem suffered greatly that day.

During the low work, I caught on a bit faster than both Lt. Breed and I expected. Once close to the field, things began to make sense. The Navy's trick of flying over fixed objects to maintain a landing pattern made sense to me. I learned visually. I could see how the airplane behaved when out-of-trim versus when in-trim. Here the effect of power on the plane also became obvious.

That day I made five take-offs and landings. The early ones repeated the previous day's oscillations. We jerked through the departure end of the touch-and-go pattern and I asked Lt. Breed, "Does your wife love you?"

"Yes, why do you ask, Schupbach?"

"Because if she does, why is she letting you fly with a guy like me?"

"I don't know why you say that, you're not doing so bad. Let me try one and you take a break, sit back and watch."

Lt. Breed flew a couple of demonstration landings, then handed the airplane back to me.

"I have it back," I said, wiggling the stick.

Somehow I cooled off enough to make some things happen. I trimmed more often, trimmed for power changes, trimmed for attitude changes, used the rudder pedals in every turn; and, much to my surprise, touched down on the runway centerline in an acceptable manner. We took two or three more turns through the landing pattern and then departed for my first landing back home at NAS Whiting Field. Coming home, I found all of our checkpoints and maintained the correct recovery speed, which impressed my instructor. With his assistance, we flew into the break: a 180-degree, left-hand course reversal over the midfield point of the runway, and lowered the landing gear. Once established downwind, he gave me the aircraft back.

"You have the airplane back."

"I have it," I said, as I began my turn and descended for the runway.

On a wing and a prayer I turned final, lined up and brought the aircraft down in the touchdown zone for my fifth landing of the day. I couldn't believe the seat of my pants.

I just took it into Whiting Field for a smooth landing. Me? On my fourth hop? Just wait till the BOQ hears about this one!

Taxiing in, I fell in love with the feeling of that soft touchdown. It tasted especially sweet after a long and difficult hop. I felt like opening the canopy, standing up and shouting "See, I knew I could do it!" I concentrated on taxiing the aircraft and completing the after-landing checklist instead.

Lt. Breed also thought my landings were good, showing remarkable improvement throughout the day. I received "one above" for my landings and that made me feel on top of the world. I was so ecstatic about my first good landing that I entirely forgot about the other parts of the flight. Unfortunately Lt. Breed didn't.

My high work did not measure up. My knowledge and recall of the Navy's procedures were clearly below average. For the hop I received "one above" and "two below" for an algebraic sum of two below on my career. I knew I could do better and I felt a childhood dream, the chance of a lifetime, slipping away from me. I was falling out of the sky. I had to do something to turn my performance around for fear of getting a down on my next ride. I knew I had to do things differently from before.

Desperation drove me. The next day, I asked around the squadron about other jobs in the Navy. This was a big no-no and soon a high and tight Marine flight instructor told me so straight to my face.

"Go over to the ground school building," he said, "and speak with Ensign Mudd. He quit flying six weeks ago; DOR'd, and now he is shuffling papers for ground school instructors while the Navy decides what to do with him. Right! He is reapplying to flight school, crying for another chance, saying he made a big mistake. Yes, he did. There are no billets available, not in submarines, not in the surface Navy, and you won't be transferred to be an N.F.O. (Naval Flight Officer.) They don't take pilot washouts anymore. So, go talk to him before you make one big mistake yourself. You got that, Schupbach?"

"Sir, yes sir," I replied as I remembered seeing the guy before. He was miserable and even told several of us to never quit the program. So much for that one!

Flying the Gauntlet

CHAPTER FOUR

The following day was my twenty-fourth birthday and to celebrate the occasion, I chose to visit the base chaplain. I walked over to his office in the bright sunshine, wondering whether or not I would wash out of the flight program or simply DOR. As an officer, I thought I might resign my commission, take the VA benefits from being on active duty and return home to Nebraska, never to see the inside of my flight suit again. I stood alone on the main north-south street of the base. One direction led to the flight line, the other sent me to the main gate and out of the program. In a few steps I would be crossing the double yellow line of caution, which divided both the street in front of my life and me into opposite directions of travel. Fortunately, my path traveled perpendicular to the roadway, buying me some time. I headed straight for the man, hoping above all hopes that he would be able to shed some light and strength into my decisions. My twenty-fourth birthday was a day of sobering truth rather than a day of celebration. I needed to know some things about myself, and I needed to know them immediately.

I entered the white, World War II era, pine building and was greeted by a receptionist I thought a bit odd.

"Good afternoon. How may I help you, Sir?"

I looked around the room, noticing the 1960s paneling, the government-issue green tile, and her inmate-manufactured, gray steel desk. The dropped ceiling's fluorescent lighting barely illuminated the room, leaving only the two lamps at her desk for reading. The window shades were full down, protecting the occupants from the heat of the day and from observation. This was a good thing. I'm not Catholic and I felt a bit uncomfortable speaking with a priest instead of a minister. However, I knew I needed to take whatever the Navy provided and make the most of it.

These visits are strictly confidential. My visit will be kept off of the record.

After a long pause, I looked straight over her head and said, "I need to see the priest."

"What? Are you here by appointment? I don't recall any other appointments for today. Would you like an appointment for sometime next week?"

"No, I need to see the priest...today."

"I'm sorry, but he isn't taking any visitors for the rest of the day. You'll just have to set an appointment and come back."

"No, Miss, I need to see the priest and you can tell him that I'm not leaving this office until I speak with him. Today is my birthday and this is my birthday present to myself," I said looking at the pale green door behind her.

With that, the middle-aged woman picked up the telephone and dialed God's extension. Her brief conversation surprised her.

"Please take a seat. He's with someone right now but will see you when he's through. It will be some time, however, as his visits are very long."

"That's OK because I need to see the priest."

I sat down away from the waiting room in an oversized chair, facing her desk from the right hand side. I waited, playing games with my cover (hat) by running my fingers around its inside brim. I thought of a million different questions to ask this man, a priest I never met before. Most of all, I felt I needed to trust him. I needed his insight and answers. I wasn't going to leave without them. I waited an hour and a half until finally, the pale green door opened and the priest came out with another supplicant. My biggest fear then overcame me. I thought that the priest might change his mind and cancel my visit, walking by my chair without giving me so much as the time of day. I neared my breaking point and fought back tears.

I stood up as they said a few words in parting and while he spoke with his secretary.

He addressed me finally. "Welcome, welcome my friend! Come into my office. Would you like a cup of coffee?"

"Thank you, sir. No thank you, sir. I just need to talk to you, sir."

"Well, come in and sit down, my friend."

We exchanged introductions as I walked into his dimly lit office. "Pardon my lighting but the sun is rather blinding."

The office was dark. Heavy, brown corduroy curtains hung on the windows and were drawn back to allow at least some of the light to filter into the room. Light streamed in between two-inch-wide Venetian blind slats. Hundreds of books were contained within built-in bookshelves on the wall to my left. *Who in the Navy has time to read so many books?* I wondered. *Will this guy understand what I'm going through as he swivels in his comfy chair? Or will he put his feet up on his desk drawer and stare out into space while I cry out for help, not hearing a word I say?*

"Please take a seat, relax, be comfortable, and when you're ready, tell me a little about yourself."

He sat across from me—there were few other real choices—and gave a brief synopsis of his background in the Navy. He worked on all kinds of ships before being assigned shore duty at Whiting Field. He was due to rotate out in a few months and I thought that was his way of saying "Hurry up, I have little time left here so I can blow you off. It's no sweat off of my back. I have so few years left in the Navy I could swim to my retirement."

I was wrong about that. By the end of introductions, this man of God came across as genuine and sincere as any other religious counselor with whom I had ever spoken. I felt my shoulders droop as I relaxed with him.

"Well," I said, "Why am I so depressed?"

"Neal, depression is a way of life around here."

That response unraveled one of the great mysteries of the Whiting Field experience. Everyone knew what we were going through. It was a program designed to put us in that condition and everyone shared in its many ups and downs, in more ways than one. I simply reacted to it, as does every person participating in such a challenging program. We spoke at length about this before I put another question to the collar.

"Sir, why is it that I need to work-out and run almost every day? I can't quite understand why I waste my time exercising. I try to take care of myself and it feels as if it's my last little bastion of hope, my last cubbyhole away from the Navy, the only privacy I get in a day."

"Well, I like to run too. It's said that it's not that you can find the time to be able to run, but that running enables you to find the time for everything else. It's not the stress of running that detracts from you, but rather the release from stress that running gives that's important. It gives you the ability to cope with the stress. Running enhances, not detracts, from our experiences and you can do more with it than you can without it, even though it takes time during the day."

"Well, how is it that the flight line feels so much like playing football? I'm a bundle of nerves until I walk out on the flight line and then it feels like the first contact, the first hit of the football game. All of the nervous energy goes away and I get down to the business at hand. Is that the way flying is supposed to be?"

"I like your analogy and I think that holds true for any number of life's challenging circumstances. Anticipation is worse than the event. We all go through it. That is, if we are awaiting a challenge. And challenge is another way of saying naval flight training. What squadron are you in, Neal?"

"VT-6, sir, the stick-with-the-greatest squadron. I'm really glad to be there and not in the attrition-is-our-mission squadron, sir."

"VT-6, flying T-34s or T-28s?"

"T-34s, sir. I tried to fly the T-28 but the class had too many people in it and someone said that 'you can always turn off the air-conditioner in the T-34,' so I volunteered for the Mentor, sir."

"Well, you made a good choice."

I sensed he was wrapping things up but I still had one more question.

"Sir, there is one other thing I need to talk to you about."

"And what might that be, Neal?"

"Well sir, I'm passing the ground school without too much of a problem, but—flying is a different story. I study my procedures all day and all night until I can write them from memory, as if they were scripted. I put in all of the effort that I possibly can; but when in the airplane, while flying, I simply have an awful time remembering the procedures. Turn patterns and level speed changes bring me down and I'm getting below average grades from simply not being able to remember in the air what I could write out from memory on the ground."

"Neal, flying is a distraction. Flying is a great, big, physical distraction. Just keeping the plane airborne is enough to confuse anyone."

"Well, yes sir, I'm trying my best just to stay alive, let alone do the procedure. But I can't remember the procedure."

"Neal, try studying with a distraction. Close the door to your room and recite your procedures to yourself while you're doing something else. Jumping jacks, sit-ups, anything to keep your mind occupied while you remember and recite your procedures. Try it and see if that helps. You need to recall while you are distracted by something else, something physical. So find something you like to do and use it to your advantage."

"That sounds right. I think you just gave me one, very big birthday present, sir."

"Oh, it's your birthday? Happy birthday and it's my pleasure to spend time together. I don't know if I consider what we said a present. That's up to you. So go out there and we'll see you in the sky. When is your next flight?"

"I don't know, sir. They're canceling a lot of hops because of the thunderstorms. It seems if you have class in the morning and fly in the afternoon, then you just have class in the morning."

"Well, Neal, be prepared for your next big hop; and if things aren't working out for you; please by all means, come see me and we'll talk things through again."

"Yes sir, thank you, sir."

We concluded our meeting with a handshake and a walk through his door. I walked past the secretary with an "I told you so" attitude. I got to see the priest despite her best efforts. I didn't look back for fear of showing signs that I wasn't focused. I already showed how weak I was by talking to the priest, or so I thought.

Weeks later, I realized how wrong I was to think of my visit as a sign of weakness. I put his words into action and things began to turn around in the sky. Indeed, the priest gave me the best birthday present. In fact, he turned around my entire flight program in a miraculous manner. His reassurances lifted a large weight from my shoulders, and his study methods proved invaluable to me. I will always remember it as the day the Good Lord acted through his kind servant and answered my tearful prayers. I'll always regret not taking the opportunity to thank him and tell him of my success, but somehow I think he already knew.

I took the priest's suggestion to heart. After all, it was the only thing I could do. I had no other choice except admitting failure, and that was completely unacceptable. I tried push-ups while reciting flight procedures but that was time limited, based on how many push-ups I could do. I tried doing jumping jacks while talking out loud, but with similar results. However, there on top of my dresser, sat a racquetball and my father's old wooden racquet. It gave me an excellent idea.

My idea was a juggling act of sorts. I decided to bounce the racquetball off the racquet while I recited my flight procedures. This quickly proved to be more difficult than it first appeared. I was able to complete only four or five bounces while reciting two or three lines of procedure, and then lost the ball into the corner of the room. I practiced and practiced, recalling procedures every night and sometimes during the day. After several days of practice, I knew I had found my mark and I became more confident and excited about flying than ever before.

I couldn't wait to try out my newfound "distracted recall" in the airplane. After several briefings and attempts, FAM 5 finally came to pass on the nineteenth of July. During the briefing, we considered the possibility of a warm-up flight, if the event went too far south. My only disappointment was waiting so long for the weather pattern to change.

We took off and actually headed south to a working area west of Pensacola. In the high work, we flew our regular level speed change and turn pattern. Lt. Breed demonstrated two new items; both were stalls. During normal flight, a boundary layer or laminate flow of air adheres to the upper skin of the wing. During a stall, the laminate flow is disrupted and air tumbles over the upper surface of the wing. A complete loss of lift occurs and the aircraft falls from the sky in a rather pronounced manner.

Lt. Breed induced the power-off stall by reducing the power of the engine to idle as he maintained a constant altitude, trading airspeed for altitude. A few moments before the stall occurred, the T-34C's safety device, the rudder shaker, vibrated the rudder pedals—something everyone can hear and feel. This warned us of the onset of a stall, giving the opportunity to reduce the nose attitude and add power before the onset of the actual stall. At the stall, the aircraft buffeted a couple of times, then pitched nose down and began a wings level free fall back towards Mother Earth. The stall recovery procedure required the pilot to apply full power, right rudder, and lower the nose to break the stall by regaining the laminar flow of air over the wing.

Lt. Breed demonstrated and I practiced several power-off stalls. Initially I found that stalls were nothing to be afraid of, as we practiced them at seven thousand feet. There was plenty of room to recover the aircraft. Additionally, we carried parachutes. We were required to bailout if we were out of control below five thousand feet. Beside all of that, "God" sat in the back seat. Oh, how little I knew!

FAM 5 demonstrated a second type of stall, the approach-turn stall. This stall illustrated to the unsuspecting student what not to do while flying in the landing pattern. It typically occurs during the turn for the runway. An inexperienced pilot adds too much rudder and raises the nose to bring the turn around while trying to save the landing. The fuselage hides a portion of the inboard wing from the wind while creating a transverse flow at a high angle of attack. Accidents occur when both of the wings lost lift simultaneously. In the stall, the aircraft rolls towards the inboard wing, and if this happened near the runway, there wouldn't be enough airspeed or altitude to recover. Unfortunately, these events happen quite rapidly and send many doctors into the proverbial "smoking hole" in the ground, thus the nickname, "the Doctor's stall." The Navy emphasized this maneuver because the Navy flew oval landing patterns.

For my "low work," my entry to the outlying field for touch-and-goes went well and so did my landings. Lt. Breed demonstrated a no-flap landing and I tried one when we returned to Whiting Field. He always gave me an early look at a new maneuver, one flight ahead of the syllabus, and this paid off with better grades.

Between my instructor's good information and my newfound study methods, my high work improved dramatically and so did my landings. I flew great, despite having been off for some two weeks. Overall, the hop went quite well. I received two above averages on this hop, surprising the both of us. I left the debrief feeling on top of the world, walking on air, and I called home with the good news.

FAM 6 came two days later on the twenty-first of July. During the briefing, Lt. Breed glossed over a third type of stall he would demonstrate, the skidded-turn stall. He said that he would "...debrief it in detail but didn't want to spoil any of the fun."

I kept quiet and went along with that explanation. While leaving the briefing shack, I overheard him joke with the other instructors about it being the day of his best maneuver, "Shadow Flight's wicked, skidded-turn stall." Suspicious, I could only smile and wonder what I was getting myself into on such a fine afternoon.

Once in the higher altitudes, we completed the basic airmanship maneuvers, the warm-up drills. Lt. Breed then took the aircraft. He began to lecture on the skidded-turn stall; a lecture that, in reality, was a snow job designed to catch me unaware. He did a very good job. The power came back first to simulate a gliding airplane. While the aircraft slowed down, he slowly placed more and more pressure on the right rudder pedal. Nothing seemed out of the ordinary until moments before the very end. Then I noticed the aircraft was in an unusual twist while the wings remained level. The ailerons held the aircraft level against the forces of the rudder-advancing wing. Lt. Breed kept up his soothing monologue until it happened.

In the blink of an eye, we snapped completely on our back and began a rapid descent toward the earth from eight thousand five hundred feet. From that vantage point, I realized there was nothing between Mother Earth and us but pine trees. We accelerated downward and I didn't know quite what to think.

However, the good Lt. released the control pressures he asserted and lowered the nose thereby regaining some airspeed. Once in balanced flight, albeit inverted, he gently rolled the wings with the ailerons to an upright position and leveled off. The demonstration took several thousand feet to complete.

I thought the skidded-turn stall was a good time overall, flipping over at warp speed, hanging upside down and plummeting toward the ground below. However, it brought home to me the problems associated with skidding the aircraft, allowing one wing to fly while the other wing stalls.

Students never practiced this particular stall. With my famous luck, during the next maneuver, I nearly did.

For the next few minutes I entertained us with my second ever power-off stall. I had to repeat the maneuver shortly thereafter. From the previous debrief, my first stall was criticized for not adding full power while giving the aircraft a foot of right rudder. My caution for saving the turbine caught up with me with criticism. So I studied for this hop by over-emphasizing the "FULL POWER-RIGHT RUDDER" call out while sitting at my desk, flying the chair and bouncing that blue racquetball five hundred times a night. I was ready for the stall, more than ready, and what followed surprised both of us.

I flew the aircraft into the stall with little difficulty. Simply by relaxing the stick pressure and allowing the aircraft to lower its own nose, I would immediately break this stall. On FAM 6 that's not what happened, at least not during my first attempt.

The rudder shaker came on as the airplane slowed, alerting me to the onset of stall. I expected this and it armed my arms and legs for reaction. The stall occurred with two buffets and then we felt the nose fall towards the horizon. However, by mistake during this critical time, I let the right wing dip slightly as we entered the stall. As I had practiced the night before, I shouted my cockpit procedures "FULL POWER-RIGHT RUDDER," while I jammed the throttle forward and stomped on the right rudder pedal at the same time. Finesse mattered little in my mind but the airplane required it.

As the motor and propeller spun up, the rudder grabbed control of the entire airplane. We literally flew sideways for a two count, until the inboard wing stalled. Then we rolled inverted and pointed straight down.

The next thing I heard was, "I HAVE IT!"

Lt. Breed grabbed the airplane from me, pulled back some of the power and rolled us back upright. He then had a few words with me starting with "SCHOOEEBAAAACH!" Oh, how he made my ears ring over that one! I thought I might receive an immediate down. Much to my surprise, I found myself trying another stall, only this time with much more emphasis on the intentional application of power and control inputs rather than my slop and slam approach to flying. It all worked out fine.

Our last item of demonstration that day came from heaven to earth—literally. We were flying a single engine aircraft and we needed to be able to land with an engine failure at high altitude, safely gliding into an airport or an unprepared field, depending on the circumstance, the pilot's skill, and a good bit of luck. Obviously, if you could glide to an unprepared field without difficulty, setting the plane down on a roadway would be easy. Thus we practiced the unprepared field landing with simulated engine failures.

T-34C: The Mentor

At four thousand feet, Lt. Breed pulled back the power and said, "This is a simulated engine failure."

The high altitude engine failure gave time for the pilot to transition to the maximum glide speed, feather the propeller (which put its sharp, knife's edge into the oncoming wind stream), analyze the winds from above, make a distressed radio call for assistance, trim the plane, and choose a field for a forced landing. Other items included locking the shoulder harness inertial restraint system, ensuring the helmet visor was down and locked, lowering the flaps when the field was made and blowing the canopy before the airframe bent with impact. This entire procedure first appeared a bit much for me to remember, but he made it all look so easy.

We departed the cornfield after one, very low approach and flew over to an outlying field called Middleton to practice our landings. Lt. Breed again emphasized flying over checkpoints on the ground to complete an oval pattern. This method compensated for the winds aloft by simply flying whatever it took to track over the same points on the ground. I took in eight landings at Middleton and one back at home plate, NAS Whiting Field. Lt. Breed took in three. I thought I had had a pretty fun afternoon of flying for my sixth flight. However, Harry Breed had a different point of view. This made for a long, quiet walk back to the debrief shack.

At the brief/debrief shack, we sat down in a small, makeshift cubical facing the green chalkboard. The review went fine until it came to my second stall; then things got interesting. In FAM 6, the stall was an introductory item. Fortunately for me, it wasn't graded because of difficulty in grading my upside down, nose into the ground recovery, other than to say it was unsatisfactory and give a "down" for the ride. I dodged that bullet.

As one might imagine, Lt. Breed wanted to talk about my un-graded, unsatisfactory maneuver. He wanted to find out what I was thinking and correct any misconceptions I might have.

"You didn't keep the wings level," he said. "This is important, Schupbach. In any stall, when the wings are level, one hundred percent of the lift generated will be utilized in a force counteracting the force of gravity. If the wing is in a turn, then a percentage of the resulting lift will be used to turn the aircraft, resulting in a higher stalling speed."

Lt. Breed paused to let that sink in before continuing.

"The lift required in a thirty-degree angle of bank turn at a constant altitude is fifty percent greater than that required to fly the airplane in straight and level flight. This is one example of an accelerated stall, the other being a hard pull-up during the stall. Both aggravate the situation, and when close to the ground, no one needs more aggravation."

I listened to the gracious Lt. as if my life depended upon him. After looking at the ground from six thousand feet, upside down and straight down through the propeller, I knew it did. I wouldn't last long in this program without mastering this newfound challenge.

Breed continued. "The other thing that took place from your letting the right wing fall is that the upper wing, the left wing, acted as the advancing wing. And what does that do for us, Schupbach?"

"Well, sir, the advancing wing generates more lift and the retreating wing is hidden from the airflow so it produces less lift for that reason. We induced a rolling movement because of the nature of the beast."

"Correct. Then what happened?"

"Well, sir, I added full power and full right rudder all at the same time... and we ended up flopping around, fumbling it all into the direction of the ground. I guess I added power and rudder a little too quickly, sir."

"A little too quickly...that's right. Now, when you put in the power, that's a good thing. Power causes the airplane to regain flying speed. Lowering the nose broke the stall from the decrease in the wing's angle of attack. But when you jumped on the rudder, we went sideways and rotated up into the sky ass backwards.

"Yes Sir."

"Honestly, Schupbach, that was a down; but I can't give you a below average because it's an introductory maneuver."

"Yes, sir."

"You know that the rudder is just a wing stood on its edge, don't you?"

"No sir, honestly I have never thought of it that way."

"Schupbach," he said looking me straight in the eye from a foot away, "you scare me."

"Yes, sir."

Unlike the flight, this FAM 6 debrief seemed endless. When all was said and done, I left feeling lower than whale shit.

FAM 7 came the very next day. This orientation flight briefed on slipping the aircraft, a maneuver that places the ailerons in a left or right turn while using the rudder in the opposite direction to keep the aircraft on a constant heading. The technique is used to create drag on the airplane while correcting for too much altitude in the landing pattern. It is also utilized during a crosswind landing.

We discussed the precautionary emergency landing or PEL. The PEL is executed in response to any number of flight problems. That afternoon we discussed indications of impending engine failure, oil pressure fluctuations, an engine chips light and a surging engine. Thus initially, the precautionary landing maneuver places the aircraft in the direction of the closest suitable field. The object was to arrive at the checkpoint over the end of the runway and at three thousand feet above the field. From this "high key" position, the pilot has sufficient altitude to safely fly a smaller, left-handed circular pattern to the runway, all the while gliding without power.

The next checkpoint came at the fifteen-hundred-foot mark on a somewhat limited downwind leg. At this point, we lowered the landing gear. In the event of a complete power loss, this checkpoint gave enough time to hand crank the gear down—as if you weren't busy enough—while making the final turn to the runway. Lined up with the runway, we lowered the flaps although they could be utilized to create drag to compensate for a high approach. All of this was a precautionary maneuver, one that was practiced many times to gain proficiency.

The last new item of the hop was the "wave-off." The wave-off, or go-around, could originate from any number of sources, for an even greater number of reasons. During flight training, we took turns standing "paddles-watch" with two large, white aluminum paddles on the left side of each field. When the student approached the runway, we would raise our paddles over our head, indicating the landing gear was down and it was safe to land. However, if the paddles-watch waved the paddles back and forth over his head, it meant that the pilot should abort the landing attempt and fly back into pattern. At night, a flare gun was used to indicate the command to wave-off. If the student ever flew past the command to wave-off or go-around from the paddles-watch, he forfeited a bottle to his or her instructor. I came so close to buying that bottle.

We flew the landing pattern at Middleton after completing our high work. From out of the blue, a strange deep voice came through my radio: "Whiskey Oscar." Lt. Breed talked in code with the runway duty officer and paddles-watch, giving the code for a wave-off.

"Damn civilians," he said to me, "they should get some new radios."

I didn't catch onto the scenario, so I dropped the landing gear and rolled into the base turn. With the landing checklist completed, I lined up on the centerline and continued my descent while selecting landing flaps. I was happy with the approach. This was one of my better patterns for the day, *spot on* for a good quality touch and go. Out of the corner of my eye, passing under the left wing, I saw the paddles-watch waving his white paddles instead of giving the two paddles up signal.

"Wave off, wave-off, I'm going around!" I shouted into the intercom system as I advanced the throttle and raised the nose. I brought the gear up, raised the flaps and took us back up to pattern altitude before initiating my turn to the downwind leg.

Once reestablished in the pattern, I heard "SCHOOEEBAAAACH!"

I had seen the wave-off, so what did I do wrong? His comment left me a bit confused.

"I have the airplane," Lt. Breed said, taking over. "I'll take a few landings."

Then he explained. "You came so close, so close to owing me a bottle of good scotch, I could taste it going by. You saw the paddles watch at the very last second. He was waving you off from the ninety while in your turn. How you ever managed that one, I'll never know. But you did and that's what counts."

I just smiled, knowing he was right. I got away with another one by the skin of my teeth.

I heard about it again in debrief but there was no damage. I did the right thing and took it around.

"You had a good pattern going and it was too bad to not have made a landing from it—but that would have meant a bottle."

We then completed the rest of debrief, and much to my surprise, began briefing for what would be my next flight: basic instruments one.

We moved over to a booth with a paper instrument panel for that portion of the briefing. Lt. Breed gave a long lecture on my next new challenge, the basics of instruments flying. When flying the next hop, I would sit in the rear cockpit with a burlap cloth draped across the rear canopy to obstruct my view of the horizon. This simulated flying inside clouds where there is no horizon. At times, even your wingtips disappear.

The good Lt. spent well over an hour going over each instrument: from the attitude gyro to the vertical speed indicator, the compass to the altimeter. I gave each one my undivided attention as he lectured about their importance.

"Of all of these," Lt. Breed summarized, "the attitude gyro is the most important. And this little pin dot, right there," he pointed to a mark at the top of a pinnacle on the stationary bar, "is called the piper. The piper is where your scan begins. The aircraft reacts to any movement measured in degrees against the piper. The angle of bank is found at the top of the gyro with the bank angle scale and the bank angle pointer. But the piper is the key to all of instrument flying."

"You must practice the proper scan at all times. Start with the attitude gyro," Breed said, pointing to it with a piece of chalk. "It goes like this: attitude gyro-airspeed, attitude gyro-RMI (radio magnetic indicator), attitude gyro-altimeter, attitude gyro-RMI, attitude gyro-airspeed, attitude gyro, and on and on, continually going around the bases.

"Yes sir, I'll buy that."

"Whenever you have a chance, scan the ball, the vertical speed indicator and the clock."

The clock, I thought, *but that is way over there.* With that, we wrapped up our hour-long discussion of the scan pattern.

Back at the BOQ, I broke out the Paper Tiger (cockpit trainer) and practiced my scan every night by naming and touching each dial like Lt. Breed did during his lecture. I also studied for ground school classes and recited my procedures for both the upcoming Basic Instruments One (BI 1) flight and the next FAM flight. Now I was tasked with either one of the two types of flying: basic instrument and familiarization. It all seemed a bit much. The moment I caught up and landed with my feet on the ground running, they gave me a different assignment to master! At the time, it didn't seem fair.

It was two days later, on the twenty-fourth of July, that I flew my first basic instruments hop. During the basic instruments flights and radio instruments flights, the student sat in the rear seat while the instructor flew from the front set of controls. The mission changed completely for this training segment. I flew only at high altitude and while "under the bag."

I strapped on my oxygen mask, checked its settings and pulled the cloth hood over my cockpit, attaching it to the top of the instrument glare shield. Lt. Breed emphasized two things while we made our way out to the working area.

"Be comfortable, don't let the instructor freeze you out with the air conditioner at altitude. And, if anything ever goes wrong with the airplane or the flight, immediately get out from beneath the bag," he explained.

Those two pieces of advice reassured me. It seemed someone generally cared for this student's welfare and I liked that idea.

For the flying portion of the hop, I practiced my scan pattern while the instructor flew a two-corner rectangular pattern. The exercise started on a cardinal heading (N-S-E-W) with controlled descents through fifteen hundred feet of altitude. At the bottom of the pattern, he waved off the approach by adding go-around power, pulling the nose up to a predetermined attitude, and retracting the flaps and gear to clean up the airplane. The maneuver ended when we returned to the initial altitude on the designated heading and airspeed.

We flew other airmanship drills, such as recovering from unusual attitudes. I closed my eyes while the instructor put the airplane in an unusual attitude and then told me, "You have it."

When I opened my eyes, I recovered the airplane by bringing the nose-high airplane back to the horizon while adjusting the power and leveling the wings. In the real world, this event commonly occurred because of a breakdown of the scan from distraction or fixation on one instrument.

The other main event of this hop emphasized the insanity of early fliers who attempted to fly on a partial panel of instruments. The T-34C came with a device known as a turn needle. This wide, black band against a white background told the smooth pilot, if he was in a turn, which direction of the turn he was in; and, when taken in conjunction with known airspeeds, how many degrees of heading change per second the aircraft accomplished. Just when I thought that flying by instruments seemed tough enough, the Navy took away the basic instrument—the attitude gyro and substituted this antique, black finger and told me to learn to fly with it! Lt. Breed's mantra echoed in my mind, "Nobody ever said this wouldn't be semi-tough." He didn't lie to me about that one.

I learned many lessons from these challenges. I actually received my best grades while working "in the chicken coop." I guess it was easier to believe that it was only a movie.

During our next briefing, FAM 9 added some interesting discussions on emergency considerations. The tactics of enlisting a buddy to check over your airplane while you were airborne was discussed. A second set of eyes that could observe the exterior of the aircraft could prove invaluable.

"When in need, how does one acquire such a friend, Schupbach?" asked Lt. Breed.

"Sir, I believe the radio would be of great assistance. Either the aircraft's radio or, if the electrical system were damaged, you could break out the hand-held PRC 90 radio and talk on guard frequency."

Low altitude engine failure was also discussed. At low altitude, there was no option of bailing out of the stricken plane; staying alive was left to pilot skill. Although a hectic maneuver, you could practice and successfully complete belly landing the plane onto an unprepared field. I always thought roads looked good because my recruiter, "The Weasel," lost a propeller and landed safely on a gravel road in the middle of Nebraska. But roads have oncoming traffic, power lines, poles, ditches, turns and bridges. All could wreak havoc on the airplane. Besides that, the Whiting Field area had very few roads.

We spun the airplane from nine thousand feet during the high work. This was a pleasant surprise; the plane performed predictably and came out of the spin with great ease. I set up the plane in a slow flight regime and then gently put in rudder while reducing power and raising the nose. The plane broke for its back as one wing flipped the plane over and started the nose heading for the ground while rotating rapidly. To regain control, I pushed nose down to break the stall and applied opposite rudder. For fun, we counted the number of revolutions we completed while falling several thousand feet. The maneuver became a favorite of mine. The whirling sights and the near weightless rotation invigorated me.

The syllabus now alternated between familiarization hops and basic instruments events. Flights were completed with other instructors. The first instructor change was quite a shock; my new instructor never flew in the fleet. Rather than a fleet tour and the corresponding seasoning, he retread into an instructor. Therefore, to maintain credibility with the students, the man prided himself on knowing every detail of the plane and he monitored each maneuver like a hawk after prey. We called these types "screamers." FAM 10 was no exception. Somehow I survived the flight. Even the debrief went surprisingly well with another "above average" chocked up in my favor.

On BI 2, I flew with another new instructor. He was the complete opposite of the previous officer. We completed the maneuvers in almost total silence except for the chitchat of getting to know each other's background. He, too, was a plowback, a flyer that never joined a squadron. Yet he came across with several, soft-spoken pointers as well as well-intentioned suggestions.

The only new drill that remained to fly was the penetration pattern, an air work drill that first became popular in Vietnam. There, the pilots needed a steep descent from a high altitude above the airport to avoid enemy antiaircraft fire. The penetration pattern included a 180-degree course reversal, bringing them back to the airport they just flew over.

Things went a bit wobbly during my first try, but I figured that's to be expected. I put in the trim for this maneuver and kept trimming to achieve hands-off flying. This created pitch attitude problems as the aircraft gained airspeed in the dive and my trim became more affected. However, I kept the plane in balanced flight. *All in all, things went well,* I thought afterwards, *for an initial attempt at the maneuver.*

Imagine my surprise during debrief when I did poorly and there had been no in- flight comments. While I never argued with any instructor, I didn't understand his grading standard. In the end, all I could do was shake it off and walk back to the BOQ for more study. Certainly a *different breed of cat,* I wanted nothing more to do with the retread flight instructors!

During the summertime, the weather at Whiting Field made you question why the U.S. Navy ever chose this location for flight training. The considerable morning ground fog literally burned off, turned into steam and cooked anyone in a flight suit. The hazy afternoons discharged large thunderstorms that clobbered our working areas. When we launched, it became routine to duck around the storms and saddlebacks, racing over them as they grew like weeds, choking off the clear, blue sky of Whiting Field.

Pilots often contended with heavy haze at altitude that obscured the horizon. This made the visual maneuvers much more difficult for the pilots who needed a horizon, a level horizon to adjust the pitch attitude and wings of the airplane. A strong line in the sky often formed a false horizon and fooled students into believing that the line represented a wings' level attitude. The sloped, cloud formations left them unknowingly in a turn, giving both the student and instructor a good case of "the leans."

BI 3 was such a late afternoon flight. The hot, Florida steam bath was in full swing and the thunderheads made mountains out of the morning's molehills. Despite the poor weather in our working area, Lt. Breed decided to knock out another X for the command. As soon as we walked out of the hangar, I viewed the blackening, silvery heavens in alarm. However, this wasn't enough to scare off Lt. Harry Breed.

Breed climbed us to thirteen thousand feet in the MOA while I snapped into my oxygen mask and placed the hood over the glare-shield. I noticed the cockpit getting darker than expected. I wasn't used to flying in the shadows of tall storms, especially while under the bag. This made me all the more nervous, remembering the constant warnings about turbulence, lightning, icing and the power these great storms produce. All of that didn't seem to bother Lt. Breed.

We began our work at altitude and I noticed my feet and fingertips getting cold. I called "God" and asked for more heat. But while I could feel the heat through my flight suit, it did nothing for my fingers or feet. My vision weakened and I turned up my gauge illumination lighting, trying to fly the patterns requested by Lt. Breed. Recalling procedures became difficult. As if that weren't enough, in the middle of each procedure he took the airplane and turned it back around, reversing our course.

"Roll wings level on a cardinal heading of east," Lt. Breed said, urgency in his voice.

"I am wings level and my compass says east."

"No, you're about seven degrees, right wing down. Here is wings level."

With that, Lt. Breed nudged the stick and centered his attitude gyro to the vertical.

"Not from back here. This is wings level, sir," I said placing the airplane in a right bank that I thought was wings level.

"Are you sure about that?" he asked, looking back to check that I was under the hood, not cheating and following a false horizon generated by the clouds.

"Yes sir."

"Alright then, come out from under the bag. Your gyro is failing. We're going to have to scrub the hop. I have the airplane"

"You have it," I returned.

I gave him the aircraft back and took a quick breath.

That's when I realized that for the past twenty minutes or so, I had heard no one else on the radio. Taking down the burlap from around the canopy, I understood why. I expected to see some daylight and at least a touch of blue sky—somewhere. What I saw was nothing if it wasn't black—black on the left, black on the right, and boiling black directly in front of our airplane. The good Lt., with his "can do" drive to complete the flight, get an X for the Command and score a brownie point, took us into the blackened MOA all by ourselves. No one else was that stupid.

We were engulfed in towering thunderstorms. Their anger could snap off our tiny wings, kill us with lightning and bury us under thick sheets of ice.

"Are you out from under the bag, Schupbach?"

"Sir, yes sir," I said, trying to disguise both my fear and complete reliance on the man sitting directly in front of me. I knew that I didn't know how we were going to fly out of this one—and I sincerely wanted to come out of it alive.

"All right, hold on tight!" he called back to me.

Lt. Breed reduced the power to idle, rolled the plane inverted and pulled back on the stick. Immediately, large bolts of lightning cut through the green-gray rain and illuminated the shrouded forest below.

Neal, I said to myself, *you bought the ticket, Neal. You volunteered, so shut up, Neal, and go for the ride.*

In a near vertical dive, the airplane rapidly increased its velocity to redline, plummeting downward at 280 knots. I heard the prop wind back up to speed as it tried to slow us down through its own aerodynamic configurations. At the time, it was the only thing on the small airplane that even remotely resembled a speed brake. But we didn't slow down and neither did the volley of lightning bolts just off our right wing, flying formation with us in a race to the ground.

I shook off my fear and began calling out altitudes from my altimeter, that now resembled an un-sprung, watch spring with hands waving wildly back at me.

"Eight thousand—six thousand— four thousand," I announced.

While I focused inside, scanning the gages, Lt. Breed concentrated on the outside of the cockpit, and tried like hell to find a hole in the base of the clouds to take us home. At four thousand feet, his only response was a single "Roger" before finally beginning our pullout. We leveled off between two and three thousand feet, running wide open for home.

Breed flew us below the cloud deck as best he could. The rain pounded an awful racket on the windscreen and the turbulence shook us without remorse. If an object wasn't tied down, it came up to greet you. We headed south towards the Brewton Airport where I thought we might land as a precaution. *But NOOOO!* Lt. Breed pushed on and I simply waved as we slipped by what I thought, at the time, to be our one chance of arriving safely on the ground in one piece.

Still escorted by lightening, we pressed on to NAS Whiting Field, our desperation "bingo" recovery field, only to determine the weather there was unsuitable for landing. Heavy rains and lightening dominated the western approach to that airport. Fortunately, the storms gave a slight reprieve and we broke out about three miles north of the field. In strong winds, Lt. Breed salvaged a visual approach to a wet runway. He did a superlative job of landing the airplane.

We walked quietly back through the rain to the maintenance hangar. Once inside, the Lt. wrote up the gyro and then we debriefed on the fly. He complained that I didn't know my procedures and I understood what he meant. I had studied for a FAM hop by mistake the previous day. I kept silent, not saying a word about anything, not even the weather. I knew I was walking on thin ice.

Later that evening, I thought of another reason for my lack of recall. I put two and two together. My extremities were cold, my vision was weak and I was disoriented. Hypoxia! At that high altitude, I had suffered from a lack of sufficient oxygen during the flight. Live and learn.

I felt lucky that evening to just have another chance at BI 3, to live and learn this flying business. All I cared about was doing better at remembering my procedures in flight. I was too young, too dumb, too naïve, and too hypoxic to understand the true danger of our afternoon's aviation cocktail. In that situation, our only escape was straight down. Not such a good plan by anyone's yardstick, but I didn't care. They had this student focused—I'll say that for the program.

The following day, Lt. Breed and I completed Basic Instruments Three without any of the previous weather problems. Once at the bottom of the penetration pattern, my dictated course reversal turned us in the direction of home. When Lt. Breed told me to come out from under the bag, I knew that my workout for the day was firmly behind me. All I had to do now was sit back, put my arms up along the canopy rails and relax. At the time, it gave me a chance to look around and enjoy the countryside from the privacy of this two-seat Mentor. All that remained of BI 3 was debrief and I could almost taste the cold beer rolling past my lips.

In all fairness, Lt. Breed had a chip on his shoulder when he debriefed the flight. He thought I was progressing, but he was still miffed about "missing the X," missing the completion from last night. While I thought getting the hell out of the thunderstorms alive was enough to convert an atheist; he didn't give it much thought, even after the straight down departure through lightning, rain and heavy turbulence. He complained that on the previous mission, I didn't know my procedures, and "...by the way, Beechcraft couldn't find anything wrong with your attitude gyro!"

The following Monday, I went up to fly BI 4 with the instructor who I thought was inconsistent and irregular in grading. The briefing went well enough but the flight was yet another incomplete due to weather. Fortunately, this man had more commonsense than iron nerve. We didn't come close to the thunderstorms in the MOA. The entire flight lasted just one half-hour, which made me feel like saying "I told you so." I didn't say anything. I was actually quite happy to be on the ground away from those powerful thunderheads.

Lt. Breed returned for FAM 11. All of the workings were repeat items, priming the student for the infamous FAM 13, safe-for-solo check ride. He didn't like my high altitude engine failure, but I did make the field. After getting hammered for a few minutes in the airplane, Lt. Breed told me to use the flaps to get down for an easy approach instead of extending the pattern out-of-bounds.

"I kept the flaps up as you suggested, sir, to keep the last bit of their ballooning effect in case we need to jump a fence or an obstacle," I replied.

Lt. Breed granted me that one and gave me another high altitude engine failure from three thousand feet. I did fine and he took the plane back and flew away from the field just when we were ready to de-tassel the corn. It was a low one and I loved it.

The next day, I flew my pre-solo preparation hop with Lt. Breed. It was a full scenario with a spin, both high and low altitude engine failures, a PEL, no flap approaches and landings, a wave-off and a review of several of our emergency procedures. The next flight would be the safe-for-solo check ride and this was Lt. Breed's one, last look at my progress. He didn't want to embarrass himself with a poorly performing student, so he threw just about every conceivable scenario at me.

We briefed extensively, discussing a wing fire along with the obvious consequences leading to a fuel-fed wing fire, a fuselage fire, and resolutions to combat the problems, and smoke and fumes elimination. All of these problems required quick action by the pilot, but the most important point was to first fly the airplane! The Navy emphasized flying the airplane first, as there was not a chance of survival if the pilot quit flying the plane because of a distraction, even a fire. Next, don the oxygen mask, ensure 100% is pre-selected, and place the emergency switch to the positive pressure position. This ensured a clean air supply, reducing chances of being overcome by noxious gases. Third, make a radio call, head for an outlying field, and prepare for a precautionary emergency landing.

"Sir," I explained, "a smoke source could be either an electrical or an engine malfunction. For the electrical portion, it would be easiest to shut down the entire electrical system. However, if the pilot notices an instrument failure or a lighting malfunction, it's a good bet that would be the source of the electrical fumes. For the alternating current components, by switching to the opposite inverter power source, it may be possible to find the source of the smoke as the power supply. If this failed, by turning off both inverters, one would have a partial panel of instruments to maintain communications capability. This is better than losing the entire electrical system."

We continued our discussion with the self-feathering of the propeller for unknown reasons. It was the same as an engine failure with complete loss of thrust. We turned our attention to the one landing that we never practiced in this airplane: ditching the airplane in open water.

While the sense of a relatively flat surface, soft touchdown, and inflatable life preserver may be reassuring, Lt. Breed pointed out the inherent danger of the waterlogged, packed parachute strapped to your back.

"If you didn't blow the canopy at altitude, release from your seat, release from your parachute, remain upright when the airplane comes to a complete stop, exit the aircraft and inflate your LPA—in cold water mind you—then a ditching scenario may just ruin your whole day. It's a whole lot better to take your plane to the beach. Maybe you can impress somebody with your airmanship on the beach, Schupbach."

"Yes sir," I said as I thought back to my problems with the Dilbert Dunker and how I couldn't find my release mechanisms as I dangled upside down underwater. There would be no safety instructors during a real ditch. I took what he said to heart. The beach alternative appealed to me.

Lt. Breed and I completed our marathon briefing in methodical fashion. We then checked the weather screen and departed for the issuing hangar. The flight line was busy with planes taxiing about in the bright afternoon sunshine. During a careful preflight, I found a glove in the wheel well, placed there by someone who was testing me. For my upcoming safe-for-solo check ride, he wanted no mistakes on my part, even more than I did. I was his student, his product, and in a large sense, a part of his reputation. There was a lot on the line for the two of us and he wanted me to be ready. After all, I had considered quitting the program a little over a month earlier. This was his last look at me.

During the high work we spun the airplane from 9,500 feet. A gentle pullout, following the addition of power, leveled us out at 5,500 feet. After recovering from the spin, we practiced a turn pattern, a stall, and finally, a high altitude engine failure. At the bottom of that engine-failure maneuver, Lt. Breed took the airplane, climbed back to 1,500 feet, gave me the airplane and then simulated a low altitude engine failure. Our progression through all of this came at a blistering pace. At this point in the program, I compartmentalized well enough to swing at every pitch, hit the ball and average one thousand.

We progressed rapidly through the precautionary emergency landing, two full-flap approaches, no-flap approaches and a wave-off or two. Finally, Lt. Breed took the airplane for a couple of touch-and-goes while I relaxed for a few moments. I took the last landing and then we departed the pattern, heading for home plate, NAS Whiting Field. During the flight home, Lt. Breed turned off the entire electrical system by selecting the battery switch off from the rear cockpit's electrical control panel.

"Hey!" I shouted into my dead microphone, and then turned my head to look behind me. This was his doing and I needed to try something to restore my electrical circuitry. Reaching down, I actuated my battery switch to the momentary reset position and released it to an ON position. The entire airplane—lights, interphone, radios and instruments, came back to life in a flash.

"What did you do that for?"

"I was just testing you to see how you would react, Schupbach. You passed."

I had a somewhat low opinion of that testing. After all, I was busy enough flying the airplane, especially working as hard as I did that day; and still he had thrown in an actual, complete electrical failure. I thought I handled it well as I made flying the airplane my first priority. That was the other point to the event. Once airborne, I didn't need an electrical system to safely return home. The correct procedure was not to sweat it—just fly it and try to correct the circumstance after I maintain control.

I flew over the water tower in a few short minutes and lined up with the runway for the break. The arrival and landing went well. Once out of the airplane, I realized how hard I had worked on this flight. Even with the air conditioner blowing directly on me, I sweated gallons through my flight suit. From take-off to landing, the flight had lasted two full hours with the entire event lasting perhaps four and a-half hours. By the time it was over and I walked back to the BOQ, I was exhausted.

I flew well enough to be recommended for the check ride, but little did I know how much pressure that check ride would entail: "Nobody ever said this wouldn't be semi-tough."

I experienced the pressure that everyone talked about two days later. The FAM 13, safe-for-solo check ride, came with a surprise that was just part of the program: a demeaning, screaming, demanding, slamming instructor from hell. My instructor was a marine captain known as Captain Corn for short. I barely knew of him from talk around the squadron, but what I did know wasn't good. To top it all off, his doctor took him entirely off caffeine two days prior to my check ride. From the start, he was not a happy marine.

Captain Corn and I briefed about the flight and he told me about his doctor's advice. I read between the lines and knew that no matter what was said, the flight would be a doozy, one for the record books. I wasn't far off on that one. With my prior knowledge of things to come and with my strong showing on FAM 12 to boost my confidence level, I decided to ignore whatever he threw at me. I would fly the airplane as I had been taught. The rest would take care of itself.

The attitude commenced as soon as we closed the canopy. I closed mine. He slammed his.

"Get this machine moving with no mistakes or you'll flunk without seeing the runway."

Fortunately, I sat in front of him and he couldn't see my smile. *OK, Neal,* I said under my breath, *it's all a big act; he's really a great guy and a softy deep down inside.* Although I later learned my assessment was correct, for the next couple of hours there was hell to pay.

The instructor's game kept the pressure on the student through intimidating remarks and loud general harassment. It worked against some; but for me, I just kept doing my job and worked hard for the best flight I could achieve. During the high work, he wanted to see a turn pattern within fifty feet of altitude and five knots of airspeed, course reversals on heading, and on and on! The tolerances were double that, but he kept up his spiel throughout the maneuver. Then came the stall "without losing a foot of altitude." *What's next?*

"ENGINE FAILURE!!! THIS IS A SIMULATED HIGH ALTITUDE ENGINE FAILURE AND YOU GOT ONE CHANCE TO MAKE IT RIGHT, SCHUPBACH!!!!"

I complied with our procedures although I was a little slow in choosing a field. I spotted one just going under the nose. It took me two full-circle turns to get down to the landing zone. There I dropped my flaps late to slow us into the cow pasture.

Captain Corn didn't take it back, but yelled, "WAVE OFF, WAVE OFF!!"

There is a first time for everything, including the student wave-off from an engine failure. This was an effective tool to build pressure on any student and surprise them in a critical situation.

I added power and flew out of the low-altitude approach. That's when I realized why Lt. Breed always allowed me to take us to the crop-tops. It was to gain confidence. I thought this backseat Bozo merely wanted to see a completion with a twist. The earlier-than-normal wave-off, from a safety standpoint, made sense. If I failed or froze up, he would have adequate time to take the airplane and recover. Fortunately, I did my job correctly.

We then went into a second engine failure, a low-altitude failure from one thousand feet. With precious little time to react, all of my skills were reflexive, which was something else he wanted to see. I also made that field and we were off to the races. Captain Corn yelled and screamed all the way to Brewton Field. I thought I was flying with a baby in the back seat who wanted his rattle.

"OK Schupbach, just where the hell do you think we are?"

"Oh, about ten miles north of Whiting Field."

"JUST WHO THE HELL TAUGHT YOU TO READ A VOR AND DME?" he screamed at the top of his lungs.

I smiled and kept us heading to the outlying field. I just had a hunch that was about our location. Our electronic equipment agreed with me to the nearest tenth of a mile. Now, I had bigger fish to fry as we moved to our landings.

We entered the Brewton Airport on a PEL landing. Midway through my downwind leg, I dropped the flaps.

"ENGINE FAILURE," he screamed. "THE BATTERY IS DEAD AND SO ARE YOU IF YOU DON'T MAKE THIS LANDING. WHAT DID YOU PUT YOUR FLAPS DOWN FOR, SCHUPBACH? YOU WILL NEVER MAKE IT; YOU WILL NEVER MAKE IT!!!"

Somehow, by the grace of the Almighty, I correctly picked my glide path and managed to slam the plane on the ground for my first of many landings. I actually wanted to slam one on, just to shut him up for a minute. It didn't work.

We took back off to the west and turned a left downwind with Captain Corn riding me all the way. After a couple more landings, two no-flaps and three full-flaps, I was whipped. I never knew flying could be so loud for so long. Then again, I knew about this pressure before I stepped into my flight suit, so I just carried on.

Once we departed, I figured the flight was a success. I knew the road home and how to fly hands-off. I took my hands off of the controls for a few moments, just to piss him off. It didn't work. He was a marine in his element, and a good marine at that.

The trip home was quick. We took an extra landing at Whiting, just because it was something new and different. I handled the twist without a problem and we returned safely to home plate. Once in the chocks, Captain Corn wouldn't talk to me. I didn't get it. It's not like I expected a band, just praise for a job well done. Shouldn't there be congratulations or something? *No!*

The debriefing went just the same, relentless, and that's when I knew I passed. I nodded my head a bunch of times and kept the conversation as simple as possible. I beat the system and they would let me solo. I was one happy man, and once again, I could just about taste a beer on my lips.

Few towns in the world cater to the U.S. Navy quite like Pensacola, Florida. To celebrate the weekend, I headed for McGuire's Irish Pub. Once arrived, I knocked back a few pints before my further adventures. A few more were surely on the horizon after my safe-for-solo check ride.

Every student who didn't fly at Whiting Field on Saturday morning flew at McGuire's on Friday night. It was close enough to Whiting Field, but not as far as the beach itself. Directions to McGuire's were simple and the times were good. After all, it was flight school, Reagan was in office, a pay hike was in the pipeline and the women were more than friendly.

One-dollar bills covered the walls and ceiling. Occasionally, a bit of the original decor showed through all of the money. Each bartender specialized in keeping your mug cold and full of beer, and each seat came with a couple of warm friends. Everyone had a group to belong to; you could have served in the same AOCS class together or been in the same ground school. We were brothers-in-arms, each of us learning how to talk with our hands, how to exaggerate our stories and to feel like a million bucks just for being alive. Flight school could do that for you if you let it, if you caught on and kept up with the torrid pace of things. No wonder the weekends at McGuire's were so necessary!

I met lifelong friends at the end of that bar. The only problems we had there were finding the signs for the head, especially after a couple of cold ones. The bathroom signs were painted on big hands with one finger pointing to the other door. Thus, if it said women, it meant for the happy patron to proceed to the other door. If the lady opened the door with the word "women" written on the hand, she was in for a surprise. The opposite was true for the men. It all took a little getting used to.

Four days passed between my safe-for-solo check ride, that true Marine Corps mental beating in the sky, and my first solo flight. The anticipation nearly killed me. I was probably more nervous over the weekend while waiting around for the "keys to the car" than before my safe-for-solo check ride. I feared I might brain-dump. Several students had "downed a ride" for things they had ice-cold the day before. How could I flunk a solo flight? After all, no instructor is present. If I just followed the course rules, made four landings at an outlying field, and came home for the fifth landing, I would pass. After that, no matter what happened, at least I could say that I flew solo. *Right*?

Wrong!

Because of the time lag between the check ride and my scheduled solo event, the command's policy mandated that I receive a second safe-for-solo check ride before I flew alone. When I found this out, knowing the sky torture from the previous ride, I practically gave up all hope of earning my wings.

How tough can they make this program? I wondered. *What reason do they have not to trust me? Plenty of reasons! What do you mean plenty? Why am I talking this trash? Neal, get out there and stand up to the challenge, again and again if you have to. Punch the camel in the nose!*

On July 24, 1981, I hiked down to the flight line briefing shack and found a pleasant surprise waiting for me. Captain Leprechaun, a Marine Corps helicopter gunship pilot, waited for me with a warm smile and some very good news. This flight was a warm-up for my solo flight, not like the check flight I flew on the previous sortie. There would be no screaming, nothing out of the ordinary; just a pleasant flight in the morning sunshine to practice a few items, have some fun between take-off and landing with spins, high work, an engine failure or two, and then proceed into the bounce pattern. A few weeks ago, those words placed a mountain of anxiety before me; but that day, I did exactly what the smiling marine suggested. I relaxed.

For the warm-up recheck, we flew to the south of Whiting Field to complete our high work over the westernmost tip of Florida's panhandle. The sky was clear and blue while the air was as smooth as a baby's behind. Captain Leprechaun sat quietly in the back and merely requested the maneuvers that he wanted to see me perform. I flew with a large smile on my face and great confidence in my own abilities. Our spins went well and my high altitude engine failure went down like a piece of cake. I flew the simulated, impending engine failure landing into NAS Saufley Field and my landings were just fine. On the trip home, once again, I flew down Interstate 10 to our check point, turned left and headed for the initial entry for the pattern at NAS Whiting. Once lined up with the field, the oval pattern was a snap until turning final. It was then that the instructor pulled the motor on me.

I flew the "dead stick" landing into home plate, something I had never done before but improvised with each passing moment. With the gear and flaps already down, I lowered the nose of the plane to increase my glide-path angle, thereby becoming more inclined to compensate for the loss of power. I announced my own feathering of the propeller and Captain Leprechaun reset the power to simulate the prop's turning knife's edge into the wind stream. Then I put out a mayday call over the intercom system, simulating an alert call to the tower, concentrated on keeping my airspeed correct, and threw away the rest of the checklist. If I flew too slowly, I would wash out my flight controls effectiveness, leading up to a hard landing. If it were too fast, I would float in the flare and land long, eating up the valuable real estate I needed to stop the aircraft.

At the bottom of the flare, I had a lump in my throat and a knot in my stomach. The pucker factor, as measured by the grip of the sphincter wrapped around itself several times, was at an all time high. I knew I had to land the plane without hesitation, but I never realized that I had done this from PEL maneuvers half-a-dozen times before. It was the surprise, the psychology of the moment that gripped me. Just when I thought I was safe to fly solo! My landing went fine, and as I taxied into the chocks, I could only think how sneaky it was for the soft-spoken Marine Corps captain to pull the motor on the final approach, just when I thought the flight was over. Nevertheless, I smiled, fully understanding the point of the exercise. I began to unwind as I went through the last checklist.

The flight debrief went quickly with nothing to report and Captain Leprechaun wished me well on my first solo flight.

"It's yours to enjoy," he said, "so make the most of it, but stay inside the rule book. Use the solo call sign and check over the plane. Do everything just as you learned it and listen to your habits. Your habit pattern will let you know if something is wrong or missing."

Those encouraging words told me I was again safe-for-solo.

Ironically, even today, I cannot recall a single memory of the solo flight itself—where I flew, where I landed four times, nor my return to NAS Whiting Field. I know that I filled out the paperwork, the Navy's "yellow sheet." The entries made it into my logbook that the squadron kept in another office. Later, I attended the "Solo Flight Tie Cutting Ceremony." Furthermore, I graduated from the squadron, earned my wings and flew in the fleet. However, I can't remember a single moment of my first solo flight. It's strange that something I worked so hard for escapes memory and can't be recalled. My paperwork for the 24th of July 1981 is the only proof. I have—nothing else.

After my solo flight, I had the next three days free from flying. I concentrated on ground school and reviewed my next flight, Basic Instruments 4. Each basic instruments flight built upon the previous and became repetitive with their maneuvers. Still, I could take no chances. After all, I narrowly escaped a downing grade on BI 3—not to mention almost losing my life during the same flight.

A cloud of unwanted curiosity hung over me because I flew well with both my safe-for-solo instructors, but the basic instrument flights weren't polished.

On the Friday following my solo flight, I learned that I wouldn't be going to McGuire's for a celebration with my friends. My daily call to the squadron duty officer revealed an instrument hop early on Saturday morning, and not with just any instructor. My next instructor was my commanding officer, "The Skipper," and I felt thrust back under the microscope for yet another examination.

To prepare for the flight, I sat in my BOQ room on Friday night and carefully sequenced the next day's flight, pouring over every detail, flying the chair, bouncing the racquetball, reciting procedures, and practicing my instrument scan on the paper instrument panel. Each maneuver had its own emphasis on specific instruments designed to work the student into proficiency; and each maneuver had its particular pattern. A right turn instead of a left turn could mean the difference in grading and the overall scoring of the hop. I studied my tail off up until ten o'clock, when I finally decided that a good night sleep would benefit me more than anything else.

Waking in the morning, I remember not being particularly nervous about the flight. I knew the CO was a fair gentleman who enjoyed his position in command, enjoyed his squadron's spirit, and enjoyed flying so much that he worked on Saturday morning. When I arrived at the brief/debrief shack, everyone had a bad case of nerves. The instructors knew their commanding officer inspected their work through my abilities. Every instructor knew of my jagged progression in learning to fly and every instructor wanted to see me fly well with the Skipper. This would reflect upon all of them. That morning, all of the instructors and students alike watched me. *What? Is there something telling about me this morning that advertises whether or not I'll pass muster?*

While I waited at the duty desk for Skipper Pellon, a friend asked me how I was so lucky.

"You know you're flying with the Skipper this morning, don't you Neal?"

"Yes, it's a tough, dirty job but someone has to do it," I said.

Someone shouted "Attention on deck!" Everyone stood and braced at attention while the commanding officer approached the duty desk.

"Good morning, gentlemen," he said. "As you were, carry on. Is my student available?"

"Sir, yes he is, sir. Ensign Schupbach is right here, sir." My buddy introduced me to the Skipper.

We shook hands and he invited me for a cup of coffee on him, suggesting that we brief the flight and get underway.

"After all, this is Saturday morning," he said.

Things went well during the brief.

"I might need a warm-up flight on this one, sir," I mentioned, "because I haven't flown an instrument hop in two weeks. I don't want this to be a reflection on Lt. Breed, though, sir."

"Oh, all right, we'll keep that in mind," he said at the end of the briefing. Skipper received the aircraft tail number from the duty plan and we headed out the door as all eyes followed us.

"Attention on deck!" was called as we left the office. Everyone stood and braced for the Skipper. Although I knew they braced for the commanding officer, I thought it awkward and funny to be walking past my instructors as they stood at attention. Their solemn faces told me how much this flight meant to each of them.

During preflight, I felt more relaxed around this man than with any other instructor. We zipped through the paperwork and walk-around. I quickly found myself strapped in my parachute and assembling the five-way restraint system of the T-34C. The Skipper closed the canopy and started the engine while I plugged in my oxygen mask and placed the dilution selector to 100%. In a flash, we taxied out to the run-up area and then on to the runway, cleared for take off.

The morning boasted calm winds and smooth air for our ascent to the high altitude working area. I snapped my mask onto my helmet, covering my face with the cool soft rubber; then pressed the emergency, positive-pressure flow switch that allowed the system to fill my nose and lungs with the cool, dry oxygen. *It's now or never,* I thought. *Just relax and do whatever is asked of you, Neal. Let the chips fall where they may.*

Once at altitude, I took the controls and the Skipper looked to see if I was wearing my oxygen mask. He then put on his mask and had me go under the bag, draping my clear canopy with burlap to obscure my vision. Once situated, he commanded our prescribed maneuvers in a calm, soft-spoken manner. The right combination of preparation, rest, nutrition and oxygen came together for some of my best airmanship in the training program. "No warm-up needed here" was the only comment I heard from him during the exercises. I flew each maneuver without correction or repeating any item. The final maneuver was the high-altitude penetration pattern, a steep descent of ten thousand feet at high speed, followed by a half-circle course reversal.

"OK, I have the airplane. Come on out from under the bag and enjoy the ride home."

We walked back into the briefing shack for the flight debrief. After the stand-down issued by the Skipper, everyone's eyes were on his face. Every instructor read his demeanor, trying to find out how the flight went, how well I did, and what their commanding officer thought about their product. He nodded with approval to his men and they appeared to relax, some even smiled at me. We sat down at a small, green chalkboard in the far corner of the next room and debriefed the flight. To say it went well is an understatement.

The Skipper covered the flight, play by play, and I received compliments from him every inch of the way. I could hardly believe my ears. Everything from my basic airmanship to my knowledge of the procedures drew his praise. I received two above-average marks with no below-average grades recorded for the event. Best of all was his comment about my penetration pattern. He wrote one word, *BEAUTIFUL!* The flight became my shining moment in the squadron. And to shine in front of the commanding officer is the best place of all.

I walked home in a dream state that Saturday morning. The warm sunshine felt like kisses from the heavens above. I compared my newfound flying skills with the same student who, just seven weeks prior, contemplated dropping out of the program entirely, never knowing what it would take to be able to hack it. My birthday present, a visit to the chaplain's office, paid off now more than ever. Ahhh—the sweet taste of success during basic instrument flying. The "put-up and shut-up" speech from another instructor paid off as well. I felt good about my progress as the command issued me happiness for the first time.

From that flight on, the instructors treated me better than ever before. They joked with me and made me laugh, loosening me up and making me feel like part of the gang, a far cry from being just another student naval aviator. It worked both ways; I could joke with them, too. On one occasion, I noticed Lt. Breed getting his hair cut at the BOQ barbershop. I immediately complimented the barber for her talents because *she could do so much with so little:* "SCHOOEEBAAAACH!!!"

The basic instrument flight regime ended with the eighth flight in the series, a basic instrument check-ride. With that series behind me, the syllabus called for the precision aerobatics (PA) flying. There would be a total of five flights in PA: two instructional hops, two solo flights and a check-ride. The events built confidence in the student, allowing him to be more aggressive with the plane; and it introduced the fundamentals of aerobatics and air combat maneuvers. Solo flights came rapidly after the introduction of the maneuvers, on the very next flight to be exact and this surprised all of us. These flights were flown as two-a-day hops.

Everyone enjoyed the extraordinary sensations of aerobatic flying, myself included. We flew loops, *wingovers*—a maneuver that took the airplane near vertical and then reversed course using a rudder input, three-hundred-sixty-degree rolls and barrel rolls. It was a maneuver similar to the aileron roll; but one that climbed the airplane while slowly rolling inverted, and descended the airplane while continuing the roll back to the straight and level starting position.

We also practiced the Navy's infamous angle of attack landing. The reason for flying in this manner was the carrier landing. During this flying exercise, the object was to lower the aircraft to a fixed point on the runway without generating a flare of any kind. I called it a *controlled midair collision, wheels first.*

During all of these maneuvers, the barrel roll was by far the most difficult. I may have completed one or two properly, but I doubt it. The airplane's wings met the fuselage at a three-degree pitch-up and this tended to destabilize the bird when inverted, pulling it back to the earth in a rapid manner. As a matter of fact, I considered myself lucky if I completed the barrel roll maneuver, but never as lucky as during my PA5 flight check.

Over the course of the summer, thunderstorms filled the working areas and the Navy closed those areas for safety. For my PA5 check flight, two of the three working areas were clobbered with storms and shut down. However, this didn't prevent my instructor from aggressively pursuing the aerobatic flight, even though everyone else required the use of the very same, very limited airspace above Choctaw Field. I thought it rather unwise to place all of the planes from three, separate squadrons in the smallest working area and then perform aerobatics. But hey, I was just the student, so what did I know?

The instructor, Lieutenant Commander Bust, had made me a bit nervous in previous encounters. This flight was no exception. We took off and flew most of our work without much of a problem, keeping a close eye out for other traffic in the area. As I said before, I didn't fly a good barrel roll and Bust decided to demonstrate one, and then talk me through the next one. As we went up into the maneuver and rolled upside down, it was easy to see his overall finesse of the plane.

At the top of the maneuver, while hanging upside down in our straps, from out of the blue came another red and white T-34C directly on our nose—at our altitude, so close that I could have hit him with my knee board.

My heart jumped out of my chest. I screamed "TRAFFIC!" into the ICS and the instructor instinctively pulled back on the stick, placing the plane in an inverted dive from which he quickly recovered.

Lcdr. Bust didn't see the other airplane and could only rely on my description of events. I don't think he believed my story but it didn't matter to me. I could only think of how stupid we were flying aerobatics in overcrowded skies. To this day, the vision of colliding head-on, wing to wing, hasn't left my mind's eye.

I still ask myself, *Neal what were the chances of successfully blowing the canopy, releasing the restraining seat straps and falling out of the rotating plane from eight thousand feet, parachuting into the bay waters while still disoriented from the original impact?* Somehow, we avoided all of that mess, most likely from my shouting "traffic" loud enough to scare the man. There was no time to take the plane from the instructor. It was a close call, a very close call...

In debrief I was awarded only one below average mark, while I still trembled from the experience.

The Navy kept up the pace of flying in a seemingly endless group of fast-paced events, weeding out those who couldn't or wouldn't in favor of the student naval aviators who dedicated everything to the program. Once past the solo flight, the hardest events came in the form of radio instrument flying or RI. Virtually everyone experienced difficulty completing either the classroom tests or the flying itself. Instead of flying through the wide, open spaces of the great blue heavens above, we were required to fly over specific, electronic tracks along the ground. To do so required the mastery of radio instruments.

From a small collection of gizmos, we oriented ourselves to our geographic position and navigated the desired track over the ground, while at the same time, flying precise airspeeds and altitudes. "Flying the needles" as they call it, requires knowledge of both where one is and where one intends to go. RI became the bust of many student pilots for obvious reasons.

I flew seven radio instrument flights and excelled at the many challenges that these flights threw at me. My grades held above average; I thought that spoke volumes for my abilities because I came into the program without any form of flight training whatsoever. The troubles that plagued my colleagues didn't appear to trip me up. That gratified me, but I was equally suspicious. *What lay in wait for me around the next corner of each flight?* I worried. When the syllabus changed, my caution proved to be warranted.

Throughout the entire flight training, the squadron drilled safety into our heads as the number one priority. Each squadron recorded the number of accident-free flight hours and prominently displayed that number as well as posters promoting safety awareness. They indoctrinated us with the message that we were responsible for the safety of the person in the picture, the picture being a mirror hanging on the wall. One day each quarter, the base held safety stand-downs. Lectures were given, flying was prohibited and wrecked automobiles were placed at the main gate with signs reminding everyone of driving safety.

The very idea of intentionally flying four feet away from another propeller-driven aircraft scared me, yet that's exactly what we did next in formation flying. The Navy's formation flying syllabus contained five flights and a solo hop. Formation flying taught the basic maneuvers of the fleet, starting with the running rendezvous and the under-run: a maneuver designed to under-run the lead aircraft when overtaking him too rapidly, thereby avoiding a collision. The standard parade position came next, with airplanes flying behind and to the right of the lead airplane. The pilot sighted specific "hard points" of the lead airplane and maintained his relative position during the flight without ever taking his eyes off the lead plane. We learned of climbs and descents; the relative power of each engine kept the planes from falling behind or pushing ahead of each other. Parade turns were taught. The difference of the radius of the turn caused the wingman to travel farther; and thus required more power for additional speed during the turn away from his position and less power for the turn toward his direction. The lead aircraft always held his power constant.

The most difficult of the maneuvers was the lead change. This maneuver required the lead pilot to look back over his shoulder and sight his wingman, pull off power, descend below the other aircraft while maintaining the correct position, gently retreat from the lead while simultaneously adding power to stabilize his relationship, then slip under the new lead airplane and take up the parade position on his opposite or starboard side.

Each flight improved my flying formation, but I had a monkey on my back. This was way too close to fly a spinning propeller next to another aircraft in my perception. My fears weren't justified—every student managed to fly formation, but they kept me honest with a healthy dose of respect for my own personal safety. Dying was the hard way to earn the "Wings of Gold" and I wanted no part of that.

The form flights went well enough to keep me out of any serious problems. They also provided me a chance to fly again with my on-wing instructor, Lt. Breed, the man responsible for my initial flying education. This happened on my fourth formation flight when he happened to be one of the instructors. I didn't ask to fly with him but my hopes were high for that scenario because I genuinely liked the man. This flight provided the opportunity to put us both together again in an airplane, flying one last flight for old time's sake. Lt. Breed felt similarly, as he put his hand on my shoulder and chose me for his student, which was quite the compliment.

I completed the maneuvers with a bit of coaching from Lt. Breed. I had the sight picture required to place the aircraft in parade, but I doubled the distance between the two airplanes. Each time he took the plane and demonstrated the proper distance, I saw my error; but unknowingly, I always allowed the planes to separate as if my eyes were too big for their sockets. Though correct on the extended line of position, I flew too far from the other airplane despite his instruction.

It then became my turn to fly lead. This also offered the opportunity to look around at the lower Alabama countryside. An assortment of buildings stood out in the distance. A heavy fence or two and low cut fields that looked like lawns appeared to surround them in all directions. Lt. Breed said they comprised a state penitentiary, a medium security prison.

I considered what their lives might be like in comparison to mine. *How cruel. How cruel it is to place an incarcerated man in a prison yard where he can watch us fly formation, working on our futures and our careers in the freedom and vast openness of the blue sky above. The sight must torture a man, as he rots away, serving time in that hell. He must hunger for the freedom we represent high above in the heavens.*

I thought of myself and knew it would crush me to exist under such circumstances. I couldn't even think of meeting the men or women who resided beneath me. Whether poetic justice or pain, that knife was sharp on both edges. But there are different forms of prison. Ten years later, my life's journey would intersect with a woman caught in a similar circumstance. Watched closely by her Russian peer group, her freedoms were bound behind concrete walls and tall, barbed wire fences. Her incarceration was political.

After we completed the flight's curriculum, the fun really started when the instructors rendezvoused at a predetermined point closer to Whiting Field. It was dogfight time and the turning and burning heated up the afternoon sky. Lt. Breed "jumped" his "bogie," my wingman, as he tried to escape our trailing efforts. We turned hard left and descended behind him only to have him apply full power and climb rapidly, trying to escape. "Guns–guns–guns!" came over the radio on a discrete, predetermined frequency. Lt. Breed bagged his colleague and then broke off for another engagement.

The mock fighting continued for ten minutes and I can't remember ever being as disoriented to where we were as then. However, we did have fun with the airplane and I enjoyed the dogfight immensely. Lt. Breed put us on parade with the other plane; we returned to Whiting Field as the wingman while the lead navigated us back home. After all of the aggressive turning over unfamiliar territory, that came as a blessing.

The lead aircraft flew the break over the field and I scanned the horizon in front of me for other planes. I timed my three-count and then broke left across the runway. This time, instead of flying it strictly under the rules of visual conditions, I scanned my attitude gyro and altimeter and nailed the break maneuver, much to the delight of Lt. Breed. Once on the ground, both inside the hangar and at the line shack, Lt. Breed told his fellow instructors that he just witnessed the best student break ever. While the tall, accomplished, aviator bragged about me to his buddies, I kept my mouth shut and simply gushed inside.

Yes, I had cheated a bit; but if you're not cheating, you're not trying. It was a moment and a flight that I will always remember. First, the reunion of student and teacher, then the formation flying, the prison scene, the surprise of the dogfight; and finally, my on-wing instructor bragging about one of my maneuvers. I performed well under his instruction, leadership and attitude, and the command again issued me pride for the day.

Although I demonstrated average or slightly better than average flying skills that day, I knew it to be my best formation flight. Unfortunately, I never defeated my overcautious attitude when flying the propeller so close to other aircraft. In the airplane, my body and arms stiffened with anxiety, which was evident on my safe-for-solo-formation hop the following flight. During debrief, I knew I flew all right; the ups and downs of flight school are to be expected. Even though I scored well enough to be deemed safe-for-solo in formation flying, on the following day, several people gently suggested that I take the airplane out and fly aerobatics instead, forgoing the formation solo altogether.

Neither my wingman nor I would have any of this advice. I thought my peers would look upon me with disdain. After working so hard in flight school, I couldn't turn back now. Perhaps the suggestion was correct for the day, but it eroded my confidence and rode with me on the solo hop. During the solo form, the suggestion showed its ugly face again.

That afternoon, I took off with my wingman and a customary chase instructor in a three-plane formation. I flew lead for the first half of the flight, flying twenty feet above a boiling cloud deck with clouds racing by us at one hundred fifty knots. The clouds' relative motion was spectacular. I flew us so close to the clouds that at one point, the chase plane called up and had me climb another one hundred feet—our altitude put him into the cloud deck, blocking his vision. I thought that rather comical.

Once I completed the required maneuvers, the parade turns, climbs and descents, the lead change became anything but funny. It easily could have cost me my career or my life. After sighting my wingman over my right shoulder, I moved my left arm aft twice while believing I reduced power for my shallow descent. For reasons unknown to me, during the descent, I gained distance on my wingman and lost him from my field of vision.

I knew he was directly above and slightly behind my position. I couldn't see him and he couldn't see me. I also knew a spinning propeller sat on the front of his airplane. I could easily collide, cutting either aircraft like a hot knife through soft butter. I dared not make a mistake, or try to regain sight and position on him. I dove down and to the right, in my own impromptu escape maneuver—escaping to save my very life.

"Come back, come back," the instructor called to me.

I looked to my left, seeing the two planes in the distance and performed a running rendezvous. From then on, I was too rattled, shaken up, and my "vision" of parade distance became even more enhanced. I trailed my lead by a greater distance than on previous flights, but we continued the flight without another word from the chase instructor.

During the return to Whiting, the chase instructor spotted an opening in the cloud deck and coached the lead into the sucker hole. While flying in formation, we descended rapidly through the hole, turning in a high angle of bank, spiraling down through the clear air. We entered the thick clouds, but I stuck with our lead aircraft, something that surprised the chase instructor after my previous debacle. I thought that particular maneuver to be both exciting and enjoyable because I could see the clouds in my periphery; yet remained locked on the lead aircraft in a steep, descending attitude not experienced in other flights.

Once back on the ground, we debriefed the flight for what seemed forever. Although the flight was a non-graded event, as all solo flights were, it was egg on my face. Afterwards, my buddy and I went out for dinner and talked it over; but I never admitted what I just said about my power setting. I didn't take enough power off of the airplane, which caused the plane to accelerate away from the other aircraft during my descent.

Back at the squadron, I was uncomfortable; people looked at me differently, more than I wanted them to.

After completing the formation-flying syllabus, I returned to complete the last four radio-instrument hops and had little trouble until the check-ride. I flew that hop with "a coasty," a coast guard helicopter pilot, who was genuine to the bone. Unfortunately that night, he got the big idea that I should do everything, including coordinating with ATC. Talking on the radio was a bit outside the curriculum of RI flying. Although this shouldn't have posed any major problem, it was the check-ride that broke many a student and we knew its reputation. I was not up for any deviation from the previous ten RI rides.

During this check-ride, for just the simple act of talking on the radio, making my own decisions and coordinating them with air traffic control, "my wheels came off." I couldn't perform the simplest items, although I did manage to get into holding correctly. I flew to the approach fixes backwards, couldn't proceed directly to NAS Pensacola, and changed runways at the bottom of a ground controlled approach, ending up in between the two runways at the decision altitude.

Coasty took over the plane and had me come out from under the bag.

"Look at where you are" he said.

The entire ride home, I dreaded the debrief and for good reason. I received my first "down" over things that I flew with ease before this check flight. The approach to Sherman field was the straw that broke the camel's back. During debrief, I felt so bad I wanted to crawl in a hole and cry.

That night in the BOQ, sitting in a common lounge with the TV blasting, I felt lower than whale shit but received little sympathy from my fellow students.

"I downed my RI 11 check ride," I told no one in particular.

"You and everybody else" was the general consensus. Those words made me realize it wasn't the end of the world after all. "You and everybody else" actually cheered me up as I drank a couple of cold beers with my buddies.

Check-itis came as a surprise to me and to all of the instructors in the squadron. Over the course of the next couple of days, I spoke with two senior instructors investigating my particular problem. We couldn't figure it out because I knew the maneuvers and procedures cold.

We sat in a small room reviewing the items, over and over again.

"You know your procedures," the reviewer finally said. "What do you think happened up there?"

"I don't want this to reflect on Ltjg. Coasty," I replied, "but he did make me talk on the radios."

"THAT'S IT, THAT'S IT," he said standing up, waving his arms in the air. He walked out of the room, announcing our discovery to anyone who would listen and they were all listening.

After that, I flew the customary, two additional practice flights and another check-ride with a senior officer: a ride I actually enjoyed. I even toyed with the commander by saying "What's that off the left wing?" and then snapped his head with a sharp turn to the right, directly on course at the moment when I knew he was distracted. It all went over well in good fun; he knew he was had. After all, I had no vision of the outside environment.

Everyone was happy to see me power through the recheck. Coasty even bought me lunch at the O'Club. Together, we celebrated my completion of primary flight training, an enormous accomplishment considering the ordeal.

My last visit to Whiting's O'Club came twenty years later after revisiting NAS Pensacola. Gone were my memory lanes; remodeling moved the function room and bar to the enlarged BOQ facilities across the street. The government consolidated bases during the 1990s, placing more students than ever on the base. Even the archrival Air Force now trained their students at NAS Whiting Field. *Is nothing sacred?*

Stark walls and cafeteria style, quick-stop dining replaced the military plaques, decorations and memorabilia, but not my memories. The surroundings faded, replaced with my mind's eye vision of the best of times at NAS Whiting Field. I took ten minutes at a table, leaned back and thought of only one thing: my safe-for-solo tie cutting ceremony.

I thirsted to be surrounded by squadron buddies again, making merry together over a beer while reliving our early days of flying. Students and instructors, all aviation colleagues now, gave one another reasons to laugh and reasons to cry, to press on, fall back, and raise ourselves above the high bar of daily challenges found on this flight campus. I could reach out and touch them all, but Lt. Breed stood apart from the crowd.

Harry Breed made good on his promise to me, writing everything down so he would have something to say at the tie cutting ceremony. It was a good thing, too. The Navy postponed my ceremony until I nearly completed the program. One entire event even canceled, all because of a previous tie cutting party when a student showed up in a flight suit instead of the proper coat and "tie" uniform. His penalty for the infraction was getting the ends of his socks cut off.

In 1981, the squadron used a large bowie knife with a sharp, twelve-inch blade for the ceremonies. The safety of the knife wasn't questioned because the instructor pulled the student's tie away from his body before cutting it in half. That summer, however, a tipsy marine took aim at this out-of-uniform student's outstretched sock and missed, striking the sock directly above the student's big toe and severing the tendon. The commanding officer placed all future "toe cuttings" on hold. Practical jokers later replaced the "I" in TIE with an "O" on the bulletin board announcements.

By late October, the squadron got back on track with the aid of a large pair of black scissors. I arrived just before the preliminary announcements. The large room filled with officers from my squadron, VT-6. Everyone knew everyone else by face if not by name. A keg of beer stood near the back wall. Each officer had a large plastic cup in hand, anxiously awaiting the stories and festivities to come.

"Good afternoon, Skipper," started the ceremonies.

The operations officer (ops boss) continued, "Ladies and Gentlemen, welcome to the VT-6 tie cutting ceremonies. We gather here today to celebrate our student's accomplishments, acknowledge their hard work, and hear some of the stories from their instructors. At some point in our lives as students, each of us has been on this small stage, earning our wings. We now return to pass the torch, giving all who are here today encouragement and camaraderie. I know that all of you are pressed for time, so let the show begin!"

The ops boss called a procession of on-wing instructors and their primary students to the small, raised platform. The instructors prided themselves with student screw up stories and few, if any, students topped their instructor's wit.

One instructor said, "He was doing fine until we entered the landing pattern...on the wrong end of the runway, facing traffic."

A student recalled, "On my fourth flight, ATC called and told me to raise my landing gear. I guess that helps make the airplane climb."

We had a good time and lots of laughs.

Lt. Breed and I were the last ones called on stage. He looked down at his scratched-up, personal notebook and recalled, "On FAM 2, Schupbach called the airplane a 'yee-haw.' I thought that meant he was thinking it was a cow he was riding back in Nebraska."

That got a good laugh from the crowd.

"He had a very heavy right foot one afternoon and we flew backwards for a bit." Shaking his head, Breed said, "I hadn't done that one before. And when he flew well on just one landing, gosh darn, that was enough to cancel out all the other grades during the hop."

After a small round of applause, Lt. Breed turned to look at me and said in an unsuspecting manner, "Well, Schupbach, this is your big moment. Do you have anything to add?"

"Yes Sir," I replied as I looked out into the audience, wasting no time to begin. "Lt. Breed is a superior pilot, a wonderful instructor and a great guy. And if you believe all of that," I said pointing my right thumb over my shoulder, "I have a used car sitting right outside." I then did my best imitation of his, "Ooooh Kaaay."

Both got some good laughs and I noticed the Skipper's eyes shown bright upon me, giving me his approval. But he didn't know I was just warming up.

"There we were, chopping the crop-tops on every engine failure, spinning from ten thousand feet and you know what he calls me? 'SCHOOEEBAAAACH!!!!'—followed by his famous saying, 'No one ever said this wouldn't be semi tough.' Yeah…right."

"At Saufley Field I practiced solo touch-and-goes one day, and a voice on the radio said, 'You're landing long; try to get down in the groove. Schupbach, is that you?'"

I responded, "Breed, is that you?"

"'IT'S LIEUTENANT BREED, SCHOOEEBAAAACH!'"

The crowd howled and I knew I was on a roll. My ego fed from the center of attention, success with my timing and the energy of the room. I had them where I wanted them, crying with laughter. Lt Breed stood to my left waving his hands in front of his body, trying to say in effect, that it wasn't true, as he turned red with embarrassment.

"Then there were the thunderstorms. Dark, I mean dark! No...black, black, black and more black! There we were in the MOA all by our lonesome. Gee, I wonder why gentlemen?"

Again laughter filled the room. Breed put his right hand up to his face and rubbed the bridge of his nose, shaking his head in disbelief of the roasting. I was on fire.

"Has anyone here ever raced lightning to three thousand feet...STRAIGHT DOWN...and won?"

Skipper Pellon, the most conservative in the group, bent over his table with laughter. He was dying along with the rest of the large crowd.

"Our next move came as no shock after that one. Brewton airport looked pretty good to me. NOT! We came home to momma and slid in safe at home plate," I said, stretching my left hand out parallel to the floor while taking a step forward. "But what does Lt Breed say through it all, in debrief one day? From one foot away, he looked me right in the eye and said those immortal and ever so inspiring words, 'Schupbach, you scare me.'"

That brought down the house. People laughed and laughed; their mirth seemed endless. Lt. Breed turned in my direction and shook my hand. We both turned and faced the crowd, soaking in the applause with large smiles on our faces. I did my job. I hammed it up and entertained the command.

The traditional vote for best stories at the finish was spontaneous.

"Breed, Breed, we want Breed!" people shouted.

He won the coveted master of ceremonies title for the next tie cutting.

Lt. Breed may have written things down, but I remembered it all. Then as now, sitting in the former Whiting Field O'Club, the memory of our *esprit de corps* brings sweetness to the very air I breathe. But for the people, it was a tough row to hoe. Remembering the challenges and the camaraderie of my first squadron, VT-6, I miss it all, oh...so dearly.

Yee-haw!

Multiengine Flight Training

CHAPTER FIVE

I received my new orders after completing the Navy primary flight training course and the intermediate maritime curriculum flying at NAS Whiting. I was sent to NAS Corpus Christi, Texas, for advanced maritime, or multiengine, training in the Beechcraft King Air C-90, known as the T-44A, which is the military designation for this aircraft. We affectionately renamed the plane after the Texas state "bird," the armadillo, calling it the *Turbo-dillo* because of its two turbine engines. The command's front office even displayed a wooden model of a flying armadillo with turboprop engines and wings.

I checked into the squadron at the hangar and then settled into an efficiency arrangement in the BOQ. There, I shared my quarters with the largest cockroaches imaginable (they do say everything is bigger in Texas), as well as other uninvited guests. I immediately fogged, foamed and sprayed every poison *de jour* found at the Navy Exchange. Unfortunately, my efforts didn't pay off. These critters were already immune to the poisons from years of exposure to the available pesticides. Instead, I mentally inaugurated a *beware-of-dog* attitude towards my issued roommates, making the best of our arrangements together.

There were several other welcoming committees at NAS Corpus Christi. First, January sent strong winds across Corpus Christi Bay, the kind that only Texas with its long, flat, treeless approach to the North Pole can generate. The wind covered everything with salt in a matter of hours and wreaked havoc with learning to fly a new airplane, a condition I experienced shortly after I began flying the Turbo-dillo. Second, my squadron smiled at new students with steel teeth. A bunch of hard-assed men, they pressured us with threats of failure and attrition, while the sister squadron across the hangar deck treated their students with more respect. I thought, *Is this the wrong community for me? There isn't a happy person in here. What's the purpose of their attitudes and how do I avoid picking up one myself?*

Last but not least, the T-28s flew in the landing pattern at night. Powered by fourteen-hundred-horsepower piston engines, this airborne committee flew directly overhead at one thousand feet. The noise from these Trojans kept everyone awake. I learned how to sleep wearing earplugs and bought a loud alarm clock.

Ground school started immediately after check-in and included a review of meteorology, an introduction to the systems particular to this airplane, and a new course in over-water navigation. Navigation was a real bear of a week all by itself.

The navigation course clearly never intended to create navigators out of pilots. Rather, it familiarized them with what the navigator's job entailed on either the P-3 Orion aircraft or the C-130 Hercules. This course alone returned us to the *drinking from the fire hose* experience of the AOCS. We were exhausted from the ordeal of the navigation course by the weekend. We flew with navigators who specialized in this unique art form; so fortunately, our understanding of over-water navigation was all that was required. Otherwise, even more training at the navigation table would have been involved.

Our systems required understanding of proper terminology, physics, applications, procedures, emergency procedures and limitations of the individual piece of equipment. These critical elements could affect other systems; and correction was rarely straightforward. What are the pilot's in-flight considerations when one of these went down? For example, if one wing failed to deice properly, why should I have second thoughts about utilizing the wing deicing system? The simple answer is the resulting imbalance. Creating one clean, more efficient wing induces a rolling movement into the dirty wing.

Another more complex example derives from the inherent design of the multiengine aircraft. If a pilot in a single engine aircraft experiences engine failure during take-off, his only choice is to abort take-off, preferably stopping on the runway. But flying a multi-engine airplane is different. Once a multiengine airplane reaches "decision speed," it can lose an engine and still stop; or it can have enough remaining runway to safely take off and clear all obstacles with the other engine's available surplus power. Prior to take-off, and once the aircraft reaches "refusal speed," stopping on the remaining runway is no longer an option. The pilot is forced to take off, flying toward safety that only the sky provides.

These speeds also depend on other factors besides available runway length—the gross weight of the airplane, altitude (affects power available from the motors), the headwind component and slope of the runway, as well as runway contamination.

Pilots observe the old statement: "If the decision speed is greater than the refusal speed, the aircraft is over weight for take-off." In short, while the airplane can be at refusal speed (not having enough runway available to stop), it may not have reached decision speed (having enough runway to continue the take-off with an engine-out condition). A plane with engine failure in this ground regime rolls off the end of the runway. The pilot's career does the same.

Ensuring safety, we studied charts and graphs to determine take-off performance data. We also concerned ourselves with two other speeds of importance. The first was the velocity of minimum control ground speed (VMCg). This is the speed required to maintain a straight track while accelerating on the runway with the critical engine inoperative, and the other at a specific high power setting.

The second speed is the minimum control airspeed (VMCa). This speed is the minimum speed required to maintain heading control in flight under the same engine conditions. If a pilot attempts to continue with an engine out while below either of these two speeds, the plane's flight controls are ineffective: too weak to counter the power of the remaining engine.

But here's the kicker. While these problems and speeds are specific to all multiengine airplanes, all reflect the basic problem of power required, combined with a moment arm. With the engine on the wing, the wing serves as a leverage device against the flight controls—primarily the rudder, as it's on the aircraft's centerline. The pilot tries to stabilize the aircraft by placing the rudder forces against the turning forces of the engine and moment arm. Thus, there is a minimum required speed for the rudder to generate enough force to overcome the engine-out operating conditions on both the ground and in the air.

After several weeks of these types of classes, we finally saw an airplane: albeit a crashed airplane. Familiarization began with a static trainer, an airplane that survived a crash well enough to present the actual cockpit to the student. Next, we moved onto the flight line with the introduction of the on wing instructor and preflight. Then, we began flying in all types of Texas winter weather, gale force or not, tornados be damned, and who cares about the volcanic ash covering our windshields! For an introduction to multiengine, it was quite an experience.

Our syllabus contained ten familiarization flights: one double-student solo at the end, five basic instrument flights, four night familiarization flights with one double-student solo, twenty-one RI flights, and four airways navigation flights. The RI22X, our grand finale, was the mother-of-all check rides.

I failed the first hurdle: the crosswind at NAS Corpus Christi. In all honesty, while at NAS Whiting Field, I never experienced crosswinds—let alone such strong ones. On my fourth NAS Corpus Christi flight however, the wind blew across the runway with authority, shifting from one side of the runway to the other without notice. Perhaps I might have done better with a constant wind from one side or the other. I put in the corrections and tracked the centerline; but at the bottom, the winds shifted or fell off and I couldn't land on the centerline. The tires weren't aligned with the direction of travel and I landed somewhere off to one side in a stiff skid.

For all my efforts (and there were eighteen landings to show for it), I received a down for the flight. This led to the much-feared speedy board with a group of instructors and two additional flights with the squadron's hatchet man, Lt. Cher. It was a trying week for sure. But at the meeting, we discovered that I knew absolutely nothing about the crosswind landing technique called the forward slip.

"Neal, during a crosswind landing, what controls the aircraft's position relative to the runway centerline?" the senior officer asked.

I knew I had two choices, either the aileron or the rudder. Fortunately I made the wrong choice.

"The rudder," I replied.

The silence was telling. In that moment, the board understood why I was called to appear before them. I hadn't been trained in the crosswind landing technique and it was obvious that I was clueless.

The senior instructor took over and thoughtfully explained the lateral component of lift from a wing tilted into the wind.

"The tilt holds the aircraft on centerline by countering the wind's push," he said. "But Neal, if we simply tilt the wing, the airplane turns. So, to counter the tendency to turn, the pilot presses on the top rudder, and aligns the aircraft's longitudinal axis in relation to the runway. This keeps the aircraft from turning. At the same time, it allows the one main gear tire to roll on the runway without being scraped sideways."

I learned that the initial objective in the crosswind landing is to obtain runway centerline from several miles away. Next, was an exact calculation of the winds and finally: the combination of aileron, elevator and rudder inputs to place the upwind landing gear gently on the ground without any telltale shaking of the fuselage. All of this requires both a constant airspeed and configuration, whether flown with no flaps, approach flaps, or full flaps. It was one heck of an afternoon around that table of overly serious investigators; but I learned some things that weren't obvious to me before.

Lt. Cher, the squadron hatchet man, supervised my next two, extra instruction flights. I improved despite his best efforts, as the winds didn't wail across both sides of the runway.

Looking back on the down, I couldn't help but wonder about my wing instructor's agenda. *It was my fourth flight in a new airplane. What did he hope to accomplish with such challenging conditions? My flying partner did better than me, but he had some prior flight time before joining the Navy.*

I can't say that the conditions were impossible, just miserable. I had to get it behind me and press on through Lt. Cher and his hatchet game, while remaining respectful and courteous throughout. I was determined that this student wasn't going to wash out.

Once again flying by the syllabus, I flew six or seven more hops with various instructors and loosened up quite a bit. I gradually found out most instructors were good guys; several had funny approaches to different situations, such as the dynamic engine cut at altitude.

One Lt. grabbed both condition levers (they control the fuel shut-off valves) and mixed-up shutting down an engine during a simulated malfunction. He was pretty hilarious about things and tried to make you laugh as a distraction before shutting down the engine—without the auto-feather system being armed. A momentary wind milling propeller and violent yawing of the aircraft ensued.

By acting deliberately, deflecting the rudder pedal against the operating engine and adding more power, I kept the situation under control. If I had pushed the wrong rudder peddle; however, the airplane would have yawed and rolled out of control in a heartbeat. That's why smart instructors anticipate and block any input to the wrong rudder pedal.

Other high-altitude simulated maneuvers included ditching, dual engine flameouts and engine fires, during which we simulated shutting the engine down and firing the fire extinguisher. All of these included memory item callouts and checklist procedures.

During our pattern work, we simulated the loss of either engine anywhere in the pattern. We flew the remaining landing pattern on one engine to a landing or a wave-off. On take-off, this presented difficulty climbing, keeping the plane in balanced flight with the rudder, while simultaneously performing an emergency shutdown of the bad engine. It's much less of a challenge on downwind because the power required to maintain level flight is far less than that of climb-out. On the turn to final, if you did nothing at all, you would make the runway.

We practiced standard maneuvers for basic instruments and added failed instruments to the situations, calling them "partial panel maneuvers." The instructor controlled a small box with special switches under his right armrest. These switches shut off the student's attitude gyro and required the student to fly timed turns, utilizing turn needle, compass and clock. Additionally, we demonstrated recoveries from unusual attitudes—nose high, nose low or a steep descending turn, using a degraded instrument panel with only a turn needle.

After basic instruments, we advanced into yet another course in RI or radio instruments. The fun began with already familiar approaches from our primary flight training. Then they added two other important approaches to the syllabus. The first was the ILS approach (or instrument landing system approach), an approach that guided the aircraft directly to the runway centerline. It provided a three-degree glide slope to a decision altitude, usually two hundred feet above the elevation of the approach end of the runway.

The second was the localizer-only approach. This provided azimuth-only guidance to the runway centerline, and therefore held higher altitude requirements than the ILS. However, from this approach, and with other non-precision approaches, a circling maneuver could be added at the end; which aligned the aircraft to another runway rather than that of a straight-in approach. We learned to fly each of these challenging approaches all on a single engine.

Non-precision approaches can be flown with a frozen-compass card; the instructor disabled that device, too. In the event of a frozen-compass card, one aligns the ADF needle with the aircraft's nose, asking for the heading from the instructor pilot who references the standby compass. From there, the student pilot adjusts turns and asks again for the heading while keeping the ADF needle on the nose of the aircraft. In this teamwork manner, the ADF approach is properly navigated despite the degradation of the heading source.

The VOR approach can be navigated in this configuration, but the tail of the VOR needle always points to the actual radial, and therefore gives a slight advantage. Still, terrific navigational skills and situational awareness to navigate the plane into landing position are required.

Both the attitude gyro and compass card were failed at the same time to further complicate matters. For that situation, the ground control approach proves most beneficial. The controller issues simple commands such as "turn left" and "stop turn," greatly simplifying the navigation problem. The student uses standard rate turns of three-degrees per second (a full needle width deflection on the turn needle) while in the pattern. On the final approach course, he uses half-standard rate turns or one and one-half degrees per second to finesse the plane across the ground while descending on the glide-slope, as dictated by the precision approach radar controller. All of this is performed at specific airspeeds, altitudes and configurations, with checklists to complete in the meantime.

The program challenge later on included "flying into the valley." The valley is in Brownsville and Harlingen, Texas, where three airports and four approaches came so rapidly upon each other that there wasn't enough time to manage each separate problem. This tests a student's ability to sort out important items while keeping the plane in the air during the most difficult times. Here, more than anywhere else, while we flew approach after approach, the instructors failed engines, turned off our attitude gyros, and created crisis after crisis just to load-up the students. I know I didn't do everything right, but I hung in there and my instructor said I didn't lose a knot on my single engine arrival. I remembered to add power and fly the airplane first, navigate second and communicate third, just like our good book said. It all works out.

It was time for the RI22 check ride at the end of the curriculum. I remember it was a windy day with thunderstorms in the area. Nervous, I fouled up the flight plan. Someone told me weight and balance was important, something I knew nothing about. I reviewed that instead of flight planning. What a mistake! My instructor enjoyed a field day with my fouled flight plan, the strong winds and thunderstorms. However, I stared down failure, flew aggressively and passed.

It was the thirteenth of May. Now, the only thing left was a round trip to San Diego. Shortly afterwards, my parents came to town and my mother pinned on my wings. That was a very proud moment for all of us in the base chapel: Navy and Marine Corps pilots getting their "Wings of Gold." My mother still has those pictures and I still have the memories.

Those first wings hang on my "I love me wall" beside my commission and Naval Aviator Designation. Although they are not real gold, they were mine. Sixteen months of hard, hard work, dedication, study and extra effort finally paid off in "gold"—crusty, chipped-up, sprayed-on gold.

What I didn't know was that my transition to flying in the fleet meant that more of the same lay ahead of me.

The RAG:
Welcome to the Machines

CHAPTER SIX

After I completed training at the base in San Diego, I drove along the coast of California, passing through the maze of Los Angeles freeways, while heading up Interstate 5 for the Bay Area. The trip took two days and I was beat by the time I checked into the BOQ at NAS Moffett Field.

The Moffett BOQ was an attractive, Spanish adobe-style building surround by a nice setting of trees. It looked more than adequate from the outside. I was wrong. The rooms were filled with metal cots and creaky old beds. Wooden doors closed with a bang and the walls were obviously made from thick paper. Moffett billeting was a far cry from the Navy housing to which I was accustomed. Roommates came and went at all hours of the night. My first night there left me longing for my lean-to tent from desert survival during SERE school. At least there I could get some peace and quiet, even when sleeping with sidewinders.

The next morning I talked with my roommate while standing outside behind the BOQ near some dumpsters. We needed an apartment and discussed which areas of town to investigate. It was then that a blond-haired gentleman in running gear came over and interrupted our conversation. He was a handsome man, built like a fullback. His love of exercise and running long distances was obvious.

"Hi, I'm Commander Stan Bark, Executive Officer of VP-31," he said smiling and gave us both a firm handshake.

"Good morning sir, I'm Ensign Schupbach. This is Tom Riley. It's a pleasure to meet you."

"Riley and Schupbach? I'll try and remember. You're here for the RAG. Well, it's a tough course, be ready for it. Everyday is a new challenge and we keep piling it on. But you will love the P-3, the mission and your time here at the RAG. You Ensigns look so young, the girls will be all over you."

"We hope so, sir," Tom replied as we both smiled and let out a small bit of laughter.

"What are your orders? What squadrons are you going to next?"

"Sir, I'm headed to Hawaii, VP-22 at Barbers Point," Tom replied.

"Steve Benkman's group, the Blue Geese. Steve and I served in Vietnam together, flew on the same crew. He's got it going out there. I hope you like the Philippines with all of the pretty girls. They deploy in April. Be ready."

I spoke up, curious as to what Commander Bark knew of my future, "Sir, I'm headed to VP-40."

"The Fighting Marlins, VP-40. Dick Overton is in charge there. I believe they are cross deploying next summer—Keflavik, Iceland. The Atlantic is good hunting, the Soviet boats have to squeeze by Keflavik to get to open ocean. Europe is a two-hour flight. London, Amsterdam, Paris, are all at your fingertips. They're also slated to be the first squadron to receive the P-3 Update 3 Aircraft. That should be something with the new innovations, software and synthetic radar. They say you can read the paint off the side of a ship with that radar," Commander Bark said as he outstretched his arm with his hand pointed up, moving it from left to right across his body.

"Yes sir," I said in a daze. *New airplanes, Europe, Iceland?* I was on cloud nine!

With those words I about died. I was impressed with the upcoming travel adventures, but even more so with Stan Bark. Not in my wildest dreams had I ever expected to meet my Executive Officer on my first day on base, let alone even before I checked into my new squadron, VP-31. There I stood shaking hands with this kind-hearted gentleman who thought nothing of being the first one to welcome a couple of new freshman to his advanced flying-campus. He knew more about my life for the next three years than I did! I loved the guy just for that twenty-minute conversation. During a job interview years later, I was asked about who made a big impression on me during my flying career and why. My quick answer was Commander Bark and it was because of that conversation.

Through pure luck my roommate and I found an apartment that afternoon. We moved in on Sunday, as it would be our last day off. Come Monday, we were back drinking from the fire hose again at the Replacement Air Group, VP-31 or the RAG for short.

We would soon learn how little we knew about flying machines. Our missions were not only about airmanship and navigation, as taught in previous squadrons during flight school. The P-3 Orion is the Navy's long-range patrol airplane. With its speed, range and endurance, it can fly over any of the seven seas in a matter of hours. This led to its many missions including: search air rescue (SAR), relocation of interesting surface contacts, open ocean patrol, low-level photography of ships (both merchants and combatants), over-the-horizon targeting, mining, air-to-sea missile attack and its mainstay, and anti-submarine warfare (ASW). We trained to find a submarine, localize her position, track her course, define her speed, and put a weapon on that target as necessary to defend the United States. During the first six weeks of the RAG, we learned the strategies and awful realities behind that lesson.

During the 1970s, the "Evil Empire" of the Soviet Union began a weapons modernization campaign throughout its entire sphere of influence. The Soviets modernized their ground armies with new armor; they developed more accurate missiles with longer ranges, capable of accurately striking Western Europe with nuclear weapons from the Ukraine. They rapidly advanced their navy's entire submarine program and antisubmarine warfare skills by stealing research and development secrets from the Navy, with the aid of the American spy, John Walker. During the same period, the United States did precious little to counter their strategic advances.

Many of their submarines were large missile platforms. For example, a Yankee 2 class submarine carried two rows of twelve missiles, each containing two, 500-kiloton warheads. If just one boat unleashed its full salvo against the United States, from anywhere in the Eastern Pacific ocean, the entire western half of America would be incinerated in a thermonuclear nightmare.

The P-3 community shared in the responsibility for countering such a threat. While our mission in the P-3 community was not as glamorous as the F-14s roaring from carrier decks, the mission was one of deadly consequence to all of America, and for that matter, to the entire world.

In addition to the nuclear ballistic missile threat from the undersea world of the Soviets' nuclear-powered SSBNs or "Boomers," the Soviet

Union also possessed both nuclear-powered and conventional diesel/electric attack submarines. These boats were primarily used for two purposes: to deny the sea-lanes to the Free World and to sink the envy of the world, the fleet of American aircraft carriers. These American aircraft carriers and their escorts represented and projected considerable power and influence throughout the world. The Soviets knew this quite well; yet, they could not produce any carrier battle groups of their own. Instead, they countered the carriers with the submerged threat of nearly 350 submarines.

In the closing twilight of the 1970s, the United States Congress fortunately sensed the disastrous nature of our military complacency. For many reasons, our defensive posture had stooped to new lows and the legislative branch acted to infuse much more money into the Pentagon's budget. Large pay increases, expanded hiring of all service men and women and increased supplies followed. Then came Ronald Reagan with his unwavering display of patriotic defense for the United States of America. We countered the Soviets' display of military might on land, at sea and in the air.

In response to the Soviets' policy of rearmament, America gave birth to a new concept for Europe. The U.S. based Pershing Two nuclear missiles on the continent. The Pershing Two could strike the Soviet Union in a matter of minutes from the European theater. There were protests to be sure. The idea that America could project its nuclear missiles without firing them from America had many Europeans afraid of the Soviets' response to a non-European decision. They feared both preemptive and retaliatory strike by the Soviets against Europe in a war that did not involve Europe.

The Reagan Administration, however, went ahead with the concept as part of a U.S. strategic defense of Europe. This made our friends in the Evil Empire quite nervous. The Soviets perceived the need to "keep up with the Jones'" and place their missiles a mere thousand miles or less from our shores. The ability to counter an American first-strike missile threat in Europe became their policy. As an analogous response, the Soviets deployed their SSBNs. The flying time for their ballistic missiles to reach the closest targets in America was now approximately ten minutes.

At the RAG, our "tactical education" consisted of brief overviews of the tactics that we employed, tactical trainers called "Weapon System Trainers" (WSTs), and an explanation of each of six tactical crew positions on the airplane. It was a lot to swallow; yet, we were expected to firmly grasp these basics before we left the RAG for the squadron. In addition to the flying, we were expected to understand all twelve P-3 crewmembers' functions and we were introduced to their various areas of tactical responsibility.

For starters, we flew with an in-flight electronic technician who repaired equipment that periodically failed during the flight or on the ground. That was easy enough to understand. We also flew with an ordnance man who loaded the airplane with our sonobuoys, both in our external storage areas and in the internal racks. The sonobuoys are expendable, floating radio stations that we dropped from the aircraft. Once in the water, the sonobuoys release a hydrophone and the hydrophone picks up the various sounds found in the ocean. The buoy then broadcasts the data back to the airplane for analysis.

The ordnance man also assisted the Tactical Coordinator (Tacco) in the launch of the internal sonobuoys, acted as our photographer, and served as an aft observer. Sensor operators one and two were our two, acoustic sensor operators onboard the airplane. Their mission involved real-time analysis of the sonobouy's information and the various sounds in the water. They categorized each frequency in regards to the target of interest. Every operating machine produces its own frequency group or signature. When placed under an "audio microscope," sensor one and sensor two picked out the noise made by a submarine's various mechanicals and exploited this data into useful tracking information—on a good day. A simple analogy would be a teenager being able to tell the difference between a galloping Harley Davidson and a four-cylinder Honda motorcycle, including their relative locations.

Sensor three was the non-acoustic sensor station. He operated the forward and the rear surface search radar. Each of these radars was so powerful that it took two grown men to pick up one of their iron-laden components: the magnetron. On a calm sea, it was said that the P-3's radar could locate and identify a floating beer can one hundred miles away from the airplane. Sensor three also operated the electronic search measures that listened for and categorized various electronic signals. Another terrific tool at sensor three's station was the infrared camera that was located in the nose of the airplane. He lowered this camera and displayed imagery in real time, as well as photographing the ocean's surface and/or any object on the surface of the ocean.

The last sensor that sensor three operated was the "MAD," or magnetic anomaly detector. This sensor detected any change or flux in the earth's field of magnetic lines. Although this sensor had to be in close proximity to pick up on the iron submarine, it was instantaneous and thus the most accurate, real-time fixing information available. Sensor three's call out of "MADMAN, MADMAN, MADMAN" always echoed like beautiful music for the entire crew. Unfortunately, because of the close proximity of the airplane to the submarine, "MAD trapping" allowed the sub to hear the sub-hunter. The alerted submarine always took evasive action to counter her detection.

We flew with an Officer whose position was called the NavComm, short for Navigator/Communicator. He was in charge of the over-water navigation aspect of the mission, as well as maintaining communication with the Anti-Submarine Warfare Operations Center (ASWOC). Without a doubt, his position was the most difficult of all those on the aircraft. There was no room for a navigation error, even on the open ocean. This would place our aircraft away from the predetermined area of highest probability for detecting the Soviet submarine. He documented all events and communicated the important ones back to the ASWOC. His job combined the double bitch of continuously listening to the scratchy, high frequency radios, while at the same time, sitting on the propeller line with four noisy propellers slapping shockwaves against his eardrums. The propellers turned at slightly over one thousand revolutions per minute, which mathematically equates to four blades, times four engines, times one thousand times per minute, or sixteen thousand slaps per minute. His old joke was, "Why do they put so much sound insulation in the P-3? To keep the sound in!"

The other Naval Flight Officer (NFO) served as the Tactical Coordinator (Tacco). He sat across the aisle from the navigator. His station was the nerve center, the command post of the entire airplane. He took the information generated by all of the crewmembers, (including the pilots) and generated an electronic picture before him. From this information, he decided on what course of action the crew would pursue. He was aided by one, very large analog computer, the CP901. However, because the frequent power surges that cursed Orion made it crash, this box of wires was more of a problem than it was worth. In the flight station, we kept in loop via headsets, a small keyboard, and an even smaller television that served as a stripped-down tactical display unit. For some odd reason, the display didn't even repeat the radar presentation, as if weather avoidance wasn't the pilot's call. The same held true for the infrared display. We did have large windows and three pairs of the "Mark One Eye Ball." More submarines than you could imagine were located visually, either from an occasional periscope and its trailing foam or feather in the water, or being spotted while transiting on the surface. We also had gyro-stabilized binoculars, which were excellent for ship recognition; and the earlier model, the P-3B, sported a bright light mounted under the left wing of the airplane.

For the pilots, the absolute best part of the RAG was undoubtedly the twelve flights in the P-3 Orion. However, we put up with more high intensity crap and workload to get to that point than you can imagine. Our first exposure to the cockpit was not as a pilot trainer, per se, but rather a flight engineer with systems and procedures exams in front of a cockpit mock-up. These two cockpit trainers were without a syllabus and they caught me flat-footed. I never knew there were so many dials, gauges and switches in the entire universe—let alone in one aircraft. While it was good to introduce the overhead panel to the pilots, the surprise tactic they employed thoroughly embarrassed and intimidated me. The nature of the beast was news to everyone, but somehow we all made it past that minor hurdle.

We were then introduced to the simulator for the P-3. It was a full-motion simulator with visual effects and could be landed quite well with the aid of the vision system. We accomplished both flight orientation and emergency procedure training in four-hour flying periods. Each student came away believing the "flying box" was more like flying a Christmas tree than an airplane, as the instructors lit up every conceivable warning light and challenged us with a multitude of problems in short order. All the while, we were still required to fly the airplane. "System discussions," in reality, were system quizzes following each warning light. Life during those eight hours, including the brief and debrief, was quite draining: mentally, physically and emotionally. Even though we didn't crash the box, we still got our lunch handed to us.

Before my first flight in the P-3 I had another unpleasant surprise. I was nervous as hell that fateful morning. My partner and I worked on the flight plan, received the weather brief, and reviewed the notices to airmen. When it came time to pick up our clearance from Moffett clearance delivery, our instructor pilot discovered that we forgot to file the flight plan with ATC. It was one of those most awful and embarrassing moments. The drinking from a fire hose pressure treatment was overwhelming and we thought we might flunk the entire flight. Our instructor had a big laugh at our expense and we felt so foolish.

After that fiasco, the engine starts went well and we were soon underway. I found the plane easy to taxi with the new-to-me nose wheel steering and differential thrust. On the ground, the large plane maneuvered quite handily. On take-off roll, I switched to the rudder for steering at forty knots and we accelerated down the runway at an impressive clip. The feeling of my first take-off in the P-3 was out of this world. The acceleration pulled me into the seat, while the sound of the props biting into the air represented pure power at its finest. When coupled with the feel of the enormous lift under thick wings, it all became one very impressive and very short take-off run.

We departed the San Francisco Bay Area via a standard instrument departure or "SID." The Woodside Eight departure led us straight ahead to seventeen hundred feet, at which point we turned west toward the ocean, heading directly for the Woodside radio beacon. We climbed to and maintained four thousand feet while flying over the San Francisco Bay. We headed south from the beacon and climbed another two thousand feet while flying over beautiful mountains and valleys covered with California redwoods.

We flew out to a "warning area," an area of designated airspace over the ocean where there was no civilian traffic at our altitude. There we practiced basic airmanship with steep turns, climbs and descents, and stalls before departing for the landing field work in the middle of the San Fernando Valley. It was my first time landing a large airplane. I accumulated a total of nine landings that sunny September afternoon with multiple touch-and-goes. The other student did much the same.

The return route took us through many twists and turns, and finally placed us at the arrival fix for Moffett Field. The instructor flew us "into position" for the approach to runway 32 right. After a touch-and-go on the right runway, we continued with some pattern work on the left runway and finally called it quits for the twelve-hour day. It was some kind of workout; and, although I was tired, it had been exhilarating!

During my second hop, I gained three instrument approaches and ten landings. On my third flight, I had five approaches and twelve landings. My fourth flight gained eight landings with five approaches. On the fifth flight, I had eight approaches and six night landings. The check ride came the next day with five landings and two approaches. All in all, it was a great three weeks of flying.

One of the most awe-inspiring things about the P-3 RAG at Moffett Field was the dirigible hangar in which it was housed. The massive steel structure was larger than anything I could imagine. In its day, it housed the U.S.S. Macon, a dirigible that launched and recovered aircraft from an internal bay. At that time, Silicon Valley was nothing more than farmland and San Jose was the nearest city. This silver hangar, made entirely of steel, had operable curved doors that rolled with steel wheels on steel tracks.

The very size of the building dwarfed the P-3 Orion. Consider that it was possible to park eight or ten aircraft in the south end of the hangar alone. The north end housed both the ground school buildings and the simulators, while the squadron offices ran along the eastern wall of the hangar. With all of these activities, and thanks to Commander Bark, Hangar One still had enough room for Joe Montana and the San Francisco Forty-Niners to practice football during a particularly rainy season.

Doors of Hangar One,
originally the home of the dirigible: USS Macon.

Hangar One was so tall that during air shows, the carnival hosted hot air balloon rides to the top of the structure! Its arch impressed me the most. It reminded me of a Cathedral, perhaps Paris' Notre Dame Cathedral with its flying buttresses of support. Impressive in the daylight, these steel beams and girders were even more amazing once the sun set. At night, the flood lighting inside the hangar created thousands of shadows behind the multitude of crossing steel beams. Although beauty is said to be in the eye of the beholder, everyone who saw it seemed similarly affected. It was inspirational.

Designated as a national historical site, Hangar One is protected from destruction by law—a very good thing. Its beauty and grace, stemming from the efforts of a long past generation of engineers and workers, stands as a tribute to their achievement in a simpler time. They, too, dedicated their lives to the defense of our nation and its people. These "can-do'ers" stood tall in their efforts, so tall that they helped to shelter us many years later. That hangar will remain standing for many others for years to come. Obviously, Hangar One spoke to me in a language all its own.

Another great thing about the RAG at Moffett was its proximity to the City of the Golden Gate: San Francisco. We did not overlook this fact. After the proverbial *Friday-night-at the-O-Club* antics, on warm autumn Saturdays, several of us drove to the city for the day. It was not uncommon for three or four of us young people to travel to San Francisco to see the sights, hear the sounds, and meet people in the crowded establishments. However, what made this so much better, so much more special, was the treatment we received because of our Navy Whites.

As four young Naval Aviators, complete with wings and butter bars, we walked into the Buena Vista at Fisherman's Wharf and the world became our oyster. In 1982, President Ronald Reagan led the resurgence of the country's pride in the military and we, so to speak, just rode in on his coattails. Everyone loved us. The girls wore our hats and their boyfriends bought us Irish coffee, while we all told our stories of commissioning, flight school follies, and the RAG with its incredible workload. We loved San Francisco and its people, and the city loved us back. Those afternoon visits in uniform were special, and we became celebrities just for daring enough and caring enough to show the flag with pride. But by Sunday night, we were back at the grindstone, faces in our books, hot and heavy preparing for the week ahead.

On Monday morning, in stark contrast to the weekends, we were in classrooms inside the massive hangar, experiencing the absolute worst part of the RAG. These rooms were hot, temporary trailers that suffered from ventilation problems. As students, we were given poorly written handouts, only a few lectures, and virtually no training aids. One of our most important missions in the RAG was to learn the dozen-plus systems of the airplane. The Navy demanded that we thoroughly understand them. Each day we went home with more and more normal procedures and emergency procedures to study, charts and diagrams to understand, and numbers to memorize from a big, blue sleeping pill—the NATOPS training manual—which was the size of a New York City telephone book. We reviewed at night, made flash cards, and crammed information about the P-3 into our minds at an astonishing rate.

This aircraft is a derivative of the Lockheed Electra Jet Prop, with a shortened body and stronger wings and fuselage. In short, I learned that these combined attributes of the P-3 made for an impressive, incredibly responsive airplane. One hundred seventeen-feet long, with a wingspan of 100 feet, the airplane stood 34 feet high. Unlike other aircraft of its size, all of its flight controls were hydraulically driven with aerodynamic trim tabs as secondary flight controls. These features, when combined with the straight wing, made the airplane extremely maneuverable, especially at low altitudes and slower speeds. Even a low time pilot could gracefully fly the 135,000-pound plane while practically touching the water with the wing tips. I quickly learned to love that airplane and still do to this very day.

The P-3 Orion was a highly complex, four-engine monster compared to the light twin-engine airplane we just graduated from. There were: flight controls systems, landing gear, an armament system, air conditioning and pressurization, the fuel system, three hydraulic systems, the inertial reference units and instrumentation, the engines, the ever-so-burdensome electrical system, and the granddaddy of them all: the most respected and feared mechanical dinosaur in the sky—the Hamilton Standard propeller. It exemplified the workload and bewilderment placed upon each student.

To begin with, each propeller controlled an engine that produced 4,600 horsepower. The plane was so powerful that it could pull its own wings off. At one time it held nearly all of the range, endurance, speed and climb records for turboprop aircraft, and it did so with ease. The P-3 Orion at sea level, while flying on just three engines, could outrun a modern jet passenger liner. It redlined at 405 knots, which is screaming at sea level, but Lockheed test-flew the bird at 485 knots to prove its air-worthiness. Besides all this, unlike other turboprops and jet transports, the Orion possessed both instantaneous power and a thick "blown wing" that rested behind the four enormous propellers.

Nothing gained our attention more in the classroom than the overly complex, *disaster-waiting-for-a-place-to-happen*, P-3 propeller system. It had four of them. To begin with, if controlling oil pressure dropped below a certain level of pressure, the propeller blades would go to flat pitch, which is just the opposite direction required for flight safety. We all knew that a flat pitch propeller, spinning in the wind, placed an inordinate amount of resistance on an airplane moving through the atmosphere. In most airplanes, this eliminated nearly all climb performance and placed an adverse yaw on the airframe. That in turn could pull the airplane into a death dive, especially when at low altitude or at high speed. Even the junior pilot in the class understood this all too clearly.

Gasps were heard throughout the classroom when this feature, a major violation of common sense, was first brought to our attention.

"Who designed this one?" was the question on everyone's lips.

Although the instructor went over this tidbit without blinking an eye, as if everyone should clearly be on board with the concept, no one was. Everyone disliked the concept immediately.

In fact, NO ONE COULD BELIEVE IT! It was true, nonetheless! To counter this basic aerodynamic design principle borrowed from *Mad Magazine*, the entire power plant had thirteen safety devices built in or added on to its core problem: the propeller itself. We all understood that thirteen safety devices were one heck of a lot of safety devices. Besides, everyone knew, thirteen is not a lucky number.

Each of these devises had to be memorized and completely understood as to their functions, the timing and triggering of their functions, the limitations behind each function, and what would occur should they fail to function. Each of us had to know the propeller in its entirety, its do's and don'ts, a whole slough of normal procedures and emergency procedures as well as the anti-icing system. Yet, this was only the propeller.

Words such as: propeller brake, negative torque signal (NTS) system, thrust sensitive signal (TSS) system, auto feather system, safety coupling, temperature datum control, over temperature release circuit, speed sensitive control, over speed protection, beta follow up, oil tank shutoff valve, fuel topping governor, fire detection, fire extinguishing discharge button, fire extinguishing transfer switch, pitch lock, synchrophasing, synchronizing, block out ranges, feather-pump pressure cutout override switch, the feather system, the feather valve and the emergency shutdown handle were now all forces with which we had to wrestle. This was *still* just the propeller! For an example, of the detail of each item (a set and subset relationship), the emergency shutdown handle had eight functions unto itself.

I distinctly remember one lecture on the propeller where the instructor discussed a mysterious "negative-torque sensing system," as it related to an even more mysterious "decoupling mechanism." In short, the engine produced power and transmitted that power via a rotating drive shaft to the propeller. Therefore, two units, the engine and propeller, were "mechanically coupled" or mechanically connected together. In contrast, our previous airplanes involved designs that separated the primary drive shaft from the power take-off shaft, through the use of blank space between the turbine wheels. In that design, each turbine wheel turned a different shaft. This arrangement was known as a "gas-coupled" or "gas-connected" design.

The efficiency of the P-3's mechanically coupled engine and its instantaneous response came with just one drawback. If the engine stopped producing power, as would be the case during flameout, the "Mad" propeller reduced its pitch to remain turning at its constant speed. If the propeller's safety devices failed, its blades reduced their angles toward a flat pitch and the propeller extracted as much horsepower from the air stream (provided by the other engines dragging the stricken plane through the wind), as necessary to keep the propeller spinning on its designated speed, called 100% rpm. Now, if the engine is mechanically connected to this dying-to-crash propeller, the propeller is required to turn the engine at its normal speed, also called 100 %. To do so, the compressor section of the engine extracts six thousand horsepower from the propeller. In order to avoid this intolerable situation, the engineers designed a device known as the decoupler: decoupling mechanically disconnects the engine from the propeller.

As I sat in class listening to all of this, the only thing I understood was the part about the "gas-coupled" design, because I had trained in aircraft powered by gas-coupled engines. I was not alone in this matter. The questions kept coming up and the instructor could not answer much about this mysterious decoupling device other than to say it actuated at a maximum of negative seventeen hundred horsepower, a confusing number to be sure because the engine produced a positive forty-six hundred horsepower.

The instructor's explanation began with negative torque and led its way through to the decoupler. It went along the lines of a Mason jar your grandmother used for canning.

"Imagine your grandmother's Mason jar," he explained. "Now, if you hold it out on its side and the left hand holds the lid stationary, and the right hand turns the jar clockwise, that is how the engine is designed to operate. However, if the right hand, representing the engine, is stationary and the left hand turns the lid in the same clockwise direction—that is our negative torque scenario. Eventually the lid will spin off of the jar and that describes our decoupler in action."

I thought: *This is a thirty million dollar airplane and not only is the RAG explaining something so serious as to cause the loss of the aircraft and entire crew via a Mason jar analogy, the guy doing the talking doesn't even have a Mason jar!*

Because the Navy had five hundred P-3 aircraft and Moffett Field was an intermediate level maintenance base, I thought that they should have a spare decoupler lying around. So I asked the instructor, "Would it be possible to bring a decoupler to class as a instructional aid?"

"Oh no," he responded, "There is no way. It would cost too much." With that I thought I would rather die than go on with another lecture.

After realizing the complexity of the P-3's propeller system, we adopted the user-friendly phrase "don't tease the animals" as words to live by. In other words, if something is working fine, just leave it alone.

Because of the unique power plant design found on the P-3, once on station 900 miles or three hours from land, "teasing the animals" is exactly what we next learned to do. Just when we understood the propeller and its inherent dangers, we literally shut one down and sometimes two. As convoluted as this may seem, three engines were at times better than four and two were better than three. All of this centered on horsepower required for flight and fuel economy.

The enormous shaft horsepower of the P-3—take 18,400 as an example, could be measured directly and instantaneously through four, large horsepower gauges mounted across the center instrument panel. The total of these readings was the horsepower required to maintain the aircraft in flight for a given condition. This became, in no small way, a detail that we quickly used to full advantage: one that made the P-3 famous in its mission of maritime patrol. Unlike most other airplanes, if the P-3 could produce the same amount of total horsepower from the algebraic sum of three operating engines (as it could with four engines at a reduced throttle setting), then it was possible to save large amounts of fuel and extend the time loitering on station by safely shutting down one or even two engines. This translated into a fuel flow of 900 pounds, or roughly 135 gallons of kerosene per hour per engine.

To save fuel, we took advantage of the fact that we read the horsepower required for flight. If it required a total of 8,000 horsepower to keep the plane airborne, this translated to 2,000 horsepower per engine when all four were turning, but 2,667 horsepower per engine if only three were turning. The basic horsepower consumed by the four combined compressors was 24,000 and it could be reduced to 18,000, if only three engines were running. If you were in a high altitude prosecution, not only could the P-3 loiter one engine, but both outboard engines for additional savings. In that flight regime, the plane's compressors only required 12,000 horsepower; and therefore, even greater savings could be obtained while flying, loitering or waiting on your assigned geographic position. These were just two of the convoluted propeller lectures presented in the hot, stuffy classrooms of the RAG. Other systems didn't even have corresponding lectures, only corresponding exams. THANK GOODNESS!

Somehow, we all graduated and went our separate ways to various squadrons. Some went to NAS Barbers Point, Hawaii, while the rest of us stayed at NAS Moffett Field. To be sure, our excellent flying education was both highly advanced and yet elementary when compared to the real world of flying the P-3 Orion. Consider, for example, that crew coordination now stretched 100 feet from the front to the back of the airplane, not just to the man sitting next to you.

Much more was yet to come. I received a change in my orders. My new squadron was VP-88 instead of VP-40, and I expected to deploy to Kadena Air Force Base on the island of Okinawa. In a few short months, I was to find out what I was missing—in more ways than one.

Our missions would be graded from outside the squadron and every point within every grade mattered. Eventually, I would fly missions on a crew hunting Soviet submarines with gear so sensitive that our tapes went to the Pentagon for analysis. As it were, the two years of AOCS and flight training provided by my government seemed like enough of an accomplishment for this young man.

The arrival of Christmas 1982 marked the end of my training in VP31. I flew home on a P-3 good deal boondoggle, which was dedicated to cross-country flight training at Christmas time. We landed in Kansas City at night. My father waited for me with his utility car, a beat up old station wagon. We drove west to Manhattan, and then took highway 77 north, bypassing the fond memories of the turn-off to our cabin on Tuttle Creek Lake. Next came the old-west town of Marysville, Kansas. We pressed on for Lincoln.

As we approached the Kansas-Nebraska border, I asked, "Dad, did Governor Thone win re-election this year?"

"No, he didn't. His bid for re-election was upset by a young, local man. Bob Kerrey is his name. He grew up in Lincoln and owned a restaurant on West 'O' Street."

"Bob Kerrey? I know Bob Kerrey!" I said. "I cleaned his restaurant late nights when I went to the university. Well good for him! He was a great guy and really nice to me. He thought nothing of spending time with me over a good cup of coffee. You know he won the Medal of Honor in Vietnam don't you?"

"Yes, and that made him quite popular throughout the state. Hometown boy done good, you might say."

A half-hour later we drove though the small town of Beatrice, Nebraska, and ventured back into the dark night on the two-lane highway in silence. Without a word being said, parallel thoughts of one generation to another, my fathers and mine, captured our moments together. My father thought of his time in the Army. He trained in Fort Riley, Kansas, just a few miles from our cabin.

I thought of all the challenges I overcame in my two years of military service and how I missed my old friends from former times. He knew how I felt without talking about it. A torch passed that night. Now I was the young man in uniform, driving route 77, returning home from intensive training as my father looked on.

We passed another familiar turn-off, "Crete Corner," the road we took to visit my cousins, great aunts and Grammy Greer. As children, my brothers and I played a simple game during the drive home from their small town of Wilber. We each wanted to be the first one to call out "I see Lincoln" when sighting the four-hundred-foot gold dome on the white stone state capitol building.

As we drove to the crest of a ridgeline, my father and I could see the lights of Lincoln reflected in the cloud layer above the city. On the top of the hill, the capitol building revealed itself, lit up tall against the night sky like a shining sword or Nebraska's landmark Chimney Rock.

Spontaneous and heartfelt, we both sang aloud, "Oh beautiful for spacious skies, for amber waves of grain, for purple mountain majesties above the fruited plain! America! America! God shed His grace on thee and crown thy good with brotherhood from sea to shining sea!"

Ten years prior, the Vietnam War divided us. But then, I understood something more about life and much more about the inside of my father's old uniforms. They just might fit me now. Looking back, that night was one, very large Christmas present for the both of us, but especially for me. And very soon it would be my turn to serve America overseas.

Kadena

CHAPTER SEVEN

It was in early February, just short of a month of my arrival at squadron VP-88, that we deployed to the Kadena Air Force Base, Okinawa, Japan. My first flight across the Pacific Ocean was an eye-opening experience; the water went on forever. We flew to NAS Barbers' Point, Hawaii. The host squadron of the month greeted us on our arrival with a set of tires and a welcome sign for VP-88. Evidently, our previous eight airplanes all required tire changes when they arrived at NAS Barbers' Point and they were trying to send a message to the VP-88 Maintenance Department. After the seven-hour flight to the islands, we spent the night in the BOQ. Our Executive Officer, Commander Fogg, flew with us, as we were the last airplane to depart for the deployment. In Hawaii, he allowed us one beer before we returned to the Navy's twelve-hour rule forbidding alcohol consumption before flying.

"Now, I want to make this very clear to everyone. We are here in Barbers Point on a mission, not a party. We are under a microscope as this is the home of CincPacFleet. I will allow a beer during the next twenty minutes, but no screw ups."

No one complained, but everyone wanted the take-off pushed back an hour. We simply purchased two beers and saluted the cause of our frustration.

We packed our twenty-three people into the crowded airplane the next day and departed for the island of Guam, four hours to the southeast of Okinawa. We flew this southern route because the prevailing head winds did not allow us to transit to Kadena nonstop. Once in Guam, we refueled and quickly departed for our final destination: "The Rock."

Large thunderstorms greeted our arrival to the Okinawa area. We worked our way around them, but we still had to drive headlong into turbulent air while making the final approach. I strapped myself down to a rumble seat located between the computer bays on the aircraft. In reality, the seat was a six-inch wide composite board with seat belts for two people. With little room to move my legs away from my chest and a warming cabin, I almost got airsick. Three other people did just that as the rises, falls, bumps and rolls overcame them. I could hear them throwing up into their Navy-issue, green nylon helmet bags. The aircraft's ventilation system couldn't keep up with the heat and the smell of their vomit. We were all in this together and likewise miserable.

We were greeted once we landed by other members of our squadron with a welcome case of beer on ice at the base of the air-stairs. Their open arms made everyone happy to be on the island with their shipmates, swapping stories and sharing good times at two o'clock in the morning. Yet our long day was far from over. We unloaded our sea-bags from the aircraft, piled our flight gear into the lockers in the hangar and headed out to the Japanese immigration office to complete the "in chop."

After clearing immigrations, the crew then went to Air Force billeting to obtain our housing. It was four o'clock in the morning. At four-thirty local time, I finally lay my head down to rest from a long week of work, topped off by three long flights to my first overseas adventure. I needed sleep so badly I could taste it.

Two and a half hours later, the Patrol Plane Commander (PPC) of our crew knocked on my door and got me out of bed. We had thirty minutes to get to the squadron wardroom, where the skipper would address his officers at the weekly All Officers Meeting (AOM). I couldn't believe it. I thought, *Why on earth would anyone want to have us at work after flying through seven time zones and the dateline in two days, while snatching only two hours of sleep before listening to a stinking speech in the wardroom?*

True to our training, we all complied and droned down to the flight line. Once in the squadron spaces, there were those who laughed at my red eyes and stooped shoulders. The news, as usual, was not much news. It wasted everyone's time and sent out mixed messages. Our skipper's goal was safety first; but, apparently, taking care of our people came in a distant second.

At the end of the meeting, the skipper stood up and enthusiastically welcomed our crew.

"Crew Two safely arrived late last night. I am proud of them, too. Here they are bright and early, ready to go to WORK!"

I thought, *So why do you call sleep-deprivation safe? Is this really taking care of your zombies? And what work is so important right now anyway?* It didn't matter. No matter how hypocritical the circumstances became, he was the skipper and that was the end of the story. We were his captive audience!

I found Kadena a very good place to be stationed in spite of my first twenty-four hours on the base. The Air Force, with all of its money and recreational facilities, owned Kadena. I had the opportunity to see many unique and entertaining displays firsthand of our aeronautical achievements and prowess. We had come a long way since the Wright brothers.

The Air Force touted a large, F-15 Eagle base across the field from us. The F-15s swooped about the base in their landing pattern, looking quite macho. The Air Force also positioned a half-dozen B-52s behind earthen bunkers just to the south of our hangar. They hid behind the manmade embankments with only their tall, shark-like, camouflaged tails protruding from their surroundings. Their presence alone was quite intimidating.

An air refueling squadron also roamed the property. This tanker squadron just looked bad—plain and simple. Their airplanes were dinosaurs and possessed the original water-injected jet engines. During take-off, while the water did increase thrust by increasing the amount of mass exiting the engine, it also created the most awful black smoke from a four-motored beast than one dared imagine. I thought little of these KC-135 creatures, except that their presence, with their special cargo, always announced the coming of "Habu."

The SR-71 Blackbird, parked to our south, was America's Mach 3, super-secret, black titanium spy plane. There was a plane I could get into! No one dared approach them. SR-71 was aptly nicknamed "Habu," after a four-inch Asian snake whose strike is remarkably deadly. Everyone who watched it fly, including the Japanese, marveled at its evil beauty. Oftentimes I found myself on the flight line preflighting the P-3 for an upcoming mission when the tankers paraded by, usually a half-an-hour before the SR-71 show began. After the tankers took off, two truckloads of armed Air Force security guards, fore and aft, escorted Habu past my position. The elongated, black airplane had three pointed protrusions, one from the nose and a black cone covering each engine intake. It passed by and dripped jelly-like fuel from its curved belly onto the taxiway. About that time, it made good sense to head for the cockpit, safely out of sight and out of mind.

The idea that the 1960s-vintage plane actually leaked fuel intentionally seemed a bit dangerous to me. But once inside the P 3 cockpit, my Lieutenant told me, "The SR-71 flies so fast that wind resistance heats the skin and expands the aircraft, thereby sealing the fuel tanks and maintaining strength in the airframe. The best place for thrill-seekers to be is outside on the tarmac."

I left the cockpit and stood in the shade, under the wing of our airplane. I just had to witness the thunderous take off and departure of this plane.

The firsthand thrill and beauty of a Blackbird departure is as intense as any NASA space launch. At first, I heard the engines spool up, followed by the muffled roar of each engine at a high power setting. The airplane began its take-off roll out of sight, but the sound of the fury to follow kept me on edge. I was as antsy as a kid at his first baseball game.

As it rolled by, the noise was tolerable for those who wore ear protection and painful for everyone else. By the time the aircraft approached our abeam position, its afterburners were literally screaming at full power. Bright blue, stove-blue flames shot out seventy-five feet behind the aircraft's engines. The individual ring patterns in each afterburner flame created a circular cascade of blue and white in the spectrum of its intense fire. The pounding roar shook the ground and my body vibrated with the fury of the blue roar.

By then, the aircraft was beyond my position, its sleek, black body merely peeking out from behind the long incendiary devices someone had the nerve to call engines. When the aircraft rotated for take-off, it swam its way into the sky much like a large manta ray glides to the surface of the water. Most take-offs were at twilight; and this mysterious, black-pointed object flew against the evening's dark blue sky, while its afterburners lit up the heavens with hot, pointed sabers.

Once safely clear of the ground, the pilot violently pitched up the aircraft and rolled into a steep, climbing turn, seemingly standing on the afterburners as if they were gas ladders to the stars. Then, at a predetermined altitude, the pilot shut off the burners and cruised to the first tanker aircraft. He was out of fuel. Habu could not take off with enough fuel to sustain the mission and full fuel tanks hindered his runway performance. We were all suitably impressed.

Respect for the Blackbird's raw power was immediate, while its cruising speed of Mach 3+ remained unfathomable. At that speed, it would take the total airspace of over four or five western states in America to turn the aircraft around. Also at that speed, with its narrow leading edge, covered engines, lifting body and curved underbelly, its radar signature was so small that it could not be detected until it arrived over a radar site. Because of both its speed and 80,000-foot altitude, it proved itself invulnerable to missile attack. The missile would be unable to catch the aircraft. Upon first detection, Blackbird would be out of range, even though its oncoming trajectory took it directly over the missile launcher. There simply wasn't enough time to enact an effective launch.

In the morning, Habu returned to its nest, though not yet able to land. Although fuel is expensive, it is lightly measured to the cost of the SR-71, and landing the plane with too much fuel was dangerous. Fuel is heavy, and an overweight landing causes damage to the landing gear and wings. The SR-71 pilots made several low approaches to the field, waving each one off. They took the 100-foot spy plane back up to a landing pattern: a vertical, standup maneuver with a half-twist to reverse course. Again and again, these pilots flew around Kadena, expending their fuel in order to land. When light enough, they made a few touch and go landings before retiring at the end of their long mission.

I could only stand on the sidelines and wave as they passed by, taxiing to their hangar. Occasionally, a pilot waved back. Even at age twenty-five, their responding wave gave me a thrill. I was so proud to be a part of the United States military team.

Australia

CHAPTER EIGHT

Our crew, led by Skipper Pardee, headed out for the land down under: Australia. It was during my third month in the squadron and my second month on deployment. For the mission, we flew two airplanes to the southern coastal town of Adelaide where the Royal Australian Air Force had an airbase, RAAF Edinburgh. The Australians flew many models of American military aircraft, the P-3 was just one of them. Our combined missions engaged the Australian Navy in joint antisubmarine warfare exercises.

The trip to Australia was a thrill a minute. Only two months prior, I had celebrated Christmas with my family on the cold, windswept plains of Nebraska. I now flew 8,000 miles from my hometown and gazed down on mirages generated by the heat-scorched, red desert of the Australian Outback. Green trees dotted the Martian red, rocky hills. They emerged from cracks and hung onto life against the windblown, solar furnace. Vast expanses of orange and red sands covered the flatlands.

The minutes turned into hours and the desert changed again, as miles of south Australia's white, salt pan slipped beneath our wings. We made our approach to the airfield with the late afternoon sun standing on our right wing. RAAF Edinburgh, our destination, stood just north of Adelaide. My wanderlust for exploration from years gone by began anew in the land down under.

Adelaide is a beautiful city, set between the Mount Lofty Range to the southeast and the cool waters of the Gulf of Saint Vincent on its western edge. The central city planner, Col. William Light, drew out the city as a grid—one imperial mile square surrounded by parklands. On its northern border, the Torrens River formed Lake Torrens, dividing Saint Peter's Cathedral from the University of Adelaide. South of the University, the city proper presented the Rundle Street Mall that was filled with flower shops, wine bars, bistros and street artists.

Victoria Square, with its open seafood market, curiosity shops and sidewalk cafés lay in the center of the city. Adelaide's Mediterranean climate complements Australia's exemplary hospitality with warm, dry days and cool, sea breezes at night. On two particular occasions, my short stay was filled with exuberant nightlife, fresh Australian wine from the Barossa Valley, women and song. It was then that I thought, *Please pinch this young Ensign. I must be dreaming!*

At the time of our first ASW mission, I was the junior pilot on the crew with 287 hours of total flight time. It was not much by anyone's standard. We took off early in the morning and headed east towards the South Pacific. The transit time was three hours to and from the area of operation, our target submarine's location. We cruised at 19,000 feet on our way outbound, which gave us a great view of the continent of Australia. Skipper Pardee kept us nervous, quizzing each of the pilots, challenging us about the performance of the airplane, fuel economy, and tactics we might employ against our underwater adversary.

The Australian submarine we sought was a particularly difficult, modern diesel/electric boat. The Australian Navy had no need for nuclear boats. Their coastal defenses were manned with a greater quantity of the less expensive, difficult and dangerous diesel/electric submarines. Diesel boats could loiter in a defensive position or transit quietly for a considerable amount of time undetected. Their acoustic advantages while running strictly on battery power were well known throughout the world. They broke their silence only during their snorkel time, submerged with one lone air intake pipe above the water to run their diesel engines, thereby recharging the batteries. Even then, when they were vulnerable, it took a great deal of effort and luck to locate the approximate position of the boat.

Added to our dilemma was the fact that we were a new crew, assembled over the course of the last six months. The text of our tasking required us to acoustically locate, track and simulate attacks against the submarine while she ran her diesel engines and while she operated on battery power. This proved to be a challenge in the beginning of the snorkel exercise, and nearly impossible while on battery power. The Australians were quite good at their game.

We arrived on station and checked in with the submarine via the radio communications plan. I remember our Tacco questioning the submarine, asking if we would be allowed to use an explosive echo range technique. This ancient technique employed a pattern of sonobuoys in the water, followed by the release of a small charge to give range echoes. The advantage of the explosive echo ranging was the available range from the strong, outgoing signal strength generated by the blast. The major drawback with the technique was the small explosion. Should their sonar operators be listening on their headsets, it could injure their hearing. At the time, it also presented several range events on a chart. The first would be the actual charge detonating; the second would possibly be the hull's reflection of the concussion. A possible third would come from the bottom of the ocean and the fourth from an undersea mountain or plateau.

We first tracked the submarine while she ran her engines near the surface. Once detected, this proved to be well within our capabilities and we enjoyed the success. However, the exercise called for the submarine to return to the depths on battery power and our luck went down with her. For ninety minutes, she had the advantage. No matter how we tried, even with explosive echo ranging, our conventional sonobuoy techniques were ineffective against the skilled submarine crew. As a submariner friend of mine once said, "Never play cards with a man who makes his living out of being sneaky." We were trying to draw for an inside straight.

As a new pilot with little experience in the matter, I simply flew the plane in slow orbits at one thousand feet, flying to waypoints the Tacco designated for his buoy drops. I truly was a bus driver at that time, while Skipper Pardee commanded from the right seat. But the Skipper played a hunch based on experience, a hunch that paid off in spades.

"Neal, turn right to a heading of north," he said.

"Yes, sir." I rolled the airplane to the right and the fun began.

From the middle of the turn, I looked outside the aircraft. In the center of my windshield I saw a small, thin periscope emerge from the depths of the sea.

"There she is!" I called out and pointed at the lone mast in the water.

We couldn't tell whether he was looking at us or not, but it didn't matter.

Skipper Pardee then ordered, "Descend to two-hundred feet, open the bomb bay doors."

He then called back to the Tacco to coordinate a weapons delivery run. It all seemed to happen within a matter of milliseconds.

I made it well within the weapons delivery envelope, but my novice skills kept me at approximately four hundred feet. I was completely occupied with the descending turn while trying my best not to sink too rapidly, thereby avoiding the surface of the sea.

The Skipper kept telling me, "Go lower. Get to two hundred feet, Neal!"

We opened the bomb bay doors just as I lined up on the target. Shortly thereafter, our sensor three shouted out, "Madman, Madman, Madman!" With that call, the Tacco simulated the release of the Mark 46 torpedo.

"Turn left, Neal, a hard left turn," said the Skipper.

I placed the aircraft into a thirty-degree angle of bank and we came around in due time. However, while in that turn, the Skipper gave me another lesson. He wanted the airplane flown at forty-five degrees angle of bank, two hundred feet above the water, while turning into the dead engine.

"Yes, thirty degrees is comfortable, but look at the long revisit time! Come on Neal—wrap it up. Let's get back in the fight."

So with his orders coaching me, I flew at a forty-five degree angle of bank, added some more power, and retimed the elevator and rudder. We rolled out from our 270 degrees of turn and headed right back into the target area.

"Madman, Madman, Madman!" called out sensor three.

We detected her again. This time we dropped a passive sonobuoy in her absolute location. It was another 270-degree turn from there, but this time to the right, lining up on our original inbound course.

"Madman, Madman, Madman!" again came blaring over our interphones. The fight was on and it lasted for more than a dozen MAD traps.

For the purposes of the exercise, the submarine's periscope came at the right place at the right time. We got lucky, very lucky. In the antisubmarine warfare business, if you want a good reputation, always choose luck over skill. When detected, the submarine commander chose to hunker down, going dead in the water to make it impossible to track him acoustically. Without his electric motors turning, the passive acoustic detection (through listening only) was not available to us. However, after a dozen or more magnetic detections, the Skipper made the decision to take up the active portion of the exercise.

From then on, our acoustic sensor operators pounded her hull with pings from our active sonobuoys and we actively tracked her for the remainder of our on-station time. Upon our departure, there were good reports received from the submarine and we, too, complimented the skill and cunning of the sub's entire crew. My first mission flying from RAAF Edinburgh was a day of high-spirited adventure. We returned to Adelaide and good times were had by all. It wouldn't last.

Our next mission kept us up late at night; and, no matter what we tried, the submarine had the game well in hand. It proved to be an open ocean search. It was quite maddening. We had no luck, droning on and on into the black night sky. It was like throwing darts into the vast ocean, hoping to spear a fish.

The Southern Cross kept us company that night, as if it was our only friend. Upon terminating the exercise, we made radio contact with the sub as she surfaced. I peered out the left, aft observer bubble window and discovered a lone white light below us against the blackened sea. I called the light sighting forward to the Tacco, but we were already departing our station, headed for home. So I took a few minutes, sat back and realized how difficult the adversary could be. Hunting the unseen, listening, waiting, disguising, localizing, tracking, and swooping down like an eagle grabbing its prey got under my skin. The hunter and prey aspect of the chase left a strong impression on me. At that moment, while flying over the South Pacific, I fell in love with the antisubmarine warfare mission. I have never let go of that love.

While we flew our night work, an enormous storm swept in from the Australian Bite, blocking our access to RAAF Edinburgh. As we approached the city of Adelaide, our own eyes could not believe the size of this monster storm. We could neither see above its smooth, gray, monolithic structure nor around it. Our radar operator, with as powerful tool as he had in front of him, could not penetrate the storm because of attenuation. The storm simply swallowed up the enormous power from the radar of the P-3 and would not allow any reflection from its backside. The rule was, "Never trust a storm your radar cannot penetrate."

Admittedly, the skipper is the skipper and it is his airplane. However, Skipper Pardee was quite gung ho when it came to getting us back to RAAF Edinburgh. There was no way to make it back, neither for love nor money—even if we had the fuel to circumnavigate that storm. On top of that, we were unsure as to whether the field would even be open. Finally, Skipper Pardee conceded defeat to the weather and we diverted to Melbourne.

The next day, we returned to Adelaide only to find our sister aircraft badly damaged from the same storm. The Australians parked their yellow gear on one side of their hangar away from the flight line. While all of the flight line gear was secured properly, one tall check stand had blown from around the side of the hangar, down the length of the flight line and slammed into the number one and number two propellers of our sister ship. It was not a pretty sight, with pieces of aluminum missing midway on two of the propeller blades, one on each prop. The good news was that the Australians knew how to fix the airplane. The bad news was the Australian propellers were not available to us because of the liability issue between the United States and the Australian government. What if one failed and the aircraft were lost? Who would be to blame?

We continued flying by alternating crews with our one remaining good aircraft. This left us more time to visit the city of Adelaide and to rest up for the next evolution, which was a good thing. How bad luck can run in threes, when you have only two airplanes, is a bit of a mystery; yet, our bad luck held. Once again, when crew two flew our next mission, Lady Luck turned against us.

We flew south of Australia, into the vicinity of Tasmania. As we descended through four thousand feet, the number three engine's number two propeller pump light came on. This warning light illuminated without any other warning lights, such as the number one pump light, as would be expected. Our flight engineer, Chief Wrinkle, performed a quick lights check as I called for the plane commander to return to the flight station. Noting no other failures, we called for the engine to be shut down.

Chief Wrinkle grabbed the emergency shutdown handle and the number one propeller pump light came on, indicating an extremely serious failure inside of the overly complex, spinning death trap. The plane commander came forward at that moment and commanded the crew to pitch-lock the propeller, thereby freezing the blade angle of the prop. The engine rpm was now entirely controlled by the movement of the power lever, and not as an automatic function of the constant speed propeller design. On top of that, the engine would need to be shut down and decoupled from the propeller before landing.

We flew the stricken ship to the RAAF Richmond, an airbase outside of Sydney, which was the nearest field for a suitable landing. The plane commander flew on the power generated by the three remaining engines, while Chief Wrinkle maintained the engine rpm on the number three motor. If the engine dropped below ninety-five percent rpm, the fifth and tenth stage compressor bleed air valves would open, as during engine start and catastrophically bleed off the engine's cooling air. Then the turbine would overheat, destroying the power section of the motor by fire. No one on the crew wanted to commit such an expensive mistake.

We arrived at the airfield just past dawn, under the authority granted to us by declaring an airborne emergency. Much to our surprise, fog covered the landing end of the field like a blanket. However, the upwind side was clear and the plane commander's hands became quite full. Still in flight, the time came to decouple the engine from the propeller by shutting off fuel to the stricken power plant. At the same time, we needed to maneuver for a seldom-practiced tail wind landing.

The command was given and the engine completely shut down except for one detail—it did not decouple. The air stream now rotated the motor. Meanwhile, the plane commander took it upon himself to perform the unusual, upwind approach and tailwind landing with a wind-milling propeller.

Much happened in the short, final approach to the field and the plane commander did a fine job handling both the downwind landing and the stricken ship: a ship in much more danger than one with a mere engine failure. Once on the ground, we taxied to parking and received a warm welcome from the local RAAF flyboys. Tired, but happy to be back on the ground, we purchased pins and patches from them. Unfortunately, we had none with which to reciprocate, something I felt bad about. We Americans did poorly at befriending our hosts.

We made our way to yet another hotel in this, our third Australian city. Those who carried ditty bags with civilian attire went on through the day exploring Sydney, the final city on our Australian tour. The others slept the remainder of the day. Unfortunately, the Australians had our airplane flying again within a couple of days. We then transited from RAAF Richmond back to Adelaide with a great personal adventure behind us; yet we wore a large serving of egg from our less than stellar ASW showing.

We gathered our support team together with the culmination of the exercises and took off approximately two weeks after our arrival. Our crew departed Australia, leaving behind the second crew and its broken airplane. It took nearly a month to complete the repairs on the stricken ship, for we had to find not just one, but two props and transportation to the land down under. This all took some kind of doing. The U.S. Air Force flew two propellers in from the United States.

Inspired by our three-city tour, our crew came up with a deployment patch from the adventures in Australia. An Australian flag served as the background with a "Crew Two" beer mug in the center. Along the bottom yellow border were listed the cities "Sydney-Melbourne-Adelaide," and along the top were the Australian words we learned while in the down under: "Chundering Cobbers."

I returned to Australia many years later, while flying for Conditioned Air. On that visit, I flew cargo from the cow town of Rock Hampton, located on the eastern coast. Rock Hampton has an Australian military base, and interestingly enough, General McArthur stayed in Rock Hampton after being driven out of the Philippines by the Japanese. It was from the Rock Hampton Courthouse that he staged his Pacific Command of World War II. There were pictures of him in the hotel where he resided and a small military museum stood a few blocks away.

I toured the museum and took a special interest in the large assortment of crew patches from every conceivable unit ever created. *Every unit but my own*, I thought. It would be a rare day when I would have the opportunity to give them one of our patches. Nevertheless, I vowed if I ever had the opportunity to return to historic Rock Hampton, I would indeed bring along a donation or two to the museum.

The next day I departed for Guam with a planeload of cargo and flew commercially back to Florida. When I arrived home in Key West, I was one tired dog. But less than six hours later, Conditioned Air telephoned me, sending me back to Rock Hampton. UNBELIEVABLE! I would leave the next day for the seven-day trip. Fortunately, I had just finished my laundry and I had some clean slacks for my uniform. But more importantly, I had been given an opportunity to give the museum some of our P-3 patches from many years ago. That night, I searched through my boxes of memorabilia and found extra Tacco, Pilot and Air Crew flight crew patches. Additionally, I ran across an extra Crew Two beer mug patch, complete with writing only an Australian would understand.

I had a mission when I reached Australia. I hoped the military museum would be open when I arrived. Once in Rock Hampton, our crew split up into separate cabs and ended up at the wrong hotel. We then transited to the motel and I held the cab for a run downtown. The driver took me to the museum. Fortunately, it was open. Once inside, I spoke with the proprietor and explained my situation and admiration of his collection. I presented the four, like-new crew patches as a gesture of good will to my host country.

The gesture went over well, making the old man smile a silly grin. The beer mug gave a big hint to the meaning of "Chundering Cobbers." Back then, we drank enough beer to testify to its validity. After all, we were junior officers trying to hold on to the last bastion of good times.

I explained the meaning behind the Australian cities and of the wording on the patch to the other Americans in the museum. The old man smiled because he had never seen a military patch, or any patch at all, with words meaning 'throwing-up good buddies' written on it. Well, now he had one in his collection along with three officially sanctioned U.S. Navy patches from many years ago. The Americans in the museum had a good laugh at my inside joke.

I didn't stay long after that, only long enough to thank the proprietor for his work. My donation of patches was a long overdue gift of memorabilia, given for the sake of honoring small friendships from so many years ago. I remembered the Australians because they were always so good to me. That mattered to a young Ensign who was unable to reciprocate at the time. The small gift of patches served as a way of closing and coming full-circle with my friends, my allies, and my comrades-in-arms. It was my way of saying goodbye to the land and the waters down under.

Diego Garcia

CHAPTER NINE

Halfway through our deployment to Kadena, our crew rotated to the British Indian Ocean Territory (B.I.O.T.) island of Diego Garcia. We called it *Dodge*, as in Dodge City, Kansas. This island lies in the middle of the Indian Ocean, approximately twelve hundred miles south of India. It is truly in the middle of nowhere, like Dodge City, Kansas.

We transited through the Philippines, as part of the long journey to the "Footprint of Freedom," as referred to the atoll. The "island nation" of Dodge was actually four or five islands on an atoll. Its thin outline in the water took the shape of Fred Flintstone's right footprint in the sand. Thus the official nickname for Diego Garcia became "The Footprint of Freedom." We still called it Dodge, however, as it gave the senior officers something else to care about.

The flight to the Philippines took four to five hours. In the early 1980s, one could not be a self-respecting WESTPAC sailor and not visit our Navy's home away from home: Cubi Point at Subic Bay, Republic of the Philippines. The facility sported a deepwater port, a Naval Air Station, a submarine repair facility and the best Officer's Club in the entire world. The deepwater port berthed at least two aircraft carriers and the submarine base was just around the corner. Here in Cubi Point, P-3 squadrons rotated through on their deployment cycle and the base also hosted detachments from other squadrons. Olongopoe City supported the bases. *O' City* was the most outlandish, robust, rocking town of the wild, western Pacific. An overflow of pent-up young men routinely swamped the local facilities in Olongopoe City.

Nothing brought more happiness faster to a sailor than a visit to this uniquely qualified land of ice-cold San Miguel beer in painted label bottles and hot, hot little Filipino girls waiting on their every beck and call. We spent the night in Cubi or more accurately stated, in Olongopoe City, during our transit to Diego Garcia. On my second visit to this island of nightlife pleasures, five of us walked into some nightclub that had piped out good music to the street and placed lots of inviting women at the door. Ice-cold San Miguel was a given. As we stepped through the door, two beauties instantly flew formation under our elbows, and remained all the way to our newly found thrones in paradise.

The bar was a smaller place, segregated into two rooms: one where most of the patrons sat in booths and the other having a few tables facing a fabulous five-piece band. The dark rooms were barely lit with stubby table candles. We could hardly see one another through the smoke and haze. Then, within a nanosecond, the beers arrived. Liberty in the Navy was as it should be that night—women sitting on our laps, cold beers in hand and a great band.

The Filipino musicians were extremely talented. It must be something in their culture or in their genes that allows them to recreate music from a recording. It sounds exactly like that recording, including the vocalist. After I danced a set with the local girls, the band played Simon and Garfunkel's, "The Boxer." I sat back down at our table, but after hearing several of the songs from that dynamic duo, I felt compelled to compliment these musicians for perfectly reproducing the music. These guys were really great.

I approached the lead vocalist and told him how I felt. His reaction, or I should say his non-reaction, took me by surprise. Had I done something wrong? It was as if my praise had fallen on deaf ears; and, in a way, it had. He stood there with a blank look on his face, frozen in place like a wood figurine. I soon realized that the musician was able to imitate the likes of Simon and Garfunkel to the point of perfection, but no one in the band spoke a word of English. I returned to our dark table and told my buddies. We all shrugged it off and laughed, ordering another round of beer. I then asked our waitresses to tell the band how much we appreciated them and how great we thought they played.

Come closing time—as if the bars ever closed in Olongopoe, the dark environment proved advantageous to the Filipinos. We couldn't see well enough to count the local currency. Naturally, there were people there who could help us. I kept track of the costs in my head and when two gentlemen came over with flashlights, I paid in pesos for the amount I believed our bill to be. The two men picked up the money and then pointed their flashlights back into my wallet. The girls encouraged us to give a few more pesos and with the currency exchange rate, it was no big deal.

However, the impatient men with flashlights again jiggled their beams back into my wallet, indicating that they wanted still more money. So there, in the wee hours of the morning, I took the hint. Peering blearily into my wallet, I kept shoveling out more and more money. After my wallet ran dry, a few of the others chipped in with some American money. Our combined efforts made the men with the flashlights smile and disappear into the darkness. We were now free to leave our booth and head for the door. At first I felt a bit ripped off by their payment plan; but once outside, we just laughed it off. After all, we were forewarned to keep our real money hidden and let our wallet money display our limitations. It was a game to be played, so long as the winner didn't take all!

The rest stop allowed everyone, including the crew and the squadron support team, time to stretch their legs, bark at the moon and stock up on San Miguel beer. I can't remember which was the preferred beer, red caps or green caps, but it sure was good beer. For the detachment to Diego Garcia, we carried ten cases of beer on a homemade rack the flight engineers inserted into the bomb bay. The flight engineers then took special care in heating the bomb bay to 34 degrees to ensure the beer did not experience any catastrophic bottle failures.

Our flight to Dodge took twelve hours the next day. A P-3 could make the journey in ten hours if the United States obtained diplomatic clearances to fly over Micronesian and Malaysian airspace. We did not have such clearances and were required to navigate by radar. We transited entirely over water, circumnavigating their airspace by flying directly down the centerline of the straits of Malacca. We had plenty of pilots, a good radar operator and a strong navigator on board. The navigator was the most important player of the day. If he messed up, the crew could conceivably run out of fuel before finding the island in the middle of the Indian Ocean, somewhere past the far side of nowhere.

When we arrived on the island, the British wanted our customs cards and spoke of their rules against glass bottles being brought on the island. As we unloaded our suitcases and gear, the flight engineers opened the bomb bay and were the first to reach in and grab a properly chilled, ice-cold beer for the British inspectors. After a formal ceremony ensued to inspect the shipment for God only knows; the rest of us, and anyone else who happened to be in the area, had a couple beers on the flight line under the wing of the plane. There we stood seven degrees south of the equator, hiding from the hot sun in our long flight suits, boots and an occasional pith helmet, tired from our twelve-hour journey, taking down a cold beer airmailed directly from Cubi Point. Nothing ever tasted better than that. The Brits could be flexible about some things. Thank goodness for small favors as moments like those made the whole journey seem worthwhile. On April 10, 1983, Crew Two arrived in style.

We packed up our belongings and traveled by cab (the cab company was run by Filipino working residents) to the main street of Dodge. The enlisted village housed our personnel in new, clean, freshly painted and well-lit, air-conditioned, open bay barracks. Although the quarters for sleeping were in a common area, they were in great shape.

The officers traveled an additional mile and a-half to the northern end of the west side of the island. On the tip of this point stood the O'Club. The officers' housing was directly to the south of the club. It comprised a village of plywood hooches, each dating back to the mid-1970s. They were raised off of the ground with concrete blocks and had porches made from a double row of stacked blocks that were laid on their sides at the base of their white doors. The designated name of each hooch was stenciled on the doors instead of the expected impersonal numerical address. These names gave each hooch the homey touch of a modern hotel name, much the same as the American POWs gave their cells names in the Hanoi Hilton. Ours was called the "Sistine Chapel." Once inside our hooch, it was easy to understand why that name stuck.

The previous residents of our hooch personalized the building, much the same as people autograph and paint up a plaster cast. Seemingly, each crew painted or inked their immortal testimony to boredom on the ceiling of this hooch. Some were more elaborate than others. The fidelity of the artwork improved as the military population gained better support and a hobby shop opened up at the PX. Eventually, out of boredom, I painted our crew patch on a large section of wall and our navigator emblazoned our names on a white background to the right side of the masterpiece.

The Sistine Chapel at Diego Garcia

The plywood accommodations added a quaint charm and mystique to the entire adventure despite their open bay, bunk bed arrangement. When coupled with sand-covered plywood flooring and windowless container design, this left quite a bit to be desired. Toilets were port-a-pots and the outdoor showers were all we were afforded. A cassette deck did its best to add atmosphere to our hooch with Willy Nelson singing "You were always on my mind," to us homesick sailors. I'm not sure that this lifted our spirits, but our crew leader played it nearly every day.

The island was a plantation at one time. Mangy chickens roamed freely and there were hoards of scrawny house cats left to fend for themselves amongst their visitors. The inner bay was a natural harbor where the Navy allowed us to swim. The dredging of the harbor left the waters clouded with silt and ruined the bottom colors with thick, white coral mud. The ocean surrounded the opposite side of the narrow outline of an island. It boasted finger reefs, clear waters and great beaches. However, after a shark attacked a Filipino swimming at night, the Navy barred us from even wading in the ocean proper.

Two other hooches, occupied by rival VP-88 crews, were across the white gravel street and to the left and right. With Dodge being a place of relaxation and with the O'Club being so near, other crews lapsed toward weight gain. Although I couldn't notice the difference because I was meeting them for the first time, the three senior officers did notice and gave them the nickname "Sky Pigs." In fact, they painted the outside of their hooch with a large squadron symbol with the stenciled notation "Sky Pigs VP-88 CREW1". Each crewmember's name and nickname was listed, and they signed "WAR ON FAT, BS Pardee" beneath. I took pictures of these practical jokers standing in front of their creation in their flight suits. They stood with pillows stuffed in their front sides, cheeks puffed out, and wearing yellow "Sheraton Hotel Djiboutiful" ball caps. It did much to raise a stir, especially since they vilified the skipper's own crew and he had instituted a campaign—actually a minor war—against fat sailors.

The business of Diego Garcia was multifold. The small island served as a harbor for ships and submarines. It was utilized as a repair facility. As a matter of fact, one American submarine made such a port call, anchoring in the harbor directly across from our beach. The island also was equipped with a 12,000-foot runway. This enormous field was utilized for strategic purposes as well as tactical advantage in defense of the Persian Gulf region, Africa, and was a strategic deterrence against the Soviet Union.

Our missions out of Diego Garcia included tactical deterrence, intelligence, reconnaissance, relocation of Soviet Naval assets, antisubmarine warfare, medevac and the showing of the flag. In so doing, seemingly unimportant countries became critical for our operations against the Soviet Navy. Otherwise unheard of places, such as Djibouti, were now valuable landing fields where a plane fueled and launched. They were on station in two hours instead of the five hours required from Diego Garcia, and loitered for eight hours instead of two hours available from Dodge. We recovered broken airplanes there too, instead of requiring them to transit back to the island.

During our time on Diego Garcia, the Soviet Navy utilized Yemen's port of Socotra, an island off of the east African coast. The port fell on the north side of the island and was just big enough to suit their purposes—refueling their ships and providing relaxation for their sailors on the Soviet comfort ships. Soviet surface combatants made use of the facility, as did their submarines. Thus it became a real thorn in the side of the United States Navy to both keep tabs on the port and on the changing positions of the Soviet submarines in the Indian Ocean.

We flew multiple trips from Diego Garcia to the island of Socotra, providing continuous coverage of the port during periods of intense interest. During those times, we worked with a carrier battle group. On one of our inbound legs, we were intercepted by two F-14s. That is an impressive aircraft grounded, but in flight it is downright awesome. The pilots flew their planes seventy-five feet from our window, about twenty-five feet from our wing tip. The aircraft first appeared as if they were just engines floating in space with a long, pointed nose advancing in front. However, the squadron symbols painted on their tails told a tale that meant all business.

We retaliated against their air show by holding up our per diem checks, money which they did not receive, and waved monogrammed hotel towels as if to say "Gee guys, where are you staying tonight?" The pilots inspected our tail number, gave us a few signs of disrespect in return, and then departed while we cruised into the area of interest: Socotra.

In an effort to remain covert for the moment, we kept our radar off and dropped sonobuoys, trying to pick up any acoustic information available from the port. We were too far from the island for that tactic to be effective, especially against engines that were not running. Our binoculars were of no use because of the sea haze and the dust blown out from the desert. The radar operator took a look into the port and found several targets, although nothing discernable. At about that time, our senior pilot had an idea.

Every geographic region of the world has specific frequencies, which are called "common and/or guard frequencies." Over the oceans, ships' common is VHF 123.45. Civil Aviation Guard frequency is VHF 121.5 and American militaries use UHF 243.0, the double of that civil aviation frequency, as its UHF guard frequency. Still others are monitored during high altitude cruise as a common practice. One of the Russian Navy's common frequencies is VHF 126.5.

The plane commander's plan was simple: "Let's see what they're talking about."

Although this plan's primary drawback was the fact that no one on our crew spoke Russian, it mattered little to the overall success of this idea. We dialed in the Russian ship's common frequency and gave it a listen. In about five minutes, we had our "Russian Intelligence" coup for the day— maybe even for the week. Somehow, someone on one of those ships in port got on the radio and sung his drunken heart out, his word-slurring heart out, not letting up on the microphone switch for nearly ten minutes. We laughed until our sides hurt and thought of what the rest of the ship must be like since this man apparently had unrestricted access to the communications room in such a condition. Somehow, the singing Russian made the twelve-hour mission worthwhile.

Our destination airfield was Mogadishu, Somalia, on another mission. In the 1970s, the Soviets were based in Mogadishu. This gave them an airfield and a friendly country to display their presence all too close to the Persian Gulf region. However, as the 1980s came along, the Somali government ejected the Soviets, giving them only a couple of days to leave the country. After they packed up and hastily departed, the Somali leadership invited the United States and its military presence into the country, specifically the airfield at Mogadishu. Socotra sat three flight hours from Mogadishu and this made it a suitable location to conduct our P-3 operations. The tasking from Diego Garcia rotated crews in and out of Somalia in an effort to relocate or find the Soviet vessels and support the American fleet. When our turn came to work out of Somalia, we packed our bags full of shorts, flip-flops, food, water, beer and tee shirts and headed for the plane.

Typically we completed missions into the Arabian Gulf, or a reconnaissance mission at Socotra, before landing at Mogadishu. This greatly extended our on-station time and made for a good day's work. During daytime, landing at the Mogadishu airport presented few problems. We had checkpoints worked out with radar and certain geographic landmarks to find the airfield. It was a visual arrival to the field from there—no sweat. At night, it was a different story.

At night, even though we flew a mission for the United States with a designated arrival time, we had to radio the embassy to ensure the landing lights were operating and to make certain a battery-powered sonobuoy was turned on. We navigated using our radio gear onboard the aircraft and found the sonobuoy located on top of the embassy. From there, we flew a desired track leading us to the airfield.

The night landing was a black hole arrival with very few visual cues. On top of that, the locals grazed their cattle on the few blades of grass adjacent to the runway. Therefore, our first pass over the field came with our landing lights on and positioned low enough to scan the runway and scare off any of our four-legged friends. Once satisfied that the field was relatively safe, our next run was for the landing. Fortunately, this technique worked for all of the crews that flew into Mogadishu. It would be one hell of a place to have an accident, as there were no hospitals, no dedicated fire department, and quite a few potential looters who might care more for your watch than for your well-being.

We parked the aircraft, put on all of its plugs and covers, and departed the field in a medium-sized school bus. The ride to our accommodations took twenty-five minutes to a half-hour. By this time, it was daylight and Mogadishu was already oppressively hot. Strict poverty practically paved the dusty streets with women and children. I waved to them and they waved back and smiled. It seemed the people existed on the sheer will to live and little else.

As we drove along the dusty road I noticed high walls with broken glass embedded in the tops of the concrete. Obviously a security measure, these high walls were everywhere. *If they simply toppled the walls on each side of the road,* I thought, *the streets would be paved instead of being made of dust. That would start their climb out of poverty.* As overly romantic as that thought may seem, this was strictly a city of haves and have-nots. Fortunately, we were part of the haves.

When we arrived at our accommodations, the so-called "Moog House," a guard carrying an AK-47 greeted us and opened the gate. He provided protection for us against the crowds. I felt disadvantaged being unarmed. Once inside the compound, we off-loaded our bags, our food, charcoal, cooking utensils, Budweiser and bottled water.

The house itself was quite large and came with a large, dirt courtyard surrounded by a high, white wall on three sides. A long white building with a shallow corrugated metal roof blocked the fourth side of the yard from the street and its people. An occasional worker or two busied themselves painting the walls inside the compound. On the outside of the house were two verandas, or elevated porches, overlooking a scraped dirt expanse. Several scrubby bushes grew by the far wall. Someone placed a gathering of rocks in a triangle as decoration. Beyond the white wall were two and three-story white houses and an occasional office building.

We entertained ourselves by throwing a frisbee around the courtyard, drinking, cooking burgers on an open fire and playing with the adopted compound dog, "Scoety," who liked our food and water. The little white Scoety charmed everyone with his good manners, pretty tan face, dark brown eyes and pointed ears. The fact that he was so happy reflected how often crews came to the "Moog House."

While it did have electricity and lights, little furniture besides the patio furniture existed. The floors of the two-story building were covered by light brown, nine and twelve-inch tile. Each bedroom was equipped with rickety, metal bunk beds housing four to six people. The bathroom was filthy. In the shower, slimy, moldy green pallets kept our feet off of the floor. When we did shower, we were under orders not to let the water run into our eyes, nose or mouth out of fear of dysentery and infections. Afterwards, we rinsed our faces and ears out with bottled water. Thankfully, we left in thirty-six hours.

The school bus arrived early the next night. We loaded up everything in the back, piled into the front and set off for the airport in the middle of the darkness. We traveled about Mogadishu decked out in our flight suits, our required uniform because part of our mission there was to show the American flag to the local population in place of the Russian hammer and sickle. I didn't give it much thought coming in during the day; so at night, I gave our departure even less concern. Then the driver turned on the interior lights of the bus and paraded his well-lit targets through the streets of this desolate, God-forsaken city. *Oh shit!* We were without any protection inside the bus and if someone with a left over Soviet AK-47 assault rifle ever decided to chase out the Americans, we were primed for disaster. The crew went quiet, contemplating the collective sense of our circumstances.

We traveled through the poorly lit streets and I noticed crowds of people circling around the occasional streetlight, watching swarms of large insects aimlessly flying about the blue light in maddening white cascades. I thought, *In life we imitate ourselves; in so many ways, imitation is the sincerest form of flattery.* Here, under the darkened sky, interrupted by the bright blue glow of a mercury bulb, the question became *Who imitated who?* Both the people and the insects were attracted to the bright blue lights against the blackened sky. Both the people and the insects swarmed under and around its glow, aimlessly milling about for the entertainment of its illumination. Yet, what did it reveal? I withdrew into my thoughts. *The insects were closer to their purpose on earth than the people; they were more in tune with the fulfillment of their lives as they were so created than were the people, caught inside the furious afterglow of struggle between the Soviet Union and the United States of America. The insects called the street their home without the pain of extreme poverty. The insects flew over the high walls at will, not burdened by the broken glass, immune to the dust, and hidden from the heat of the day in their habitat. The people were trapped to the dusty ground of their plight; and no matter how hard they tried, they were denied their flight from their habitat and left only to form rings of mankind under the blue mercury light at night and watch those who can fly on by, just like our crew did now.*

We drove down the main street and passed these scenes at every street corner with a lamppost. Finally, the driver turned onto the pitch-black road that led to the airport and I saw no more of them. Every one of them could see us. In that setting, I became even more concerned for my own safety. Crewmembers, each in our own way, realized that we were completely defenseless. Our position was illuminated and we could not see any of what went down around us. Fortunately, we never encountered resistance to our visiting Mogadishu, Somalia.

During our three hour preflight, I performed yet another grenade-check on the exterior of the airplane. The plane sat unguarded for over twenty-four hours. Could you trust anything without your own security? No one had an answer to that question, certainly not I.

We tried to depart from Somalia on time, but for some unknown reason, the number two prop's electronic control system burned some wires. The electrical side of its complexities therefore could not function and the airplane was hard down. There was no way around that one and we all knew it. We were stuck without enough provisions and water to carry us through a maintenance evolution from Diego Garcia.

Our flight engineers, who doubled as our mechanics, headed over to the Italian Air Force as the night turned into dawn and asked for tools and some assistance. The Italians were our allies, of course, and were eager to help. Through a simple barter system, we traded our remaining fresh fruit for one of their wiring harnesses. We knew that our flight would not involve a mission. Once back at a maintenance facility, we could replace the impromptu loaner parts with new ones.

It all worked out fine until the engine's maintenance run burned up more wiring and the Italians were fresh out of parts. Fortunately, when the Soviets departed Somalia, they didn't have time to repair two helicopters that were sitting one hundred fifty yards away from our airplane.

Someone came up with the idea, "Well, parts are parts."

With that being said, our two flight engineers walked down to the Soviet helicopters and scavenged more wiring for the repairs. In every other location, a simple light bulb failure in the wrong system would ground a plane—but not here. It is simply amazing what we did to get out of Mogadishu, Somalia. Being part of that crew, I certainly shared their motivations.

Once satisfied with the airplane, our "Mogadishu special," we taxied the aircraft the full length of the runway, performing a safety sweep for animals. With wing tanks full of fuel, a high-speed collision at the short end of the runway would bring a fiery end to us all. Each of us knew, but none of us ever talked about how the animals were able to walk right back onto that runway beyond the edge of our ability to stop. At lift-off, I breathed a sigh of relief, as getting out of Somalia eased both my mind and my spirit. Because I had little sleep during the previous day, I remember the mission as a head-nodding bruiser.

That proved to be my last trip from the East African coast. The night mission turned into a day mission and as we headed east, it slowly reverted back to night at Dodge. Our navigator shot star fixes with his sextant for our guidance. When we finally arrived at the hooches, we dropped our bags of dirty gear, threw off our sweat drenched, greasy clothes and one by one headed for the outdoor showers.

It was while standing there in the dark of the night, that I realized the luxury of our "Sistine Chapel" and appreciated the simple beauty of the tropical island of Diego Garcia. Under those southern stars, I envisioned myself for the first time as just a man along side the indigenous peoples of the lands we frequented. I wanted to get back into the warmth of that humanity and fly out of the hard, cold steel of the past two years. Alone with my thoughts I asked myself, *How do I make a big red heart fit inside a small green flight suit?* In the military, compassion and sympathy are forbidden signs of weakness while anger and aggression come praised as strengths. To go against the flow meant certain ridicule and open attack. Yet I wondered when, if ever, my seniors discard the burden of "buying the program" and see others as themselves: human beings with real needs, emotions and pain? I slept without answers apparent, my journeys left me too exhausted for the struggle.

Being "home" again was a real eye opener. I awoke in the morning to the gentle mewing of kittens under our hooch and the crowing of a distant rooster and I realized I could no longer think only in terms of the mission and the machines. I had to deal with the impoverished peoples we visited. However, the question in my life became how to hide the sympathy of my heart. It would be seen as a weakness among my peers, leaving me vulnerable. I never found an answer to this question. That morning contained a new dawn.

After returning from Mogadishu, our crew stood many ready-one alerts, watches that required us to preflight the airplane and then go immediately into crew rest to be able to fly twelve-hour missions at a moment's notice. The Navy wanted to have a crew airborne within one hour of notification at any time, day or night. At first this seemed like gravy, with five hours of work followed by crew rest. However, boredom slips in and being on a one-hour leash is no fun, especially within the close quarters of the hooch, even with the beach in front of you.

To combat boredom, I dedicated many days to painting our contribution to the Sistine Chapel: the perfect Crew Two symbol, the Australian flag with a beer mug. That is, I worked at perfecting it until our senior officer decided that it no longer boosted morale. Rather, he found it a waste of time. According to him, while in ASWOC and at the hangar, our real efforts should be directed toward performing nonexistent ground jobs, showing someone that we were really part of the Navy Team and not a bunch of freeloading air-dales. Perhaps I was mistaken, but I thought this was ridiculous and counterproductive. The system worked fine without us working eight days a week; you can't fix what isn't broken.

This concept of our eight tactical crewmembers needlessly interfacing for hours on end, "staying current," seemed particularly absurd to me because the ASWOC had very little need for all of us groveling through their workspaces. Once there, what could be done in a fifteen-minute brief took all morning. I lost respect for the organizational style and its implementation because of this so-called "face time." On top of it all, there was just one Soviet submarine in the entire Indian Ocean to worry about, with the remote possibility of another coming from Cam Ranh Bay, 2,500 miles away. *So where is the war?* I asked myself. There we sat, gaining face time for days until the ASWOC threw out the junior officers. Even then, our "Fearless Leader" came home mad because we were not in the ASWOC showing face. On the opposite days from alert, we flew "bounce hops" and I think that made Fearless Leader even madder through sheer jealousy of our required non-productivity. But, hey, we were pilots and pilots required training and proficiency flights, despite what anyone else might think.

When we did launch tactically, one of our missions in the Indian Ocean included a top-secret rendezvous with an American attack submarine. On that particular mission, the Navy failed to inform us about the elevated classification, but we didn't talk about mission particulars in the first place. However, approximately six months after flying the mission, and back in the U.S., the squadron security officer came around. He required all of us to sign a non-disclosure statement for a mission we flew together. Yet, he could not tell us which mission we were signing for, why we were signing for it, or any other detail other than the fact that it took place with our crew somewhere over the Indian Ocean. I didn't argue with this bit of Naval Intelligence. "Clam up, sign up, put up and don't look back." At least I thought I knew which mission we weren't allowed to think about.

Another mission included the photoreconnaissance of all targets within five hundred miles of the island. There were two primary targets of concern. First were the merchant marine ships, bringing Diego Garcia supplies. Second, were the rich vacationers on their yachts, tied up in the shallows of the northern atolls, displaying all for our pleasure and enjoyment. Many of these boats had wind generators to power their batteries without a diesel generator. I thought that to be the top of the game, even as I flew a thirty million-dollar aircraft, with the U.S. government buying the gas. The grass is always greener on the other side of the hill.

We also launched on a medevac mission to Cubi Point, Republic of the Philippines. One of the Filipino contract workers literally ate a bad egg. The Filipino ingested an egg that he previously buried in the sand for several weeks, a traditional Philippine delicacy called a "baloot". However, something went terribly wrong. I felt so sorry for the poor fellow being carried up the stairs to the airplane. His stomach was the size of a basketball and he cried out with severe pain. A doctor and two corpsmen attended the patient, while we flew the ten-hour mission restricted to ten thousand feet, where the air is choppy and rough. This was necessary in order to maintain sea level air pressure inside the cabin and not further aggravate the patient's swelling by a higher cabin altitude. Diego Garcia is not a place to get violently ill!

By the time we arrived in Cubi, the patient had improved and the junior officers (J.O.s) felt good about our mission. However, our senior officer questioned the need for the evacuation, as if he, too, went to medical school, or that a doctor's diagnosis and medical opinion would be more valuable had our patient worsened or died in flight. At least he could have measured the contract requirements between the governments involved and the good will derived from the mission. It seemed that using a war bird for a humanitarian relief mission, a medical emergency no less, was wrong in his eyes. I just shook my head in disbelief at his making a sow's ear out of a silk purse. What did he know except that he wasn't interfacing in the ASWOC?

On a brighter note, our return to Cubi gave the J.O.s an opportunity to restock our supply of San Miguel, along with a full night on the town in Olongopoe. We returned to Dodge with yet another bomb bay full of ice-cold beer.

But all good things must come to an end; and so, too, did our detachment to Diego Garcia. On May 23, Crew Two departed the "Foot Print of Freedom" for Patia Beach, Thailand, on a boondoggle our maintenance officer finagled out of the command. This particular escapade let us all experience the beauty and charm of Southeast Asia's countryside. We stopped at a shrine for our cruise book crew photo and made two additional beer stops before reaching the hotel. After all, no one wanted to drink warm beer and the driver knew the storeowners—most likely his family, so everyone benefited from the stretching of our legs.

Once in the hotel, there was the traditional crew cocktail party, massage tables, foamy baths for those so inclined, and room 222 for the foolish. I stayed with the massage table and left it at that. The shopping included gemstones, rings, and gold and silver bot chains. The precious metals were of high quality; but, with an Ensign's salary, I only purchased a small silver bot chain necklace.

We departed for Kadena the following day with a technical stop in Cubi Point. The senior officer wanted to make it as brief as possible, but the plane commander made it my job to take back as much beer to the squadron as possible. The job was no small undertaking. I knew everyone was on board with the plane commander's idea and that all would be copasetic with this spirited shenanigan. After all, it wasn't a secret and not one out of twenty-three people objected to having a few more cases of San Miguel for the squadron picnic. So, after fifteen minutes on the ground in Cubi, I departed the airplane with a half-dozen cases of empty beer bottles. My next destination was the base class six store, via the on-base taxi drivers.

I managed to fill three grocery carts with bottled beer. Then I slowly made my way through the night back to the taxi. Thankfully the taxi was a van.

At the taxi-van, one of the carts slipped out of my control, rolling down the slope of the hill and off the curb, spilling its contents everywhere. Several bottles broke and others foamed past their caps, leaving a sticky residue behind.

When I arrived at the airplane, more trouble ensued as the senior officer was pissed. Customs arrived at the plane while I was gone. The Air Force customs agents looked for me and no one knew exactly how to explain my absence. (Like it or not, the senior officer was fully aware and in on the deal from the get-go.) I suppose there is nothing like an O-4 covering for an Ensign, except for a possible customs violation. The senior chewed my ass, but I completed "the mission" and the fifteen cases of beer made it onto the aircraft tucked under our suitcases, sea bags and maintenance equipment.

"Just trying to please the plane commander, sir."

We arrived in Kadena an hour behind schedule but who cared? Even Skipper Pardee greeted the aircraft and crew with warm enthusiasm. We enjoyed good success in the Indian Ocean and our crew even completed a top-secret mission, interacting with a U.S. submarine.

Shortly thereafter, disaster loomed as the skipper stood at the bottom of the stairs, pressing the flesh with the passengers and crew. The U.S. Air Force customs personnel came aboard for our paperwork and ran a dog searching for drugs through the airplane. Everyone else vacated the plane and I was in charge of clearing customs with the Air Force. *Great, how do I out-bluff this one?*

The senior airmen sat down with me at the rest area table. Together we scoured the stack of documents. Fortunately, all of the paperwork appeared to be in order. That made my life a whole lot easier. The other airman led the dog up the aisle of the aircraft, past the hidden beer, and that made my life a whole lot harder.

This second gentleman had a difficult time handling the animal because, as any dog owner can attest, dogs like beer and this one was no exception. The German Shepherd followed his master's lead up and down, back and forth, all the way to the flight station. Unfortunately, the dog kept returning to our stack of bags, under which the fifteen cases of smuggled San Miguel beer were hiding. This made me sweat blood, but I couldn't show it, not then, in front of the inspectors.

Admittedly, trying to smuggle beer into Japan is a foolish prank, when all the Okinawa officials really wanted was the courtesy of a declaration to their judge, a deep bow, and a small duty paid as a gentleman. However, somehow that made the beer taste bad. So the game became one of hide-and-seek played against one tough dog. Fortunately, the dog was well trained and did not sit down in front of any one bag, indicating a drug alert. He merely kept his nose in front of them. If the dog had it his way, he would have stood there all night, inhaling the delicious spilled beer aroma, maybe even getting one or two for the road.

In the meantime, the skipper stood at the base of the air-stairs in conversation with the plane commander, saying, "Gee, during this deployment, we have had our bumps along the way, but fortunately customs has never been a problem."

"Oh, yes sir. We want to keep it that way, sir."

I diverted the customs personnel away from the stack of bags by demonstrating the computer bay doors, the storage racks, and the various nooks and crannies throughout the aircraft. However, unless he was literally dragged away by his trainer, the German Shepherd never strayed from our bags.

Finally, the senior customs official said, "Well, this just about wraps things up. We were hoping not to repeat last week's incident with the C-141 crew."

"Oh, what happened?"

"We caught them with too much beer on board the cargo transport. They had it stuffed behind the insulation and under any seat that wasn't glued down."

"What a shame. You know, now that you mention it, we have about fifteen cans of assorted beers in a cooler in the back. Here, let me show you."

With those select words, I went over and lifted the cooler lid, demonstrating my good will and full cooperation.

"Oh, no, that's OK, we aren't concerned about that. We are really after crews that are bringing in a dozen or so cases of beer. That is our big bust."

"Oh no, not us. We like things nice and quiet around here."

"Alright! Let's go some place where we can finish the paperwork and get off of your airplane. It all seems so easy."

With that being said, I opened the door, saluted the skipper and the plane commander, still standing at the bottom of the stairs, who smiled a nervous smile and showed the two off of the plane. The first customs officer walked backwards down the stairs, while the second carried the animal because the German Shepherd was afraid of heights. Someone was needed to keep the dog from even thinking about falling. Personally, right about then, I would have liked to trip the animal out of sheer revenge. Instead, I followed them back to their car where they caged the animal, and then invited them to my office in the hangar.

When we were safely inside my office, I closed the door, allowing the senior enlisted fellow to sit at my desk and complete his paperwork, stamps and signatures. As I busied them in the office, the skipper, satisfied with the smooth inspection, departed for bed. The rest of the crew heaved a big sigh of relief.

"Gee, I wish all of our inspections went as smoothly as this did. You guys are great," the customs officer said to me.

"Well, we aim to please."

With that, I spent a few more minutes reviewing every detail with the men and showing a genuine interest in their jobs—a smokescreen by any other name, but it worked. Whew, what a relief!

While I snowed them in the office, the rest of the crew formed a fire brigade, passing the fifteen cases of beer down the air stairs and into a waiting pickup truck. It sped off into the night. To this day, I have no idea where the chief petty officers hid the beer. I was one popular Ensign at the squadron picnic.

There ended the fun half of the deployment. The second half of the six-month cycle was difficult. It was punctuated by the loss of two aircraft by a sister squadron in Hawaii. We heard the rumor of a gear-up landing in Hawaii only to have our fears acknowledged by our own command. Then Skipper Pardee met me at the bottom of the air stairs one night.

"Neal, you don't think any of *our* pilots could make a gear-up landing, do you?"

I paused for a minute. "Yes sir, I think it is possible for anyone, including our pilots, to land a plane gear-up."

With that, he just smiled a wry smile that made me wonder what he was thinking. To be honest, I didn't know what to think about the guy; I couldn't read him. Skipper must have been a good poker player. Was it an open question or a probe? I will never know.

Two weeks later, my plane commander stood on board the aircraft and during a planeside brief, he lowered the boom. The ASWOC confirmed the loss of another plane from the same squadron. It exploded into the side of a mountain on the island of Kauai, just west of Oahu. There were no survivors, just the beginnings of a long investigation. We were all stunned and it made for a very long evening of flying. Many were friends and acquaintances. Everyone on the airplane took the news of the losses personally, especially knowing it could happen to us.

The accident with its large loss of life created great cause for concern in the entire P-3 community. We waited many months for the accident report and the longer we waited, the more people speculated that the new radar system they employed might not depict terrain properly. I received only briefings from the classified document and never read any of it personally. But in short, the terrain was charted, the radar functioned properly and a tactical aid to navigation radio station (tacan) operated just a few miles away. The real culprit, respect for the obstacle, was absent by all crewmembers. As Staff Sergeant Black said, "They paid for their transgressions." They paid all right, with the high price of their lives.

During the investigation, I learned of the deaths of three of my former shipmates. The anguish became intensely personal. It knotted my stomach whenever I thought of them and I knew I would never be the same again. In their memory, I vowed to never let go of a navigational fix. Understanding my position over the earth became a heartfelt, professional priority. I still pursue this with passion.

My peers have often seen my passion in aviation; but they have never understood, until I explained the reason behind its intensity. This accident and the needless loss of life is the source of my passion with all of its intensity. I never let it go, nor will I ever do so. I operate in this manner. It is my sincerest, final salute to honor my lost friends in the spirit of Naval Aviation.

This place is dead.

CHAPTER TEN

Twenty years after our small homecoming from the Kadena deployment, NAS Moffett Field called to me for a different reason. I was drawn to go back, it was time to share my history and remember the past with Ginger, the love of my life. I didn't anticipate how this journey would impact me. What followed came as a twisted surprise, not from old familiar surroundings but from memories within.

Ginger and I vacationed with her family in the summer of 2003, near Half Moon Bay in northern California. Ginger insisted that we visit San Francisco. Happily, I found my old local haunt, the Buena Vista on Fisherman's Wharf; where, as ensigns, we had worn our whites in the bar and were treated like royalty. Sadly, only the Buena Vista resisted the unbridled growth that swamped the rest of the city. I mentioned my prior visits and observations to the bartender. He gave me a free drink and thanked me for remembering those days gone by.

We toured the San Francisco Bay area the following day. That morning we drove south through the city and picked up the woodlands of Skyline Drive. The winding road took us to Mountain View and Sunnyvale, which was the home of my military service at NAS Moffett Field.

When we approached the front gate just before noon, the new reality of September 11th greeted us with security barriers and car searches. Gone were the traditional Marine sentries, now replaced by civilian security guards earning extra pay on top of their retirements. After fifteen minutes of checking our trunk, the undercarriage and my paperwork, we proceeded through the gate and drove the boulevard surrounding the parade grounds that led to the silver and black Hangar One.

On the right, we passed the Bachelor Officer Quarters where I stayed in 1982 and met Commander Bark. The sight gave me the heartfelt desire to look him up just to say hello and brighten his day. He lived within a few miles in Cupertino, but our time that day was so limited that it wasn't possible to make that connection. The enormous redwood trees of Big Basin State Park, Santa Cruz, and a sunset drive on the Pacific shores of Highway One still beckoned us.

Ginger thought the golden adobe structures of the base were pretty. I pointed out a few sights as we drove past the tall flagpole standing in front of what once was the Commodore's office. On the left was a vacant structure that had served as the Officer's Club. Farther along the drive, we found the small commissary or base grocery store. Directly in front of us stood Hangar One. From inside our car, it was taller than the eye could see.

During our short drive I noticed the distinct lack of activity. Gone was the hustle and bustle of the nine fleet squadrons stationed there during the 1980's. The noise of their ever-turning propellers gave way to silence. NAS Moffett Field seemed a military cemetery of sorts.

We turned left, driving parallel to the giant hangar, and stopped at the three-way intersection. The tree-lined road to the left led to the NASA Ames Research Center, where engineers proved the space shuttle's design in the enormous wind tunnels. To the right, the perimeter road wound through a collection of buildings and past a fire station, looping around the runways to the golf course and the other two dirigible hangars.

We turned right and took another immediate right into a large parking lot shaded by the cold steel of the Navy hangar. Rust usurped the black painted top and streaked the silver sides of the structure.

I parked the car, withdrawn into my thoughts and feelings, unable to tell Ginger how disappointed I was. We stepped out and walked down the flight line adjacent the east side of the hangar. My instincts pulled at me as we traveled on the sunny side of the hangar and toward an obscure doorway, where I thought we would enter the large structure. Although I didn't realize it at the time, that wasn't what really drew me there. My senses brought me to that door, but for reasons other than a tour of a vacant building or a walk in the sunshine. With Ginger as my sounding board, I was forced to a confrontation with my past.

The door was padlocked closed and warning signs stood on posts behind its windows. The State of California had found dozens of carcinogenic chemicals inside the old hangar. As we stood next to the enormous hangar, I said, "This place is dead."

Hangar One from across an empty NAS Moffett Field

Turning to Ginger, I continued, "Back then, nobody cared about those chemicals, cancer and people. Twenty years ago, the entire ramp area here was full of P-3 aircraft, maybe twenty of them, with another five in the hangar. Across the field were another six squadrons with nine planes apiece and three more were always on deployment. The Navy: that's all we were ever told to care about, our naval careers and nothing more."

We walked south with the sunshine on our faces, in between the eastern side of the off-limits hangar and the empty flight line. The yellow painted warning lines boxed us into a small corridor. I remembered how I learned to taxi the P-3 on that flight line. Now those lines were faded and peeled back, taken away by the elements.

Empty concrete pads stretched for hundreds of yards, northwest towards the San Francisco Bay and southeast in repetitive squares, stopping just short of the perimeter road. Acres of land now sat vacant and covered over with concrete for no apparent reason. I perceived this as a series of large tombstones lying on their sides.

Ginger turned to me there.

"Neal, after all of these years, why do you say that you couldn't care? What do you mean by saying that you can't care about anything more? Life is full of caring, giving and sharing."

With the warm sunshine on my face and the corrugated steel building behind me, I took a breath and began a long story.

"Twenty years ago, we just got home from a six-month deployment to Okinawa and beyond. Personally, I had been as far away from home as Somalia, to what became known as "Black Hawk Down" country.

"All of us were anxious to get away from the squadron and go home for a couple of weeks to be with our families. The last thing any of my shipmates or I wanted to see was the inside of those green hangars across the field. For myself, I needed two things: my own bed and a motorcycle. I wanted to see California on a BMW motorcycle and let my head air out from the intensity of our six-month deployment.

"Our skipper had other ideas. He wanted to impress his boss at Wing 10. We called it *Brand X* for its roman numeral sign."

"Everyone wants to impress their boss, Neal. Why should he be any different?"

"Ginger, it was bad, really bad. Two years of murderous infighting and it all started twenty years ago with our return to Moffett Field. In less than a year, I developed my own mantra. *I never learned how to hate until I came to VP-88.* I made a promise to myself that I would never own a hand gun so long as I was in that squadron!"

Ginger stopped in her tracks, knowing I struck taut chords. Our visit to NAS Moffett Field now served many purposes. We just discovered its primary objective: to begin a healing process for injuries received twenty years before. My hidden and painful wounds had reopened by the familiar ground I treaded.

With Ginger at my side, I discovered that the very sight of this duty station lanced scars as painful as fresh, open flesh. She knew in an instant that this was my time. With her help, I was able to confront the ghosts of my Moffett, to rinse and remove the salt water from my open wounds and to begin anew.

We turned around and walked back to the car parked at the north end of what once was the RAG. The warm sun felt good on our backs as the cool San Francisco Bay breeze gently kissed our faces. I knew I would try Ginger's endless patience with the catharsis of my stories. I pressed on, knowing that she cared, trusting her and loving her love for me.

"My crew was the last crew to leave the island of Okinawa. Watching everyone else depart for our California homeland made me all the more homesick. When we finally launched on our long transit home, it wasn't a moment too soon. We flew to Hawaii for our rest stop and to clear customs before landing here at Moffett. After all, wives and friends awaited our return. To delay our people at the bottom of the stairs while customs' officials searched our baggage would create conflict.

"The next day, we departed Naval Air Station Barbers Point, Hawaii, late in the evening and flew east toward the California mainland. Our seven-hour journey landed us here at NAS Moffett in the morning. We gained three hours from the shifting of the time zones. I remember flying through the night, watching the dawn break through the clouds. We were tired to the bone, but the feeling of the new day came with heartfelt thanks to be going home to America.

"At the same time, I made out the tall, Sierra Nevada mountain range three hundred miles from our position. The peaks first appeared as if they were clouds, but their majestic strength lingered while others changed and I knew I was looking at my homeland. Everyone who could fit into the large flight station looked out at our first view of America. The sun kept the mountains in silhouette and the cockpit grew silent but for the constant noise of the four, large turboprops droning on into the morning light.

"We switched the radios over to Oakland Center's long-range frequency and it was like speaking to an old familiar friend whose voice was long overdue. From there, our next welcoming came when Oakland's radar vectors gave us a shortcut to Hooks Intersection, the initial approach fix for the airport," I said, pointing south over the Santa Cruz Mountains.

"Crossing Monterey Bay gave us a good view of both Santa Cruz and of the coastal city of Monterey. The sight boasted of everything that was good in America: the bay hugged our airplane with the Santa Cruz Mountains, the sandy half-moon coastline, and the craggy coast stretching to Big Sur. After that we cleared the flight station and prepared for landing on the far runway over there," I motioned to the spot, "—runway 32—right. It gave us a short taxi to our parking in front of hangar three."

Once back in the car, we drove around the long loop of the base. We headed south toward the base operations building and a P-3 that stood on static display. I stopped to show my former airplane to Ginger. After taking a walk around the airplane, we stood under the right wing and gazed at its two enormous propellers. Moments later, a smile cracked my face and I laughed.

"Now I understand why you like things so quiet!" she said.

Hugging her, I tried to convey my appreciation of her perceptiveness. As we embraced, Navy jets landed. Their high-pitched engines shrieked as they taxied onto the nearby tarmac. It was indeed time to depart for quieter spaces.

We stopped short of the car and I pointed past the jets, across the field.

"That's where I'll take us next, hangar three. Once, it was also a dirigible hangar, built as an enormous wooden arch with that green copper roof. It stands together in parallel with hangar two on the eastern side of the station."

Taking a left-hand turn, we departed the display parking lot. I remembered a different time as I drove the perimeter road with a heavy heart.

"That day we landed at Moffett homecoming, the wives and children of the married guys were waiting for the plane to arrive. After six long months, they stood patiently in the doorway of the enormous wooden hangar. They were so anxious to see their loved ones. As the props spooled down, they approached the airplane, forming a semicircle.

The Commanding Officer, Fogg, led the passengers and crew down the stairs to the families. I was the last one off and standing on American soil never felt better. I thought, *Let our long overdue vacation begin!*

"Our plans were interrupted when Commander Fogg deleted and virtually destroyed our traditional post deployment vacations. Instead, the squadron stood extra ready alerts, backing up the squadron already standing the one-hour ready alert. On top of this "ready posturing," one Friday afternoon after a flight, I heard scuttlebutt about 'cots in the hangar.' Evidently the skipper ordered cots brought over from the other side of the field. He wanted his men to sleep on the hangar deck instead of at home in their own beds!"

"Neal, that's terrible!" Ginger was shocked to anger.

"Fortunately, the Captain of the Wing performed his Friday afternoon tour of the hangar decks and saw it shaping up. He put a timely end to the idea of our crews spending the night on the hangar deck just days after a six-month deployment, instead of being at home with their wives and family. He may have influenced Fogg into finally giving us ten days of vacation, too. But I don't know how that came down.

"Skipper Fogg's hangar-overnight and vacation snafu set the stage for one of the most bizarre requests from any Commanding Officer. Commander Fogg went outside the squadron and enlisted a survey team to take a survey of the morale of his sailors. It came back so black that one member of the survey team said that she 'was surprised there had not been a mutiny among the officers.'

"Unfortunately, her assumption was incorrect. One Lieutenant had quit mustering at the squadron within the previous year, nine months prior to the survey. Yet the survey changed nothing and the squadron battered on, carrying morale in a bucket. The first joke on the hangar deck was, 'Two more working days till Monday.' The other joke was, 'The floggings will continue until morale improves.' Both were very true.

"That autumn, even more bad news came to us from outside the squadron. It was handed down from Wing 10. Somewhere, somebody with clout and stars to back every word decided that the deployment sites needed expansion. This included Diego Garcia and Adak, Alaska. These two islands became full-time deployment sites instead of detachment facilities. At first, this seemed exciting. More deployment meant more flying. However, implementation of this policy became an absolute nightmare."

Ginger listened patiently, paying attention to my words with the gentle kindness of an angel. Her compassion allowed me to continue. I gained heartfelt relief knowing that someone outside the squadron finally listened to the musings of this man. This journey shaped up as some kind of car ride!

"After our first month back in America, the only constant left unshaken became Monday mornings, when the command held the All Officers Meeting, or AOM, at eight o'clock sharp. All of the senior officers spoke and like clockwork, by a quarter to nine, the operations officer always stood up to say: 'What is the bottom line? Be flexible as flexibility is the key.' This expression just about made me ill but it was standard issue, boilerplate language code words for being out of control.

Sometimes, all I could do was shake my head in dismay at it all and silently question the madness.

"Then five minutes later, like clockwork, Commander Fogg stood and addressed the group. Ginger, I know this seems insignificant, but the squadron had just returned from the Pacific and we were laden down with cameras, stereos and inexpensive electronic alarm wristwatches. Everyone now wore watches that beeped on the hour, every hour, unless the wearer deselected this feature. Because no one ever read the owner's manual for a simple watch, every time the commanding officer spoke a chorus of beeps interrupted his monologue.

"These small interruptions annoyed the skipper. He always stopped and asked, 'Is it my turn to stop talking? Is it my turn to sit down?' No one ever answered those questions. This scene replayed for several weeks and I left my watch in my desk for my own safekeeping. At least, I could claim that I didn't even wear a watch. At the AOM, I would be safe in the area of wristwatches."

I shook my head thinking back on my naiveté.

"Wrong! Enter Doc Pale, the squadron's very own flight surgeon. Doc Pale was a great guy with a bit too much money and far too many hours of liberty on deployment. He also was a gadget freak who acquired every last gizmo sold on Okinawa. The Doc was a real pro at this, too. His watch had to be the watch to beat all watches. The damn thing practically flew all by itself. He used it for everything—from scuba diving to health care, athletics to his alarm clock.

"Unfortunately, the good doctor set this miniature football field of black plastic and battery for his Sunday morning alarm clock, nine o'clock sharp. On the following Monday, Doc Pale interrupted Commander Fogg's recital with his nuclear powered wrist alarm. All I could think was, *Oh shit!*

"Our own personal H-hour began in full. The skipper stopped mid-sentence, dead in his tracks, while everyone looked around for this virtual orchestra of electronic sirens. Out of sheer fear I even looked at my own naked wrist! Fifteen seconds later, Doc Pale discovered he was the culprit. The skipper turned beet red. He didn't even ask his usual two questions. Rather, he threw out the entire squadron of junior officers from the wardroom and the meeting continued for hours with only the senior officers present. We returned to our shops in shock and dismay, scared of what more would follow. For all of us, *the shit had hit the fan.* From that day forward, life was spent mopping up messes instead of enhancing the capabilities of the team. As a junior officer, I wasn't briefed about the Skipper's two-hour plus extemporaneous savagery. However, from that day forward, attention to detail meant micromanaging minutia."

My story entertained Ginger and she asked for another one. I tried my best to mix it up as every cloud has a silver lining. I slowed down our traveling speed to relax and take a drink of water as we drove along the south fence road. I noticed the new rail line just past the fence. The migrant farm workers no longer tended onions in the fields along the edges of the runways as they did twenty years before. Nor were there planes in the landing pattern. NAS Moffett seemed so quiet; I took pause noticing all the things that were missing. *Why were they that significant then?* I wondered. *Why was everything significant then?*

"Fogg's biggest crime was his battle cry: 'Compete!' He pitted his men against one another like a cockfight. We lived, worked and flew in close quarters, and competition for the sake of career survival became the status quo. Fogg led the squadron away from the team concept and into a Darwin society—the Jurassic Age."

Ginger and I turned the far corner of the perimeter and headed north towards my old squadron hangar.

"Our post deployment training cycle lost eight months, reduced from eighteen months, to just ten months. However, the number of inspections, qualifications and evaluations remained the same. In other words, we were inspected, qualified and evaluated the same number of times in ten months as we were when our training cycle lasted eighteen months previously.

"For the eleven crews, the qualifications were a seemingly endless series of hoops to jump through. We flew flight training simulators, training flights, submarine tracking, photoreconnaissance of shipping, mine laying and torpedo attacks, to name a few. Additionally, there were three corrosion inspections, qualification boards for each crew member, one instrument proficiency flight exam, and an open-book test and a closed-book test for each of two NATOPS flight exams."

I took another drink of water before continuing.

"The granddaddy, son-of-a-bitch of them all, was the dreaded NTPI."

"What's an NTPI?" she asked.

"Well, the TPI stood for Technical Proficiency Inspection and I can't tell you the rest."

Out of the corner of my eye, I noticed Ginger staring out her side window into the distance. I knew I was overbearing but I kept talking as I had a captive, but sympathetic audience.

"Worst of all, was the fact that most of this occurred on an unscheduled basis and we were left without a monthly, or even a weekly plan for our daily events. Asset availability dictated tactical qualifications, and of course, that quite literally came on a catch-as-catch-can basis. Our long range plans and assignments were subject to constant interruptions and oftentimes the *plan of the day* was issued by the Operations Department at seven o'clock or later in the evening, after most people were already home. Calling the duty office became a lifeline. All too often I learned of a five A.M. briefing at eight o'clock in the evening. This left me the choice to study more or sleep less, an aggravating situation, especially for those in relationships."

We turned left onto a small road that passed several nondescript, white portable buildings. These were all that was left of the major land-based, antisubmarine warfare center of the west coast. Hangar One now stood in the distance. Hangars Two and Three were both off to our right, their massive concrete doors closed tightly shut. The squadron insignia's faded paint still clung to the faces of the flat door supports. I stopped at a small cable gate and turned the car around.

We then parked in a small lot a hundred yards behind the cable. I asked the two Air Guard's enlisted personnel, "How do we get into the hangar? I just want to show my girlfriend the insides of where I used to work."

The two Guardsmen pointed us back down the road to the cable gate.

"Park here and your identification card will get you inside the building," one of them said.

After thanking the gentlemen, we strolled holding hands under the bright California sunshine, and made our way towards the hangar.

Hangar Two. An identical Hangar Three stands to the immediate right of Hangar Two.

"Ginger, on top of all of this—as if we had nothing else to do, the squadron sent four of our nine airplanes to the Jacksonville Naval Air Rework Facility for major overhauls. The Command then accepted two hangar queens from the RAG and gave orders to return them to flying status. We were even expected to return them to antisubmarine-capable aircraft, if possible…planes that arrived in non-flying status!

"I couldn't understand why the skipper placed the bar so high for our maintenance personnel. I realized, with fewer airplanes to maintain, our staff would be available. I balanced that with our training cycle, reduced by eight out of eighteen months, which appeared to be fair. However, as a junior officer afforded little respect, my logic never made it past my lips except with other junior officers. Our Commanding Officer's arm was filled with helium and he joyfully volunteered us to repair two hangar queens, two old airframes used for spare parts, both at the same a time.

"Overtime? No problem. More often than not, at quarters on Friday afternoons we were told to plan for a 'working weekend.' That was a policy for surges, flaps of flying against an important submarine target, not routine operations. Under our given conditions, it translated into never being able to accomplish the task. There was no reward for reaching a goal and everyone simply slowed down."

As Ginger and I approached the gate, several other National Guard personnel walked toward us from the hangar.

"Sir, this is a restricted area. May I see your badge," the senior enlisted said.

"I don't have a badge, only my reserve ID card. I was hoping I could show my girlfriend the inside of hangar three. I used to work here back in the early eighties. It's a trip down memory lane, so to speak. Can we get over there?"

The sergeant looked a bit more serious but remained polite.

"No sir, I must ask that you vacate the premises. These are secure grounds. You're not supposed to be walking here."

"I won't bother to ask why," I said, turning to Ginger.

She understood. The times had changed. Our simple desire to view the inside of a seventy-year-old wooden building was not allowed after the September 11th disaster.

"Everything is even more paranoid now than it was then," I remarked, returning to the car with Ginger.

"What do you mean by that? Neal, things are in the past."

"I know, but out of all of this, that was the one thing no one understood. Why on earth was the skipper so paranoid? All decisions went to the senior officers and beyond. Our training was marginalized, replaced by five additional months of standing one-hour alerts. Even our senior enlisted popped for smoking dope. But there was no intervention. I drug tested thirteen times in the same year. Yet I was told it was my fault that two of my guys got caught. Nothing made any sense."

"Well, I'm hungry, how about some lunch." Ginger suggested.

"All right, let's check out the golf shack, find out if its still there. The Moffett Field golf shack should be just around the corner."

The small facility had changed into a fast food bar. The waiters were gone, so I seated Ginger at a table next to the large, bay window facing the course, while I ordered a couple of cheeseburgers at the cafeteria style counter. Ginger wanted French fries; I had a side of onion rings.

"Neal, tell me more," Ginger said, before taking a large bite out of her cheeseburger. She *was* hungry!

Although I didn't want to complicate our simple lunch, I was gratified by her interest and continued my tale.

"In the middle of the winter, everyone changed ground jobs and I became the Public Affairs Officer. Being ambitious, I thought the job was a good deal. I wanted to make some changes in the squadron's self-image. The previous PAO did a decent job, but beyond the newspaper, I had special projects in mind and thought I could do better. I filled the coffee mess with healthy food instead of the usual Pop Tarts and Snickers bars. I set up a squadron photograph after a dress blues inspection. All things considered, it turned out quite well, even with the two-headed man practical jokers and a few stray walk-a-bouts. And knowing I was under the gun to promote our enlisted personnel and squadron morale, I placed articles in the NAS Moffett Field fish wrapper."

I popped an onion ring into my mouth. While chewing it, I thought about what happened next.

"What surprised everyone was the first time the base newspaper printed my stories. The base public affairs office saved up four or five of them. By this time, my CO was hot about my lack of publications! Then, however, they all ran simultaneously in one newspaper. One squadron having so much publicity at the same time made an all time record. Morale shot up; people walked around the hangar reading story after story. After a while, even the Wing Commander knew my name and where I grew up. I was on a roll and happy for it."

Ginger just smiled. At least I wasn't venting anymore.

"But then it happened."

"What happened?"

"One morning, I took a couple of draft articles up the chain of command. What a mistake. The office was empty except for Commander Bark and the skipper and their offices shared a joint entryway. With the doors open, the skipper heard every word of our conversation after Bark invited me in and looked over the articles with interest. I remained standing near the doorway.

"'These are good, Scoop,' he told me. 'I like this one. But let me ask you something.'

"'What is that, Sir?' I said.

"'Scoop, can you imagine what it's like to be gay?'"

"Ginger, that came out of left field. I stood frozen not knowing what to say. I knew, of course, both gay officers and enlisted men in the squadron. Unfortunately, the military hunted down these dedicated service members. Some did fantastic work and were far more ambitious than the rest of us. Yet, they were considered security risks. For them to acknowledge their sexual preference, attend certain parties or be photographed around San Francisco bathhouses by the Naval Intelligence Service meant the end of their careers. Ginger, just weeks prior to this conversation, two junior enlisted processed out of the squadron for just such reasons."

Ginger stopped eating and was toying with her food.

"Well, I said 'No, Sir, I'm from Nebraska,' trying to artfully dodge the question. Although straight, I became nervous and looked over my right shoulder. I could see the skipper watching my every move. Another man waited for the executive officer in the hallway behind me.

"'I mean, Scoop, can you imagine taking it up the ass?' he asked me.

"'It's not my cup of tea, Sir,' I replied.

"But my dodge didn't work."

Ginger's eyes were as big as saucers.

"I wanted to say to Commander Bark, 'Sir, I'm not gay.' But I feared both the question and the audience. On one hand, to be sympathetic might offend Commander Bark, and on the other, I didn't want to be seen as antagonistic to an underground community. Confused by it all, I glanced at the skipper and saw disappointment in his eyes."

"Disappointment?" Ginger was stunned.

"Yes. Each time I said 'it's not my cup of tea,' in response to Bark's repeated questioning, I could feel the skipper's interest build. Oddly enough, the fact that I didn't take a position in defense of the gay community that day may have hurt me."

"How so?"

"Right after that, a couple of dirty tricks occurred. I shouldn't relate them, but their timing is quite interesting."

"Dirty tricks? I thought there was honor in those white uniforms."

"So did I. But my navigator, then close friends with the skipper, and a 26-year veteran Warrant Officer, left one of his secret codes on an aircraft. He blamed it on me. This occurred in Hawaii, in front of the enlisted crewmen. We recovered the codes without much effort, but he spread it around that I was responsible for losing them, poisoning my reputation. They were his codes, damn it! He signed for them! And I listened to that crap for a year and a-half, much to my dismay. It was quite a stab in the back!"

Ginger sat with her mouth open.

"Then the senior enlisted in my office told me that while I was away, my boss removed the commanding officer's color photographs from my locked file cabinet. Every deployment sight had color photographs of the various COs in the Pacific theater. But my skipper's photo appeared in black and white. How could I tell him what my enlisted men told me? As an officer, I felt that I needed to shield them from the command and not ruin their careers. I knew there was trouble ahead. I put in what I could but all roads to success were blocked."

"Did anyone else complain about what went on?"

"I never said a word to command. Maybe that was a big mistake, but I preferred to keep things quiet and just hope they would go away. One man who did complain was a former Army helicopter pilot nicknamed 'The Magnet'."

"What do you mean?"

"Magnet flew helicopters in Vietnam, got out and then joined back up in the Navy. He had a great head on his shoulders. He knew what was important. Your buddies kept you alive, not paper work. The man knew it all too well with his 37 air medals from fighting in Nam. He had even more air medals than the skipper who also fought bravely. That is puzzling. Shouldn't the two be more alike?"

"What do you mean?"

"Magnet flew in the battle of Khe Sahn. The badly outnumbered Marines held three supporting mountaintops. The communist fighters hollowed the mountains inside out from below. They could tunnel up anywhere and did so for thirty days. In his words, 'It was a fucked up situation.'

"Magnet was shot down five times but never got a scratch. He doubled up his protective vests, sat on them, and even wore them around his legs. 'Hey it's all you got and at least it's something,' he used to say.

"Magnet lost a whole lot of people all around him. He told stories of the glory seekers and the high price they paid, and made others pay during the war."

"Why are you telling me this?" Ginger asked.

I stopped talking and stared out the window. The natural setting of the golf course comforted me for the moment. After carefully considering my reply, I answered.

"Magnet could smell bullshit from a mile away. He, too, could never figure out VP-88. Then it happened. In a way, the man just snapped. We were on deployment in Misawa, sharing a large room in the Officer's Club with another command. It was a hale and farewell party and the room was packed."

"What did he do that was so terrible?"

"He stood up to the command in his farewell speech, in front of two squadrons, and let them have it.

"'Back in Viet Nam, we used to shoot our officers for less shit than goes down in this squadron,' he said in a loud, commanding voice. The speech went downhill from there.

"We both never knew why the place went off the deep end in its sweat, its paranoia, and unnecessary overwork. 'Either you found the submarine or you didn't' was my opinion. The missions depended on the efforts of men. Working someone into an early grave before a mission made no sense to me. It reduced the chances of success."

Ginger stared out the bay window, and then shook her head. "Let's go, let's get out of here."

"All right. But do you know what I think was the driving factor in this whole mess?"

"No."

"I couldn't figure it out until ten years later. I sat in a crummy hotel room in Buffalo, New York watching CNN news. They covered a San Francisco march supporting President Clinton's 'don't ask, don't tell' policy. And who do you think I saw in a Navy captain's dress uniform?"

"Neal, I don't know. The Magnet?"

"No, Skipper Fogg! That's when I put two and two together. I suspect he supported gays in the military all along. In 1984, his political views were as outlawed as a three-dollar bill. If a superior in his chain of command knew of his support, with a mark on his fitness report, he would be non-competitive. His career would be ruined. Support for gays under Reagan was suicide for an officer. The skipper had too much at stake, too many years in the Navy to become a casualty for their cause. And I, for one, believe he was found out. This made him paranoid, afraid for his own career."

"So what did he do?"

"In order to shake the heat he overcompensated and worked his squadron to death. Everyone sweated every detail until they, too, became paranoid.

"With that one news clip, everything came together for me and made perfect sense. In the 1980s, gays suffered great discrimination from the government they chose to serve, including giving up their very lives. They still do. Fogg was sympathetic to their plight and paranoid. His views made him a target of discrimination, too."

Ginger and I departed the golf shack in silence for the main gate of Moffett Field.

After twenty years of holding back, talking only between squadron mates, I finally shared just ten months of this one man's command and released my hidden demons. It took being physically present on the air station to force me to deal with my emotions. I bottled them up for all those years. Yes, that day, it was good to see Moffett Field—good to see it dead.

Fogg was married with children. He could have been bisexual; I don't care to know. As an officer, I didn't care to know about anyone's sexuality. I used a host of names when referring to gays, but I consider all sexuality a matter of privacy. My colleagues felt the same way.

By chance I discovered the truth behind the insanity—sympathy for the homosexual communities. My commanding officer quietly opposed the intolerance generated strictly by a prejudiced government policy. His quiet support could well have cost him his career.

The consequences of his conscience, unfortunately, were intolerable for both himself and his men. The Navy paid a high price for this policy. In a twist of its application, the government's antigay policy ruined morale, careers, and American military capabilities.

That trip was the last time I visited Moffett, a time I was happy to see forever gone. Later, through the release I gained from my conversations with Ginger, I now find myself wanting to go back to tour the hangars and remember the good times with the junior officers with whom I served.

After the way we were treated, I never thought this possible.

Misawa

CHAPTER ELEVEN

Our crew barely got our feet on the ground after our return from the Kadena Deployment before we were buried in the Misawa Deployment. Our first flight assignments were to the east of Japan. Missions were on us day and night because of our close proximity to the Vladivostok and Petrapovlov Soviet Pacific submarine bases. After several surface surveillance missions, our underwater searching took off in a fury.

The Soviets deployed a modified Echo Two submarine and we were assigned a search area posthaste. The Antisubmarine Warfare Operation Center (ASWOC) briefing officer instructed us on our mission requirements, limitations and communications plan.

"Gentlemen, we have positive intelligence against a new target, code named Sierra 18. Sierra 18 is a nuclear powered Echo Two Mod, fresh from over-hall in the yards. You are to locate, classify and passively track this target. Under no circumstance are you to over fly the target. MAD is not authorized. Radar is not authorized. If you visually acquire the target, turn away from his position so as not to alert him. Sierra 18's last known position is an area of high probability only. You will be the first to fly a mission against him. Your call sign is Alpha Two Quebec."

Steve, our senior pilot and mission commander, turned his head to view the crew and spoke in a subdued voice, "This is our big chance to look good. Let's not blow it."

"You will launch at 1800 hours with an on station time from 2000 until 0200. Your relief, call sign Bravo Three Yankee, will arrive at 0130, and the swap procedures are outlined in the briefing documents. Normally we read the entire package to you; but gentlemen, we are short on time. If there are no questions, let's break up into the tactical groups and continue."

We split into small groups with the junior pilot and flight engineers leaving the ASWOC to safety check the aircraft. The acoustic operators and sensor three headed to the back of the ASWOC for their individual briefings. The Tacco and Navcomm stayed behind for their specific details. Steve and I headed over for a weather briefing and filed a flight plan. In forty short minutes, we met up on the aircraft. Fortunately, we flew the one-hour ready alert aircraft. It sat in a fully mission capable status, saving us two valuable hours in our pursuit of the Soviet submarine.

Crew One launched into the foggy night sky in less than two hours from our initial notification. The cockpit flew to the on station position at nineteen thousand feet. The Tacco worked feverously, planning his initial buoy pattern. The navigator guided us to the designated search area while maintaining constant communications with the ASWOC. Upon our arrival on station, Steve brought the aircraft down to five thousand feet for our initial buoy drops. A loud bang sounded throughout the aircraft as *cads* (explosive charges sealed in steel chambers) fired away. They jettisoned the sonobuoys from launch tubes in the belly of the aircraft.

We deployed the initial search pattern in thirty minutes. Our two acoustic operators poured over the data the buoys echoed back to the aircraft. The entire mission hung on finding the right frequencies, and thereby detecting Sierra 18. For over an hour, we orbited in slow flight above our field of buoys while sensor one and two worked their graphs.

Sensor one called up, "Tacco, we have contact!"

One of our buoys heard the submarine.

"Contact? Which buoy, where?" Tacco replied.

"Buoy fourteen sir. I am sure it's him. We've had him now for some twenty minutes, both primary and secondary lines of interest."

"Flight, this is Tacco—turn north to buoy fourteen. I am generating a localizing search pattern now. We will drop four more buoys."

The Tacco sent positions to our tactical display and indicated where he wanted to drop our next buoys. We flew over those positions and within minutes of their deployment, three of the buoys held contact with Sierra 18. The hard part was over. Then, we simply classified the target and refined its position until our relief airplane arrived two hours later.

Later that night, we passed tactical data over encrypted voice communications to the oncoming aircraft, ensuring a positive hand off or swap. After separating our aircraft by twenty miles, crew one began its climb out to transit home at twenty three thousand feet. The other plane simultaneously descended to five thousand feet in the opposite direction to continue the prosecution.

Upon completion of our search period, not only had we located this submarine on its transit to on-station, our crew classified the boat as well. In the two hours that followed, the cabin crew documented all of the details of the prosecution while the flight station flew the airplane back to Misawa. High spirits of success beamed from every crewmember. We proved ourselves to the ASWOC and to our squadron that night. The command shone like a bright star because of our hard work.

During the course of the next few prosecutions, other crews let the submarine slip away into the silent ocean depths. Our crew regained contact or "relocated" the submarine, even gaining visual contact of her radio mast plowing through the surface waters on our very next launch. Two joint U.S. Navy/Japanese Maritime Self Defense Force events allowed us to continue the prosecutions. On one of these flights, we extended on-station and diverted to naval facilities near Tokyo. On two others, we prosecuted the submarine alongside the Japanese. It all fell into place.

Tactically, each assignment challenged us. Back at ASWOC, our crew was greeted with large, wolfish smiles. During later separate events, we chased two Soviet submarines, finding a third underwater contact for which prosecution was disallowed.

"Never mind, Crew One," we were told.

This led us to believe it was a friendly U.S. boat. Except for that one, it seemed we could do no wrong. As a matter of fact, on our first trip into the Sea of Japan, we got a new fix on two other Soviet Kilo submarines transiting together. We gathered the first ever, acoustic information against these particular targets. Additionally, we located a third previously unknown sub coming out of Vladivostok. We were rolling. Three subs located on one mission became the Crew One's hat trick, something that made all of us proud.

After all missions, however, the real challenge for the flight station was our return to Misawa. Sea fog always blanketed the base. Weather station reports called the ceiling zero and the visibility zero (no vertical clearance from the cloud base and no ability to discern objects horizontally)—the classic "zero, zero" approach. Under such conditions, the Navy allowed us to fly the full GCA approach (Ground Controlled Approach with guidance from a ground based radar operator) to an altitude of one hundred feet. They allowed such a low altitude because of our experience level and our two "NATOPS QUALIFIED" pilots who, quite frankly, were still young enough to believe we would live forever.

Although some people dipped below these altitudes—the lowest of aviation minimums, our crew kept the minimums, making it in with technique. The first such approach required runway lights to be turned up to their full bright position. I was amazed they weren't on full bright in the first place. Simply put, the brighter the lights, the farther the lights penetrated into the fog. *The crew has to ask for this luxury?* For our second trick, we darkened the ship inside and out, turning down the cockpit lighting and turning off all of the landing lights, strobe lights, the red, green and white navigation lights, and the rotating beacon. This kept the lights from obscuring our already diminished visual range. This is comparable to driving in fog with your low beams, instead of using high beams because it blinds the driver. We had to think outside the box in terms of aviation, getting used to landing without landing lights. The third technique was to raise my seat to a higher position than normal. Although ergonomically awkward, this allowed me to look directly at the runway passing beneath the nose of the aircraft. Consequently, the runway lights were closer to the cockpit because of the diminished slant range to the aircraft. Oftentimes the flight engineer, sitting between the pilots, never saw the runway lights before touchdown because his particular windscreen view increased his slant range to the runway.

The landing pilot flew ground-controlled approaches manually from the left seat, while the non-flying pilot backed him up from the right seat. The trick to hand flying was to configure the airplane early with flaps in a full "land flaps" position, landing gear down, and being on speed with the landing checklist completed before commencing the final let-down to the runway. Some people said this burned excessive fuel, but it was better than a pilot needlessly balking the landing and executing the missed approach.

Once in this configuration and on speed, there were few variables to manipulate for an accurate approach. The feather-light feel of the airplane became apparent, the sound of the propellers a buttery whirl. Slight heading changes were controlled with light pressure on the yoke and rudders. The aircraft's sink rate and its relationship to the glide-slope on the controller's radar screen were easily controlled. With ever so slight adjustments of the four power levers, we flew closer and closer to the ground, giving our complete trust to the voice of the approach controller.

The final controller began his radar vectoring with a radio check and a wheels' check. "This is your final controller. Wheels should be down; how do you read?"

"Loud and clear; three down and locked."

Then he issued lost communications procedures and missed approach instructions, in case we lost radio contact for five seconds on final approach or did not acquire the runway. We could break off approach at any time, if we felt uncomfortable with the situation. But the Japanese air traffic controllers were exceedingly good at their job and we worked together like a key in a lock.

"Coming up, coming up and on glide path. Begin descent, heading 271 on glide path. Drifting slightly right of course…turn left heading 268…going below…slightly below glide path…on course…slightly below glide path…come up…coming up and on glide path…on course." Their voices got into our heads during every ground-controlled approach. Our concentration could not have been higher.

In the rear of the airplane, the entire crew knew the score for arrival; they knew our past schedules and knew how tired they themselves felt at the time. Not surprisingly, every workstation listened to the air traffic controller talk us down to one hundred feet. Occasionally, we did not acquire the runway and on one specific occasion, we lined up over the edge of the runway. On that one, I was the "cockpit observer," standing on the flight engineer's pedestal, calling for the wave-off. We were too far right of the runway centerline for a safe landing. Being that close to the ground, and having one wheel over the grass instead of the runway was frightening.

Ten minutes later on the next approach, I found the runway environment first because of my vantage point, standing up on the six-inch high pedestal.

I called to the flying pilot, "Field's in sight, on centerline. Flare!"

He made a great landing, all without seeing the runway for himself.

When we came to a stop, visibility was rotten and we were stranded. We couldn't see well enough to taxi the airplane and we had no auxiliary power unit to generate electricity. Just to keep the lights on, we kept two engines running, one as a back up. With the propellers turning, it was too dangerous to send a tug, driver and linemen out to the runway to retrieve the airplane. So, there we sat for another hour, waiting for the fog to thin enough for us to taxi. We had time to take a breather—to calm back down from our adrenaline high and chill out.

To say we relied heavily on each other for our very lives would be an understatement. Our youth and overall lack of flight time made these events remarkable, yet that was just what was expected from each of us. A glance at the low incident/accident rate numbers might suggest that the recovery at Misawa was routine procedure. However, it was anything but, and made possible only because of our professional training, fierce concentration, and everyone's overall desire to stay alive.

In Misawa, Crew One's biggest boondoggle began when we traveled the Pacific while chasing one particular submarine. Our second flight of a new series took us to Guam where the submarine gave us the slip. But much to our delight, we relocated her during a third, open ocean search flight. We were hot, exhausted from flying at all hours of the day and night, although our spirits could not have been higher. However, the flight station knew our plane would not hold up much longer because of our ailing number three engine. It barely produced required power on take-off. The question was when, not if, it would quit.

We continued chasing this sub from a fourth base of operations NAS Cubi Point, in the Republic of the Philippines. Coincidently, a large hurricane blanketed the region, hampering our efforts. This didn't impede our launch and recovery sequence in the slightest. The Navy simply issued us "disposable raincoats"—plastic bags—for our walk to the airplane and preflights. Someone placed a box of these white elephant condoms on a chair outside the door of the ASWOC. We took our survival switchblades, cutting holes for arms and head before donning the high fashion item for our walk out to the airplane. However, this hardly mattered, tropical rainfall being what it is. The ramp flooded and the rest of our flight suits simply wicked up the water, drenching us to the bone. Fortunately, the weather was warm and our spirits were up; we just laughed about our improvised rain gear.

The flying conditions were tough at best once airborne. We bounced and shook our way to on-station and dropped our sonobuoy pattern as best we could under the hurricane. The flight station found a buoy that wasn't floating under a band of thunderstorms and set up our orbit over it. At our location, the low-level wind speeds of the hurricane were in excess of sixty knots and the shaking of the airplane kept us more than occupied. The P-3 rode like a MAC truck. Our awkward crab angle, tracking to the buoy, provided laughs and badly needed entertainment. Slaphappy, we were fatigued from all of our flying.

On our last flight of the series, we again launched into a night thick with wet stormy weather. This encore mission called for our pinpointing the transiting Echo Two MOD Soviet submarine. Dead reckoning gave us another search area to investigate. Just as luck would have it, formations of stacked thunderstorms radiated out from the center of the hurricane, crowding the area. Once on-station, our mission required us to keep our radar off so as not to alert the submarine to our presence.

While we complied with the original orders, luck favored us—the submarine came to the surface, revealing her location. It was our chance—a darn good one—to regain acoustic contact for a fourth time, except for the line of thunderstorms between the target and us.

Shackled with the order to control our radar, our tactical coordinator stepped in to speak with the mission commander.

"Steve, bring us into the game. We need to punch through the storms and work the other side of the showers," he said. "We need radar to avoid the storms."

Despite orders to the contrary, we lit off the high-powered beast, sending the submarine back down into the deep. Yet, from our fixing information, we came across his position in a relatively short amount of time. Orders required us to remain passive in our prosecution, to not alert the target to our presence. Our radar, however, already alerted the submarine, so the Tacco made another counter-decision to utilize active sonobuoys and place "pingers" in the water. His small pattern of active sonobuoys immediately found the target, as if it were preordained, and we were back in business for the fourth time against an adversary whose location was originally unknown. We tracked him for several hours, putting the submarine squarely back in the Navy's relocation game, like sticking a pin on the map. When our relief crew showed up, they didn't want to utilize radar to penetrate the line of weather out of fear of alerting the submarine.

"Go ahead," our Tacco responded, "he already knows we're here. I've been pinging on him for a couple of hours now."

That ended Crew One's absolute best month. Next flight out, the number three engine finally gave up the ghost and we aborted take-off. At the end of the runway, in the engine run-up area, we confirmed the engine required changing and we were hard down for a couple of weeks. Our weakened beast could not be serviced; engines were unavailable in the Western Pacific. This stranded us for two weeks at the home of the Navy's best Officer's Club, Cubi Point, situated across the bay from Olongopoe City. Throw me in that briar patch, it was time to relax!

Our efforts won us the highly coveted "West Pac Crew of the Month" award and later, the squadron's "Crew of the Quarter" award. It was more than any one of us ever expected, and it was only our first month of the deployment.

Adak

CHAPTER TWELVE

Adak, Alaska, is of strategic military importance to the United States, located on the southernmost regions of the Aleutian Islands chain: fifty-two degrees north and one hundred seventy-seven degrees west, to be exact. During World War II, Adak defended Alaska from a Japanese conquest and protected Seattle from aerial attack. The Japanese occupied islands to the west of Adak and attacked islands to its east in a brilliant display of Japanese naval airpower. For years at a time, Americans occupied Adak and camped out in subterranean sod Quonset huts with no amenities whatsoever.

As far as the Navy was concerned, Adak was a strategic island because of its location. We could launch and recover airplanes into the Northern Pacific Ocean, the Bering Sea and the Western Pacific near the Kamchatka peninsula. We even flew into the Arctic Ocean from Adak although returning to this isolated island then required landing and refueling. The Navy required the P-3 aircraft to be "on top" of the island with 21,000 pounds of fuel. This was one-third of its total fuel capacity, to satisfy if needed, the flight to the alternate Elmendorf Air Force base located in Anchorage; which was three and a half hours away. This fuel requirement limited every mission. With no other reliable field handy, that was part of the experience of flying in Adak.

Adak weather was nearly always the same—bad. The rain came in sideways, thick clouds broke at nine hundred feet. When there was fog, it could own the place in a matter of minutes. The few sunny days required the operations officer to be in the tower, while pilots flew the touch-and-go practice-landing pattern. Under his watchful eye, we practiced landings until we burned down to the 21,000-pound mark. Then the operations officer had to verbally approve every take-off below bingo fuel.

The worst part of flying in Adak, however, was actually flying in the Adak region. The island follows its horseshoe-shaped mountain range, allowing only one way in and out, without exception. To make matters worse, the high-peaked island of Atka sat east of Adak, at the mouth of the horseshoe, and guarded Adak from careless airmen who might try a long, straight-in approach.

*NAS Adak. Visible are the Razorbacks, Finger Bay, the Runways and Mount Moffett guarding Runways 5 and 18.**

The P-3s' onboard radar helped us circumnavigate Atka and we flew back to the south, picking the final approach corridor to the field. Adak now sported four runways; the straight-in flight path was runway 23 while all others required circling in extremely tight proximity to the mountains. On one portion of the single approach, the airplanes flew below, and perhaps one hundred yards to the south, of the big green monster, Mount Moffett.

*U.S. Navy imagery used in illustration without endorsement expressed or implied. Photographer Unknown.

The winds always blew rain through the dark gray of low clouds. At the bottom of it all, next to the straight-in runway, lay a steep rock hill called "Tacan Hill," because it supported the tacan navigational beacon. Once the pilot landed on the slick, ice-covered runway during the winter, Tacan Hill momentarily blocked the wind from affecting the aircraft. This caused the crosswind-control inputs on the plane to cock the plane crossways down the runway, scaring everyone half to death. After the pilot corrected for this condition and straightened the plane from sliding sideways, the aircraft emerged from the protection of the wind shadow. The pilot then reinstated or, more accurately, reinvented his crosswind correction to compensate for the cocked aircraft. He had to keep it from drifting off the side of the runway, while holding the four motors in maximum reverse, to avoid using the brakes so as to not lock his wheels and blow his tires.

Many people warned, "You haven't lived until you see runway 23 centerline of Adak, coming through your side view window." They were right.

Back in the summer of 1984, when Crew One first arrived in Adak, the circling runways 18 and 36 were the only runways available. The straight-in runway 23 was under reconstruction. The base of Mount Moffett lay directly before runway 18. It supported the lead-in lights to the runway. Those lights served as obstruction lighting for terrain that began a steep rise at the very edge of the end of the opposite runway. We called those lights "The Stairway to Heaven."

The construction trenches shortened the near end of runway 18 by one thousand feet. We flew a left-handed, curling slope down the stairway to avoid the dark mountain to the immediate right of the airplane, while simultaneously skipping over the three trenches to land on what remained of runway 18.

Hangars and base facilities stood to the left of the shortened arrival end of runway 18. The base BOQ and steep terrain obstacles stood immediately to its right. At its far end lay a short gravel overrun, sloping down to a paved roadway running alongside Finger Bay that was approximately one-half mile across. A rock mount rose from the bay, guarding the left side of the departure end of runway 18. Straight on, beyond the bay, stood the jagged ridgeline. These six to nine hundred foot tall peaks were suitably called "The Razorbacks." These obscure obstructions just smiled at you during night launches, waiting to put their teeth into your wings.

All this meant that upon lift-off, the desired track climbed until the landing gear retracted into their wheel wells at approximately three hundred feet of altitude, placing the airplane over the edge of Finger Bay. The pilots then commenced a sharp left roll into an immediate thirty-degree angle of bank for one hundred fifty degrees of heading change. If an engine quit during that time, all previous rules such as "Sit on your hands for a moment, maintain wings level, climb to a safe altitude before instituting any changes, clean up the wing by raising the flaps," went right out the window.

The mountains ruled, requiring pilots to maintain airspeed in a steep turn next to the water, slowly climbing the heavy airplane while maintaining precise navigation on an instrument departure. Developing a sink rate from a wind-milling propeller, or decreasing the rate of turn, spelled disaster in a matter of seconds. All of this might well go on, as the fire horn blared one hundred decibels into the flight station and red warning lights distracted the pilot from his instrument scan, terrifying everyone on board.

The opposite runway, runway 36, was prohibitively dangerous for night approaches but beautiful and exciting for a day landing. The approach started with a straight-in runway 23 approach and then broke off to the left, maneuvering inside the horseshoe of green, windswept high terrain. We utilized checkpoints to assess our runway progress because the flying pilot couldn't see the runway until he rolled out on centerline. It was a matter of completely trusting the teamwork of others. Flying in Adak, Alaska, was no joke.

For this approach, the aircraft flew over the water in a thirty-degree intercept to the mouth of Finger Bay. From this position, while flying directly at the razorbacks, the pilot rolled the airplane to the right and descended toward the water. The seven-hundred-foot rock mount in Finger Bay became the center of a circle about which the pilot flew a constant radius descending turn to obtain the desired track over the ground. About that time, I always prayed to God, "Lord, please don't rearrange the rocks or the runway!"

Technically known as "contact approaches," these runway 36 and 18 maneuvers came during landing practice, as well as at the end of our nine-hour flights, with or without a low ceiling or a driving rain. These circling maneuvers required flying below the approach minimums with reference to known objects. A contact approach can only be requested by the pilot and cannot be suggested by the approach controller. However, the Adak controllers took this rule one step further, raising the minimums, so the pilot had to request the contact approach upon every arrival. As a matter of fact, the approach controllers would not issue a full approach without the pilots asking for "the full approach to a contact approach." Instead, the air traffic controllers issued minimums so ridiculously high that they left the airplane stranded in the clouds, or flying to the alternate landing field one thousand miles away. The air traffic controllers did not want the responsibility for the approach guidance. Pilots had to clearly state their contact approach requests on tapes, creating evidence that the contact approach was requested at the end of the approach.

From its onset, this position made me uneasy about the ground-controlled approaches and alerted new pilots to the very real dangers we faced. *Why would they require the request instead of giving a standard approach?* I wondered. *Wasn't there someone who could simply order them to issue the full approach? If not, why not?*

The controllers liked the situation even less than we did; but of course, the worst thing they could do was fall out of their chairs. Not so the flyers! The worst we could do was crash...and burn...and die!

On one particular flight we were honored to be with Executive Officer, Commander Bark. After touring the region of islands to the west of Adak, we flew toward our return approach corridor. Visibility outside the corridor was quite good with a two-thousand-foot ceiling. Even NAS Adak called their ceiling at 900 feet. We got in line for recovery. Unfortunately, the operative term of "got in line" meant that we were in trail to a Boeing 707, a jet with very old and dirty engines. Those engines created soot to which water vapor from a saturated atmosphere readily adhered. This generated a prolonged fog in the funnel of the approach corridor. We didn't know that at the time.

The B-707 made it into Adak without any problems; he maneuvered over the Stairway to Heaven and down to the runway without a hitch. However, my approach and landing was the most difficult and dangerous flying I have ever accomplished. It was the only time that I nearly rolled off the far end of any runway. I trained in the Navy hard enough to be too stupid to be scared—at first.

We asked for a GCA approach to a contact maneuver for runway 18. During the approach, I configured the airplane with full-down "land flaps" for three reasons. First, I didn't want to have an abrupt configuration change during a critical time of flight; second, I wanted to be able to fly more slowly to reduce the radius of the required turns that lie up ahead; and third, the full flap setting reduced our stopping distance. When the shortened runway came coupled with a chance of landing long, I wanted to stack the deck in my favor. However, what we really needed was about ten more minutes between the B-707 arrival and us.

While the controller did a marvelous job of talking us down to minimums, we flew in the exhaust and subsequent fog of the B-707, a meteorological phenomenon that caught everyone by surprise. I became suspicious of the weather. *Just when are we going to break out?* I asked myself. *Just when are we going to break out?* We were flying into the original blind canyon, an ever-so-narrow box that tightened with the loss of each foot of altitude.

My tension increased proportionately; yet I buried it and continued, concentrating on my instruments and the lone voice of the final controller. While we expected to break out of the fog at 800 feet and execute a safe and simple maneuver, this was impossible because of the B-707s trail of fog. Instead, we broke out at roughly three hundred feet, far below the circling minimums for a crossing runway—especially one protected by mountains, just as a golf green is protected by sand traps. I took a mental snapshot. In front of us lay the closed, straight-in runway; Tacan Hill stood to the right of our position, and some low lying buildings, the base exchange, commissary and hangars lay to our left. I had to act and react.

With no time to hesitate, I took the plane down to 250 feet, slipping under the remaining ragged layer of clouds.

I envisioned a mirror's image "S" turn to gain track distance, enough distance to align with the runway. As I did so, I turned left away from the Stairway to Heaven, because I couldn't curl between Tacan Hill and Mount Moffett where the Stairway to Heaven stood tall and bright. This was opposite all previous training, except that in the end, I would be descending to the runway while looking at it from out of my windows in those last two hundred feet of altitude. It would be the simple, oval landing pattern we practiced in primary flight training: practiced in a single engine, four thousand pound airplane three years ago. In retrospect, it was a ridiculous thought.

There was barely time to think; but that's when the fun really began. Simultaneously, I brought on a handful of power to maintain airspeed. In this high-drag configuration, the airplane wanted to slow down and descend rapidly, neither of which I could allow. As we turned left over the end of the beach, my mind's eye spotted my curving course in front of us. It didn't matter in the least that we would fly over half the island's population in the village below, thundering across them with engines cooking at high power, flying over so close that some might think they could hit us with a stone. Now my body was as taut as piano wire. I had only my mindset and goal in sight. I visualized my flight path to a familiar point in an oval pattern, the landing and the still possible escape maneuver, flying down the runway and departing as if on a "normal take-off run from runway 18."

I turned to my right, beginning a shallow descent from 250 feet. We flew over the civilian area at two hundred feet, headed directly for the Stairway to Heaven with Tacan Hill on our right side. Approaching the centerline of runway 23, I threw the aircraft into a steep left turn, pressed firmly on the rudder and reduced power. At the bottom of the turn, I leveled the wings, pulled off the remaining power, put in an opposite crosswind correction, and touched halfway down the shortened runway. From there, I came on with maximum reverse. As the aircraft approached the end of the pavement, the patrol plane commander yelled "brakes" and jumped on the binders, something we never practiced, not ever! We were taught the brakes were too powerful for the plane, but this time they felt great. With my hands full and my mind focused on our arrival, I didn't remember the brake pedals. I never used them before and didn't think of using them then, but our teamwork paid off.

Fortunately, we came to a standstill, sticking to the pavement! Motionless, we all took a moment before the plane commander sprang into action.

"Let me show you how we cool off our brakes," he said as he pulled the outboard engines into reverse and set a bit of forward power on the inboard engines, blowing cold air on them.

I began to breathe again. After our brief pause on the runway, I turned the airplane around and taxied back to the right-hand turn off to the tarmac. We completed our checklist items, while waiting for a lineman to guide us through the array of small excavations on the ramp area. My heart was pounding, my skin wet with ice cold sweat beneath my saturated flight suit.

P-3 departs NAS Adak from runway 23 in a left turn-out,
avoiding the oncoming mountain. *

*U.S. Navy imagery used in illustration without endorsement expressed or
implied. Photographer Unknown.

Not only did we operate with a restricted runway; but we also taxied through a maze of deep cutouts, placing them between our wheels, guided by some of the most junior enlisted personnel in the squadron. On the ramp, one false move spelled disaster. If a landing gear fell into a construction hole, at least one, if not both spinning propellers would strike pavement, break off and fly through the fuselage.

That gray day, there was little debrief of the approach and landing, even from the executive officer, who sat on the radar bay directly behind me. My plane commander mentioned that the XO's eyes were as large as saucers during the maneuver. Other than that, not a word was said, even though we should have called for a wave-off. The missed approach was a simple left climbing turn, to fly out the approach corridor well above the terrain—a piece of cake.

To this day I don't understand our reasoning to press the approach, when the weather was far below the safety minimums for maneuvering the aircraft. Were we trying to impress the XO? Were we trying to impress ourselves? Did we feel the pressure of repeating the approach with the minimum of four hours of fuel on board? Did our bingo alternate's distance and the XO's schedule weigh on our shoulders? I never asked and I was never told. To this day, I am simply thankful that everything worked out.

That night wasn't any different from other nights around the BOQ. After receiving our next day assignments, we sauntered into a BOQ room converted into a grubby little lounge to watch deployment movies—*Caddy-Shack, The Blues Brothers, Animal House*—and some porn flicks. My colleagues drank beers, but my assignment as morning duty pilot prohibited my consuming alcohol. No matter, I was beat and I turned in for the night—there would be tomorrow.

Maintenance control released me from my taxi pilot duties late the following afternoon and I found myself back in the BOQ. I headed to the Officer's Club for a round of eats, drinks and socializing. In Adak, "club" was just code for a dark, typically red-carpeted bar and high-spirited Naval aviators. It hosted all the base officers, not just the flyers, and could be counted on for a cold one, a couple of pretty women and some good sea stories in between.

Within the club's dark depths, I sat back against the wall and, after a few minutes, several crewmembers joined me. Not long after, the XO entered and took up his favorite position, sitting with the junior officers who were always good for a laugh. The XO stood with his men, believing in camaraderie before rank.

It was twenty-four hours after our fancy arrival, yet we hadn't said a word about it—good, bad or otherwise. It weighed heavily on me, however, replaying over and over in my mind's eye. I withdrew from the group, yielding to a long, drawn-out stare that only the XO, from his days in Vietnam, really understood or gave a damn about. I usually drank Sapporo beer, but scotch on the rocks was required that day. The ice in the bottom of my glass clinked from a slight palsy in my hands and arms.

"What's going on, Scoop?" the XO asked, slipping up beside my chair and startling me.

My real concerns for the flight were honest ones. It took twenty-four hours for my nerves to finally kick in and I think he noticed. Even then, Bark didn't say a word about the event; he didn't have to in order to get his point across. He flew with his face in the wind, living in the moment, enjoying wine, women and song. I looked up at his smiling face and felt compelled to finally agree with him.

I walked over to the corner of the bar where several young ladies stood. Setting aside my scotch, I ordered a beer for myself and asked one of them if she would like anything.

"A coke," she said. "I go on duty in a couple of hours."

While waiting for drinks to arrive, this beautiful young Lieutenant corralled me over the P-3.

"Hi. My name is Maria. I see you're a flyer. What kind of flying do you do?" she said as she pressed her soft breast against my left arm. Her wet, red lips glistened under the overhead colored floodlights and her breath was hot.

I swallowed and said "P-3s" thinking it a bit obvious because it was the only aircraft stationed in Adak.

She already knew most of the answers to her questions, giving me sly, wanting looks from behind her high cheekbones.

She finally asked, "Tell me, why did an airplane fly so low over the base exchange yesterday? It shook the ground, the building and scared everyone inside and out. What sort of practice could the Navy be doing?"

I pulled back in a moment of hesitation, but then gave her my best shot. I calmly explained our situation to the full-lipped, young beauty. I looked into her large, brown eyes surrounded by deep rose-colored cheeks and black hair that softly gathered behind her head.

"We got caught in a fog bank to down three hundred feet. When I broke out, the traditional route to the runway was blocked. We were too low and too tight to turn right. What I envisioned for the line up, necessarily curled back over the base to gain a position for my final approach to the runway."

As all pilots do, my hands communicated as well as my words, until she interrupted.

This woman beamed me an enormous smile before embracing, bending me over backwards, and enveloping my mouth in the sweetest, wet kiss Adak has ever encountered. What a kisser! The girl wrote the book on this vital form of foreplay. With her tongue in my mouth, I smelled the wisp of her elegant perfume and thought I was in heaven. I tried to wrap my arms around her, but they wind-milled as I nearly fell over, sober at the bar. When she let me up for air, we were the focus of attention.

"Can I have your room number?"

"Go to the far end of the third floor. Mine is the last door on the right. You'll find me there tonight."

Coke in hand, she wheeled away, leaving me dazed and holding the bar tab. Mesmerized, I watched my mystery "Maria" glide across the room. She walked back to her smiling girlfriends, pulling all eyes with her. I never knew what she said to them but I understood what they were asking!

I returned to the table and the XO—a lady's man—stood up, swinging out a chair for me. Mystified, he wanted to know what I said to the woman.

"Scoop, in his flight suit, walks up to the bar and, pow!" he exclaimed. "He nearly gets laid in front of everyone—in Adak, Alaska, no less. I never saw such a thing. Scoop, what's your secret? What kind of line did you lay on her?"

"Well Sir, she wanted to know about yesterday's flight over the exchange and commissary, so I told her."

Commander Bark smiled with a twinkle in his eye. I could tell he approved of my approach to life, at least that night, in the bar at NAS Adak, Alaska.

"Did you hear that?" he asked, turning to the others. "Scoop told her about our flight yesterday."

A normally rowdy bunch, the others sat quiet in the noisy bar, disbelief written all over them.

Far off and forgotten Adak served many purposes for the Navy and the P-3 served as the platform to pull off most of those missions, the reasons why so many people called this cold rain and windswept island home. We flew against the Soviet submarine fleet, relocated their surface assets, and flew outside the 12-mile limit in what was acknowledged as "free flying airspace" along the Soviet border. (This was by agreement that every country must allow foreign aircraft flight to within twelve miles of its borders.) To carry out these close-to-their-border flights, the military set up a system of watchful eyes—a whole cascade of assets to monitor each American asset to be on the lookout for trouble well before it happened.

The entire, peacetime flight blanket program developed out of lessons learned from the 1967 U.S.S. Pueblo incident. Communist North Korea intercepted, boarded, and pirated the ship, claiming it was spying in North Korean waters. America claimed the Pueblo was intercepted in international waters. It didn't matter. They held our people hostage and possession is nine-tenths of the law. Eventually they coerced the ship's commanding officer into confessions out of fear for the lives of his crewmembers. To be blunt, we were caught with our pants down.

An inadequate warning system was one of the first painful lessons learned from this incident. Prior to this takeover, North Korean activities went unmonitored. Little wonder the Pueblo was caught off-guard! Had we been more vigilant, most likely the event would never have occurred.

The Pueblo incident pointed out another valuable lesson. One asset, a "lone ranger," cannot adequately perform missions in defense of the United States. Different well-coordinated and well-protected types of platforms, within radio range of each other, are necessary during close transits of hostile states.

Communications were absolutely essential for this peacetime flight blanket program to fly. While in flight, we simultaneously monitored a UHF radio, a VHF radio, two scratchy HF radios and four turbo props—all slightly above ninety decibels. It was a headache waiting for a place to happen. We were required to immediately report any degradation in any of our gear through any number of encoded messages. If the Air Force lost any of its key capabilities to monitor us, they were required to command our extraction from the peacetime patrol area. If someone determined the communists launched decidedly hostile aircraft against our presence, despite our being in international free-flying airspace, the U.S. immediately recalled its assets.

It wasn't uncommon, however, to sight Soviet Mig aircraft near our position. They, too, had the right to fly in the international airspace and they exercised that right. While we flew our Boeings, Lockheeds, and MacDonnell-Douglas aircraft, they flew their Tupelovs, Migs and May aircraft. It became a regular high-altitude, super-power air show when we were all in the air at the same time, playing cat-and-mouse over the North Pacific and Arctic oceans. But most often, baiting the Soviet with our presence in rough weather was a lonely pain in the ass. The Soviets' supersonic jets could easily overcome our slow moving P-3 turboprop. In comparison, we resembled Linus and his security blanket flying Snoopy's doghouse instead of a credible, survivable platform.

Whether Adak launched these missions, or they initiated from any number of other locations, each mission had one common beginning: every airplane launched on time or it did not fly. That was the first granddaddy rule of them all. The next set of rules was the communications plan, the in-chop (check into theater of operations) procedures and constant monitoring of the "soup-of-the-day broadcasts." Seven hours of that gave everyone problems and drove us all half crazy. (Whoever had the job of sitting at a microphone and broadcasting that trash 24/7 must have done somebody wrong.)

The last rule was to do exactly what you're told because it may save your life.

"Yes, sir!" became our constant anthem.

P-3 stands one hour ready alert while another crew
practices landing in Adak.*

We flew our designated tracks from Adak. West of the island, the higher latitudes allowed for shorter mileage transits over the same degrees of longitude: an advantage we effectively utilized despite our enormous, alternate landing field fuel requirement. But no such mileage advantage exists when flying north. The lengths between degrees of latitude never vary between the equator and the pole. Therefore, when we needed to fly into the Arctic Ocean, Eilsen Air Force Base, located just outside of Fairbanks, hosted our activities. In late August of 1984, our crew departed Adak and flew to Eilsen for such missions. Our assignment was antisubmarine patrol.

*U.S. Navy imagery used in illustration without endorsement expressed or implied. Photographer Unknown.

The peacetime flight blanket covered our missions. We were ordered to locate and track two, modern Soviet ballistic missile submarines while assigned a location north of Wrangle Island, in the southern Arctic Ocean and northeast of Siberia. Still under the ice, we knew the submarines headed for the Bering Straits.

The cold was a cruel adversary. Our need for staying warm during preflight was a real challenge throughout the cold Fairbanks nights. A hooded sweatshirt combined with a pair of jeans under the flight suit and leather flight jacket retarded the bitter chill, until the flight engineer turned the air conditioning full down, claiming his gauge indicated it was hot in the electronics bays. I saw neither the logic nor the humor in that one.

The cold temperatures also shrunk the seals in the propellers and elsewhere, so we let the engines turn and warm up for ten minutes before advancing the power levers. This required the propeller to change the pitch of the blades. Another challenge was keeping the P-3 flying as long as possible. For that, we shut down one engine, sometimes two, and flew the remaining engines. Last, we needed to drop our sonobuoys in between the ice floes where they deployed their hydrophones in seawater, not on snow-pack. The try—try again method was utilized. If one missed the mark, we simply dropped another.

Launching from Eilsen, we headed northwest, just north of frozen nowhere. During the week of its fall season, the landscape wore time's passage as we flew over the Brooks Mountain range. The trees were turning colors on that first flight, while on our second, they were bright yellows and snow was scattering the landscape to our north. The slopes seemed dusted with an airbrush of fine mist on the third and fourth missions. Snow marched south and crept down those same, soft mountain slopes. This beautiful and enchanting progression was a fair reward for flying against the frigid Soviet Union.

"Hey Scoop, this modern 'boomer' must be headed for the scrap yard!" one of the crew called out. "It's a loud one. Why do you think they put to sea?"

We relocated one of the massive, Soviet Delta class submarines. Our sensor operators (we flew with the leading acoustic technician in the squadron) couldn't believe their own equipment. The submarine made so much noise that it took the better part of an hour for us to actually agree that this was indeed the target of interest. From great distances, this Soviet submarine's broken ice cream machine revealed its position to its every adversary. The Soviet sailors must have known that they were sitting ducks. I can only imagine how they felt.

The Soviet Union Navy could not keep up with the United States, no matter how proud their sailors, no matter how much manpower and money they diverted from their people to put ships to sea. Their maintenance requirements crushed their crews' best efforts as surely as sea pressure would. No matter how hard they tried, the Soviets could not keep up their aggressive deployment cycle. Despite that fact, this Soviet submarine carried twenty megatons of nuclear weapons capable of reaching deep into America's heartland along with men willing to launch them.

We bunked in the Eilsen BOQ when we returned, which consisted of a village of small, multi-personnel cottages. The private rooms came complete with bright red carpet, a psychological ploy to make you think warm. There was enough steam heat to keep you warm with the windows open while you slept.

During off-hours, I cleared my head from the internal noise of the squadron and returned to my own sense of humanity by hiking across an open field where an enormous flock of wild geese practiced their versions of landing. Some came down with webbed feet spread out beneath them. Their tail feathers spread wide and their wings lifted in a strong arch, using their bodies to rip up the air in an effort to bleed off energy, airspeed and altitude for a spot landing. Two geese made their flare look easy, while others took their practice with several abrupt bounces off the earth, honking and squawking all the way into the crowd. Others—I suspect the more practiced and mature of these aviators, flew in on a silent breath, slipping effortlessly on the glide. Then, with a feather's touch, they settled into their crowded field of friends without making a sound.

Man's fascination with flying is understandable; this flight was quite a sight. The large conclave was gathered for migration south. When I walked between them, they veered off as one, moving apart with a dignified waddle, allowing me to approach their numbers in safety. All too soon, it was apparent that I violated their secure space and hundreds took off at once. It saddened me to see them leave; but the grandeur of their massive launch, that lofty departure, filled me with joy. My heart took flight with them.

The twilight of that early September in Eilsen, when the Aurora Borealis was active, proved especially dramatic. Night after night, I stood directly under a canopy of electric reds, yellows and greens. It looked like an artist might have whisked a paintbrush back and forth across the canvas of the night sky. The red colors slowly changed shape, but the greens raced across the heavens. Each display made a crackling sound; and, had I not heard it for myself, I would have doubted the possibility. The northern lights spoke to me and charged me with the wonder of all of Alaska's fantastic magic. It was easy for me to understand why so many called it "God's Country."

Our flights in this particular series ended when the local Eilsen flight surgeon interviewed us and then grounded the entire crew for fatigue. We flew as much as we could, a hundred hours in less than thirty days, and had become a danger to ourselves in doing so. Some of the crew chain-smoked to stay awake and the tactical coordinator chewed through antacids like they were candies. The effects of our night and day schedule changes were written in broad lines across our faces.

We returned to Adak the next day where, fortunately, the straight-in runway was now open for business. After working so hard at flying our contact approaches, I felt somewhat cheated of that challenge when flying the straight-in approach. The straight-in runway made our precision flying feel too easy despite our immediate proximity to the mountain.

With the tempo of our flight operations relaxed, I understood that a few days face down behind closed doors came with the grounding orders. That only made perfect sense. But how I could be so wrong! In ironic compliance with the orders from the flight surgeon, once back on the ground in Adak, the crew stood twelve-hour watches mixed in with our ground jobs. We worked fourteen plus hours a day to comply with the order that grounded us for fatigue. The command overruled the flight surgeon in order to impress someone special.

Incredibly, I flew again in less than forty-eight hours. Extracting blood from a rock was Commander Fogg's specialty. *"The floggings continued until moral improved!"*

Key West

CHAPTER THIRTEEN

In October of 1985, I received orders from the Navy to transfer from the high paced NAS Moffet Field sea duty with deployments, to a slower, easier shore duty without deployments at NAS Key West, Florida. The Navy transfers pilots every three years, shifting assignments throughout their careers. My flying days in the P-3 Orion seemed quickly to come to a close. I found myself on house-hunting leave for ten days to secure a new dwelling in Key West.

I flew the Eastern Airlines red eye to Miami, then rented a bright red, T-Top muscle car and drove 160 miles to the Naval Air Station on Boca Chica Key. The Keys were quite impressive. Grand expanses of water lined both sides of a two-lane highway. The brown flats of the Gulf of Mexico sat off my right arm with the crystal blue waters of the Atlantic Ocean and Florida Straits on my immediate left. Bridge after bridge retreated in my rear view mirror and counting down to zero, my excitement built with each passing mile marker. With a blue sky overhead and the sun at my back, the end of the road was my only destination.

Once in Key West, I checked into the command before heading to the BOQ, (Bachelor Officer Quarters) located at Trumbo Point on Key West proper. Packed full of Naval and Marine Corps aviators, the "Q" was the largest building on the island: six stories tall, it encompassed three wings of rooms. Although I made a reservation well in advance, I barely got a room. Not having slept on the red eye, I took a short nap before calling my sponsor, Lt. Jack Peaton.

"Neal, glad you made it, but I'm unable to show you the town this evening. I promised I'd spend the tonight with the family. Check out Captain Hornblower's for jazz however. I am sure the music will appeal to you." The Lieutenant gave me my first night's flight plan for exploring Key West.

I thought it a bit odd that I came all the way from California and my sponsor didn't have the courtesy to spend a couple hours with me. We had spent hours talking on the telephone and he even sent me a welcoming package, introducing all the base experiences and the nightlife of the city. He was my point of contact for my transfer to Key West, a one-man welcoming committee already stationed there. But what did I know about his schedule or lifestyle anyhow?

His directions were simple enough: "Go to the end of Duval Street, turn left and Captain Hornblower's is the third building on the left, second floor. But to get the full effect of Duval, take Truman Avenue through Old Town, park on Simonton and walk the length of the downtown district."

That appealed to me, but I had no idea what was in store for me. That night, Duval Street truly was an end all, gay burlesque, eye-opening experience for this Naval aviator—far crazier than San Francisco's Castro district. My Key West *Ying-Yang* life experience began that night.

Here at the edge of the earth, as seen from the west shore piers, a life of casual tolerance and openly gay, in-your-face, nightlife appeared to be the norm. I was the outsider. Duval Street was torn up, under construction, as the city was replacing storm sewer lines. The mile-long construction site transformed Duval into a stopgap, makeshift outdoor mall, complete with loud music blasting from male-crowded bars and balconies overflowing with catcalling, half-naked, drunken fools who admired my baby moons.

I felt a bit nervous, but Duval was the best-lit street for blocks. I took my chances walking it, checking out the action from a safe distance. Block after block, historic ship captain's houses were converted into run-down drinking establishments. Those few serving food did so only on street level. Indolent owners, aided by relentless saltwater and sun, allowed these buildings to deteriorate. The silvered wood of neglect was everywhere, as was the dust rising from the middle-of-the-road trench. Storm sewer pipes lay helter-skelter in nearby piles, as if thrown down in a game of pick-up sticks that children used to play.

Do I really want to live here?

Live music blared out of "The Bull," a pub at the corner of Caroline and Duval. Its carved mascot, which was a red-eyed, raging bull replica, protruded from the exterior wall on Caroline Street. The Bull featured open bay windows, a corner stage and a large bar, perfect for beginning the evening. I cooled my heels with a cold beer, all the while enjoying the music of a female guitarist and conversing about potential real estate with a few of the redneck locals. After all, this was a house-hunting trip, not just a party town extravaganza—or did I have that backwards? I observed my surroundings. The women were either with someone or genuinely uninterested in my gender, while the men stuck to their smiles, those who were able to hold their heads up. I left for Hornblower's after just one beer.

I crossed over to the right side of the street toward Sloppy Joe's, a large establishment everyone mentioned. Despite pictures of Ernest Hemingway, its most famous patron, I thought the big, square bar rather mundane after poking my head in.

Another guitar player worked the crowd with little success; the bartenders and waitresses worked the crowd with greater success, and the smoke worked all but the sprinkler system, thoroughly defeating my eyes, nose and throat. So much for introductions, as—once again, I left for Captain Hornblower's after just one beer. This pattern of barhopping, hardly methodical, allowed me to take in the rest of the village.

I finally found the old brick bank building that Lt. Peaton gave as a landmark. Turning left, I passed a large, inviting balcony, overgrown with tropical plants that welcomed me, as did the incessant rotation of ceiling fans and women. A large and colorful sign, suspended from an overhang, announced "Captain Hornblower's." Assured that I found the right place, one recommended by a navy pilot, I relaxed. This was my type of crowd, the straights or breeders, as we were referred to. Not!

A nice jazz club, Captain Hornblower's opened late and was frequented by the other half of the gay community—tough lesbians. Just striking up a conversation with a few of those women was enough to send cold prickles down my spine. At one time, Key West was a Navy town with little other income besides serving grits, grunts and key lime pie. Not any more!

That night I discovered that the gay community, with its formidable wealth from up north, had migrated to this tolerant, tropical island that was coincidently located on mile marker zero, a warm spot near the end of the earth. I coupled that tidbit of information with my other observation:

the town was virtually under siege with backhoes, open trenches and large storm sewer pipes—an underground renaissance of infrastructure.

This upheaval signaled that the town was not going away; it was rallying, as the community took interest in the fundamentals of restoration. The city wasn't going under, rather it stood in the midst of a potential revival on an island that had run out of land.

Do I really want to buy a house here? I wondered. Over a couple of drinks, I carefully weighed what I was getting myself into. I might have walked into a two-edged sword. My answer came in the next few days when I found a new, affordable, two-bedroom townhouse. I purchased it as a dead horse loan between duty stations with $3,500 down, money that I borrowed from the Navy. I'd be moving in by July.

With a housing brochure in hand and a few tales to tell, I returned to Moffett Field at the end of my leave. Life would be different way down in the south of sunny Florida, in "The Conch Republic." Living there interjected a radical contrast, like night evolving into day, between my new circumstances and the lives my abandoned VP-88 shipmates would endure in Adak, Alaska. They had to survive winter in the BOQ, something I would remind them about, while trying to keep their spirits up.

Once back at Moffett Field, I checked out of command in early November, wishing everyone the best of luck in their upcoming deployment to Adak. I almost laughed at my sarcasm, but I held back and came across sincerely.

"I will be thinking of you while I'm in Key West," I said to the wardroom. "Good luck with all of your prosecutions."

What I really thought was, *You poor souls got the short end of the stick. Winter in Adak is brutal; and if you can find the backside of an oilier bobbing about in the storms, you will be doing well. So just forget about the submarine threat until April. Press on with the readiness drills and simulated qualifications during the next four months from inside your BOQ room. I hear Adak television has more than one channel these days. You have that going for you.*

I felt like saying all of that. I knew it would get a laugh because everyone knew it was true. But I didn't, fearing that my orders would change overnight to an eighteen-month tour of Antarctica.

I drove from Moffett to my next training station in Dallas, Texas. Along the way, I spent two nights in snowbound Flagstaff, Arizona, and one night with my aunt in Albuquerque. Once in Dallas, I found that the Navy crammed a two-week simulator course into seven days. Learning about the next airplane I would fly—Beechcraft's Super King Air, B-200, was a tough as nails experience with all new aerodynamics to master, systems to learn and limitations to memorize. The Super King, or C-12 in military terms, is a twin-engine, tee tail turboprop built to airliner standards of comfort and reliability. It could really perform in a pinch, something I would soon find myself putting to the test.

The C-12 had an overabundance of power and the wings of a sea gull; its avionics were far superior to that of the P-3. The autopilot coupled to the flight director and flew ILS approaches when needed. That was very rare in naval aircraft but came stock, as standard issue, in the purchased, off-the-shelf Super King Air. The plane sat seven passengers and three crewmembers and cruised 255 knots at 25,000 feet. For once, someone got it right the first time. In that short week I was both dog-tired and suitably impressed with the two million-dollar machine.

After Dallas, I drove to NAS Norfolk, Virginia, for further training in the designated C-12 RAG. The RAG consisted of one week of ground school followed by six days of flight training in the actual aircraft. The ground school was a repeat of Dallas; but for flight training, as any pilot will tell you, there is nothing like flying the actual aircraft. We flew first in early morning when the air was still. During the afternoon, things got really choppy over the contrasting warm air of the city of Norfolk and cool waters of the Chesapeake. Those times were for the advanced syllabus. We finally flew one hop at night for a night familiarization and then a check ride. We flew engine-out work and touch-and-go landings, viewing the Chesapeake Bay from above. In all, I flew six flights in seven days for a total of forty-nine landings. Better yet, I met some really wonderful people who recruited me to work at Norfolk at the Navy's Air Safety Center. It was tempting, but thinking of my new house and of all of the flight time I would acquire in Key West, I declined. They countered with a type rating in the Convair, but I remained unmoved.

Over the course of the next three days, I drove myself down Interstate 95 to Highway 1, the overseas highway, and finally arrived in Key West late one evening. I came to work the next morning thoroughly exhausted from the drive. I could have taken longer, but I wanted to save my leave for real vacations instead of travel and time given to proceed to my next duty station. Lt. Jack Peaton was happy to see me, as I was soon to be the only other plane commander of the C-12 on base. The other pilots were helicopter draftees who showed off by flying both H-3 helicopters and fixed wing aircraft on the same tour, sometimes during the same day.

On a Saturday morning, I walked out of my BOQ room and headed downtown to a French pastry shop. I ordered my soon-to-be favorite lunch—spinach and feta cheese croissant with rich black coffee—at the French Croissant. It was a small, three-table café filled with hot ovens, hotter French women and just baked, warm, filled pastries. After devouring the croissant on the shop steps, I toured the length of Duval, heading south to the Atlantic Ocean. I found a small beach and a charming old mansion on the west side of Duval. For obvious reasons it was called the Southern Most House. Opposite, across the water, stood the pier and gazebo of the Hotel Reach and down the street was the monument of the southernmost point in the continental United States.

I returned to the coffee shop for one last cup of Joe before reversing course and heading down to the northern end of Duval. I passed several curiosity shops, an off-limits sex shop, bar after bar, a couple of restaurants, two closed hotels, fifteen tee-shirt shops and a handful of boarded-up old houses. The latter appeared to be nothing more than termite tenders and windowpanes. Walking past The Bull, I smelled emanations from both the sewer that pooled at the street corner, despite newly constructed storm lines, and Friday night's beer still residing on the floor, walls, and anywhere else a patron might have slopped it.

A smallish looking place called Rick's was further down on the left side and across the street from Sloppy Joe's. A woodcarver busied himself there, engraving mermaid figurines on the ceiling's support pillars that studded the dark wooden bar. There was a small stage in the back, a bit of sluggish air conditioning, and a pretty lady serving cold beer on tap. On that beautiful Saturday afternoon, this sailor—patrolling for liberty, didn't need any more of an invitation than that.

I sat there talking with one bartender or the other. A professional multi-tasker, I tried to learn the lay of the land, all the while checking out the ladies on the sidewalk and paying attention to the woodworker, chiseling away at his latest creation just a few feet from where I sat.

Then it hit me. I was content sitting there on the warm streets of Key West while my squadron buddies deployed inside the soft ice storm of an Adak winter. I thought about it for a while, finally coming to the conclusion that they really needed cheering up. I was the man to do it, even from five thousand miles away.

Next to Rick's, there was a tee-shirt shop that also sold postcards. Not just any postcards, but the kind you see in south Florida, advertising tropical palm tree lined beaches, sunshine and surf, all directly behind the big breasts of a half-dozen lovely women clad in miniature bikinis, thongs, or nothing at all. I ventured over to the stands, purchasing the best and brightest variety of Florida booby girl and sunshine postcards that Key West offered. Blondes, brunettes, and redheads—these outlets had them all at five for a dollar. There were at least a dozen of them. And why not? The post office was a short three blocks from where I sat and I would be raising the morale of the United States Navy, three hundred men at a time.

Returning to my bar perch, I began my six-month communications project with my old squadron buddies stationed in Adak. I signed for my mission on every postcard. It was the least I could do, jacking them up, inch-by-inch, foot-by-foot. I knew my captive audience was hungry for mail, starving for a laugh and thoroughly disgusted by a predicament that would not go away any time soon. Every card was as vital to them as the air they breathed. I knew it; they knew it.

What I didn't know was exactly how bad things had deteriorated over the course of the first month. To start, it was December and the winter solstice bore down upon them with very short days and massive amounts of thick precipitation. The planes and crews could fly, but there were no targets to fly against. The ready alert crews dutifully pre-flighted their airplanes, yet they saw little action. The training department had no support airport within eight hundred miles suitable for pilot training and the worst was yet to come.

The squadron allowed twelve-man crews to workout in the base gym and play basketball for their exercise. This opportunity gave everyone a chance to forget the world around them and get badly needed relief from ground jobs and inactivity. But, as anyone can tell you, basketball is a contact sport, complete with injuries—especially ankle injuries, which are just part of the game.

What the inventors of basketball did not count on was the crew readiness system invented by the Navy. To maintain readiness and receive qualifications for events, roughly seven of the twelve-member crew, by name and position, must actively participate in each graded event to receive a Qual—the gold star at the ASWOC. This directly reflected on the commanding officer. Everyone knew that, especially Commander Snow.

One fine winter's day, a crew played its game of basketball; and, as fate would have it, the flight engineer leapt up for a rebound, stretching high into the stratosphere while another player or two did the same. One of them had to come down first. The flight engineer, who held the "tactical seat" for the crew, came down with the ball feet first, landing on someone's foot instead of the flat floor of the basketball court. He sprained his ankle.

This should have been anticipated. Certainly it is common to the sport, more common than not. However, during the dead of winter, Skipper Snow had not considered the dangers associated with basketball in Adak.

Commander Snow leapt into action when he learned that one of his beloved crewmembers sprained an ankle. The flight engineer, laid up and unable to fly for several days, denied the entire crew and squadron the ability to gain a gold star; although, it was a remote possibility in the first place. Believe it or not, in the dead of winter on Adak, Commander Snow outlawed basketball to promote maximum readiness. Drinking alcohol, watching repeats of the same movies and reading my postcards from a bar located in sunny Key West were their only diversions. My efforts to boost morale were a Godsend.

I wrote to the wardroom as a whole at first. When the cards arrived, they were read aloud and displayed at the all-officer meetings, where everyone enjoyed and profited from a heterosexual's sense of humor. Later, I wrote to individuals, even sending gay cards to a few select lieutenants, those who could stand the ribbing. Whether they were gay or not didn't matter, just knowing that someone took the time to jack you up was enough to put smiles on everyone's faces. Whenever the Adak mail contained my postcards, "Roll Call!" became the battle cry up and down the halls of the BOQ. The junior officers piled out of rooms, braced against hallway walls and received their reality check from Key West.

It became a game. In a sharp military manner, each man stepped forward from their brace, pivoted and marched forward to the individual with the mail. They pretended to be back in AOCS basic training, greeting the officer with the greeting of the day, talking in the third person, receiving the cards with flat palms coming together chest high and parallel to the floor, performing an about face, displaying pictures to everyone, and reading whatever it was that I had to say. It didn't take much to keep these guys and gals entertained.

Well, I just couldn't resist the temptation. Some thought it vicious and not at all funny or in good taste. Maybe they were right. Yet, for those who constantly lived on the Navy's short leash, whose entertainment consisted of top secret inquisitions of new junior officers or occasional runs to the base exchange where copious amounts of alcohol were available, my postcards of women on the sunny beaches of warm Florida, with socially inappropriate comments made them all laugh their butts off. So what was so wrong about supporting the fleet? At least it gave them something to talk about and took their minds off their justified gripes.

At a party in California the following summer, several people told me that my mail was one of the few things that kept them sane.

Once established at NAS Key West, I took up office residence in the operations building, which jutted out into the flight line area at the end of the main road. Adequate for our needs, the office housed three naval aviators, one helicopter pilot, and two C-12 pilots. Gray government-issue desks, black rotary telephones, dirt-brown carpet, and lockers filled the room, as did a range of intrusive noises from aircraft on the flight line and runways.

Three individual concrete strips served as runways in Key West, the longest of which was runway seven at ten thousand feet, while the two shorter strips were eight thousand feet in length. When the fighter jets utilized the short runways for takeoff, their afterburners were at full power on the other side of my building instead of the typical, reduced power setting one mile away. Oh, *"the sound of freedom"* at its finest!

Not so coincidently, NAS Key West housed an aggressor squadron that flew all the different types of foreign aircraft to challenge our F-14 pilots in air-to-air combat maneuvers. Key West, the east coast "Top Gun" base, came complete with telemetry data radar, plenty of open ocean airspace to rip up in pursuit of the ever so elusive bogies, hundreds of square miles of water to shoot up while practicing gun work from fighters, and thousands of square miles of open water in which to go splash. The entire office filled with the deafening roar of one type of jet engine or another, vibrating our pens and pencils, shaking our windows, and generally raising our anxiety levels five or six times per day. It was something to get used to, reminding me of a Woody Allen movie where as a child, he was raised under a roller coaster, explaining the onset of his many neuroses.

The initial jet training of NAS Key West, combined with all this noise, vibration and futile anxiety heightened our chances for a similar response. During wintertime, student jet pilots came down in droves to fly their T-2 Buckeye trainers in suitable weather, free from the fog and ice that plagued many of the training bases along other parts of the gulf coast. "FCLPs" (field carrier landing practice) occurred on a daily basis during the winter months. The visiting squadrons placed six, ancient, straight-jet, twin-engine airplanes in the oval landing pattern at one time, generating over one thousand take-offs and landings a day at the base. Over and over, they flew around the base at low altitude, simulating their work around the U.S.S. Aircraft Carrier. These students also launched from Naval Air

Station Key West for their first carrier landings—their moment of truth. The worst was yet to come.

The very worst flight line office noise came from the H-3 helicopters. These large beasts of burden, the workhorses of the Navy, performed search air rescue in Key West. Properly maintained, they were also capable of antisubmarine warfare in the fleet and utility transport. For example, the complete rotor head was changed out every one hundred flight hours to prevent disintegration. The high maintenance of these birds included washing and preventive greasing of every moving part. They washed the beast after every flight to prevent salt corrosion. We, in the flight line office, thought they washed the helos just to raise our anxiety level a few notches above the water line left by the thundering jets.

For their washing at the birdbath, the station utilized the ramp space next to our windows. The pilots kept the engines, the main rotor above the helicopter and the tail rotor turning, while parking the helicopter directly above the drain facing away from us. The enlisted activated a fire hose and sprayed down the bird for its daily clean up from the salt-saturated air. This seemed reasonable enough until the application. The crews invariably placed the tail rotor, whose five blade tips spun at the speed of sound, next to our windows—only twenty feet away. The helicopter was so loud that its noise drowned out the other aircraft, even fighter aircraft. This wash rack routine lasted from thirty to forty-five minutes, and I swear the helo pilots did this just to play games with us fixed wing drivers. It was an impressive air show at NAS Key West, but I often wore earplugs in the office, speaking loudly on the telephone while performing the ground job.

My primary job known as the ground job was "NALO" or Naval Air Logistic Office coordinator. I interfaced with staff in New Orleans for tasking and requests for air logistics movements of our own. The Navy's C-12 program was spread out from base to base. Flying as a station pilot for the Navy meant that you reported to the commanding officer of the air station. Our tasking, however, came from the Naval Air Logistics Office in New Orleans where all flights were coordinated.

The airplanes were assigned to the air stations and that caused a bit of a rub. The base command did not control the airplane and it was not the commanding officer's own private mode of transportation to take whenever and wherever he pleased. This frustrated just about every base command because they could neither control what they felt to be their asset nor the pilots who flew it. The captain made requests to use the airplane through NALO, just like everyone else, unless it was for training hops.

We NALO pilots were an oddity unto ourselves. We reported to everyone, were responsible for everything and accountable to all schedules. NALO wanted things to run on time, whether the field was socked in, lit, or even open. Our can-do spirit, training, and a section of limitations guided us like radar throughout the system: just file the flight plan, fuel the plane, board the passengers and get the job done.

All this made flying as a NAS Key West station pilot one of the best deals going in the entire U.S. Navy. Our destinations included: Navy Norfolk and NAS Oceana, Virginia; Cecil Field, Mayport, NAS Jacksonville and Opalaka, Florida; NAS New Orleans, Navy Dallas at Love field, NAS New Brunswick, Maine; Guantanamo Bay in Cuba, NAS Rosie Roads in Puerto Rico, Honduras; and Andros Island, located in the Bahamas.

Each destination had its own unique challenges, whether it was the dense fog of NAS Norfolk, the poor approach and wide, last minute heading change to avoid the hills and Cuban troops at Gitmo, or the four thousand foot strip with no approach at night at Andros Island. There, the field was surrounded on three sides by fifty-foot palm trees and marked only by smoky yellow flames from a few smudge pots set out along the runway edges. Yes, each environment—and there were many—challenged us to push the limits of aviation, flying in a "light twin" turbo prop. I enjoyed it all—all except for a couple of flights that nearly ended in disaster.

On the first troublesome flight, we traversed Florida zigzagging our way through afternoon thunderstorms that crowded out the summer sky on a daily basis. The C-12 could not fly above the storms. Therefore, if you wanted to get anywhere by air, it required flying around storms using on-board weather radar. We were south of Tampa, the lightning capital of the world, when our trouble began. I relieved the pilot in command a half-hour before. He dozed in the rear of the plane while I sat with the playboy officer in the flight station. The PO was a helicopter pilot who viewed the C-12 as his own private airplane with no rules, similar to how helicopters operate when over an open ocean at one hundred feet on a sunny day. However, we were neither over an open ocean nor at ground level. Rather, we were working with air traffic control at twenty-four thousand feet, flying in an alley sandwiched between menacing thunderstorms.

Florida thunderstorms really mean business in the afternoon and that occasion was no exception. The storms spit out hail for twenty-five miles downwind, produce sixty knots of vertical wind shear, cause severe turbulence in and around their environment, and always contained enough lightning to power a night football game. But the PO didn't care and he didn't want to hear my tested and proven words of wisdom.

"Stay away from hook-like reflections on the radar, sir. They represent the anvil tops. Flying under the anvil puts the aircraft downwind of the storm, exposing us to hail, damaging winds and lightning, sir."

Not! The PO said phooey to all of the literature, all of the documentation of previous disasters, and plowed ahead over my objections. I didn't sign for the airplane and he outranked me. As usual he did whatever he pleased—but this time he got caught and nearly killed us all.

The PO flew to one side of the storm, the downwind side, directly under the anvil head of that monster. I was nervous but there wasn't much I could do. When we came abeam the black evil, the sky lit up, a large flash crossing our windscreen all the way out to our right wing tip.

"Shit," I yelled, "we've been hit by lightning!"

The PO thought nothing of it, projecting his nonchalance all the way into NAS Key West. I was pissed, but there was nothing to do except trade seats with the pilot in command and hope for the best until we safely reached ground.

Lightning is a destructive force in almost any setting. Heat generated by its current flow can weld metal parts together: parts such as flight controls. It can punch holes completely through wings and ignite fuel in the aircraft tanks. It destroys sensitive radios and avionics; and in the case of the C-12, it burns engine bearings, causing them to flake while magnetizing the drive shaft and gears in the gearbox, along with a host of other life-threatening problems.

For us, this lightning strike did all that and more. Upon landing, I wrote up the event and the initial inspection revealed that both propellers demonstrated entrance markings from the lightning. The right wing tip was blackened and the flaps had seventeen exit holes on their trailing edges. The following day, our mechanics informed us that each power plant required replacement and new propellers were on order. We were fortunate that both power plants had not failed during the flight—their oil screens were full of metal flakes from the engine bearings coming apart in flight. Although time was not on our side that sunny day in Key West, God must have been. I was happy for His Grace, despite the playboy officer's attitude.

For our few training hops, we took the helicopter pilots assigned to fly the C-12 into the pattern for landing practice and flew the precision approach circuit for their instrument currency in the airplane. Oftentimes, at the end of a long day, we combined the flights and shot several approaches because we had the opportunity to ferry the airplane back to Key West. Cross-country flight trainers were fairly rare; but if we did have to train, and the sky was full of jet drivers, we found other fields to practice our landings. Also, there were the Friday afternoon, short-legged flight trainers, "one landing specials," as we used to call them.

Friday afternoon flights were especially planned to spy, to get a leg-up and the word out to all of those on base that owned a boat. After all, this was Key West and the place was overrun with fishermen. The biggest and best fisherman was a middle-aged, retired navy senior chief—our best mechanic, who moonlighted as a fishing guide for some good bucks. The whole base of boaters was in on the deal, the Friday afternoon flight "club." This is what I heard.

When the airplane was available, Commander Pabst took time out of his oh-so-busy Friday afternoon pre-happy hour schedule and flew his training hops with one of our qualified plane commanders. He called it a bounce hop, although there was only one landing coupled with possibly one approach back to the airfield. The entire purpose of the flight trainer didn't have much to do with aviation, although he did record an approach, a landing, and an hour or so of flight time for his currency records. The flight provided weed-line reconnaissance for Saturday's launch of the Navy's impromptu powerboat fishing regatta.

Once out over the Florida Straits, he flew along, searching for floating lines of weeds and debris in the water. Finding them, he took radial and distance readings from the Key West Tacan Station, surveyed the competition from the air, and headed back to base for his one approach and landing. His system worked!

Upon returning to base, Commander Pabst charted out his positions and gave the geographic coordinates of his tacan fixes to all those with a need to know. The helicopter pilots did much the same thing, but moved in closer with the H-3's, especially when a tournament was in town. It was fish spotting on government time and not a problem, as the flight time was required. Commander Pabst hid his genius well, both in fishing and flying. Doubling up on everything was perfectly legal, every inch of the way. He was quite good at it all!

Trips to Navy Pensacola provided another avenue for C-12 reconnaissance. NALO assigned the flights; so, as long as we were going there, we loaded a special, oversized cooler through the rear cargo door of the plane. Our trusty mechanics provided us with the cooler and blocks of ice for the long ride home. After all, oysters must be stored at the proper temperature.

The day before we flew the trip, someone called a NAS Pensacola helicopter pilot, affectionately known as "Blades." He didn't like that moniker, but in the Navy a nickname stuck. He earned it because of a nick received from a tail rotor during one bad night of flight training. Evidently the instructor in the helicopter thought they had hit the tailskid, a bar that stands out vertically which prevents the helicopter boom from striking the ground. Blades went back with his flashlight to check for damage and then remembered where he was—directly beneath the spinning tail rotor. He carefully looked around, but the spinning rotor impacted his visor cover on top of his helmet. This sent him to the ground. Blades was one lucky son-of-a gun; he got away without serious injuries.

It was too bad about the nickname because Blades was a great guy about everything. He met the Key West station pilots with large gunnysacks full of fresh oysters. The sacks weighed at least 200 pounds, explaining the reason for the oversized cooler full of block ice. We didn't have much ground time in Pensacola; but with the aid of a yellow towing tractor, I darted over to Blades' car, picked up the bags of precious cargo and transported it back to the cooler waiting outside the airplane. Restrained by a net, the cooler and its contents were parked in the back of the plane next to the life raft.

Upon our return to Key West, all of the pilots rendezvoused at Commander Pabst's residence for some of Pensacola's finest. Evenings like these made being in uniform a bit special. It boosted morale, upping our work performance. In short, these evenings made us forget the gravity of our naval responsibilities for a while and putting some fun back in our lives.

These two short stories contrasted with two others I *heard* about and nearly *read* about. The first was a recurrent training session at the simulators in Dallas, Texas. The second was an emergency flight to Andrews Air Force Base, transporting a leukemia patient to the National Naval Medical Center in Bethesda, Maryland.

In order to remain current with the plane, the Navy required us to attend a brief ground school every year, including three recurrent simulator sessions. The government contracted with Simuflight for this service and it worked well for everyone. We received the training without paying for the outright purchase of the simulators or instructors, while Simuflight received our business. Even the hotels made out, as the Navy guaranteed them business, contracting a fixed price within ten dollars of each other.

I received my written training orders and flew commercially to Dallas. Per these orders, I rented a car on the government's dime and proceeded to a Holiday Inn where I had stayed during previous simulator sessions. It cost a bit more, ten dollars more per night than the other hotel, wherever that one was located.

It was only after checking into class the next day, rental car in tow, that I learned the other hotel was right next door to the Holiday Inn and provided free transportation to and from the simulators and the airport. So much for communication! Two senior officers stayed at this less expensive hotel and they made me feel quite uncomfortable with my financially incorrect decision. But what did I know? I had my orders in hand, authorizing my choices. No one had put out any word on the cheapest and easiest solution to our Dallas housing requirement. I was there for three days of intensive study, not a boondoggle. Besides, I flew so much of the time in Key West, my next assignment or week of assignments might be buried in the paperwork people threw on my desk, which I found after returning to base that night around 9:30 PM.

I felt good knowing I worked hard at Simuflight to receive the best training and annual qualification in accordance with my written orders. Until I overheard several coworkers talking about it, I thought little about Dallas after turning in my travel claim for processing.

"He had it in writing," they said, "and it was approved. He did nothing wrong. The rental car was on his orders."

My boss came down saying, "Neal, I'd like to see a copy of your Dallas orders."

He read them and walked out.

I hardly believed all the heat generated behind my back over a rental car and a ten dollar extra hotel room, obviously sour paper for which someone thought someone else had to be held accountable. *What a penny-wise and dollar-foolish system*, I fumed in embarrassment. Fortunately, I only heard about it. In the end, orders came down that no one would be authorized a rental car without the expressed written consent and signature of the commanding officer.

The second story I heard about came with an emergency call from the base PO or playboy officer. Command received a phone call early one afternoon from a flight surgeon that just diagnosed an enlisted man's wife with leukemia. NAS Key West had a hospital, but the building was condemned years ago; besides, it didn't have the expertise to treat serious diseases. In the doctor's opinion, the woman needed rapid treatment and he requested the command to fly the woman to Maryland for treatment at Bethesda. Simple enough. I made a couple of phone calls to NALO, while the mechanics towed the airplane out and fueled it. We would fly the mission at sea level pressure inside the cabin, cutting all the corners through the East Coast warning areas under the authority of our medical emergency and land in Andrews Air Force Base.

Before I knew it, however, the PO came to my office to personally plan this trip. It wasn't out of the kindness of his heart. The PO wanted to overnight at NAS Norfolk. That afternoon I worked between his conversation, telephone calls from NALO, the medical center at Key West, the hangar, and the captain himself. At one point, I took both of my telephones off the hook to focus on our needs and planning. The medical center cried for the flight, the command authorized the flight, the PO wanted the flight for his own ends, and NALO wanted the flight, but only with message traffic to support it.

At the time, our message traffic required an optical reader. This meant exacting forms and special type. In 1986, email and fax machines had not arrived in Key West and this left the command in a lurch. In the time it would take to draft and type a message, drive it around the entire airfield to have it scanned, sent, and read at NALO, with an about-face reaction from NALO back to Key West, everyone but NALO figured we could already be in Andrews or our patient would be dead.

My overriding priority was transporting the patient to Bethesda. I sized up the large oxygen bottle standing by the aircraft and did what my command asked of me—without the NALO paper excursion-diversion. After all, this made the playboy officer happy, too.

During the trip, we flew through the military practice areas off the East Coast, technically called warning areas. As it would be the shortest distance to Andrews from Key West, I requested the routing and stipulated our medical situation on our flight plan, utilizing the appropriate medevac call sign. All went according to plan over land, but once back over water, east of the Carolinas, the controllers wanted to know if we really did have a medical emergency or not.

What kind of question is that? I thought. *Who do they think I am, a doctor or a pilot?*

"I believe we declared the emergency on our flight plan," I responded. "We have a doctor, a nurse and a very large oxygen tank accompanying a patient, who is lying on a stretcher strapped to the floor of the airplane."

That seemed to convince them of our plight, but it also raised some eyebrows.

When we arrived at Andrews, the patient and medical team deplaned before I stepped out of the cockpit. I feared that our air crewman, his clothing soaked in the oxygen-rich atmosphere that he was exposed to during the flight, would light up a smoke; so I quickly caught up with him before he could incinerate himself. He might have also tried to fuel the airplane, creating an equally horrifying scenario.

Fortunately, we trained at the same school. He did the appropriate thing, aimlessly walking around for fifteen minutes, allowing the concentrated oxygen to dissipate into the atmosphere. He refueled the airplane later on while I filed a flight plan to NAS Norfolk. The PO made an important phone call, possibly to Key West to report on our success and the health of the patient—but I doubt it. He was all smiles by the time we headed back into the night sky.

Back in Key West the next afternoon, NALO was on the telephone, inquiring as to why we flew the "unauthorized mission."

"I handled it the best I could, sir. It was an emergency and the command authorized the mission. That's correct, sir. We didn't have time to go through normal channels and protocol. The flight surgeon wanted her in treatment at Bethesda that evening."

As a rule, Key West paperwork consisted of wrapping up your catch-of-the-day. But when paperwork turns south, even in Key West, somebody wants someone else to pay for the embarrassing lack of paperwork.

This paper chase went on for weeks before the PO chimed in.

"We could have driven the woman to Miami," he said. "There the medical augmentation plan covers her treatment within the military contracts."

He blamed the decision to fly the patient to Andrews AFB on me!

"I am not a doctor and I did not place the request for her medevac," I responded. This was my only shield against the numerous arrows heading my way from all sides. At that point, it became personal. I felt I had done the right thing, while under guidance from my commanding officer and in aid of a deathly ill dependent. Much to my surprise, I heard about this one for a long time and nearly read about it.

In July of 1986, I took a few weeks leave, traveling to California and riding my motorcycle back to Nebraska. I couldn't miss my father's retirement. Luckily I found two convenient military airlift flights, the first on Friday to NAS Jacksonville and the second on Sunday to NAS Alameda in California. In between, I stayed over at the NAS Jacksonville officer's quarters and entertained myself at the O'Club.

I was minding my own business, talking with another pilot at the bar late that Saturday afternoon when the Naval Reserves from the NAS Jacksonville medical staff entered the lounge. Out of the corner of my eye, I glimpsed a streak of red hair that captured my attention. I was a sucker for redheads.

This time it'll be different, I told myself while I simultaneously realized I was already in deep trouble. She had spotted me too. After a few minutes, this radiant young Lieutenant Commander, with her crystal blue eyes and voluptuous curves called out across the Jax O'Club Ready Room in my direction.

"Excuse me, excuse me!"

I turned on my barstool, surprised to realize a senior officer was calling me over to her table—a senior officer I was happy to oblige.

"Lieutenant, we have a question here. Would you come over and join us?"

"Of course," I said and grabbed my glass, feeling lucky anticipation.

I respectfully addressed the senior officer at the table out of professional courtesy, recognizing his rank as a navy captain.

"How may I help you sir?"

"My name is Carl Daven, Commanding Officer NAS Jacksonville Field Hospital Reserves," he said as he shook my hand.

"This is Fred Gaugen," he continued signaling with an open hand toward his right, "Donna Becker, Fred Mansphere, John Whitehead and David Fritz."

"It's a pleasure to meet you sir. I'm Neal, Neal Schupbach and this is my friend John," I said and looked to my colleague at my immediate left. My eyes then snapped back to the beautiful red head and caught her eye.

"You're a pilot aren't you?" she asked.

"Yes."

"We're medical corps and we were debating whether pilot's wings had one anchor or two. You wear glasses but fly?"

Somehow the dichotomy of her question was totally forgivable.

"That's right. The eyes are the first thing to go and I forget what's after that. My twenty-twenty went during my third year in the Navy," I said as John walked around the table and came up behind Lieutenant Commander Becker. Captain Daven signaled to the waitress for two pitchers of beer with his left hand and I noticed his academy ring covered the white stripe of his wedding band. John pulled a chair along side Lieutenant Commander Becker, sat down and began flirting in a breach of protocol.

"Neal, sit down and join us. The night is young," said Captain Daven in an inviting tone.

"Yes sir. With pleasure sir." I pulled a chair to the now overcrowded table.

The pitchers arrived and much to my delight, so did Donna Becker—right on my lap. John's early advances worked to my advantage. She thought little of my newfound bar buddy and later called him "creepy."

Surprised by the informality shown by the beautiful redhead, I behaved myself for just a few short moments and then played with her leg with my left hand while drinking beer with my right. Donna didn't dodge my advances and I thought that to be a good sign.

The table buzzed for an hour and then Donna said, "Would you like to see my new car?"

"Why, of course," I said expecting to see something rather simple.

We left the group and crowded bar, walking outside through the back of the club. We took time to overlook the broad expanse of St. John's River.

Donna led me on a circuitous route, walking under tall pine trees that whispered in the wind. *I hope this means she has something in mind.*

Ten minutes later we stopped at the side of a beautiful, blue sports car. "What do you think? Do you like it?"

My jaw hit the ground.

"Like it? Babe, I love it!"

I stood before a brand new Nissan 300ZX Turbo. I was awestruck.

"Would you like to drive it?" she asked as she held out her keys.

"No. No way! This is your treasure, not mine. But, can you do me one little favor? I want to at least see the engine on this beast. Can you and pop the top?"

My mouth dropped open when the hood came up.

"Seen enough? Lets go for a ride. I know a good wine shop."

"Yes sir!"

Donna drove us off base to a small wine shop a few miles away. Vibrant hues of various wines shone along the upper shelf, lending a warm, welcoming ambiance to a perfect evening.

"Back in Mississippi, my mother decorated the kitchen windows with mason jars filled with colored water," Donna said as she looked around at the room's beautiful décor.

"We could do that in our house," I said without a thought.

"Our house?" replied Donna as she turned and gazed into my eyes.

I was caught in the act—the act of falling in love.

"Yes, our house," I said as I kissed her for the first time.

"Watch out, I'm a sucker for redheads," I whispered as we parted.

"I'll remember that *Brown Eyes*."

One thing led to another and so it began. Before I knew it, I was involved in a long distance romance with Donna. She came down to Key West or I flew up to NAS Jacksonville on a regular basis. On weekends we visited each other via Piedmont Airlines and space available transportation from the U.S. military.

Our relationship was unique. As my senior, she required my salute when boarding my aircraft. I was the boyfriend aviator, flying her directly to the romantic isle of Key West in a 2.5 million dollar airplane. At times it was as if the plane was ours, not some loaner from the government.

In Jacksonville, we enjoyed seafood dinners on the beach served up by a big, husky guy named *"Chap, as in stick."* He was our favorite. In Key West, I cooked lobster tails on my back porch and we savored the sunsets at the nicest establishment in town, Loui's, Back Yard, where the terraced decking overlooked the water. After sunset, the gazebo at the Reach Hotel served wine on the oceanfront where we could watch a full moon rising.

In the space of a few short months, things got serious between us. Much to my surprise, while we were talking one night in front of the stereo, Donna popped the question. We planned a March wedding. The equinox, the 21st of March, fell on a Saturday and that seemed perfect for us as it symbolized equality and balance in our relationship.

I suggested our ceremony be in the very room where we proposed, the living room of my small townhouse. We invited a small circle of friends and immediate family. Navy whites were the uniform of the day. I rubbed my hands from nervous energy before the ceremony. My best man was my Navy flying partner and the base chaplain performed the ceremony—after he returned home and retrieved his shoulder boards. Donna's walk down the aisle proceeded through the kitchen hallway.

My seventy-year-old neighbor, Rose, demanded that I kiss Donna twice because she thought my first one was a weak attempt.

"Come on Neal, we want to see a better kiss than that. Give her a big kiss!"

Three of our invited guests arrived too late for that demonstration because they flew a last minute search air rescue mission in the helicopter. That was neither a surprise nor a slight for a Navy bride and groom!

We honeymooned at the new, "old" hotel in town, La Conche. Our refurbished antique section even provided a canopy bed. For those three days, I was never more relaxed.

I never worked harder at trying to stay alive in an airplane than I did one time coming out of Key West. That one flight to NAS Jacksonville and one mistake nearly cost me my life and that of those on board. That day is burned into my memory.

The previous day, Dirk Bridges and I took off from Key West, flying to NAS Roosevelt Roads in Puerto Rico. It was to be an uneventful ferry flight, a four-hour trip that pre-positioned us for our mission the following day. We would take an admiral, his staff and all of his classified materials from Rosie Roads to NAS Jacksonville, with an intermediate stop in West Palm Beach to refuel and process through American customs. Once in Jacksonville, Donna, then my fiancée, would board the plane for the ride back to Key West. The lost weekend would be ours. My plan sounded simple enough, a few flight plans to file, catch a weather briefing in the morning and give Dirk, a helicopter pilot, some badly needed practice at landing the aircraft. *A piece of cake.*

Dirk took the night landing at Rosie Roads and flared a little high, something all helicopter pilots need extra practice to overcome. Obviously, flying fixed-wing differs from hovering in a rotary wing aircraft, especially when it comes to touching down. We spoke about it and I thought nothing of the landing after that. I knew that repetition hones proficiency and on the following day he would have three more landings.

Dirk, however, really didn't care about flying fixed-wing. He was passionate about the helicopter program, even after barely surviving a nighttime helicopter crash while entering the high seas on its side. Despite the crash, he mastered that bird, caring less for this one. Still, I tried to give him all four landings planned for the trip.

We went to base operations and received the required weather briefing in the morning. There was nothing unusual there, for either West Palm Beach or Jacksonville. We filed the stopover flight plan and pre-flighted the airplane before meeting the admiral and his staff at the end of the red carpet. The admiral sat on the starboard side of the aircraft, over the wing, while his aide sat in front of him next to the cockpit. They could observe everything that went on over my shoulder. That made me nervous, but there was nothing I could do about it. The accompanying staff took up two more seats directly behind me. The remaining seats became cargo bays with seat belts used as restraining devices. Their suitcases joined our life raft in the back of the plane.

The sun was brilliant and visibility unlimited when we took off that day. We motored four hours to Florida's West Palm Beach, a lengthy flight by anyone's standard, especially compared to the admiral's standard of jet service instead of our slower turboprop. Dirk flew the leg, and although his approach to West Palm was acceptable, he flared a bit high once again. Dirk recovered by pushing the nose over, but then over-rotated for another try at the flare. He repeated the pushover-pull-back technique, turning the smooth flight into a roller coaster ride. He came just slightly short of smacking the tail by landing on it instead of the wheels.

I was more than concerned and assisted the next gyration by limiting the amount of pull he could apply to the control yoke. My blocking technique worked, but by this time problems compounded. We ran out of airspeed, altitude and ideas—all at the same time. The airplane jolted on landing in an unsettling manner, far from making an impressive landing. The admiral pinned me to the deck with an intense, dirty look. His silent message came across loud and clear.

I felt under the gun to complete the follow-on flight to Jacksonville. Despite what I had promised Dirk, the next leg would be mine. Back in Key West, he would again take over the landings, even with my fiancée on board. But there would be no repeat of the last set of landing attempts with the admiral.

We pre-flighted for the next leg, fueling the aircraft with just-full wing tanks, plenty of gas, but none in the auxiliary tanks—those located inboard of the engine nacelles. My weather briefing from Roosevelt Roads kept me legal for the second leg. Reassured, I felt confident. There were no reported systems affecting our arrival.

While I spoke with the fuel truck driver, Dirk spoke with a civilian behind the front desk of the handling company. He checked the weather.

"Neal, the weather in Jacksonville looks bad, really bad," he said as I came back inside.

The admiral seemed anxious to get going. He paced the floor with anticipation, sending frequent hard looks my way. I couldn't access a naval weather briefing, one that would contain a "WW" or weather warning. I surmised that I would seem irresolute if I approached the admiral, requesting his judgment. He owned the airplane and wore an expressive "Let's get going" determination about him. I chickened out. After all, the last landing was enough to warrant hell to pay, so why fool with it? In the Navy it's better to die than look bad. I took the old weather briefing—*it looks good enough*—and ignored Dirk's advice—*what did he know? He had made a bad landing, anyhow.*

We took off with only one person in our group knowing just how bad the forecast weather could become. That person wasn't me and it was a stupid mistake. I allowed a foolish lapse in protocol.

We flew past Cape Canaveral and up the eastern coast of Florida on that sunny day. It was smooth flying until we letdown into the Jacksonville area and headed for Navy Jax. I noticed the tall, dark cumulus clouds in front of us and brought up the weather radar. It displayed plenty of maneuvering room out to eighty miles, but my intuition kicked in. I had a bad feeling about the weather ahead. It appeared to be more of a system than individual storm cells. That spelled trouble.

I flew further on into the darkening sky, accepting radar vectors from Air Traffic Control to bring us into the Navy Jacksonville airport environment for the final approach. At eighteen thousand feet, I looked up from my instruments and radar and saw the sickening green cast in the billowing clouds off of my right wing. They look bruised. Further up in my field of vision, I saw circular "ball" clouds. I knew from growing up in eastern Nebraska that those clouds meant severe thunderstorms, possible hail, and damaging winds. What I didn't know was how rapid conditions were deteriorating all around me.

From out of the Gulf of Mexico, a system of warm, moist air blew into the western corner of Florida, forming a layer above the colder February weather pattern. The interaction of these two atmospheric conditions culminated at NAS Jacksonville while clobbering its surrounding sister airfields: NAS Mayport to the east, NAS Cecil Field to the west and Jacksonville International to the north. In the meantime, a line of strong thunderstorms filled in behind me, blocking my exit.

"NALO 312," a transmission came through.

"There is severe weather in the Jacksonville area. NAS Jacksonville is closed. State your intentions."

"What are our intentions?" Dirk asked me.

I wanted to get away from Jacksonville to the east.

"Our fuel is limited. Request radar vectors to NAS Mayport. Hopefully the weather system is north of there," I replied.

Dirk repeated my request to ATC, "NALO 312 requests radar vectors to Navy Mayport."

ATC responded, "Roger, NALO312; fly heading zero six zero and descend to two thousand feet."

"Heading zero six zero, down to two thousand feet, NALO 312."

Dirk then called the base on a separate radio.

"Jacksonville NALO312 is diverting to Mayport."

"Roger, NALO. We'll call base ops for you and tell them you are coming."

Now the fun really began.

We encountered moderate turbulence on our short trip over to Mayport. Dirk lacked experience in two-piloted crew coordination practices of fixed wing flying. The plane shook and kicked about. Lightning filled the blackened afternoon sky. The autopilot kicked off several times and I hand-flew the airplane, feeling the weight of the entire world on my shoulders. A strong sense of isolation overtook me like never before. Failure was not an option. There was no giving up. I had no choice but to press on and perform, to function to the best of my ability under these circumstances. Failure could mean crashing, dooming us all.

Feeling this way doubled my workload in an already bad situation. I was really sweating it. After all, I had an admiral on board who was less than impressed with the team. He and everyone else on the airplane could hear and observe our every effort and the weather had gone to hell in a hand basket. I allowed myself a nanosecond of pity and then got back to flying. I quickly got back to the basics. I even recited the quiet chant I learned while flying basic instruments, *"attitude gyro, airspeed, attitude gyro, altimeter, attitude gyro airspeed, attitude gyro altimeter, heading, attitude gyro,"* moving my eyes around the instrument panel in cadence with the words, occasionally looking at the radar.

The weather had worsened considerably by the time we arrived in the Mayport terminal environment. My concentration and chant fatigued me, as my secondary instruments, heading and vertical speed, began to take on less and less significance. I only wanted to keep my airspeed up, the wings level and the pitch of the nose in a flying attitude. I was literally down to the basics, supporting life with the very basics I knew. *What more can I do?*

The airplane had to ride the storm waves, the updrafts and the downdrafts, accepting each with little correction. Otherwise, one of the wings might overstress and snap off, sending us to an early grave.

I had to descend during the approach to Mayport to land; but, in all honesty, I wanted the altitude for a protective buffer against striking the ground. Realizing this, I decided to climb-out, to go around and reformulate a plan "C" with ATC.

"There are tornados reported in the Mayport area," ATC said on climb-out. "State your intentions."

Dirk keyed his microphone. "There are tornados reported in the Mayport area. State your intentions." He repeated the controller's communications to me, but keyed his mike out of fright.

The repeated verbatim message added quite a bit of confusion to our controller's workload.

"Now someone up there is mimicking me. NALO, are you the parrot?"

Once we got it all straightened out, I keyed the microphone and asked for the weather at NAS Cecil field, an airport with a very long runway. Fortunately the weather report came back better than the last two fields. I elected to take vectors to Cecil for the approach and landing.

In the meantime, to facilitate the proper handling of the admiral, Dirk called Mayport ground operations.

"NALO 312 is departing for Cecil Field."

Donna also got word from Mayport base operations and drove across town to Navy Cecil. She worried about her future husband flying around in a sky as black as pitch.

Our trip over to Cecil seemingly took forever. I could not push the airplane to its cruising speed. At that speed, the weather could break the airframe. Instead, I lumbered the plane and passengers along at 180 knots, following radar vectors at four thousand feet, keeping my attention fixed on the basics of aviation and one small radar screen.

As a rule, I couldn't rely on the ground-based radar, but I had to trust someone. The rain obscured everyone's information. It became a guessing game. I finally set the radar on its lowest range and worked my way back up the mileage scale to a setting that provided useful information.

In all my days of flying, my workload was never higher than on that missed approach and diversion to Navy Cecil. My biggest dilemma quickly became the status of NAS Cecil. *When we arrive, will the field be open or socked in by these violent thunderstorms?* Cecil or bust!

The low altitude flying quickly drained my tanks of precious fuel and I worried that I might be out of options. In the Cecil approach control sector, the weather report came back with a four hundred foot ceiling, heavy rain at the field and strong winds. It all sounded good to me. Of course, at that moment, I was still flying in the thick between the storms. At least the winds rammed straight down the runway.

For the approach I held the flaps for a no-flap landing. *It will be safer flying in such strong turbulence, with flaps retracted,* I thought. *To assure their retraction in case of a go-around to yet another field, somewhere far down the road.* I knew my fuel would be exhausted in short order, if unable to retract a jammed flap. I configured the airplane as late as possible, dropping the landing gear below one thousand feet and advancing the condition levers for the propellers to spin at their maximum rpm, their most efficient performance at lower speeds.

We flew the first GCA approach, listening to a distant voice—all that separated us from our Maker. If our radio connection broke, there was little left for me to consider besides flying west and finding a small strip or a highway—with an admiral on board. I kept the speed up, way up to 140 knots, yet flew a shallow descent for the glide path. This alerted me to the headwind component, a strong headwind that blew my aircraft one step back for every three forward. I kept at it until we hit moderate to severe turbulence, somewhere below six hundred feet.

The plane shook violently. I added maximum thrust to escape from the ground. Fortunately, the Super King Air lived up to its name and reputation as we powered our way back into the sky for another turn in the GCA pattern. Between the ragged layers of low clouds, I caught sight of the field, usually a welcome sight. But right then, contrary to what we wanted, it was best away from the ground. I couldn't trust the winds and the rain for landing.

I radioed, "NALO 312 is going around."

The controller came back. " NALO 312 turn to a heading of one eight zero, and state your intentions."

"Dirk, ask him for another approach to a full stop. Tell him about the weather, too," I said.

Dirk responded, "We would like another approach to a full stop landing. We experienced severe turbulence on final."

"Roger. Missed approach instructions remain the same. Stand by for your final controller."

We turned downwind for anything but a routine ride to the base leg. Ten seconds after I rolled wings level from his turn, all hell broke loose in the airplane. Charts and approach plates went flying, and anything else that wasn't tied down.

I held on to the yoke so tightly that my fingerprints imprinted on the black paint. My total concentration was focused on the attitude gyro. It held the kernels of truth between living and dying; but, much to my horror, the loud and violent vibrations visually blurred my gyro. The whole plane vibrated like a paint shaker. *When will this end? Will my attitude gyro function after this, or will I be staring at an orange "off flag" across the instrument?*

Thank you, God! When we came out of that burst of turbulence, the gyro still functioned and we continued south into another burst with severe disturbance once again erasing critical information. I swallowed hard, swallowing the knot in my throat, and held on, maintaining what I had set up in the first place. I tried my best to maintain the last heading, to change nothing until I could see again.

Ground control came back with a vector, turning us east, but I refused until things settled down. I kept my wings level, maximizing the vertical lift on the plane and minimizing any change in directions. I complied moments later with the vector and the final approach controller kept me in a turn to the final approach course in one maneuver.

"This is your final controller; wheels should be down."

"Three down and locked," Dirk replied.

"Coming up, coming up and on glide path. Begin descent: heading three—five—four. Going slightly below—slightly below glide path. Now going further below. Decrease your rate of descent."

On this approach, we once again rode the winds like a wild bull. For that reason, I used the same configuration as the last approach. This time, however, I concentrated on pushing the airplane down the glide-slope, forcing it through the updrafts, being keenly aware that powerful downdrafts could push us into the trees.

"Coming up. Now just slightly below, slightly below glide path. Heading three—five—eight. Coming up and on glide path."

The seemingly endless approach went on and on until, at four hundred feet, we broke out and Dirk called out, "The field is in sight."

I looked up at the runway and added even more power to travel down the glide-slope for what I envisioned as the correct runway intercept point: a point we barely made before touching down. I threw the engines into reverse, although the airplane required hardly any to stop. Our ground speed was so slow we stopped without any opposition on a flooded runway, no less.

When we taxied into the loading area where the admiral's ground staff waited for him outside base operations. I shut down the left motor and feathered the right, maintaining electrical power on the plane. I turned around to the admiral.

"Sir, I know this isn't Jacksonville, but we've landed safely."

He looked up from his book and smiled from ear to ear, leaving me to wonder. *Had he, too, concentrated through his fear, intently reading throughout the entire north Florida adventure?*

After that harrowing journey, everyone piled out of the airplane posthaste while ground personnel brought up a handcart and some tarps to keep the admiral's luggage and classified materials dry. I sat alone. Alone in my cockpit, I drew in more than a few deep breaths. In order to bring us safely back to earth, I had to force two approaches at Cecil. I lowered my head and gave thanks to God for getting us safely back on the ground.

For all of my training, study and simulators, every bit of what I learned—and then some—was applied on that flight. I scraped the bottom of the barrel for what to do, what to do next, and what to do afterwards.

Somehow the Good Lord helped me hold it all together through the worst of things. I was alive, living proof of His good grace.

"Mr. Schupbach? Mr. Schupbach, what are you doing out here all alone? Are you going to come inside? There is a lieutenant commander inside asking about you, wanting to know where you are."

I pulled my head up and looked back at the young airmen.

"Yes, I'll be coming right along. I need to check the weather. Can you put full main tanks and thirty gallons in each aux for our trip back to Key West?"

"Yes sir, but the field is closed for another fifteen minutes. We'll have just a short time to take off before the next storm system comes in."

"I'll check with the weatherman, but first I need to see that pretty commander."

We departed the plane and I walked across the ramp to greet Donna, the love of my life. She never looked better. She outranked me, so I gave her a salute instead of a kiss, a greeting that became our insider's joke. I guess that's what love in uniforms does for a person.

We had cheated death that day; but in just forty-five minutes, Donna and I would be airborne, flying home for our lost weekend in Key West. I knew I could compartmentalize, but this was ridiculous. I amazed even myself with my desire to fly so soon after a nearly disastrous flight. We had to make our weather window!

Despite being a military facility, the calm blue waters and sunshine of Boca Chica Field, NAS Key West, looked unusually inviting upon arrival.

Back in the maintenance office, Commander Pabst asked, "Neal, after twelve hours of flying, how did you keep the airplane so clean?"

I only smiled, but the next week I broke the secret to him.

"On a wing and a prayer."

In Key West, the small things make you think. For example, on nearly every night flight back to the Keys along Florida's west coast, we saw the lights of Miami from twenty-five thousand feet. But there was no glimmer of the lights of Havana. This fact gave rise to my speculation as to Castro's enforced poverty on the residents of his worker's paradise.

It made me think of the Somali people standing under streetlights with nothing to do.

Why don't the cities of Cuba have streetlights?

While stationed at NAS Key West, the Navy and Coast Guard constantly intercepted Cubans on a near-continuous basis, floating on mere inner tubes tied together to make rafts for their crossing of the Florida Straits. By their very presence, this exodus told a story of hunger, inhumanity, oppression and desperation. Why else leave everyone behind? Why risk all, enduring the burning sun and pounding waves for days, just to come to the land of the free, the shores of America? Could Cuba be financially worse off than Somalia? I doubted this. Look at all of the Soviet assistance they received. Still, it made me wonder what was going on in Cuba.

Then one day, a Cuban General surrendered himself and his family on the flight line of NAS Key West.

It happened one afternoon as I spoke with a superior officer. Someone came in saying, "Hey, we have a small passenger plane squawking highjack, ten miles to the south of the field and closing, sir."

This activated the security response plan. It didn't involve me, but I couldn't help but investigate. I went outside to the southwest corner of the operations building and met up with several sailors and another pilot. There we watched as a small, twin-engine aircraft rolled to the center of the runway and exited the field onto the outer limits of the tarmac.

Once arrived, the pilot cut the motors. Soon after, the door opened and a dark-haired man stepped out onto the concrete tarmac. Raising his hands into the air several times, he signified his surrender. Two senior chief ordinance men, with experience dating back to the Vietnam War, ran across the tarmac carrying shotguns raised in one hand that were pointed to the sky. The dark-haired man again raised his arms in surrender. After that, I borrowed the binoculars.

"My God, he's in uniform and has stars on his shoulder boards," I marveled.

When his wife and family emerged from the small airplane, things became very clear. He was defecting from Cuba, taking them all with him on a daring, low-level flight from Havana. Fleeing the elite society such as a general commanded in Cuba, they defected to the closest location America had to offer: Naval Air Station Key West.

Astonished, I thought, *They are part of a privileged society. Why on earth would he risk the lives of his family to escape the very government that bestowed a better life on them, a lifestyle that most of their countrymen didn't share?*

The general's plane was small, but it shouted big questions about life on the other side in a communist dictator's paradise called Cuba, only ninety miles away.

The base handled the whole affair with great efficiency. Although the newspapers and national news knew of the possibility of a defector, no one in the Navy either confirmed or denied his existence. Instead they housed him in a comfortable, secluded residence on base and began his debrief. Three days later, government officials tasked me with flying him and his family to Homestead Air Force Base, just south of Miami, for further debriefing. He was a real catch, a coup for the United States. This military man would spend a long time discussing Castro, Cuba and the communist world's intentions at Homestead. First I had to get him there.

No big deal, right? Not until "the protection" assigned to guard these people showed up. Instead of using the air stair door, we could have justified opening the cargo hatch for this FBI agent. Obviously, he was undercover; no one would suspect a 350-pound man capable of running down bad guys. He flipped open his identification, wanting to board the airplane. I walked past him and stepped onto the aircraft first, hoping and praying that the plane would balance. Fortunately, the copilot was already seated in the front of the plane. Otherwise, with the agent weighing down the rear, the plane would have tipped on its tail, causing complete embarrassment to us all.

Once forward, I turned and greeted the children who, after all of their adventures, appeared frightened and subdued. I shook hands with the general, welcoming him to America. Scanning the passengers, I wanted to rearrange everyone. I needed to have the mother and her two youngest sit in the rear of the plane with the FBI agent over the wing. Socially, I just couldn't make that happen. I didn't speak enough Spanish to communicate my desires and I doubted the FBI agent could squeeze down the aisle between the seats of the Super King Air.

Thankfully, the children sat on their parent's laps up front. This was a small thing, but small things can make a difference. *The plane will balance out more,* I thought, once I sat down in my pilot's seat. *We won't be so far out of limits.* Wishful thinking.

I noticed the nose of the plane rose higher than any other time I had been in the King Air. Taxiing out, using the pedal-actuated nose wheel steering, I could not effectively steer the craft. Maneuvers to compensate and correct were required. I reverted to differential power and braking to guide the plane to the runway. Once on take-off roll, I pressed the control column forward instead of aft to improve the ground handling of the plane. I then added ten knots to the rotation speed and gently lifted the airplane from the earth to avoid stalling the airplane from over-rotation. Thank goodness it all worked or all of us would have been dead at the end of the runway—terminated from the FBI protection afforded us.

The FBI presence was a little thing, as if they doubted our flight going to Homestead. Where else would I take the general and his family—back to Cuba? Our anticlimactic Homestead arrival was quiet and uneventful, almost routine—a good thing, I suppose. Back in Key West, everyone had a laugh and something to say about the way I handled the airplane.

"Neal, we could see the nose in the air and the tail just above the ground," one said.

"Yeah, I noticed your difficulty steering the laden Beechcraft and heard your differential application of power between the two motors," another said.

Some even wondered if we would make it off of the ground.

Key West was a very good duty station for me. It was there that I met Donna and where we married, living in my first purchased and mortgaged home. Nevertheless, and for several reasons, I knew that this would be my last tour in the regular Navy. The military is essentially a dictatorship and the politics of the dictators were unpleasant, as so described from my Key West experiences. This type of environment stood on top of the weeding out, the wedding cake of making rank, where selection for promotion drove an unnatural, competitive wedge between the officers.

There were two particular sayings in my previous tour that rang especially true and typified this attitude—"VP eats their young" and "You make rank by stepping over dead bodies." Neither of these work rules appealed to me, then or now, nor will they ever appeal to me in the future.

While in Key West, flying was truly my primary job. I was constantly in the air. Throughout the rest of the Navy, flying is a collateral duty. As an officer, ground jobs were most important, much more so than flying. Navy pilots wore multiple hats, working multiple ground jobs they were rarely schooled for. More often than not, these ground jobs conflicted with our flight scheduling.

Navy pilots answer to multiple bosses, setting us up to fail. The result? Conflicting ground assignments without regard to having sufficient time to properly finish anything. Designed by thoughtless managers steeped in unwavering tradition, this work climate was frustrating.

Then there was a certain commanding officer who openly played favorites with his junior officers, even inspiring them to fight among themselves so that the "best" rose to the top. Both of these management ploys are terribly wrong. In the military, the man next to you might be the one you relied on for your very life. He might save your ass and become your hero. To pursue a career, we were told to outgun our colleagues, effectively trading our heroes for gold! In many respects, this policy reminded me of a particular football practice, pitting teammates against each other. Amazingly enough, these policies came from people with personal combat experience who knew better.

Serendipitously, in 1987, the airlines were hiring pilots at levels never seen before. After consulting with Donna, I put in my request to be released from active duty while holding onto a reserve commission.

Much to my surprise, the playboy officer called me into his office.

"Lt. Schupbach, this is not the way one departs the Navy. You're supposed to ask for an audience with the skipper and come in your dress blues with hat in hand. Coffee and long conversation is the order of the day instead of surprising people with your paperwork found on the bottom of the stack. I should kick this back to you denied."

"I am sorry, sir," were the first words I could muster. "I never was much for formal protocol. I guess I could have done better."

That wasn't how I felt, but it sounded good at the time. After all, this man tried to kill us with lightning and ruin me with his own cover-up, flying an impromptu medevac mission to Washington with his own motivation in mind. Anyway, it all would be over in six months. I would walk away from the Navy as a veteran.

What I didn't know was that ten months later, I would experience real tyranny and dictatorship in my own backyard. With Russia and the East Bloc as its allies, a dark land took on America and nearly cost Europe a third conflict in fifty years. Castro's Cuba stood ninety miles from Key West, close enough for people to brave inner tubes on the high seas, human smuggling in small boats, or escape, as did the general. The Florida Straits are a formidable, shark-infested barrier. However, my next destination, surrounded by guns, concrete and barbed wire, shot its citizens who tried to escape.

The next four years in Berlin forever opened my eyes and brought me an awareness I could never have imagined.

Berlin

CHAPTER FOURTEEN

The first time I saw the Berlin Wall I thought it was a construction site or a sewer project. My view was from the air, looking down on the well-lit strip that glared up into the night. An unusual darkness blanketed the eastern side, while streetlights and cars dotted the bright western edge of the zone. It didn't occur to me at the time that the reality of the clay-colored, broad swath of barren soil could be anything sinister. I never imagined that the glimpse of the wall from between the clouds was anything other than a team of workers hustling deep into the night. Little did I realize then that unseen workers sat in darkened towers and the glow of sodium bulbs were in reality, prison lights: a prison enforced by deadly mines, machine guns, attack dogs and man's inhumanity to his fellow man.

We turned left on the standard instrument departure from runway eight left and headed for the north corridor. The lowering clouds of East Germany limited me to a short look at things to come. I did not know that I would witness tyranny first-hand that night and be given the opportunity to change my attitude towards every freedom, need and longing I took for granted. I then lacked the heart to understand what I would soon experience. A change of heart would come with time. Until that night, I could only speak with my colleagues, the German flight attendants, to begin to understand my first observation of the *Wall*.

Days before that first flight, our pilot group attended briefings from the Pan Am Berlin Chief Pilot, Captain Pretz. These meetings stressed the unusual nature of our political situation and how it applied to our flying. We flew the Berlin air corridors that were first proposed and agreed to before the end of World War II. Three, twenty mile-wide air corridors extended out to West Germany like spokes from a broken wheel. One led to Frankfurt, another to Buckeburg near Hannover, and the third emptied near Hamburg. The Soviets strictly enforced these lanes of flight. Captain Pretz cautioned us that the Soviets launched Migs to intercept so called perpetrators. They practiced their intercepts on passenger airliners found in East German airspace.

While in these corridors, we flew flight levels with the standard altimeter setting of 1013 millibars. However, while over Berlin, planes flew with an altimeter adjusted to the barometric pressure registered by the control tower. This gave the pilots their altitude above sea level, which was critical information for approaches and landings. To further complicate matters, the flights were at unusually low altitudes, restricted to ten thousand feet for the entire length of each corridor. We flew the northern two corridors at even altitudes plus five hundred feet when westbound, and at odd altitudes plus five hundred feet while traveling eastbound. We flew the southern corridor at even altitudes westbound and at odd altitudes eastbound.

The air traffic altitude flight restriction of ten thousand feet came about shortly after the war, when the Soviets noticed non-pressurized aircraft naturally flew lower than ten thousand feet. The "evil empire" saw an opportunity to harass the allies in their efforts to support Berlin. The Soviets reclaimed the altitudes above ten thousand feet and *shot down* a British transport to prove it. Rather than going to war, the allies voluntarily restricted their aircraft movements to the newfound rules. Only during times of military exercises in East Germany, where the firing of artillery into the free-flying airspace posed a hazard to aviation, did the Soviets allow for aircraft above their iron ceiling.

There were few exceptions to these rules. We quickly learned that there was no lowering of political restrictions for icing conditions, turbulence and thunderstorms. We were allowed to deviate outside of the corridors for thunderstorms only at our own risk; or turn-around within the corridor, or enter a completely different corridor other than the one called for on our flight plan, with a great deal of radio conversation and headaches. These were very rare exceptions.

As if these restrictions were not enough, the city of Berlin proper had yet another flight restriction placed upon it—a forty-mile diameter circle. One could not fly outside of this circle. Everyday an American C-130 aircraft flew to its far perimeters, demonstrating the use of the airspace and our rights to operate in free-flying airspace. Obviously, routine surveillance became part of the exercise as the aircraft literally flew from inside the Iron Curtain.

The Berlin Air Safety Center or BASC was centered in all of this point-counterpoint. At the BASC, all flight plans were physically handed to the Russians for their notification and "approval." However, none of the flights were ever officially approved. Rather, the Soviets returned the flight plans with "safety of flight not guaranteed" stamped upon them—on a good day. Interestingly enough, the BASC maintained the only continuous human contact between the Allies and the Russians after the close of the war. It even provided twenty-four hour a day diplomatic contact during the Berlin airlift in 1948. We toured the BASC as a part of our Berlin indoctrination.

As it turned out, the BASC situated itself in a small corner of the former German Supreme Court building. After a formal tour, we were shown where those who attempted to kill Hitler with a bomb in 1944 were put on trial. The courtroom ceiling displayed a beautiful decorative angel. For the trials, the Nazis painted her wings black. We visited other chambers where the guilty were hung with piano wire or garroted. All in all, Hitler punished more than eleven thousand people for their involvement in the conspiracy. This included Field Marshall Erwin Rommel, the "Desert Fox," who they allowed to take poison shortly after his arrest at his home near Stuttgart.

I later sat in the back of a darkened airplane, contemplating the stark realities of my new job. I thought about what I had just seen and heard. Yes, in the past I flew for the U.S. Navy hunting Soviet submarines. Yes, growing up in America, I knew right from wrong. But had I ever placed myself so close to the other side, the "evil empire?" No! Because I had never been exposed to the hideous nature of the previous generation's war and aftermath, I easily came to the wrong conclusion when first sighting the Berlin Wall.

My colleagues corrected my interpretation that night of what I witnessed from my window. From that moment forward, I wanted to learn more about the many breaches of ethical conduct totalitarian regimes brought to their constituents on demand. I wanted to learn and I wanted to travel. I couldn't wait to share the knowledge and experiences with my wife. The divided city was to forever change my outlook and life.

The divided city (British, French, American and Soviet sectors) rebuilt its economic heart within the British sector after the war, a borough called Charlottenberg. The Central Business District focused on the German answer to the "des Champs Elysees": the "Kurfuerstendamm". The Ku'Damm, as the Berliners so affectionately called it, boasted of grocery stores, small shops, sidewalk cafes, restaurants, businesses, and the largest department store on the continent—the Kaufhaus de Westens or Ka De We.

Almost every building was newly constructed. A massive November bombing raid in 1942 blew up or burned down every building from the Mitte district, the city center, two miles to the east of the Kurfuerstendamm and to well past a mile to the west of the Ku'damm. Over a thousand airplanes took part in the raid, leaving in their wake only a damaged bell tower: the remains of the Kaiser-Wilhelm Memorial Church. Three blocks from the bell tower, five buildings dating from the turn of the century were miraculously spared utter destruction, one of which contained our apartment.

Finding this apartment was no small feat. Because of its limited space and the Berliners' love of open parks, West Berlin had a persistent housing shortage and land came under the watchful eye of the authorities. Rent controls were in place and living accommodations could not be converted into office space. This was a two-edged sword. On one hand, price controls were in effect; but on the other, renting the furniture and closets to the tenant provided the solution. With the aid of colleagues, I read three or four individual contracts before viewing the apartment on the Ku' Damm. Fortunately, I did not buy into any of these money traps.

The Chief Pilot's office assisted newcomers to the city, handing out telephone numbers and addresses for apartment hunting. It was there I found the telephone number for our apartment on Berlin's most famous avenue, the Kurfuerstendamm. I called and a gentleman answered. His fluent English was a big help and he directed me to the address of #29 Kurfuerstendamm. It was not easy finding the apartment, especially at night. I was unaware that the entryway came at the end of a long hallway created by two trendy shops. At wit's end, I took a chance with the mirrored doorway at the end of the hallway and rang what I perceived to be the bell.

The English-speaking man answered through an intercom and I explained why I rang the doorbell. He told me to wait for a couple of minutes; that he would come down and let me in to the courtyard. The whole scenario seemed a bit odd and I became anxious. After all, this was a foreign country and I was not fluent in the language. A series of clunks and mechanical noises came from behind the one-way mirrored glass door.

A bearded man with a soft scratchy voice and an American accent answered the door and I introduced myself. He showed me through a hallway leading to a courtyard. We then retreated and walked up a small flight of stairs to a vintage 1910 external elevator, complete with a pressure plate, folding double doors, and "humongous" pushbuttons.

"Don't worry, it is safe," he said as he closed the external door and two internal half doors.

Stepping off of the pressure plate created another loud clunk, as did the door closing behind us. From that point, we proceeded to climb yet another set of stairs. While walking up the last staircase, I noticed the ornate wooden railings and Herr Pleate told me about himself.

"Excuse my English," he said in an accent as American as my own. "I lived in Utah for three years and learned the language without going to school. It may sound broken to you."

"Oh no," I replied. "And it is certainly much better than my German, of which I have no understanding. Actually, I wondered why your language sounded so familiar. It isn't the British English of my coworkers."

"Well thanks. I really loved Utah. You could buy a 44 magnum practically in the grocery store, take it to the desert and shoot all day without any questions being asked. Here in Germany, it's not the same.

You need a permit for everything. A bow and arrow is considered a silent weapon. It's the 'nothing goes country.'"

Once at the top of the stairs, we stood between two massive wooden doorways. Herr Pleate opened the one on the right and changed the subject to the history of the apartment building.

"During the war, this place was hit only by a fire stick; you know, those phosphorus incendiaries the British used to burn down German cities. Bombs were used to blow the tiles off of the roofs and then the planes that followed dropped these fire sticks. Evidently, the people at the time extinguished the fire with buckets of sand they stored in the attic for such occasions."

"Yes, we certainly rearranged the furniture during that one," I said.

With that being said, Herr Pleate took an immediate liking to me, even though I displayed a bit of nervous apprehension.

"Call me Stephan," he said.

"Oh, how rude of me, my name is Neal," I said and we shook hands.

"Well, let's go in. We share a common entranceway with a little old lady named Frau Penska. She is a great old gal and has the smaller of the two apartments. Hers' has the three doors in the entrance on the left. Yours will be the two on the right with the one forward being the main one."

Before we entered the entryway to the two apartments, I looked at the ceiling above me. I noticed old rococo plasterworks, a luxury forbidden by cost in today's environments. The entryway also revealed a rococo ceiling and herringbone-patterned oak flooring. Old, heavy wooden side doors contained beaded glass windows. Every piece of framing displayed slick yellow paint complementing the wood floors.

I walked through the fifth door of this journey and entered a small, dark hallway followed by two more large wooden doors, also with beaded glass windows. Beyond, the large apartment that followed could best be described as a Korean kaleidoscope of wallpaper and tacky decorations. Stephan laughed about it all as he showed off a large living room that was the size of a small ballroom. It came complete with blonde oak parquet floors, enormous windows overlooking the courtyard, and a beautiful ceramic, gas fireplace. Whorehouse red, silk-flocked velour wallpaper dominated the room, covering the walls up to the fourteen-foot high rococo ceiling. Fortunately, three out of four of the walls were paneled oak, which the Korean interior decorator painted off-white to eye level.

Stephan—by now we were on a first name basis—and I took a moment out and had a good laugh.

"Come on, let me show you the rest of the place. You won't believe it, trust me! I mean, here is what I use for evidence that money doesn't mean all that much. She threw all of this money in here and look at what you come up with!"

We then went through the red bedroom and the green bedroom. Each came complete with yet again, rococo ceilings and silk wall paper from floor to the top of the twelve-foot ceilings.

"Impressive in the dark, I bet. I can't wait until Donna sees this one," I said.

"Oh, you are married?"

"Yes, almost newlyweds, and I think I will need to get her approval for this one."

"Well, that's OK; I will hold on to it for you."

We walked to an internal hallway that led past the second entrance to the red bedroom and stopped at the bathroom. I noticed a very long bar used to open and close a small window far behind and well above the toilet. The tile was dirty, the wallpaper displayed pink, paisley curly-cue designs and the bath had no shower. Most of the plumbing was exposed and the lighting appeared to be a holdover from what the Russians left behind after they looted Berlin.

We progressed down the filthy, dark, yellow hallway that boasted a deep brown ceiling cap.

"This hallway reminds me of something the Viet Cong would use to get around during the war," I said.

"I agree."

We then entered the kitchen, which came as a shock. I could hardly believe my eyes. After all I had seen so far, nothing stood up to this calamity of colorful tastelessness. A variety of four different colors of white and blue tile covered the walls to a height of five feet. Then psychedelic green and turquoise flowered wallpaper took over, covering the upper portion of the twelve-foot wall, crossing the ceiling and down the opposite wall to the tile. It nearly dripped with cooking grease and black soot from the European practice of heating with coal. The effect gave the kitchen that extra special touch of charm. As for amenities, the stove appeared to be something out of a Barbie doll collection, as did the refrigerator.

The typical Berlin kitchens and major appliances were much smaller than their American counterparts, this kitchen being an exception. This entire apartment was much larger in its creation and its large rooms indicated luxury. Frau Penska's apartment originally was part of our own, but now was walled off creating two living quarters.

The sink displayed open plumbing. Illuminating all of this was one, lone light bulb dangling from an electrical line that emerged from the grease-slimed ceiling. I didn't notice the floor.

Stephan continued, "In Germany, closets are counted as rooms and they tax you on the number of rooms in your home. It's different than in America where you have walk-in closets the size of small bedrooms. That is why we have great big sideboards like this one here in the kitchen, and the other in the living room. Stouber wants to move to Portugal and I know he will leave them behind. I think you will find this place large enough, even for you Americans. I mean, we Germans don't have that many things. We don't move around a lot, so we have about eighty or ninety square meter (800 to 900 square feet) flats here in Berlin and we think that's great. This place is one hundred and fifty meters. You would sublease it from Stouber because he rents it from the insurance company and has the primary lease."

"Well, I have to wait and ask my wife about this one," I said again as we walked back into the dimly lit living room. "She is sensitive about where she lives. I mean, this place would be fine for me, but I don't want to make a mistake and move in where she will be unhappy."

"Well, the rent is approximately eight hundred dollars U.S. and this includes the heat. Lights are part of the bill, and once a year they settle up with the prepaid fixed amount. I will keep it for you, no problem. Just bring her down. You have my number and we will work things out with the lease."

"Okay, until next time," I replied.

"You will have to use the stairs this time, but I will get you a key to the elevator when you lease the apartment."

With that, Stephan led me back out through the three doors and two hallways, pressed the timed light switch and sent me on my way down the eight flights of stairs.

I made my way to the entryway, but then I turned around and peered back through the glass of the courtyard doors. It all seemed quiet enough. *Should I trust this guy and the wacko flat from hell, or just forget about it?* I wondered. *Housing is just too tight to walk away from this one.* I turned and headed for the outside door that led to the Kurfuerstendamm.

When I opened the doorway, I noticed the long, highlighted hair of a tall woman with her back turned towards me. She wore what appeared to be an expensive, albeit imitation, fur-collared coat cut slightly below her waistline, a short skirt, and fishnet stockings.

"Guten abend," she said upon our first eye contact.

"Ah, hello," I responded. She stood in the hallway next to the mirrored doorway. She seemed to have no obvious purpose in being there as I passed by and made my way back out to the broad sidewalk. I walked by a restaurant called Papillon and then passed some sort of hotel that had entirely too much activity in front of it. A corner BMW dealership caught my attention with its sporty motorcycles and fancy automobiles on display. As I stood there looking at the cars and bikes, my inner voice said to me, *Neal, I think you have found your way into the red-light district of Berlin.*

Donna did a lot of marriage counseling, so I considered that this one might be a really tough sell. I could imagine my argument of: "Honey, there are no other flats available and you'll find the size and price very attractive," might go over like a lead balloon. Her reaction to the entire scene surprised me.

How much farther off the mark could I be with Donna? I tried my best to get on her good side by saying such things like: "Now watch out for the crowds. The hustle and bustle may not be for us. Donna, the number nine bus stops right here on the corner and it takes me directly to the airport."

However, for the life of me, I could not bring myself to tell her about the hooker working in front of our door and Berlin's number one whorehouse three doors down to the west. It didn't matter.

One look at the Kurfuerstendamm and she became enthralled. The Germans decorated the city's main street for Christmas. There were strings of white lights in every tree on the sidewalk. People shared hot-spiced wine, chestnuts roasted on open fires and the traditional Christmas market opened just three blocks from our potential apartment. Donna simply loved the city scene too much to be denied. Even the whorehouse came with some attraction and interest.

We greeted Stephan in the restaurant called Papillon, located between our entrance way and the house of ill repute. He bought us a couple of drinks while we chatted. From our booth near the front windows, we watched the sidewalk action within the Christmas scene. The unusually long-winded Stephan explained how the restaurant became a lovely sidewalk café for eight months of the year. I finally got a word in.

"Well Donna, I guess we can sit out on the sidewalk, drink wine and watch the hookers work through the night!"

Donna, being a trained observer of human behavior (clinical psychologist), thought that was a good idea. So with that being said, my fear of the lady at our doorway rapidly subsided. Our conversation became more interesting as the evening wore on.

Stephan asked us if we believed Lee Harvey Oswald shot J.F.K. Donna let this slide, but I openly stated that analysis was quite impossible, beginning with the conspiracy theories of popular lore. Stephan took this as a cue to tell us about Kennedy and Berlin.

"John F. Kennedy. First of all, instead of saying, 'I am a Berliner' in his famous speech to the divided city, what he really said was 'I am a jelly roll.' So much for that one! The people responded with all of their hearts and simply enshrined the American President for standing with them against the communist dictators in the east. Berlin clearly became the symbolic pivot for the people of Eastern Europe."

"You see," he continued, "what most people don't understand, especially the Americans, is that while people were locked behind the barbed wire of the Iron Curtain, Berlin offered them the one last capability for escape to freedom. They would come into East Germany, or be from East Germany, then make it through the roadblocks and checkpoints and enter the city. From there, these refugees could fly out on an American or British airplane and settle in West Germany, a country already swamped by refugees still struggling to rebuild itself from the ruins of World War II."

Stephan paused to smoke his near constant cigarette and collect his thoughts before further bending ours.

"The real problem came as one of obtaining logistical support for these people from a country broken in the first place. At the same time, the American political situation became one of keeping the Soviet political influence deterred in Western Europe, especially West Germany. If the west stood around and did nothing, then the communists and their ever-present propaganda machine would be able to generate great inroads into the German society and voting booths. This was unacceptable, but a real possibility to the NATO Allies."

Stephan sipped from his drink before he began again.

"However, the American administration also faced the critical problem of immigration. From all of the eastern Europeans migrating through the city of Berlin, clearly the balance of all of Europe once again pivoted on German soil. Very few people outside of the Kennedy administration knew of the surprise deployment of the Berlin Wall. Those who did know of the plan saw it as something they could do nothing about. They also saw it as a way to relieve themselves of the mass migration through their occupied city and into one of their most important allies in Europe. Additionally, the Wall would double as a propaganda campaign. The Soviets' public relations blunder, so to speak, had a silver lining. The Berlin Wall would help solidify support for the presence of foreign troops in Europe, the existence of NATO, and relieve the West from the costs of the immigration dilemma."

"Stephan, you are a very interesting man," I said.

"Well thank you, but the point is that the American public didn't know, and neither did anyone else for that matter, that President Kennedy anticipated the Berlin Wall and gave it a sleight of hand approval. It solved more problems than it created."

After setting the Kennedy record straight and another drink, Stephan invited us to go with him to East Berlin via the railway stop called Friedrickstrasse.

"The famous 'Check Point Charlie' is off-limits to you, even though you are Americans. This is because you are residents of Berlin. The German authorities have placed stamps in everyone's passports, registering every household and worker in the city, and the country for that matter. That changed your legal status and so forth. This has its advantages and drawbacks. Trust me, Friedrickstrasse is just one of the drawbacks."

After our drinks, we bundled up and trudged off to our large apartment that was just a few doors away. Once inside the apartment, Donna had a field day with the colors and style of the decor.

"Someone must have thought they were royalty to believe this is the *real* them," she said viewing the hysterical collage of colors. Within a few minutes of looking around, she saw enough to satisfy her and the apartment deal went down.

"I'll arrange for everything and act as your interpreter," Stephan said. "But let me show you a portion of the divided city of West Berlin."

We returned to the hallway and found our way back into the Ku'Damm night scene, the Europa Center and the spirit of Christmas. That night the lights of Berlin shone in Donna's eyes. She lit up and thought the city to be her playground. For the next four years it would be.

It was time to have Pan Am move us into the apartment, unpack and clean house. After several trying days without daily telephone conversations, mail and relatives near, Donna became so lonesome for her buddies that her smile quickly faded. I put my foot down one evening in an effort to turn her attitude around, just before leaving on an overnight flight to Zurich.

I think it helped, for idle hands are the devil's workshop, psychologist or not. When I came home late the next morning, the house was miraculously transformed into a home. I was impressed, but she was pissed. I caught a few words of it too. Life, however, goes on and I learned once again what it meant to be a newlywed.

After a week or two, we finally found the time to travel with Stephan to his other hometown, East Berlin. Late one afternoon, shortly before Christmas, we met at our apartment and proceeded to a nearby S-bahn, or surface train station. It was our first journey to the East German Capital City via the entry point of Fredrickstrasse. Stephan kept the conversations as light as he could, a challenging feat for him I might add; but only while we waited for the train. Once aboard we received yet another education of the times.

Stephan quickly became someone special in our lives for many reasons. Here was a guy who, as a child, rode his bicycle under the Brandenburg Gate where the Berlin Wall now stood. He had a unique passion about everyone and everything in his life. He hated the communists, made jokes about Hitler, and knew far too much about each of them and the current political situations for casual observations. He spoke three languages fluently without any formal education. Indeed, he called himself "The Breeze" (as in the Lynyrd Skynyrd song), although at times we wondered if it held a deeper meaning. His knowledge of militaries, politics and the inner workings of our government in a city full of history, confrontations and conflicts with little resolution kept us guessing about our newfound friend.

We boarded an East German S-Bahn. The cars were old, poorly lit, and offered no amenities except for some electric heat under each seat. Although I was bundled up, the heaters felt good radiating on the back of my legs and they warmed the air rising between the slats of the honey oak benches. Stephan talked non-stop telling us about the border crossing exactly at the moment we entered East Germany, where the Wall stood and how the train took another ten minutes or so before we arrived at the customs area.

Once at Fredrickstrasse, we noticed how brilliantly lit the East German train station appeared.

Stephan explained, "This is to aid the guards who stand above, looking down on the platform and the train, so no one can lay on top of the train and escape. The train also follows especially lit tracks, illuminated from underneath the rails. Guards posted beneath search for anyone who might hang on to the undercarriage of the cars or locomotive," he said as he pointed out guards in plain clothes on the platform. Now came the hairy part.

Upon entering the "processing facility," we were led down several flights of stairs. At the next checkpoint, we were required to purchase thirty East German marks for the price of thirty West German marks, or twenty American bucks.

At this checkpoint, Stephan said, "I might have a problem. Two or three times in the past I exchanged my currency only to be told that I could not enter the country and that I would not be receiving my money back. All of this after my strip search."

The price of poker just went up. Donna and I simply shut up and kissed the money good bye. On the free market, the exchange rate with mark to mark came at six to one. We realized this would be the least of our worries. Our guide might not reach the other side and we would then be alone at night on our first visit to communist East Germany. This did little to calm our nerves.

After exchanging currency, we proceeded one by one through the customs screening area. A restrictive passageway stood there, about as wide as the hallway leading to my kitchen and just about as attractive. The German guards, who incidentally acted illegally according to the agreement with the Soviet Union, stood above us and behind an elevated wall of concrete and glass. They carefully went through all of the pages in our passports, one at a time. They also eyed the mirrors that reflected from behind our heads, observing the entire length of our bodies. Each turn of a page came with another long body scan. The degree of intimidation was frightening. They knew their business all too well.

Somehow, we survived the "treatment" and proceeded to rendezvous with Stephan in the normal train station of East Berlin. Now, for the fun of it all! We worked our way through the East German Christmas market that paled in comparison to the West. We were accustomed to colored lights, bright illuminations, sidewalk houses selling Santa's wares and the like. In East Berlin, there were far fewer of these. Instead, the magic of Christmas appeared dictated. The signs and decorations were old and tired. They appeared to be recycled year after year.

We walked for several blocks as part of our tour with Stephan. With great pride, he pointed out a church that stood before Columbus discovered America.

"Berlin is celebrating seven hundred and fifty years. How old is America?" he asked.

We continued past the city center "Mitte" and headed for the Hotel BerlinerStaat. The damp, cold air of the December evening made us quite uncomfortable so we walked at a vigorous pace. We were focused on the tall building where we would dine.

Along the way, Stephan pointed to a particular building called the Intershop.

"This place is really known as the 'hard currency store.' Up until the late seventies, it served as an East German government profit center. The East Germans could shop there, but they had to exchange hard currency for coupons. Not at a very interesting rate of exchange, I might add. That was the only way they could purchase goods made in the West. The state had the monopoly in the Intershop and they knew it."

"You see," Stephan continued, "the communists knew the West Germans provided money in West Marks to their relatives in East Germany, and they wanted to have it for their own. Thus they set up the coupon system for the East Germans. With an East German passport, Germans could surrender West German Marks for coupons to shop for western goods in the hard currency store."

"How much was the cut?" I asked.

"I don't recall, but the jackasses skimmed from their own people so the leaders could shop at the Intershop. Later, in 1985, they eliminated the need for the coupons and passports. They saw a greater profit potential with an open door policy. However, I would like to point out the fact that they still will not allow a westerner through Fredrickstrasse with more than fifty marks of purchases. Anything of real value has to stay in the country. They just want you to purchase some little toys and dolls and the like. What you don't spend, you have to return."

"What?"

"Any East Marks that you don't spend before you leave the country have to be returned or 'donated' before we get on the train tonight for West Berlin."

"They buy them back from you?"

"No. These are donations and they tell you that. You will see it when we return to West Berlin. There will be a stand for your marks. It is illegal to take them out of the country because then you could bring them back into East Germany. They don't want their own money."

"OK, now I have heard everything: a country that doesn't want its own currency. What will they think of next?"

As we walked by the Intershop, we noticed that few people frequented the "hard currency store" where only western currencies were accepted. East Berliners didn't even window shop for what they could not afford to purchase. Only the ruling elite, the true communists, had such everyday privileges—their reward for being officials in the communist party. Later that evening I devised a simple test to see if this hard currency story was indeed correct. The result both educated and embarrassed me.

We entered the Hotel BerlinerStaat from the east. The lobby came across as stark, German architecture with white marble floors, a few chairs and fewer amenities. As we walked through the first floor, I noticed the Germans practicing energy conservation with a distinct lack of lighting. The gloomy atmosphere and cool temperature did little to impress either Donna or me.

"They call this the picture show," I said under my breath.

We rounded the corner and waited for an elevator. I noticed that there were very few females in the hotel and an even greater shortage of suitcases.

Stephan remarked, "It's a good thing this hotel is over fifteen stories tall or we would have to take the stairs."

"Why would we have to take the stairs?" asked Donna.

"Because in the communist countries, any building with fifteen stories or less is not required to have an elevator. All of the East Berliners carry their groceries and such up the stairs."

"I bet that makes them a hardy bunch," I said.

A grim smile was Stephan's only response.

When we arrived on the top floor of the hotel, we immediately understood why Stephan Pleate brought us to the Hotel BerlinerStaat. The restaurant sat on the 26th floor, overlooking both cities, and was simply beautiful. The staff treated us as if we were royalty. Each waiter wore international flag pins, thereby denoting the languages they spoke fluently.

Stephan explained, "The man with the Russian pin doesn't speak very good English, but he enjoys his job because he gets to tell the Russians that there are no seats available, even when the restaurant is only half full."

However, an American presence was popular and almost everyone spoke English. We were their contact with the West and Americans left tips in hard currency. Even American military personnel frequently dined there in uniform, according to the protocol. So we sat with our friend and worked our way effortlessly through a seven-course dinner with wine and champagne, as we enjoyed the view of West Berlin at Christmas time.

Through it all, understandably I needed to make a call to the W.C., phonetically spoken "Vay Tsay" as it came to be called. While in the water closet, I greeted a cleaning lady with a "hello" in English. A short gal in her fifties, she did a good job but cowered by her mop at the sight of my western presence. Upon entering, I was ready for her with an East Mark. Before my departure, however, I rolled a dollar bill into a shaft the size of a pencil. This was my experiment: a gift of a dollar bill. I was ready for her, or so I thought, as I handed her a dollar that she would not immediately recognize.

As I stepped out of the W.C., she unrolled the green paper note and began shouting for all in the restaurant to hear "Danke, Danke, Danke!" thanking me for the most generous gift during this, the season of giving. I was embarrassed by the attention I received. At the same time, it struck me as quite odd that the gift of a single dollar would receive such praise and thanks. I turned toward her. She had her hands clasped together in front of her chest and stood with bent knees. She continued to shout "Danke, Danke, Danke!" for the single, solitary dollar I gave her as a washroom tip. This reminded me of the Intershop, the hard currency store, and the disparity in the quality of goods available to the common man, the everyday East Berliner. Frozen in that moment were the tears locked inside me for this woman, and her shocking display of gratitude for a simple buck. I didn't know what to say or even think.

I turned away from her and returned to my wife and German friend. They commented about my withdrawn mood. I sheepishly apologized to Stephan and Donna, explaining about my dollar donation. Donna didn't think much of it, but Stephan told me off in a quiet way.

"I told you the possession of hard currency was nearly forbidden in East Germany. OK, that was fifteen years ago. Sure, if you have any given to you by your western relatives, you might; and I emphasize *might*, be able to find someone to buy something in the hard currency story. However, this is going to raise some questions. How did this money come into the country and what are you doing with it? It is strictly monitored, almost controlled here in the East. What you just did isn't against the law by technical standards. But why do you think you have to trade west marks for east marks? So the fat cats have some money to buy western goods, Neal. They don't want to have others out-shopping them, so to speak. There is not an unlimited supply. This is not 'The Land of the Big PX.'"

I was quite mortified, feeling stupid for my childish prank. I had tested the system to get a reaction—a reaction I didn't anticipate. It also revealed how overbearing Stephan could be. *Live and learn*, I thought.

Aloud, I said, "Are they going to arrest me?"

"No, but you can bet that the military sit at designated tables for a reason, if you get my drift."

I lifted up the tablecloth at one corner, pretending to peer under the table for hidden microphones. We all laughed at my gesture and with that, Stephan ordered a round of iced vodka.

I was amazed that our bill came to twenty-seven U.S. dollars for the three of us.

"At that price, it's no wonder they have a Wall!"

We placed some East Marks on the table as a display. As we left, I palmed a five-dollar bill to our waiter, half out of courtesy and half out of spite for the communist system in this city. The streets were vacant and dark as we quickly backtracked to ward off the chill and make the next train. Only the cold of winter escorted us and we were quiet, each wrapped in our own thoughts. We were not free to stay out late in East Berlin, although I was unaware of that at the time. East German law required that we be out of East Berlin by midnight. The last train left at ten of twelve. Stephan kept track of the time and trying his best to keep us out of trouble.

Once on the train platform, the glare of Fredrickstrasse and the icy stares of border guards once again unsettled me. We boarded the train as we focused our paranoid attention to the guards. Our conversations were muted. When the train pulled out, we slowly crossed the especially lit section of track just as Stephan told us we would. We traveled for about ten minutes before he indicated we were back in West Berlin.

Donna and I breathed heavy sighs of relief. Stephan merely shrugged his shoulders saying, "That's the way it goes sometimes."

We stopped in at the Papillon for a nightcap after we left the train. There, Stephan told us the true story behind the Hotel BerlinerStaat.

"The hotel actually doubles as the Stassi headquarters. It's the East German Secret Police office building and all of the people running about the lobby are working communists, *spies* for the other side."

"What?"

"Neal, all of those people are agents, creeps. There are no real guests in the hotel, so to speak. It all came to you in the form of a charade."

My skin crawled. We had dined with the enemy of the United States, the enemy of the American people. Our own enemy surrounded us at all times on every floor.

Shortly after, we thanked Stephan for his hospitality and left. Our walk home was a short and quiet one as we each reflected upon the realities we discovered during the evening—realities our classic educations somehow glossed over. By the time we entered our apartment, however, we agreed that Stephan Pleate was the most sociopathic individual we had ever met. Stephan cared little for people and less for their circumstances. We felt he could be trusted, but only so far. Even so, we did trust him; and, at the same time, we knew he cared for us. With time we found ourselves caring for him immensely.

Over the next four years, when Stephan stayed the night, we welcomed him with open arms and gave him the red carpet treatment. Good times were had by all! In fact, as time went on, we wanted to see more of him despite the fact that he often left in the middle of the night only to return shortly before sunrise. We were curious about this behavior. Yet, we simply never asked the kind of questions we didn't want answered and we believed he wouldn't want to answer in the first place.

There was something about him—something that required respect despite his lack of formal education. Stephan was extremely knowledgeable about current events and fascinated by the cold war and its east/west politics. He wasn't the kind of person you would want to meet in a dark alley. Rather, he was the kind you would want for an escort through the dark alley. That night, East Berlin served as the dark alley of communism with his escort as our protection. Our visit became a field trip away from the security of learning in a formal classroom.

In March of 1988, my wife Donna came across an opportunity to work in Berlin for the University of Maryland. With her Ph.D. in psychology and mathematics background, the opportunity to instruct came naturally to her. She wrote her own course curricula as she went along. This presented a challenge, for even this certified, classic "A" type personality, a challenge she could not resist. During one term, she even wrote and taught three separate courses at the same time. It just about killed her, but I never saw my wife happier than when she worked as an instructor for the University of Maryland. This came about for many reasons.

The city of Berlin forbid Pan American World Airways wives from working. Thus employment came as a real treat for her, as it would anyone. Donna found that she loved instructing at the college level and her students loved taking all of her classes. The social interactions with other Americans gave her a real boost as well. The University's pay wasn't exceptional; but, as newlyweds, every nickel counted. The benefits, however, were awesome.

The University of Maryland presented courses for the military throughout Europe. It came to be part of Army life for the soldiers and their dependents. As an enticement for working overseas for the benefit of the armed forces, the military issued dependent identification cards to all who supported their efforts, including University of Maryland instructors. This put the individual and their family members under the local Status of Forces Agreement or *SOFA*. SOFA came as no small thing, especially in Berlin, and it made the Germans jealous as hell.

With the new identification card, we could now shop at the Army Commissary, which gave us significant savings over our local economy food bill. This also gave us access to products from home, such as peanut butter and aspirin. Neither were available locally or, as in the case of aspirin, were available in Germany but for outlandish prices. We gained access to the American, British and French Base Exchanges as well. Cigarettes and alcohol were tax-free. For example, I bought Smirnoff Vodka at the British Base Exchange for the phenomenal price of fourteen dollars for a three liter bottle. (A very nice birthday present for Stephan, indeed.) Another surprising benefit was that the U.S. Government paid for all of our public transportation in Berlin—buses, subways and surface trains. When asked, we only needed to show our dependent ID card to the officials, even when transiting East Berlin on the subway. The granddaddy benefit of them all, gasoline, came to us through the PX network rather than the German street price of four dollars a gallon. And at stateside prices! Thank you, U.S. Army and the University of Maryland.

There were more monetary benefits for us because of Donna's teaching position. We were eligible to receive a refund of the German Value Added Tax or VAT. This tax, similar to a sales tax, was compounded through the manufacturing, wholesale and retail transactions and it added an additional seventeen percent to every item purchased on the German economy. We simply saved our receipts for every purchase above fifty marks and periodically visited the refund office for our money back guaranteed. One visit in particular occurred a few days after the cut-off date for the refund on a washer and dryer I purchased. It was a significant amount, 140 marks or roughly eighty dollars. The Germans disallowed the refund because the receipt had expired. I challenged the ruling because I had not taken delivery until a later date and could prove it. My challenge became persuasive enough to allow for the full refund of my Value Added Tax. Life was good!

Further still, we gained access to the Berlin Army hospital free of charge. We were eligible to use all of the military's recreational facilities throughout Europe. The American, British and French Officer's Clubs were at our fingertips. We especially enjoyed the British club with its delightful balcony lounge, popular for relaxing before dinner. Formal British waiters politely informed you when your seating became available. Waiting for a table became an attraction all its own.

The most interesting benefit of the SOFA agreement resulted because Berlin was an occupied city. Troops from the four victorious allies—France, England, The Soviet Union and the United States—literally occupied Berlin. The American Commanding Officer, a two-star General, could have a person shot in West Berlin. For West Berlin, this meant that the Americans ran the show, short of civil administrative policies.

Under the SOFA agreement for Berlin, the Berlin police could not arrest those who carried military identification or had the SOFA stamp in their second passport (yet another story.) Nor could the police affect their vehicle. If you parked on the mayor's front lawn, the local police called the American Military Police but they couldn't lift a finger against you. We were literally immune to the clutches of the police. Additionally, the legal system petitioned the American military to gain permission for a SOFA member to appear in German court, something that just did not happen. The Germans didn't even bother with that one. All of this came in very handy for Donna and me.

Shortly after Donna took her teaching position and qualified under SOFA, three gentlemen in dark suits and long overcoats appeared at my front door. I had let them in the street door quite by accident. One of them spoke to me in German and showed me a small brass tong, about the size of a feeler gauge with an even smaller star raised on it. I did not know what they wanted or what the spiffy key chain meant, but I was soon to learn.

"Defraudation."

"What?"

"Defraudation."

"Huh?"

"Stephan Pleate, does he live here?"

"No, what's this all about?"

"Fraud."

"FRAUD! Let me go get my wife."

With that I walked back into the apartment and spoke with Donna, who was equally confused. Before I could return to the door, the gentlemen let themselves into the entranceway and were scaring my neighbor, the seventy-year-old Frau Penska, with their key chain.

Immediately, their attention turned back to me.

"We must search your apartment."

"Why?"

"We must search the apartment for things left behind by Herr Pleate."

"Well, OK. There is a large closet full of things that are not ours. I mean, we are not renting that closet and the previous tenants stored some things in there."

"Excellent, where is this closet? My men will search it immediately!"

"It's in the kitchen, follow me."

I escorted them back through our whorehouse red apartment to the kitchen closet. Even in their somber mood, they could not hold in their laughter at the previous tenant's decorations.

Once in the kitchen, we moved a wooden stand that stood in front of the closet door, and with a newfound gleam in their eyes, they opened the white door decorated with hand-painted sunflowers. They found wooden chairs, tables, bolts of wallpaper, half-empty paint cans and rusting tools: all covered with pigeon feathers and droppings. A few nests were also discovered as birds came and went through an open window.

The men rolled their eyes and went into the closet with their flashlights glowing. Their eyes squinted through the stirred up dust. I came to my senses as the humor of the situation overcame my fear of these keystone cops. I knew the items were Stouber's and had nothing to do with my newfound friend, Stephan. After twenty minutes of making themselves filthy, each man concluded that there was nothing to be found in the disgusting guano pit.

I chatted with the senior inspector during this time, making myself amenable and gaining his favor. Rather than leaving the mess behind, he instructed his men to close the window behind them and replace all of the items into the former pigeon coop. We all walked back into the living room and the three spoke in German while surveying the large red ballroom.

"Well, that's all there is to show you. The rest is all of our things," I said.

"We are the police!" the senior inspector said with strong German authority.

"We will now begin searching the entire apartment for evidence of defraudation!"

Donna and I looked at each other and said in harmony, "BUT WE'RE STATUS OF FORCES!"

Donna reached for her purse, pulling out her military dependent ID card.

"Yes, we're SOFA, we're SOFA," I said over and over.

The three amigos were stunned. What those four little letters meant to them, S-O-F-A, appeared like hard time on their faces. If Donna filed a complaint with the American authorities, their search or even their presence in our apartment without American permission was a serious offense. As it stood now, these cops had committed a crime.

"May I please see your passports?" the inspector asked.

We both retrieved our passports, opening them to the two, full-page stamps that declared us protected under the SOFA agreement.

The senior inspector examined each and said, "How is this possible? You have separate last names. Herr Schupbach, you can't be under her sponsorship!"

Again with perfect timing and in harmony, Donna and I held up our left hands, displaying our distinctive, tiger-striped wedding bands, and said, "We're married!"

The inspector held up his banded hand with a puzzled look. There stood the three of us, hands outstretched, gazing at our wedding bands for about five seconds. The other two policemen turned away, holding back their laughter.

"How is this possible?" the inspector wondered out loud. "In Germany, the woman always has the man's surname."

"Well we have a photocopy of our marriage certificate right here in the back of our passports," I said. "We taped it in there just for these special occasions."

The man again examined everything in quiet disbelief. Fortunately, there were sufficient stamps between the two SOFA stamps and three, circuit county court recording stamps to satisfy even this hard-nosed German policeman.

He finally said, "May I please make a telephone call? It won't be long."

"Oh sure," Donna said, pointing out the green phone across the room by the windows.

After listening to his German conversation, none of which I understood, I became curious. Nonchalantly, I walked over and read the phone number recorded on the small window on top of the telephone. It was Stephan's. The police had raided his small apartment at the same time as ours. Now they had a problem. SOFA. Replacing the telephone receiver, the inspector gruffly asked to be let out.

Trying to remain as polite as possible, I replied, "Oh, but of course, my friend."

I escorted them out of the apartment, through the hallway and downstairs to the old elevator. I opened the outer door with my ancient key. One of them opened the inner doors, clunked down on the pressure plate, brought on the other two gentlemen and closed the inner doors. I closed the outer door and motioned for them to push the large button labeled "1." The inspector complied and I finger-waved good-bye as they quickly sank out of view beneath my feet.

"WHEW!!!"

I turned and ran back up the stairs to be with Donna. Nervous and upset from the experience, we were both relieved. Somehow the SOFA agreement worked as advertised.

"Now why on earth would they want Stephan for fraud?" we asked each other.

Someday we certainly would find out. After a half-hour of jittery conversation, Donna calmed her nerves by taking a long hot bath. With adrenalin rushing through my system from these most unusual circumstances, I changed into sweat clothes, needing to take a long run in the damp cold of Berlin.

That day I ran about as fast a long distance as I ever have run. I raced through the trails of the Tiergarten, a large park, quickly ending up on the left side of the Reichstag that overlooked the Spree River and the Wall. I was out of breath, but calming down—a very good thing.

But all good things must end and this one did rather quickly. Looking past the first concrete barrier, I noticed a guard tower. Something else caught my eye. I realized that the guard in the tower held a pair of very large binoculars and he was staring directly at me, observing my every move. Now, more terrified than ever before, I sprinted across the large front lawn of the former German parliament building, rapidly cutting off his line of sight. After a brief pause for a street crossing, I tore my way through the winding trails of the park, making record time back to the apartment. Obviously I had seen more than enough of the German authorities for one day. Oddly enough, they represented both sides of the Iron Curtain.

Throughout modern life, all of us acquire governmental and corporate means of identification. After living in Berlin, I can honestly say this is a universal truth. Our fellow man wants to be informed of whom he or she is talking to, thinking of employing, with a background check of sorts usually performed. However, for my wife and I, this became the theater of the absurd. From living in Berlin, as well as America, I accumulated no less than twenty, separate identification documents in a little less than six months. Granted, I brought many with me from America.

The first identification we carried was the common driver's license. We never acquired the German driver's license. The second ID is also a most obvious one, an American passport.

The third ID card I carried was the Pan Am Express employee card, commonly referred to as the Company ID card. Pan Am raised the lettering on this card so their employees could write their own tickets and travel for free, thereby avoiding the bureaucracy of a travel office for employees. This was an extremely good deal. Pan Am employees and their dependents traveled anywhere in the Pan Am system for free.

For the fourth form of identifying myself, the United States government required me to carry my pilot license. Simple enough. The fifth form of ID was the FAA requirement of a First Class Medical Certificate. This and the pilot license were often required along with the company identification for free travel in the cockpit jump seat. These provided free courtesy transportation to the bearer. It was such a deal!

The sixth form was simply a radiotelephone license provided by the Federal Communications Commission. This yellow card is also required by the Federal Aviation Regulations. The FAA loves its paperwork. The seventh card may or may not be a strong identifier, but is included as part of the job: an Airline Pilots Association, (A.L.P.A.) Union Card. There is nothing much to say about that one unless an aviation attorney is needed.

The eighth card was the Tegel Airport Security Identification badge issued by the West Berlin Tegel Airport security forces. This computerized credit card size photo ID came with a magnetic strip on the back and identified me as one of the good guys to the airport security system as well as the airport police. It also allowed me to pass through what became affectionately known as the "time machine."

The time machine was a vertical cylinder with one opening. Its objective was to identify friend or foe, allowing only "friendlies" to pass through its vertical coffin of glass. Only one person could fit in the upright tube where they were filmed each time they entered the time machine. The machine accepted their card and electronically matched their face with the photograph. It then rotated the cylinder to the quarter section, which allowed one person to enter the "time zone." The entire process reminded me of Maxwell Smart, Secret Agent 86, on TV back when.

Once in the time zone, the individual pushed a red button and the cylinder rotated 180 degrees allowing them to escape out the other side. They were then free to roam through the baggage areas, the offices and eventually out to their aircraft. Many a soul became entrapped in detention in the dimensionless security of the time machine. If you were at all claustrophobic, the time machine undoubtedly challenged your mind. ID number eight—an ID only a robot could love.

With any job comes the health insurance identification card, which is number nine on the growing list of our required documents.

The tenth ID came as a gesture of courtesy from the U.S. military. Due to the nature of the occupied city of Berlin and its required air support from the victorious allies, Pan Am was able to negotiate certain on-base privileges. These privileges included use of the base PX for shopping, the package store for libations, and the "The Harnack House," or Officer's Club. Pan Am pilots could also access the highly prized Berlin American Golf Course. To do all of this, the military issued Pan Am pilots a yellow identification card, complete with photograph, in return for their services in support of Berlin. This coveted ID card made life tolerable for the Americans, as it brought a touch of home and community to the ex-patriots. The "yellow card," even with its many lined-out restrictions became my tenth form of identification.

The Status of Forces Agreements bestowed several other forms of identification, the first of which came as a second passport, complete with two full pages of stamps. This second passport provided a layer of security. We were under the S.O.F.A. agreement, but we could also travel on our original passport and not be identified by terrorists as a member of the United States military. ID number eleven did have its pluses and minuses.

The military also issued us brown dependent ID cards complete with photographs. These were good in Berlin, throughout West Germany and the rest of the world. They provided many privileges. Life was good with ID number twelve!

Donna provided another health insurance card, identification number thirteen, the Berlin MEDDAC Card. This card, issued by the Army hospital, came as a benefit from her working for the University of Maryland and later for the Army hospital. It allowed us unlimited services in the Army hospital, thereby avoiding the German medical system entirely.

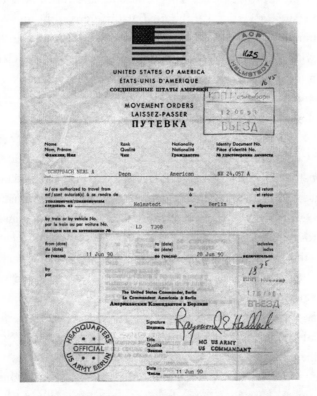

Travel Orders:
for military personnel driving from West Berlin
through East Germany to West Germany.

For travel to East Berlin, the government of the United States wanted to prove a point; and passage through Check Point Charlie became the pinnacle of that confrontation. The East Germans manned the border crossings in Berlin along with the guard towers. This was illegal according to the Four Powers Agreement. However, it would look bad if the Soviets openly administered the checkpoints, so they placed the East German guards there to save face.

The Americans didn't recognize East German rights to oversee the movement of personnel throughout the city and they also felt they should not be required to show official American documents to the guards, who were illegal in the first place. To go around this roadblock, the Berlin Command issued a yellow cardboard ID (different from number ten) to military members and their dependents. This fourteenth cardboard ID, complete with photograph, had minimal printing in English, German and Russian on the card. It was issued to thwart the illegal actions of the East German border police. In fact, while traveling through the checkpoint, we were only to hold this picture ID against the side window of the car or bus and not look at, or even acknowledge, the East German border guard. So, there, Mr. Communist, we throw this identification in your face! This ID also demonstrated the silly games each side played with each other.

Because of our special status, to travel by car through East Germany to West Germany, we were required to possess—you guessed it—a fifteenth form of identification. "Travel Orders" were pieces of paper printed in the three languages: English, German and Russian, with an American flag depicted on them. Some company clerk typed your name on the travel orders and placed the stamped signature of the commanding officer, a two-star general, at the bottom. Thus the border guards knew of your special orders and could identify you as someone whose car was off-limits for the most part.

Between the license plates and the travel orders, Donna and I demonstrated to both the illegal border guards at Berlin's Check Point Bravo and the legal border guards of the East German-West German border crossing at Check Point Alpha, that we were allowed to transit East Germany by car.

We were always under surveillance at any rate. Our transit time was carefully documented by all sides. If we traveled too fast, the East Germans accused us of speeding. If we traveled too slowly, they accused us of contacting an East German agent or something of that nature. The American authorities also kept careful watch of personnel traveling in East Germany "under orders." No one wanted their people detained by the communists; this would be in violation of agreements and give headaches to everyone involved.

The United States Naval Reserves became the sixteenth form of identification we carried. The seventeenth card was a bank machine card. I include this because of the PIN number and its power to access money throughout Germany. Outside of Germany, we carried Eurochecks; those, when presented with the bank machine card and passport, could be cashed for the equivalent of up to six hundred West German Marks in other currencies. They were backed with a guarantee of the bank that issued them. We also carried ATM cards—ID number eighteen—for the American Express bank on base. They handled our American currency needs for our savings and checking accounts.

The ubiquitous nineteenth identification is business cards, but everyone carries these, so this isn't much of a tale.

I include for the twentieth identification as a photocopy of our marriage certificate. It identified us as a legally married couple although we did not share a common name. This was mandatory in Germany. Without it, our different last names would cause many problems and roadblocks with the Germans.

As far as most Germans were concerned, they needed none of this governmental malarkey to understand that we were American. We could be spotted a mile away by our clothes, our walk, our personal space and our accents. Everyone knew who we were without any of these special pieces of paper.

We flew to Paris to rent a car—our first mistake. This flight to Paris came at a highly discounted airline interline rate. Donna and I wished we could have said the same when it came to the price of the rental car. One option would have been to have a relative rent it with our credit card number from the United States. The disadvantage of flying standby worked against us, as we did not know exactly when we would arrive, no matter how hard we tried to plan. It was as if Air France owned the rental car agency and made up for the ticket prices through the rental agreement no matter how you cut the deal. Two hundred dollars a day for a rental car is so expensive that I thought the contract came with a driver. The tiny Renault only had a radio; but then, we didn't come to France for music or creature comforts. We came to explore the Chateaux of the Loire Valley.

Donna took many years of French in school, reading the language and pronouncing the words with ease. French is not hard to read, but because most of the French alphabet isn't pronounced, we had occasional problems on the freeways leading from the airport and around the city of Paris. I drove the car and she navigated. That worked out well as driving anywhere in Paris is difficult enough. But when the signs were pronounced in French by Donna and read by me in English while driving, things got a bit dysfunctional at one hundred twenty kilometers an hour.

Donna, with her infinite education, did not understand that Neal, with his less-than-perfect comprehension of the language, couldn't translate the distinct lack of English pronunciation of the French road signs. This went on for at least a half-hour as we circled around the city and headed out for Highway A10 and Orleans. After an abundance of face twisting conversation and much ado about nothing, other than the confusion a third language brought to our lives, I felt at a disadvantage for not taking French in school.

While each of us was correct in our own minds, and Donna was correct in her own voice, this did little to assist either one of us in our high-priced circumnavigation of the city of Paris. When I did break the code, asking repeatedly for the English pronunciation of the wording we were looking for, Donna was unable to shift from French to bastardized English because of her years of training. Two strong personalities struggled that afternoon as we made our way to the south of the city. I think the only positive communication we exchanged on that drive was when she confirmed that we were to take the A10. Until we drove on that highway, I was convinced the journey was doomed to fail. With great faith, I pressed on. Donna was too excited to be denied.

We drove toward Orleans and found that our AAA Europe Road Atlas, though quite accurate in many respects, did not display the mileage we were traveling. Therefore, we drove for what seemed to be an eternity before reaching Orleans where we turned right and continued towards

Blois. We switched highways to the N152 and stopped in Beaugancy for our evening supplies of bread, cheese, wurst, wine and a few bottles of water. Once we had that in hand, Donna and I drove to a local campsite near the city of Mer. There we found remarkably affordable camping with full facilities along the Loire River. The European summer twilight lasted well into the evening as we resolved our differences over a picnic table and later in an orange pup tent.

The weather that evening welcomed us with an embrace, as only the French countryside is able, followed by a perfect night and a morning made in heaven. We awoke to a misty morning that filled the surrounding lawn and woods with the soft kisses of the river. We came to see this magnificent valley of France merely for its architecture, but this extra touch surprised and delighted us. After cleaning up, we tried to finish the French bread that we so carefully wrapped for the morning. It was no use, however, as the reputation for the breads of France held true and the need to buy bread every day became plainly obvious. Overnight, the slender loaf turned into an off-white, elongated brick that was without hope. We saved our dental work for other French culinary attractions. But it mattered little with our destination at our fingertips. We packed up for a true day of fascination with France.

Donna commanded that our first stop be the Chateaux Chambord. It was her childhood dream to visit this historic site. When I first saw the magnificent white palace, I easily understood why she held it in such favor. We viewed the palace from across its moat where rising daybreak steam hinted at undisclosed mysteries through its veil. The palace stood above a tall, stone foundation and three stories stretched between four towering turrets. Above, countless windows protruded from the sloped, black slate roof line followed by at least twenty pointed gables, rectangular chimneys, rounded bell towers and six crosses of Christ—religious symbols watching over the chateau from every vantage point.

We toured Chambord's beauty from the inside as well. Donna and I crossed a stone pathway that spanned the moat, entering the white goliath in awe of what we experienced. Donna knew the palace contained a helical double staircase, something I had never quite comprehended when she spoke of them. Then we saw them.

These magnificent, white stone staircases stood polished smooth, complete with stone banisters and curved, supporting stone. Their slight slope led gracefully to openings from the central stairwell where spectacular white hallways with square carved reliefs, eight abreast, repeated on a low coffer vaulted ceiling. Children played hide and seek on the twin, intertwined staircases. They were fascinated with the confusion generated by the double helix construction just as we were.

We discovered the balcony overlooking the central courtyard outside. Elevated walkways went everywhere, overlooking both the courtyard and the surrounding grounds. Above us, white stone figurines and intricate French stone workings yielded a busy, but beautiful effect. The Chateau de Chambord was all the more impressive for its weather-pitted stone and black moss. Thousands of forested acres for hunting and manicured landscapes for recreation surrounded us. Overwhelmed with its beauty, I thought there was little else the valley could offer visitors. I was wrong.

There are at least forty such displays of the King's opulence. The cost, whether in dollars or francs, is beyond comprehension. The knowledge that this one chateau came from the hard work of the poor, who paid their taxes to remain one step above the level of animals, boggled my mind.

From her studies of French, Donna knew about many of the chateaux through pictures and reputations. Chenonceaux was no exception. We also knew from brochures that there were camping grounds on the premises, next to the river Cher. However, what we did not know, but discovered during the palace tour, was that a laser light show was in store for those who waited until sundown. As we intended to camp, the decision to stay was a *fait accompli*.

The Chateau Chenonceaux, built over the river Cher, once served as the only bridge between Montrichard and Blere. This saved it from destruction by revolutionary parties in 1793. As we walked the riverbanks, we observed the arched, bridge-like foundations created from red stone jutting from the water. This was the gallery. Nine windows on each side illuminated the gallery from the first floor. Five were square and four contained arched glass set in rounded, miniature supporting turrets towering over and complementing the pillars of the bridge-like building. Nine windows illuminated the second floor and smaller portals set in shapely gables crowned the black roofline.

As with Chambord, the building was constructed with white stone, utilizing square windows and large gables. The black slate roof accentuated its ornate but graceful skyline. That afternoon, the entire structure reflected beautifully in the lens of the river Cher. There were four, square chimneys protruding from the main building, which comprised three stories, two above the bridged roadway. The main building square also had four turrets, attached at each corner, and three, square gables with large square windows and tri-pointed crowns decorating its roofline as it faced the river. This building housed the Chapel addition, the Library, the Salles des Gardes, the Chambre de Francois I and the Salon Louis XIV.

The main entrance to the bridge way faced the front. To its left was the addition of the Chapel, to the right, the classic turret Salon Louis XIV. The Library and the Chambre de Francois were in the far corners. Salles des Gardes was in its very center. We entered the mother of all covered bridges through that chamber. Surrounding this beautiful building was the river Cher. The chateau was further fortified by three moats that also protected the garden (Jardin de Diane de Poitiers) with their drainage canals.

The long hallway that crossed the river was tiled with alternating rows of blue and white square tiles, standing on point, traversing the length of the hall. Small benches stood between the windows below a ceiling comprised of painted timber: the beams laterally traversing the hallway in a simplistic but strong masculine fashion. The great hall served as a military hospital during World War I and portrait medallions hung on its walls. We joked about there being water in the basement, but we also imagined the damp cold of a winter morning's fog.

The gardens of Chenonceaux were laid out in four regular triangles. They were protected from flooding by large stone terraces planted with willows, nodding flowers and sculpted hedges that curled into an inward spiral. Small, pruned trees, maintained by many gardeners, dotted the most beautiful landscape.

With the tour behind us, Donna and I settled in for the night at our campsite. We then hiked back and sat on a stonewall that paralleled the river and overlooked the Chateaux. The sky turned many shades of blues, yellows and reds before growing dark, just in time for the laser light show. A small island in the river illuminated the beautiful white reflective stone screen of the Chenonceaux Chateau with a bath of warm colors. The reds gave off a glow, as if the many years of war were angry at the building. The blues cooled the scene like the water it spanned and the greens accentuated the old building with thoughts of life and a reminder of the gardens we now enjoyed. Shadows formed by the gables and floor ledges haunted our senses, as the warm evening gave over to the cool of late night. By the time the show concluded, wisps of mist rose from the river and a shallow layer of fog moved toward us.

Donna and I soaked in as much of the French countryside and Chateaux as two people could possibly handle. We accomplished the impossible in two and one-half days, looking at the most fantastic renaissance architecture the world has to offer. From the churches to Versailles, Chambord to Villein, we drove by and visited so many sites that our eyes could not take in any more. The question then became what to do next?

Both of our fathers were veterans of World War II, each serving overseas in the European conflict against Hitler. During the 1980s, Donna and I both served as officers in the United States Navy. It seemed appropriate to me that we visit some of the battlefields where Americans paid the ultimate price to free this most beautiful land. There certainly were enough of them. France has a great history with the American soldier. An ally during the American Revolution, she came to America's aid, tipping the balance of the war against England in the colonies' favor. Americans later reciprocated, fighting for the freedom of France twice in the twentieth century.

The most famous battle of World War II, fought during the liberation of France, was a long day's drive from the Loire Valley. When I suggested that we visit Normandy, I thought that Donna would object for any one of a dozen reasons. However, when I asked if she would be interested in visiting the memorial, the cemetery and Omaha Beach in Normandy, her answer surprised me.

She said simply, "We can go to Normandy."

Back in the car, we headed out to our next destination, the beaches named Sword, Juno, Gold, Utah and Omaha.

We drove on back roads for the better part of the day. The roads were narrow and gave testament to the expression "all roads lead to Paris." We traveled through the French countryside, from small towns to small villages, counting the hours of what should have been a short trip. Our large map gave few distances accurately. We were at the mercy of the accelerator and how fast we dared drive our undersized automobile.

In the early afternoon, we knew we were quite close and rather than stopping for a late lunch, we continued down route N174 and then picked up the D514 along the coastline. We began to see signs of the battle of Normandy, which were mostly cemeteries. We knew precious little about the true composition of the troops who fought and died here. The cemeteries bore witness to the fact that more than just Americans and Germans fought in the great invasion. Of course, we understood that the British were greatly involved. We were surprised to find the Canadian dead, the Polish, the Czech and the French all in their own separate cemeteries.

These cemeteries were scattered in various locations away from the areas of fighting. Yes, even the Germans had their own cemetery, buried in a manner respectful of the absolute horror of the invasion on this most beautiful seashore. Donna and I stopped at a number of smaller burial sites, noting the markers and the headstones. It made an impression on me. I thought, *After the guns were silenced, mankind recognized the eternal brotherhood of man. Here it is proclaimed that the war and its companies of the lost were too great a burden. Yet, while still segregated, all must have dignity in their rest.*

We got back into the car and pushed on towards the cemetery at Omaha, the main attraction for Americans. Having grown up in Lincoln, Nebraska, I lived just sixty miles from the city of Omaha. The special curiosity of Omaha Beach entered my mind and it was then within my reach. I always wondered why the Allies named a beach Omaha. I never learned why, but I suppose that it just served as a code name, as good as Utah or any of the other code names throughout military history: a simple coincidence for the site of America's bloody landing in the spring of 1944.

We arrived in the middle of the afternoon. The sky was partly cloudy and a high overcast threatened from the west. After parking the car, Donna and I joined hands and quietly walked to the entrance of the American cemetery above Omaha Beach. We walked into the graveyard together, she reading the brochure aloud as I tried to follow along while capturing the moment in my mind's eye.

I first noticed the crushed red rock pathways and thought of their symbolism, paving our walkway with the color of blood. There was a reflecting pool with lily pads surrounded by the red rock pathways. All eventually led to a mausoleum flanked on each side by headstones and two of the tallest flagpoles I had ever seen. But I was surprised to note that the French flag was absent. When a foreign country hosts the American colors, such absence is uncommon and conspicuous.

The lawn above the resting soldiers was perfectly groomed. Someone carefully trimmed around each headstone and there was neither debris nor grass stains on the white marble. The gravestones themselves were in remarkable condition. They stood perfectly vertical, as if set just yesterday, utilizing a delicate plumb. So, too, was the precision of their layout, straight on a taut string in every direction.

Donna read aloud the history of this site with its nearly ten thousand permanent residents. The site was chosen for its command of the very beach on which so many met their end. From her reading, we learned that contrary to popular opinion, the French indeed remember the American effort and the American soldiers. The French were horrified by the cost and the sacrifices made for them at the Battle of Normandy. So they did what little they could do to honor and forever cherish, not the British nor the Canadian, but the Americans who died on their shores.

The ground where we stood was not part of France, but rather belonged to America as a protectorate. France ceded the American cemetery at Omaha Beach to America. In so doing, the French memory was the gift of American soil to these dead Americans.

The magnitude of the loss shattered the two of us and sent us apart. For our visit to the American cemetery at Normandy, those were our last steps together. We were not alone in our reaction to the cemetery. Others did quite the same. As I walked forward to one of the large memorials, I didn't realize that I was alone. I looked over the scene and I took in the vast sea of stones, marking each brother in arms. Occasionally, there would be a Star of David, denoting where Jewish soldiers lay. I looked back over my left shoulder and saw my wife on the edge of the rise, on the ridgeline walking toward the west. I knew it would be something different for each of us to experience. Then, as I looked around, I saw no one standing with anyone else. No two people walked together. No two people congregated at a single site. No two people even spoke to one another. I saw men and women, separate and apart. All walked by themselves and quietly communicated their thoughts with their God and these men. Only then did I realize that I was alone.

Sometime after seeing how the cemetery divided everyone, my feelings changed. I pondered the significance of the French donating this land to America, in recognition of the price Americans paid for this small piece of real estate. A freedom purchased by soldiers who paid the highest price—they paid for it with their lives.

I felt a shiver run through my spine and then my senses played tricks on me. I felt as if I was standing amidst a large choir. The voices were not heard, but felt in a soft resonance within my bones. For all of their sacrifices, somehow…someway, God allowed these men their statehood, to stand and sing as a choir to the Lord, their God. I looked around and saw in the faces of others, the sound of their silence and the sound of the soldier's choir. As captivating as it was mysterious, we all heard it in our own way.

I went to the ridgeline, and from a military standpoint, admired the remains of the German fortifications. They built many pillboxes and heavy gun emplacements out of layers of concrete, literally pan-caking the gunrooms with protection from allied bombing. I walked down the trail to the beach, where I then joined my wife in admiring the beauty of the ten thousand meter expanse of sand, the crashing swells, and the north breeze with its salt air. That day, it was a place of beauty. But in June of 1944, we knew this beach on which we stood had been an open slaughterhouse for Americans.

History told us that much to the dismay of the Americans, they hit the beach unprepared for the magnitude of the defense. We could see the defenders' advantage. The slopes were lush with vegetation, camouflaging the machine guns that cut them to pieces. That previous evening, the Allies bombed and shelled where they thought the Germans were. By chance, the Germans were not in their barracks but on night patrol, practicing the defense of a beach invasion. Colonel Luck, of the twenty-first Panzer Corps, positioned his men in the defenses built by Erwin Rommel himself. The next morning they were untouched and in perfect position for battle as the Americans appeared through the early light of dawn.

There were twelve strong points covering predetermined lines of fire with a variety of assault weapons, including Germany's best—the eighty-eight-millimeter gun. Machine guns were spread through trenches dug in the hillside, 150-feet above the beach. The two weaknesses to this perfect line of defense lay in the number of defenders and their lack of air power. All else remained completely intact when the men arrived.

We knew that where we stood, Americans died by the thousands. At a low tide that fateful morning, there were hundreds of yards of open sand to cross. Protection lay only behind the obstacles the Germans planted in the water. The heavy guns from the American Navy were silent for fear of hitting these soldiers. Unfortunately, the Germans and their command of Russian and Polish prisoners of war were not silent. Rather, they gave the orders at gunpoint, to fire as soon as the men were exposed to the long, heavy walk to the shore.

For two hours they landed without the support of naval gunnery. Finally, the battleship Nevada, with her fourteen-inch guns, shot from a distance. The U.S.S Arkansas joined her in a simultaneous volley. Destroyers followed with their shallow drafts and came to within nine hundred yards of the beach and shot at point blank range. Their targets were gun emplacements, areas designated by binoculars viewing the actual American riflemen. Their five-inch guns fired thousands of rounds, miraculously hitting their targets with ease. However, they fired two hours too late for the first men on the beach where I stood.

I paused to consider what these men must have been thinking, if they even had time to think. Or, were they by the thousands, simply too scared for thought?

"Who could have let us down?" they would have thought. "Where can they be, these men who sent us here to die without even a chance for survival? Have the generals forsaken us? Is there no God on this coast of France?"

The vast waterline stretched between points ideal for defending the shore. We walked a bit farther to the east and looked back at the soft waves. Donna and I were very quiet, removed in our thoughts. From her darkened and soulful eyes, I could imagine her troubled thoughts. This beach belonged to the G.I.s of Normandy. It was hard to walk and stand where they once lay. Americans darkened these sands with their blood by the barrel and yet they still kept coming. Were we ever to understand why?

Donna and I left the beach and climbed the cliffs by way of a winding trail. We bypassed the cemetery and returned to our car. Once inside, we retraced our drive to the beautiful city of St. Lo and found accommodations for the night. Our hotel had many balconies and one came with our room. In the long twilight of Europe, the view of the city was magnificent. Floodlights illuminated the church steeples and public buildings stood against the evening sky with jagged silhouettes enticing a longer stay. A warm evening breeze ushered summer across our balcony, while we looked out over the city and shared a bottle of white wine.

Donna asked, "What was your favorite part of the trip? I bet its Normandy, right?"

"No" I said. "Normandy was too depressing for me. My favorite part was the Chateau at Chenonceaux, the one built by a woman. I thought it was the most beautiful, being built over the river itself. I loved the fireworks and laser light display."

"I did, too, but I still think you enjoyed Normandy the most."

I held my breath for a moment and resisted any urge to go down that road. It would lead to a dead end, as surely as the beaches of Normandy did for the many. Instead of replying, I took a deep breath and fought back an urge to cry. I knew that between the exhausting day's drive and my strong emotions for the American battlefield, it would serve no purpose to add such a conversation to our evening. Besides, I wanted to savor, not ruin, the twilight sky of St. Lo. However, in retrospect I believe she was right.

In the morning we drove back to Paris and flew to our home in the occupied city.

The Fall of The Wall

CHAPTER FIFTEEN

The summer of 1989 came as a very good thing. Back in America, I attended upgrade training for captain of the ATR-42, a job I wanted badly. We expanded to four aircraft in Berlin and the new responsibility came with increased pay and incentives. I could not wait to get the training behind me. During that summer, I kept a close eye on the television as much of the news coverage dealt with my own back yard: Eastern Europe.

Since 1945, Eastern Europe was the enigma of socialistic society. Americans, as well as the rest of the free world, were in the dark as to the actual goings-on inside the states of the Iron Curtain. The Soviets suppressed the bad press written about their dictator, Joseph Stalin, and erected a prison camp complete with barbed wire, guards, dogs, mines and buffer zones against the people of the Eastern European States. This came about in the name of protecting the Soviet Union, which had been invaded twice during the first half of the twentieth century.

With that excuse, the paranoid Stalin based each foreign government under his control on a single party system: the Communist Party. To find reason to fear communism, one need look no farther than the 1948 Berlin Airlift, the 1956 uprisings in Budapest, Hungary and the 1961 Berlin Wall for examples of the murderous waves of communist power. As the summer of 1989 came about, my eyes focused on two things: upgrade training and the ramifications of Hungary dismantling its Iron Curtain.

That historic summer found Glasnost influencing events in the Eastern Bloc. Hungary unilaterally dismantled its Iron Curtain with the West. Eastern Europe, sensing an opportunity, began its historic journey to freedom. For the first time in decades, the East Germans could legally travel to Hungary. They crossed over to the West by either hiking across in the early days or by train and by car in the later days. With an open border accessible to them, thousands of East Germans legally crossed the border into Hungary and then wasted no time fleeing to Western Europe.

This hole in the dike became a growing concern for all of Europe, especially for Germany. The refugees were welcome in Germany under law and so they streamed into the country. This overloaded a system caught completely off guard and unable to keep pace with the changing times.

Each new day brought news of struggles for retention of power and the failures of each government to control its people. Their protests, their desire to be free, and their rights to control their own collective destiny were simply too great to overcome without the Soviets' use of brute force. Everyday the newspapers were full of stories and photographs about the rusting Iron Curtain, the exodus from Eastern Europe and the "German Question." Each story generated questions that no western politicians dare utter solutions to, or understand the final answer of, until they became afterthoughts too late to conceive.

On the fateful ninth day of November 1989, I flew across the East German border eight times and saw not a single difference from the previous two years. After parking the aircraft, my copilot and I checked our flight cases inside the trailer beside gate sixteen at the Tegel Airport. We went our different directions from there. Before I left for home, I stopped in at the Pan American dispatch offices under gate twelve on the ground level.

The conversations there had been ongoing for weeks: *The Wall will never fall in East Germany...It is the Soviets' prize and their fear is a strong, unified Germany...Who can blame them after twenty million dead?* That night, all were in consensus.

Hungary, Czechoslovakia, maybe even Poland might have their limited freedoms, but never the Germans, as the Soviets would have NATO living in their own backyard, instead of the opposite. No, not in our lifetimes.

We all agreed as I leaned against the counter that day. The Berlin Wall and the German borders would remain for many years to come. It was inconceivable that the Soviets would remove their troops from East Germany. Just how wrong could we be?

That very hour, perhaps even as we spoke, the first East Germans crossed through the Wall at the French checkpoint, leaving East Berlin,

344

and making history in West Berlin. No one yet knew this to be the case. As a matter of fact, even the East German guards at that crossing did not know the exact truth behind the story the East Berliners were telling them: "The government announced that East Germans have the right to unrestricted travel starting today."

One guard replied that he had heard something of that and did not believe it. From their insistence, a small group of East Germans made history as the guards came together in a quick meeting of the minds. They decided that if they were going to be wrong about letting them pass, that would be their fate. This was a time to stand up for what people were saying and be counted for being right.

With the cooperation of three border guards, the French checkpoint in East Berlin allowed the collapse of the Berlin Wall, all based on a rumor that several people reportedly saw on television. That rumor did in fact hold water, and came as a shock to everyone. It was not an intentional release by the communists on their grip of power, but rather the result of an accident that the communist media broadcast from the government headquarters in East Berlin.

Earlier that year, East Germany's leader, Eric Honecker, was stricken with cancer. The resulting vacuum of power led to the rise of Egon Krenz. He was a younger man with no real stomach for the iron fist tactics required for stopping the drain of citizens leaving East Germany. He and his staff tried to emulate the newfound openness of Glasnost by holding daily press conferences or briefings concerning the daily events of the Eastern Bloc. This spun out of control. On November 9th, Krenz was faced with the question of "What should we tell them today?" He had no idea.

The communists racked their collective heads, as one low-level staff member read off a series of proposals, none of which satisfied the party chief. Then one came across, as if Radar O'Riley had his hands on it, slipping it by the colonel for his signature before the Officer-in-Charge knew what he was signing. It roughly stated that starting that day, the East German people would have access to limited travel to the West, directly through the borders of the two German states. Krenz approved this statement for release to the press without giving it much thought.

His staff took the green light without a complete analysis of the statement with Krenz. Thus, no one in the East German government was prepared for what transpired in front of the television cameras. Once government officials read this statement, there was no hope of putting the genie back in the bottle. The cat was out of the bag—big time. The first to hear of the matter came to the Wall and argued with the guards for their release from East Germany. The guards, too scared to be wrong and wanting the news to be true, went directly from worst to first. They made history on that momentous occasion, all by an accidental slip of the grip by the iron fist of the East German Government.

While I traveled on the number nine bus home, the inhabitants of the city—and almost everyone else—were about to have our lives permanently altered because of events just a few miles away in the Mitte district of East Berlin. I stepped off the bus that warm fall evening, walked across the Kurfuerstendamm, exchanged greetings with the hookers standing at the corner of Uhlandstrasse, and proceeded into my apartment building. It was around eight-thirty in the evening when I entered our apartment.

I slipped out of my black sweater and trousers and took a shower. Changing into jeans, I began packing for a mini-vacation Donna and I planned to take—a flight to Brussels the next morning. With those small tasks behind me, I plopped down on the sofa and turned on the television to watch the latest news on CNN.

The news came as a startling shock to me. I was accustomed to the East Bloc collapse, but never thought I would be living in the middle of the historic opening of the Berlin Wall. After all, I grew up watching movies about the Wall. Fellow countrymen killed over eight hundred people during their attempts to obtain freedom! There were escape attempts, even in my days in Berlin. But there it was, big as bright red apples on CNN: THE BERLIN WALL HAS FALLEN!

I couldn't believe my own eyes and ears as I sat in the middle of Berlin, Germany, and watched the news detailing the fall of the Berlin Wall, a wall I just flew over for the umpteenth time in my career. *How can this be?* I wondered. Just about this time, Donna came home from teaching and entered the apartment. I sat on the couch, transfixed to CNN.

"Good evening," she said, leaning over with a kiss.

"Donna, the Wall has fallen!"

"What wall has fallen? Where?"

"Donna, the Berlin Wall has fallen!"

"Where... which Berlin Wall? I was just outside and it all seemed normal to me."

"Donna, the Berlin Wall has fallen. Just listen to CNN!"

I turned the volume back up. When she heard the CNN news she said something completely unexpected.

"This won't cancel our long-delayed trip to Brussels tomorrow, will it?"

Thus Donna and I began our first, post Berlin Wall argument—all over a trip to Brussels, Belgium. We went round and round for about ten minutes as she had her heart set on seeing the capital of Belgium.

Could these historic days have any substitute? I thought, saying, "Donna, we can go to Brussels any time, but it is only once in a lifetime, once in history, that the Berlin Wall falls. Can't we postpone the trip and visit the Brandenburg Gate and Check Point Charlie in the morning instead?"

With those words, common sense prevailed, but not for long. We drank a splash of wine and toasted the fall of the Wall in our red living room. Afterwards, Donna and I went downstairs to share the evening with our friends at the Papillon Restaurant.

The news had everyone talking. My poor command of German prevented my participation; but by their actions, everyone validated the news broadcast. We left Papillon around eleven-thirty, walking past our lady of the night who worked our sheltered entrance as if it were her own; which it probably was anyhow. Riding the external elevator up to our apartment, we went to bed content with the knowledge that the Wall had fallen and that we would visit it in the morning.

Donna and I slept with one small window open while the rest of the double windows were each latched closed. The green bedroom had its windows facing out into the courtyard in the opposite direction from the Ku'Damm. This position made it a very quiet bedroom and the thick brick walls further muffled all sound from the street. Only an occasional entry into the courtyard or the sound of the elevator was heard. As usual, the cat slept at the top of Donna's head while I slept on the side next to the door, closest to the windows—that is, until later that night.

Around two-thirty in the morning, I awoke to the distinct sound of car horns, many car horns sounding without ceasing, something I don't recall ever hearing before that night. Because they were loud enough to wake me, I thought it significant and wondered what might be going on down on the Kurfuerstendamm. Then I remembered the news of that evening. *I must see this for myself* I thought. I was still three-quarters asleep, only able to muster my bedroom slippers and bathrobe for the journey out to Berlin's most celebrated street. No matter, the Wall falls only once and I did not want to miss a minute of history.

The cat woke and left Donna's pillow. As I walked out the front door in my bathrobe, our cat sported a look that said he thought I was crazy. I puttered on out the series of doors, took the elevator down and made it to the silvered door. I then suddenly realized how stupid this American would look on the Kurfuerstendamm in the middle of the night wearing bathrobe and slippers; but I heard the noise from the cars and the temptation was too great to ignore. Opening the door, I was met by the nightly woman of ill repute who greeted my sleep filled eyes with a laugh.

"Guten Abend, was dinks du mine Herr?"

I responded, mumbling out of drowsiness and disbelief, "Hallo, Guten abend."

I turned my attention to the street and what was happening on the Ku"damm.

Why don't these people go away? But then I remembered it was their city, the Germans' city. This was the first night that it was returned to them whole in twenty-eight years. They should be celebrating and they were. The eight-lane boulevard overflowed with automobiles, circling endlessly up and down, from the Memorial Church to Kaiser Wilhelm Strasse. More and more tried to enter the mayhem on each street corner but there was no more room. Each blew their horns, slapped their roofs and flashed their lights in celebrations of joy.

"Ja,Ja, Die Mauer ist Kaput!" (The Wall is Broken!) was my response and I repeated this to the whore as I went back inside my apartment building. She laughed again at my state of undress. The night and my outfit must have clashed, but I really didn't care on that early morning of November 10th.

Upon entering the apartment, our cat Sherlock was waiting for me where I left him, as if to ask, "What's up? I've never seen you go out into the night in your slippers and bathrobe."

I ignored him. So as not to disturb my wife, I disrobed as quietly as a church mouse and snuck back into the bedroom. However, Donna must still have been miffed about missing Brussels.

"The next time you go out in the night," she said, "please don't take the elevator. It makes so much noise that it woke me up!"

"Yes dear."

A moment later, after slipping back into bed, I gave her a hug.

"Are my feet cold?"

Noise from the street filled our apartment when we rose the next morning with muffled crowd chatter mixed with the car horns making slurry of both sound and excitement.

Donna and I kicked back a breakfast of my home-fried potatoes, garlic and cheese. As the morning wore on, we needed to know of the happenings on the Ku'Damm and at the Wall.

"Let's walk through the Tiergarten, down 17 June Allee, to the Soviet War Memorial and Brandenburg Gate," I said. It would be a long walk, as we discovered. We were not prepared for what we would find on the streets of Berlin.

Donna and I made slow progress through mobs of people in front of our building. With some effort, we crossed the crowded Kurfuerstendamm in the middle of the block. Things were quite different that Friday morning. People congregated in front of virtually every store we could see. Car traffic, normally efficient, slowly mixed with the pedestrian traffic and together oozed their way in all directions. This struck us as odd, quite unlike the Germany of yesterday where everything had its proper place, order and reason. In a country where jaywalking simply did not occur, the newfound atmosphere was like a street carnival or a disorganized parade. A party atmosphere had set in, posthaste!

Realizing our walk to the Brandenburg Gate and Check Point Charlie would be an all day affair, we worked our way through the crowds to the Kaiser supermarket to purchase some bottled water and we picked up a bit of snack food. The East Germans were there as well, shopping in droves. This was no surprise. By law, West Germany gave each East German one hundred West German Marks when they crossed the Iron Curtain. That day they spent this money purchasing food.

The availability and vast selection of grocery items was the beginning of their indoctrination to the West. At the checkout stand, we waited behind an East German family that purchased some meats and cheese to make sandwiches. Their next shock occurred as the cash register drawer opened. The children were used to the dull, drab appearance of East Marks, and now a drawer opened before them full of West Marks. Seemingly thousands of West Marks overflowed from the drawer of this register.

Their eyes lit up wide as saucers as their little mouths dropped open. The father, standing frozen in disbelief, held one of the children in his arms. He had never seen such an amount of hard currency in his life, even in his dreams. His wife was speechless and the family held up the line for a couple minutes, staring at the unimaginable wealth found in the teller's drawer. Although inconvenienced, not one of the customers complained. We all simply bore witness to the day's events. As Donna and I paid, we remarked that we, too, hadn't seen that much money in this store before that day.

On our way out the door, we went back down the Ku'damm to witness the beginning of the end of World War II. From the Reichstag to Check Point Charlie, we were bound for an historic experience. We walked through crowded streets to the middle of town where we turned left and headed past Berlin's main railway station. From there we entered the Tiergarten, crossing a footbridge over one of Berlin's many canals. The park was crowded so we decided to make our way to the broad boulevard of 17 Juni Allee, the Victory Column, to take a clear run to the Brandenburg Gate. Or, so we thought.

The Brandenburg Gate, November 10, 1989

There were people everywhere. Everyone walked in only one direction—east! After we passed the corner round about the Victory Column, I exclaimed, "Donna, there are people on the Wall!"

"Where?"

"Down there, at the gate. Let me get my binoculars out."

We stopped in the middle of the closed street, about a mile before the gate itself, which stood on the eastern side of the wall.

"Donna, take a look. There are people standing on the wall!"

"Wo?"

"Dah!" and I pointed with my outstretched arm and index finger. My wife took a long look through the small glasses, adjusting them to her vision.

"OH, DAAAAAAH! YAAAAAAH! Wir haben leute an der Mauer!" (We have people on the Wall.)

With those words firmly etched in our American minds, we walked in utter disbelief towards the political happening of a lifetime. The Berlin Wall had fallen and we witnessed the events of the day. We were participants in East meets West politics. Before that day, it was unthinkable.

As we walked closer to the gate, I recognized someone standing on a news platform: NBC News' Tom Brokaw. The superstar came to Berlin the night before to shoot video at the Brandenburg Gate. Talk about timing! Tom Brokaw scooped the first hard look at the major story of the decade. We approached his platform from the left side, taking care to step over the cables, while slipping by the throngs of onlookers. The overwhelmed NBC staff tried their best to provide security, build the platform, and simply keep the lights on for the television camera. NBC had rented two generators for Brokaw's power supply, but they were in constant danger of being cut off by the crowds of people walking on the power cables.

We made our way to the wall where so many people stood. It was quite the backdrop for Brokaw's feed to the States. There were people climbing up to the crowds standing on the Western Wall. There were people dancing, fire breathers, jugglers, hippies, businessmen and children. Here and there were a few people from East Germany. Others smashed sledgehammers against the concrete with wild, spirited blows. The East German guards were nowhere in sight. They kept to their watchtowers. Eventually, they would form up into a line, yet another wall or human shield in a show of force and solidarity, demonstrating the defiance and stupidity of their superiors.

At one point, I found the scene surreal.

"Donna, pinch me. Donna, pinch me," I kept repeating.

But Donna was caught up in the events and she didn't hear me. She stared at the people celebrating near and far, dancing on top of the Wall. Hers was a gleeful look of both joy and disbelief. I tugged at her sleeve and our smiles came together with an embrace. Two former naval officers, kissing and hugging, caught up in the celebration in front of what would soon become the photographic symbol of the defeat of Soviet Communism in Europe. That seemed the only appropriate thing for us to do, to savor the moment in lover's passion. Out of joy for the world, I wished that moment with my wife would last forever. I was far from being alone on that one.

We walked to the right of Brokaw's platform, took a few pictures of NBC's star anchor, and watched him set up and then shoot several feeds.

He appeared very tired, as if he and his team had been up all night. His demeanor, while polite, made him come across as a stretched-thin professional. Obviously, he knew this moment, this exclusive report, was a highpoint in his career. With the sound and the fury of the growing crowd, I wondered if he might be concerned for his own safety.

As I stood a few feet below Mr. Brokaw, I wanted to talk to him. I wanted to tell him to go to the stores, to the supermarkets and photograph the children.

I wanted so much to say: "The story of today is in the children's eyes. Watch them stare up at the food that is available to them for the first time. They are fascinated with the smell of wursts, mesmerized by the abundance of meats and cheeses, and wanting the previously forbidden citrus fruits. For the first time in their lives, each little boy and girl is able to reach out and touch bananas and oranges, lemons and limes. Watch for their reaction to the cash register. Not the machine, but the cash: the hard currency seen like never before by both the parent and child. There lay the human interest story of the day, their nightmares coming to a close. There is your story, Mr. Brokaw."

However, I kept my big mouth shut and simply observed how a news story came together. The backdrop and story line couldn't be more dramatic. It was history in the making. Somehow, he would have to find out for himself what I couldn't yet fully understand or even begin to explain.

We left the festivities at the Brandenburg Gate and headed off to the right, away from the Reichstag, paralleling the wall. Donna and I continued walking to the famous Check Point Charlie, so named, as it was the third checkpoint from West Germany. Check Point Alpha came at the East German border, while Check Point Bravo stood as you entered West Berlin from East Germany on the western side of the city. Therefore, Check Point Charlie was the crossing between West Berlin and East Berlin, and coincidently, it was located in the American sector.

The crowds were passable and we noticed the unusual scene of construction workers placing jackhammers at the base of the Wall. Then the noise began as they attacked the concrete structure with a tenacious vigor seldom seen in construction work. We walked past the planned opening of Potsdamer Platz and headed for the corner of the Wall near the Museum of Terrors, the former Gestapo Headquarters.

Rounding the corner, our excitement began to build. We didn't know what we would find at the checkpoint, but we guessed that the scene would be festive in atmosphere, unlike the previous day's lockdown.

We were correct. Once at the checkpoint, the usual German rules of order and discipline were nowhere to be found. A continuous stream of Trabants, Ladas, Skodas and Wartburgs—the East Bloc cars, slowly poured out from the East German border. Every car honked its horn and flashed its headlights in celebration of their first visit to West Berlin. People stood on the sidewalks, clapped their hands and stomped their feet in celebration with the new arrivals. I could not resist the temptation and why not? So I slapped the roofs of the slow moving cars and shook the hands of the occupants, welcoming them to their first taste of freedom. And believe it or not, on that first morning of freedom from communist rule and a communist economy, West Berliners handed out pink flyers to these liberated Germans as they crossed Check Point Charlie—pink flyers for McDonalds restaurants!

Check Point Charlie, November 10, 1989

We stayed at the checkpoint for a half-hour and then tried to make our way back home. The crowds were everywhere and the going was slow. Soon after leaving the area, we decided to take the U-bahn (subway) home, or at least into downtown to survey the scene from there. We were brave souls, I must admit, as the trains were completely overcrowded. The stations were full of people standing six-deep, waiting for the next U-bahn to arrive. The German authorities even added cars and extra trains to the schedule to accommodate the overflow, but it was no use. The party was on them. The train ride took longer than anticipated and in every corner people were spirited with the new day and the end of communist rule over East Germany.

When we arrived at Wittenburg Platz, the subway platform again overflowed with people. By the time we walked to the top of the stairs, our expectations of normal were skewed enough to simply relax and take it all in. We could have taken the three-stop Uhlandstrasse line to our home, avoiding the crowded streets and festive atmosphere, but we chose to experience the day for all it offered. After all, the Berlin Wall falls just once! Tauentzienstrasse, the street in front of the subway at the center of downtown, emulated a pedestrian mall during the holidays.

That Friday afternoon was one gigantic party, serving as a warm-up for the weekend. Because Charlottenberg is located in the British sector of the city, it became the British responsibility to provide some sort of hospitality and relief for all of the people. They did so by setting up stands, distributing free coffee and assorted breads until they ran out and could be supplied again from large lorries.

At the Europa center, two semi-trailer trucks distributed food from their rear platform. Long lines snaked their way around to the receiving area. The crowds began to press. To relieve the situation, or at least not exacerbate the circumstances, the British began throwing the donations from the trucks. This kept the pressure off of the people pinned against the rear bumper of the vehicle and alleviated a potential disaster. There were hungry people everywhere and these small sandwiches and gestures of kindness were genuinely appreciated.

A McDonald's restaurant stood around the corner from our apartment and had the dubious distinction of being the first McDonald's to ever sell out of every item stocked. There wasn't so much as a French-fry left in the place after Saturday, and no way to bring in another truckload of food because the crowds blocked access to the street corner.

Across the street, crowds of East Germans gathered at the local BMW car dealer. These people, if they even had a car, drove tiny wooden pressboard vehicles powered by twin cylinder, two-stroke motors. They were very curious to view the big BMW cars and their power plants. The salesman provided them with their first glimpse of western technology when he opened the hood to the fuel-injected, twelve-cylinder engine. I was impressed but the East Germans were floored. Their eyes bulged as their jaws hit the floor, staring in disbelief of the quality, power and luxury this automobile's power plant displayed.

Up and down Uhlandstrasse, the scene remained the same. Throngs of window shoppers admired the items that they were previously forbidden to own. Lines formed everywhere as the East Germans came to spend their government-granted gift of one hundred West Marks on small meals and snack food. Most bought fresh fruit, a delicacy provided only during special occasions by their former rulers.

I went by myself to the Wall at the Brandenburg Gate the following Sunday. People continued to celebrate everywhere and crowds upon crowds of people stood and removed pieces of the Wall. The scene repeated itself to the right of the gate at intervals chosen by the construction workers involved in the demolition. Immersed in the thrill of it all, few noticed the condition of the East Germans, but I noticed.

Each was timid and bewildered, yet dressed up for the occasion of their first taste of freedom. Beyond their dated suits and shoes were the impressions they made—impressions left upon me. From their lack of fruits and vegetables, and an otherwise vitamin-deficient diet, their hollowed faces lacked color and resembled Crisco shortening. Obviously, the East Bloc knew hunger and malnourishment from their communist regime.

In the distance, between the newly improvised gates, throngs of people continued to pound the concrete wall with hammers, mallets, chisels, and crowbars, as they smashed their way through the twenty-eight year long nightmare of their relatives. With the blows of large sledgehammers, concrete chips flew off in all directions, exposing the unpainted gray concrete and steel reinforcement bar. Ironically, these people actually stood on East German soil while attacking the inter-German border, the barrier simply called "The Wall." No one then thought enough to care or give a damn about borders and barriers, or the ever-present East German guards, not even in the slightest.

After I surveyed the scene to the right of the gate, I noticed an empty guard tower to its immediate left. Its square, dark brown, two-story base supported a white top with sliding windows on all four sides. The windows gave access for the occupant's machine-gun to be used against anyone found on the wide expanse of open field that lay between the inner and outer walls. A double steel safety railing crowned this devil's tower and a large searchlight mounted on top reminded me of a bright jewel embedded in a crown. *Beware of its powerful sparkle,* I thought, *as it is the sparkle of the hunt—the hunt for you and your death.*

I knew from previous exploration that another tower stood just past the Reichstag, by the river Spree, and behind the wall now blocking my view. I walked to my left, toward the Reichstag, where those who hammered at the spray-painted monolith remained. Even without construction equipment, their efforts broke through the concrete curtain in three days. As I approached the Reichstag, a fence separated me from a forest of trees on my immediate left. Fifteen white crosses hung on this fence in remembrance of the fourteen known, plus one for all other unknown victims, who died during escape attempts near the area of that location. I then remembered other crosses I'd seen along the riverbank on the far side of the Reichstag. There, eight crosses remembered seven names, the eighth being for the entire unknown who died there at the hands of the communist gunners.

I passed the first memorial, walking toward the river for a look at the tranquility of the water. I needed soothing in relief from the events of the day. Halfway there, between the hate-painted Wall and the soot-covered Reichstag, just at that narrow, eight meters across, I stopped and stood between the first major victim of Adolph Hitler's official onslaught, the German State, and his last victims, the East German State. There, with a gray sky above and the cold damp earth of November below, between the two sets of painfully sad crosses and the hardened cements of the two Germanys, it all came rolling back to me in my body, soul and spirit.

I remembered the long hours I'd spent in the air chasing the communist submarines. I remembered the years of training my government had invested in me. Millions upon millions of Americans served in America's Armed Forces; and the greatest sacrifice was given by hundreds of thousands of American men and women who fought against both the Nazis and the Communists. All our collective years of service and sacrifice came together in that moment and I suddenly understood why. The freedoms I took for granted, my ability to speak, to learn, to travel and even to eat, instantly became amazingly precious to me. I thought, *Today, the East Bloc people can taste freedom for only the first time. I take it for granted nearly every day.*

All of these thoughts going round in my mind came with an immense feeling of responsibility, a responsibility to give thanks to Almighty God, knowing the worst threat for billions of people was finally behind us. So I stood there, surrounded by it all, with people walking about while the sounds of hammers collided with concrete, and bowed my head in prayer. At that moment, I prayed and gave thanks to the Holy Father. I thanked God for a standing army strong enough to keep those BASTARDS away from me! As bad as that sounds, I found that thanking God, the giver of all life, for the power of our weapons—not in irony, but perfectly appropriate on the afternoon of November 12, 1989.

The bad days were behind Germany now, but few could believe their misery had ended. I noticed three men wearing their best suits that Sunday night on the Kurfuerstendamm as they stood in a cold, light drizzle, quietly laughing and enjoying themselves. By their proper appearance and pasty white, malnourished complexions, I surmised they were from the East.

"Welcome to West Berlin," I said in German, walking up to them.

They didn't react as if they heard me, so I repeated my greeting, trying to be a gracious host of some sort. Once again, the finely dressed East Germans ignored me and it dawned on me as to why.

Each of them was eating an orange, laughing and cajoling one another, all about being able to possess and consume as many oranges as their hearts desired. These three men were jubilant; they were simply ecstatic, partying over their newly acquired bag of oranges in the dark, cold drizzle. In their excitement, they ignored all others; their attention was focused on their oranges, something we in the West took for granted everyday. I left them to enjoy their newfound treasure, surprised and walking away without ever being acknowledged.

The Walls Could Talk

CHAPTER SIXTEEN

I first visited East Germany the following month and drove north of Berlin to a small, remote town famous for its concentration camp—Sachsenhausen. The decades of neglect the communist government provided its citizens were apparent. The roads were winding, narrow and in disrepair. Each building touted dirty, soot-covered, crumbling facades. The air smelled of burning brown coal and turpentine, the turpentine odor emanating from the blue, two-stroke smoke of the East German cars. Disheartened young men stood around drinking beer in the morning with nothing else better to do than look mean, tough and angry as I passed in my western car.

The concentration camp provided many shocking reminders of yet a third Germany, not of the East or of the West, but of the Reich—the Third Reich. I entered the camp and walked into a room designed for height measurements and photographs of the new arrivals, mostly political prisoners. A box camera sat on one side of the room across from a white wall with black hash markings. The prisoners stood on this side of the chamber for their group line-up shot. The hash markings provided camouflage for their assassins' gun barrels and they were tricked into placing their heads firmly against the wall for accuracy, the supposed accuracy of a camera. All were then simultaneously shot in the head from behind.

Outside of this building, an oval track ran with no beginning and no end for prisoners. Tall walls surrounded it. It must have been a third to a half-mile in length. It served as a proving ground for shoe designs and many victims were walked to their deaths in the effort to build a better boot for German soldiers.

Torture chambers were located underground, near the south side of the complex and the remains of the crematoria were on the north. Another building sat in the middle of this compound and along the western wall. It was used to train surgical doctors. Large rooms, virtually man-made caverns, were at one time filled with the bodies of victims stacked one on top of the other, from floor to ceiling. The German doctors learned anatomy and surgical procedures from the cadavers of thousands of dead inmates. A brochure stated that even to this day, dogs would not enter the clean, whitewashed building because the smell of death still permeates the concrete.

When the Russians swept through Sachsenhausen at the end of World War II, they wanted to tear down the entire facility. The local Germans, however, requested that it be preserved in memory of its victims and as a reminder of the evil thrust upon them. Obviously, the Russians honored this request; but in so doing, they propagated their own insanity. In a quiet, contemptuous testimony against the communists, the buildings of the concentration camp were better maintained than those I viewed in the village of Sachsenhausen, forty-five years after the war ended.

All of my discoveries combined to make a long drive home through the once forbidden, highly secretive East Germany. It was a bitter pill to swallow. The year before, the communist authorities would have arrested me for traveling in East Germany by myself without a visa. Now that the Wall was down, the picture show of East Berlin no longer played in the European theater and the idea of the reunification of the two Germanys was beginning to take hold. Soon, the "Two Plus Four" talks would begin, formally ending World War II and the Cold War for that matter. It was all too much to completely fathom.

Little did I know, however, that my newfound education was only beginning.

I arranged my schedule to have a few days off early the next summer for time to spend by myself on a bicycle trip through West Germany. Unfortunately, Donna had nothing to do with my athletic undertaking. One Friday morning, I flew to Hamburg and then took a train to the beautiful city of Lubeck, West Germany. The restored city of Lubeck is quite marvelous. Its main gate, constructed with two enormous towers, stands as a German landmark.

I began my bicycle trip there, pedaling through the gate in the early hours of the afternoon. The day was magnificent with a sunny blue sky, cool breeze, and some fine paths and roadways to keep me occupied. To spend a few days alone on the open road with my trusty cycle was a much-anticipated pleasure and adventure.

Several hours south of the city, I exited the main highway and used back roads, levies and ingenuity to make my way to my first destination: a small town called Luneburg. Donna and I had visited Luneburg once before and found it enchanting. The old city had survived intact during the war because it was too small to be a significant target. The fifteenth century buildings were made of old, teetering brick and slate roofs. The cobblestone streets and every detail of the city center were magnificently authentic. Luneburg once again quickly became a jewel box for my curiosity.

I arrived late in the day and rented a small room with a bath down the hall. Garaging my bicycle proved to be the only obstacle. My German hosts had a small shed off to the side of the hotel and when all was said and done, they were quite friendly and genuinely impressed that an American came to their little village on a bicycle. Of course, there were other cyclists: Europeans who virtually rode professional circuits for their summer tours. I was viewed as someone special and wherever I went that evening, they rolled out the red carpet.

The next morning, after a traditional breakfast at the pension, I headed out of town to the west. My map showed a large park I thought would be good for riding. The park, however, came with a bit of a surprise. I didn't realize how large an area it actually occupied. As there were no retail sales outlets, not even some simple *imbiss* (light meal or snack restaurant), I feared running out of water for drinking. I also kept one eye on the sky because the weather changes rapidly in northern Germany. Several times that day I pulled off the road and waited for a shower to pass. Fortunately, no major weather system clobbered my vacation.

At the end of the second day, I found what appeared to be a farmer's bed and breakfast. After securing my room, we put my cycle in the barn. I had a room with a bath above a small barn. Clean, comfortable and breakfast included, what more could I ask? The price came to fifteen dollars.

Around the corner stood a very nice restaurant where dinner was served on a large, stone patio. It set back from the small village circle with a stonewall around it. The evening light made the beautiful setting even more enchanting. I dined alone and slowly worked my way through a good meal. The satisfying food and Mosel wine did wonders for my overworked body. For the first time, I found my German better than the host's English, so I quietly left the restaurant and went for a walk inside the miniature village.

The farmhouse, the restaurant, and the few other buildings of this tiny village encircled a beautiful, old, ivy-covered church. The steeple bell tower rang out into the evening sky, announcing the hour with old world charm. The churchyard had two large trees and it was surrounded by a small picket fence. Inside, the fence was a graveyard on the north side of the sanctuary. The doors to the church were locked, but that didn't stop me from trying to peer through the windows.

I continued my self-guided tour and ventured into the graveyard. There were headstones remembering many generations of families. Whole clans lay in nearby burial plots. The dates spanned from the seventeen hundreds, but many also appeared to be from more recent times. I came across a section of the yard devoted to the German war dead from World War II. These carefully preserved gravesites and their immaculate headstones dated from the war years, 1939-1945. Some headstones revealed the rank of the soldier who had given his life for his country, just as soldiers of other countries and other generations had done before him. As a military man, I gave my respect for their service without judging their uniform, cause or conscience. I would not judge these fallen German soldiers. They rested there in a rural graveyard at their family church. I respected their call to duty.

If they were in error, they paid for it dearly, as the penalty lasts forever, I thought.

Returning to my room, I could see the faces of people staring at me by the soft, torch lights of the restaurant. I didn't think twice about their interest; in my mind, these collective onlookers were part of the scenery. I retired to my barn room where the animal noises lulled me to sleep. In a matter of hours, I would understand a bit more about this small town and region.

I awoke early the next morning to the sounds of cattle nearby and roosters in the distance. The countryside was universal in that respect. It reminded me of my home state of Nebraska when spending the weekend at my grandmother's house. I rose earlier than my liking and for the proprietor's liking as well, since breakfast had yet to be served. I busied myself with my preparations for the day's ride, packing my clothes and changing into my cycling shoes. I found the early morning quite cool for shorts and I wore a sweatshirt to breakfast.

The Housefrau did her best to serve two couples from Germany and me. However, her glances in my direction left me with the distinct impression that I came under suspicion. She clearly wanted me out of her house and off of the property. It didn't take long for me to put two and two together and realize my offense. I had entered their churchyard and observed their losses as a spectator, completely without invitation or any outward sign of remorse.

There will be no reprieve, I thought. *These are their war dead and I am descended from the generation that fought against them.*

The purpose and the cause of their deaths didn't concern me because each was a tragedy. A family felt the loss of a loved one still on that day, and this American cyclist obviously came across as an uncaring intruder. So, I finished breakfast as quickly as I could. I then dared to pay my bill for the accommodation.

I walked back through the large living room that doubled as the dining area, heading for the back door. At the barn, the somewhat friendly farmer helped me reclaim and reload my bicycle with my gear. Waving farewell, I started off on my third day of the trip. I detoured, still fascinated by the church, which I circled several times, appreciating the different views of the trees, the ivy, the stained glass, and of course, the churchyard. I didn't wish any disrespect toward these people. I would rather drink a beer with them than anything else, but a war got in our way. Those were words that couldn't be said and most likely shouldn't be said in this small town—at least not by me. After a few laps around the parish, I ventured out on the small road leading south.

I headed for Soltau, another smaller town near the autobahn from Hamburg. Once I arrived, I located a grocery store and purchased lunch from the shelves. I bought two large bottles of water for my afternoon ride and consumed a third bottle during my lunch. A small park across the street provided me respite for my lunch and rejuvenation. After an hour and a-half, I stood up and rode to the center of town, picking up Highway 3 to Celle and beyond. The larger highway provided a good shoulder and I encountered little traffic, making for a pleasant journey.

I saw my first sign for Bergen a few kilometers past Soltau. A few more minutes down the highway, I saw my first sign for the concentration camp at Bergen-Belsen. I wasn't sure if it would be a monument, an intact facility worth visiting, or simply a memorial to the camp's victims. I had roughly an hour to decide whether or not to visit the site of Nazi atrocities. There began my internal debate. Would I visit the site to pay my respects and gain more understanding of the reasons behind the cruelty inflicted there? I weighed that against the pain already found in my visits to other Nazi concentration camps.

My map showed me the journey to the Bergen-Belsen concentration camp. It would take me a few kilometers out of my way. For at least an hour, I rode on toward that fork in the road. To the right lay Bergen-Belsen and to the left, the road took a direct route to the beautiful city of Celle.

I remembered visiting the remains of the Gestapo's headquarters, now referred to as the "Museum of Terrors," located in West Berlin near Hitler's bunker. A hotel served as the Nazi's secret police headquarters and interrogation center for those who were held in the interest of the Third Reich. All that remained from the war were the basement cellars. The Germans told the stories of those walls as best they could describe.

I remembered my previous two visits to Sachsenhausen, north of Berlin. On my way out, I skipped the movie. Going down Highway 3, I had an ongoing debate again as to whether or not I had seen enough. Should I subject myself to viewing more of the crimes of a dictator gone mad?

I thought of how rapidly the insanity took off, not in 1941 but actually in 1933, less than a month after the madman came into power. As I rode on into the afternoon, I thought of our visit to Dachau in 1988, the first of the concentration camps. I remembered how the Americans left only one or two examples of the prison barracks. The entire prison yard was full of them once. The administration building remained as do photo displays of the atrocities. Behind that building, prisoners were taken for "special treatment" (the code words for executions, usually by hanging.) While Dachau wasn't a death camp, it routinely worked prisoners to their death and shipped the survivors off to another facility to meet the inside of a gas chamber.

The Dachau tour took us underground to a medium-sized cave illuminated only by prayer candles. From what appeared to be an altar of sorts, a white curved object projected through a hole in the ceiling. After leaving the cave and walking back into daylight, we saw a Star of David on the top of the white object. The meaning of the scene was quite obvious. The only way out of the darkness was through the chimney!

My wife headed back to the administration building that day and I ventured toward a more permanent group of one-story buildings. I then entered a white room with two doors, one opposite my entryway. The walls were smooth. In the far right corner were some iron reinforcement bars, crisscrossing each other at the entrance to what appeared to be a large air vent the size of a crawl space. At that moment, I froze within an electrified, ethereal strangeness.

If it is possible for the heart to stop, the spirit to scream, the soul to shatter, and for a man to leap out of his skin all at the same time, then that is what happened. Simultaneously, my head snapped around for the entrance, my hands virtually flew off of my outstretched arms and my feet jumped out of their shoes. It was only then that I realized my first authentic reaction to a Nazi gas chamber. Or had I been there before?

I hurried through the next door, gasping for breath, while viewing the still intact, multi-chambered cremation facility. My brochure stated that the gas chamber in Dachau never claimed a victim, but rather it served as a storage facility for those awaiting incineration. As I stood where those victims were burned, I pondered reincarnation. I reflected for a moment on all that I valued. There in Dachau, I knew I found an admission stub, a ticket to hell. I knew the exit had been through these ovens. How ironic that the coal fire's breath came from where I now tried to catch my own breath. My mouth was parched and my cold muscles seized up.

I slowed my cycling cadence and caught my breath, buried deep in unison with my memories. I wanted to cry but my eyes refused; they were as dry as sandpaper. *How can I put myself through such another trauma?* I asked myself. *Why should I beat myself silly with the morbidity of yet another K.Z. (concentration camp)? Haven't I had enough for one lifetime?*

My internal debate proceeded down the road with the cycling of my wheels. This journey was to be a relaxing, mini-adventure through the back roads of Germany. Then I drew the most painful arrow left in the quill of my debate: Terezinstadt.

Donna and I had stumbled upon Terezinstadt while driving along Highway 8, north of Prague. We came across a peculiar looking building made of brick with a starburst shape. It appeared attractive to us, so we turned the car around and drove back for a bit of exploring. Little did we know what we would find through our architectural curiosity.

Originally, the building was a prison. As a matter of fact, at one time it housed the men who shot Ferdinand and started World War I. We found this interesting as we purchased tickets and allowed our leaflets to tell the rest of the stories. When we found out what the facility became during World War II, we asked each other: "If these walls could talk?" Among other outrages, the Nazis took over the prison and used it as a concentration camp for the Jewish children of Czechoslovakia. *If these walls could talk.*

I found out that the walls could indeed talk as Donna, the clinical psychologist, translated her observations of the children's art. That weekend, the walls spoke and young voices told their tales to me through their art.

The prison yard was segregated into many regions and this made it ideal for the purposes of the captors. During the first couple of years, the children were held together with elders and the camp became a propaganda tool for the Germans. To promote their cause, they allowed the Red Cross to visit several segments of the facility, proving it wasn't a death camp. Unknown to the Red Cross, the associated death camp stood just a few miles away and these prisoners were routinely taken from Terezinstadt for extermination and the disposal of their bodies.

What they displayed to the inspectors were children and adults in cohabitation under suitable living conditions. The children were well and being educated by the adults. Their education came about through the insistence of the prisoners that the children be given the best education allowed under the circumstances. Reading, writing and arithmetic were taught along with religion, history and art. The art now became a battleground as I approached the turn for the Bergen-Belsen memorial.

For all of the facts the walls of Terezinstadt held in silent memory, those same Jewish children stood before the two of us with a perspective like no other, coming back to life from their dreadful reality buried in the past. Their communications, literally from the minds of the dead, became my breaking point. Over the course of the next few miles, I remembered what they had said and how they said it.

The conflict of visiting yet another camp resided in my heart and head as I bicycled toward a new K.Z. Its burden crushed my spirits like a wrecking ball.

Adolph Hitler decided to use Prague in a very unique manner. He established a collection of items from his victims there, beyond Germany's borders. Personal items from various Jewish communities were gathered and taken to Prague to be displayed as a museum. Not just any museum, but rather a museum built for a race he hoped to extinguish: the Jewish race. The site of the museum was the Jewish Cemetery in Prague, a fitting tribute to their passing.

Donna and I toured the cemetery one sunny Sunday afternoon. Over the centuries the Jews completely covered the large graveyard with their headstones—headstones that touched each other from front to back. Over time, it became a beautiful display, something neither one of us had ever seen before. People lay small stones on the headstones, each with a piece of paper underneath, offering a prayer for the dead at each gravesite. The scene went on for several acres and became a rolling sea of remembrance. The unique statements were very touching.

The museum stood in the middle of the graveyard, and stood approximately four stories tall. There were artifacts from all over Europe, Frankfurt, and Stuttgart—anywhere the Nazis could steal the lives of their own people. Each was carefully documented as to its origin, function and authenticity. I found the knowledge of both their origins and of the original caretakers quite disturbing. However, it was not as shattering as the art of the Terezinstadt children.

Donna and I walked the stairs of the museum as she read aloud from a leaflet. The artwork of the Terezinstadt children lined the staircase. Even the artwork of children became artifacts in the minds of their captors, artifacts from an "extinguished" race. The Czechs now displayed the paintings and artwork in chronological order. With just one question, this became the hardest visit of all.

I asked my wife to explain what they meant and what could be determined from the children's art. I regretted her answer because she interpreted the truth with poignant accuracy. In her voice lay the testimonies of victims as seen through the expressions, the eyes, the art, and the lives of young children.

The children's art demonstrated psychological transitions and pieces were displayed alongside the newsletters. The artworks were snapshots that came from within the children and about their camp. Through their selection of figures, subject and colors, the children documented their surroundings, their feelings, anxieties and problems. The early drawings, those found on the first flight of stairs, were of children playing, of flowers and better times. As we progressed up the stairs, the latter drawings were of death and pain, utilizing black inks and lifeless forms. This art and its interpretation revealed the minds of children in just one of Adolph Hitler's concentration camps. Indeed, through Donna's voice, those walls could talk to me. They spoke of more than I wanted to know.

I cycled on, traversing Germany down Highway 3. I thought of all these things, still wondering if I should visit Bergen-Belsen or pass it by. I asked myself whether I showed cowardice by avoiding such a burden.

I asked, *Why did I ever ask such a question? Now I have to listen to the innocence of children, victimized from the inside out as told by a clinical psychologist!*

As I rode along, I compared this to the experience of Dachau where I leaped out of my skin, to Sachsenhausen and the operating room and to the various chambers in Berlin. I concluded that the children were the worst of all. The dead children spoke to me through what some regarded as artifacts. Their art came alive through the interpretation provided by the voice of the woman I loved. That day, their mind's eye was enlightened to me. Those walls could talk. As I traveled further down the road towards yet another concentration camp, they spoke again and again to those who cared enough to listen. They spoke to me.

A fork in the road loomed ahead. I cycled up to it, stopped and straddled my bicycle while I studied the road signs. I knew Bergen-Belsen stood just a couple of kilometers down the small road. I knew it would be appropriate to stop at the site and say a prayer for the victims of Bergen-Belsen. It would be a good thing. I also knew that I knew too much. I wrestled with too much information for my own good. At that fork on Highway 3, coming from one German cemetery that morning, my decision to go to yet another German concentration camp came and went.

I decided to avoid the camp and its monument, ride on to Celle and take the first train back to Berlin. While I journeyed, I struggled to remain dignified and respectful of the sacred ground I traversed. For the next hour or so, I also tried to maintain my self-respect in choosing my course.

I took the road most traveled. I only wanted to go back to my home, close the door and take pause. I knew I had given "understanding" my all. I also knew that this time I had been beaten, no scoreboards required. I steered to the left, took the popular road and rode the train back to my home: Berlin.

Ants

CHAPTER SEVENTEEN

The bankruptcy of Pan Am and its failure became imminent in November 1991. The company offered us a free move back to America and it was time to bid Berlin a reluctant goodbye.

Donna and I left Berlin for a small town in southern Maryland called, of all things, *Hollywood*. We reasoned that Donna could laterally transfer to a position on the local Navy base, which at least left one of us employed. Hollywood, Maryland was a far cry from Hollywood, California—let alone the glitter and excitement of Berlin. I began flying with a small commuter airline serviced out of JFK that kept me sleeping many a night in the basement of the old TWA building. The isolation of Hollywood, along with near constant flying keeping me frequently away from home tore our marriage apart. Donna took off for greener pastures and I switched jobs, obtaining new employment at a company called Conditioned Air. I stayed behind, loving the quiet, rural charm of Maryland.

Southern Maryland, dotted with beautiful farms, woods and water is a time-forgotten land. The Amish have their horse-drawn carriages and farmers of all faiths have their large barns made of long wooden slats that reach to the sky, interrupted by shiny tin rooflines. The vertical and horizontal brown tree lines vie for attention, announcing greener things to come once spring anoints their large branches with leaves and flowers.

My lonely house nestled between the Patuxent and Potomac rivers was built on a flyway. The Chesapeake Bay glistened in sunlight a few miles further east. Every spring, migratory songbirds made the yard their playground, reminding me why I lived away from urban sprawl.

Likewise, each spring reminded me that the ant farm I unknowingly purchased with my home awakened, making my yard their collective chow hall. Off the little critters marched, finding an overabundance of old wood and railroad ties. Beams that used to support freight trains now prettied up my lot and served to combat soil erosion. But those million or so ants found a gourmet meal in them. As you can imagine, armies of high-stepping red ants recharged by warm weather emerged seemingly from every corner, crack and crevice of the earth to attack my yard's integrity. That was until Big John arrived from Kentucky.

At least one roommate looms large in every single's life. Mine was Big John. Big John earned his name for two obvious reasons—his size and first name. An original, he felt that the only woman he could love was his mother, that all women were bitches— including his mother—and that an occasional same sex poster-calendar was appropriate hanging next to his beloved Harley Davidson. Big John loved mechanical things as much as he loved his mother. I think both got him into trouble. As a matter of fact, I threw him out over his love for mechanical things—and lodging a couple of dogs behind my back.

Somewhere between Big John's Kentucky childhood, my Coleman cooking gas and the ant farm outside my garage spurred a spark of imagination that overcame this young man. This combustible combination drove Big John to burn about seventy-five feet of ant-dominated terrain. This was appropriate in Kentucky perhaps, but amid the thick timber surrounding my wooden abode—well, let's just say I prefer the modern Diazinon method.

At the time of the conflagration, I was flying through the subcontinent of India, making a freight stop at the Madras Airport prior to returning home.

"Big John, what happened?" I asked, seeing my scorched land.

"Ants. They were everywhere. Ants, ants, and more ants! So I took some of your gasoline to them and solved the problem."

"You also blackened the yard all along the driveway," I accused. "But, thank the Lord, you somehow managed not to burn down the woods, my house included!"

"Yeah, but there were ants. I mean ants like I never seen them before, carrying off everything from your yard to their holes in the ground!"

"OK, OK, now that there are no more ants, I won't bother to spread the cure-all I keep in the garage for just such occasions."

I stomped off into the house. That night, "Sixty Minutes" broadcast a segment concerning India. Having just returned from the subcontinent, their lead piqued my interest. In some ways, I regret watching that program. Yet, for better or worse, staying informed in today's society is the price we pay for living in our information age.

"Sixty Minutes" Mike Wallace pulls very few punches; and as the program's producer would have it, Mike upheld his reputation for the sake of India on location. In the overcrowded confines of their clinic offices, he interviewed medical personnel performing ultrasound imaging and demonstrating their technique for determining the sex of an unborn child. Simple enough. The camera revealed many other clinics, all too ready, willing and able to assist expectant mothers in learning this. The camera also exposed abortion clinics essentially coexisting with medical clinics. The segment confirmed what I already knew from my limited time in India. There, life is dominated by the male gender from conception to the grave.

"Sixty Minutes" went on to document use of the dowry. Prearranged marriages or "sinister" courtships are ways a family can rid themselves of a female. Akin to reverse alimony for men, this legal tradition justifies the need to feed oneself through an upfront, on-the-table, open bribe. Couples not wanting the burdensome financial obligation of a girl-child seek to learn the sex of their unborn child. If you are lucky, you are one of the surviving females.

Survival is the operative word for many women in India. As Wallace reported, many do not survive once a dowry is exhausted. The "couple" live above their means until nothing remains. Then the man murders his wife.

Indian women are often victims of "kitchen accidents" by becoming covered with fuel oil, as a common scenario. Suddenly, her large dress is drenched with flammable liquid; and then, as if by bad "luck," the cotton dress ignites like the wick of a lantern. "Sixty Minutes" interviewed several of these women fortunate enough to survive. Each said the same: "It was a fuel oil accident."

Among other beliefs, a widely held one is that the husband needed a new dowry to survive. The logical conclusion? The husband plots the "accidental" death of the woman, his wife. Struck down by "loving" husbands, the victims' faces mirrored their pain and agony. Bandages told the rest of the story.

I thought about my recent flight in and out of Madras, India for cargo. Equipment pulled up alongside the port side of the aircraft and the shuffle began. FedEx, UPS, Emery—they all require identical, heavy loading gear for raising, lowering and positioning large containers and flats of stacked crates on and off the aircraft. Once on the ground, in Madras and throughout India, these heavy items sit untouched by automation. Automation? Why bother when you have one billion hungry people who can work?

India relies on people power. Hell treated the ramp dogs better than these sweat-soaked and swaddled warriors. This working, lower caste suffered humid, dust-filled air and a blazing hot sun that baked the white-hot concrete beneath their sandals. We gave our cokes and crew meals to all of the workers who wanted them. They all wanted them; it became our good deed for the day. One of our mechanics brought along a sack of dog food for the animals. Now, even the skin-and-bone dogs were happy.

I left the plane with our flight release in hand. An operations driver waited, his jeep barely running. No doubt he ran the engine all day rather than risk starting the dilapidated vehicle more than once a day. The British jeep dated back to the colonial period— sometime before Ghandi. In its own way, however, it seemed a quaint relic. I felt part of a living museum while sitting in that jalopy. No top, no windows, no windshield, no doors and the damn "bonnet," a luxury item, was tied onto the front bumper with twine. The drive to the operations building became an adventure.

It was the "highway from hell," or so my kidneys thought. We bounced wildly about, circling the aerodrome, as the driver worked his way over the patch worked asphalt in a counter-clockwise direction with the taxiway on our left, a concrete wall to our right. A scenic route: vultures' stripped carcasses littering the approach end of the runway threshold. The road became a dust factory, covering both of us with a fine powder. No matter, the driver ignored the conditions—he never knew better—and peppered me with questions about America.

At the operations office, a teletype clacked out my weather brief for the remainder of the trip. Paper notams (notices to airmen) hung limp on clipboards attached to the wall. A senior gentleman, one with many years of service at the "terminal" worked in the back and away from the officials. His job, the only real job, kept the paper moving from one official to another. Each smoked more than a few cigarettes before ceremoniously stamping their pious approvals. This transformed my neatly printed stationery into an official document. My paperwork returned to the original gentleman who organized everything into a badly tattered folder before pleasantly presenting it to me. My gut told me, however, I wasn't any closer to leaving India than when I first arrived.

I quickly reread the flight plan and release, signed both and prepared to leave. I anticipated that Conditioned Air would have my flight plan on file with the Air Traffic Control of India.

"Excuse me, sir. You must file an ICAO flight plan," the gentleman said while handing me three blank flight plans and two pieces of new carbon paper.

"Please fill out this important document in triplicate."

The other officials smiled behind their rubber stamp collections, smiles that gave me reason to pause. Though imitation figureheads, these paper lions still wielded a form of power. They could thwart my efforts, throwing their weight around that filthy office.

Signature in place, I returned everything to the senior gentleman who walked the papers over to the three official desks for proper anointment. One copy went to the headcheese; the senior gentleman kept one for himself, returning the third to me.

"Yes sir, all is finished," he said. "Your flight will be waiting for you when you call. Our frequency is one-twenty-three-ninety-five. Have a pleasant journey."

Before leaving, I asked for directions to the restrooms and was pointed down a hallway to the last door on the right. With paperwork in hand, I proceeded with caution. A riddle passed from the old man's eyes, a riddle whose answer came as I entered the room. I stopped dead in my tracks and gagged—the smell overpowered me. Two windows illuminated the ten-by-twelve foot room. The room itself served as a toilet, one outrageously neglected outhouse. Evidently, few people used the small concrete trench along one wall that appeared to be the sanitation device. Everywhere else lay everything else. *What pigs!*

I stormed out past the officials and returned to the broken but undeniably able jeep for the ride back to the aircraft.

"Let's go!"

With my stomach in knots, my nose in shock and my bladder way out of bounds, I hoped the flight plan would fly and the fuel would be on board. *Cargo? To hell with the cargo!*

The driver returned along the same narrow, bumpy road for what seemed to be an eternity. I could just see the plane coming into sight, still a mile from our position. Once there I would relieve myself. But suddenly the moron slammed on his brakes. His palms came together and he nodded several times in a ritual of prayer. That's when I spied incense burning on a narrow shrine. Much to my surprise—the little I had left, the driver reached into the back seat for his bag. Getting out of the vehicle, he pulled some wafers from the bag and left them as his offering. Only then did we continue with the business at hand.

At the plane, the fuel agents still sat on the ground in the shade of the wing. Nothing moved these guys. Apparently they didn't accept the company credit card for fuel payment. A captain's check was my only option. So it came to pass, after a badly needed pit stop on my part.

"Captain, we are getting the go juice," I was informed, as one of the other co-pilots copied down the flight plan from the radio. The agents completed their assignment without any bribes; the cargo handling equipment disappeared and the clearance for engine start came and went without a hitch. This was quite an accomplishment, considering we were the only aircraft on the cargo tarmac.

The taxi clearance came slowly, however. Ironically, in a land blessed with the atomic bomb, a space program and one billion people, we were delayed because the air traffic control system didn't use radar. Still, no one was happier to be leaving India than I!

Once the aircraft was in motion, I was elated, or so I thought. The airplane's path took us close to a construction site near the passenger terminal. A section of removed tarmac needed fill. This project exemplified the manner in which a division of this society fed itself.

Back and forth, back and forth, they wove in broken formation between a large pile of river rock and the square cut out of the tarmac. Their work ended when the level of fill reached the orange mark on a survey stake. We sat in quiet disbelief while I taxied the MD-11, passing the spectacle off our left wing.

"They look like ants," my co-pilot said, "Ants, ants and more ants, in a continuous line."

In that moment, to our amazement, we quietly realized that we weren't watching ants or beasts of burden toiling in the hot sun. Rather, we saw women, women with children tied to their backs and at their sides, carrying baskets of river rock on their heads.

The sudden change in volume from a television program switching to a commercial startled me from my reverie. Between "Sixty Minutes" and Big John, the unforgivable memory of that view from our silent cockpit overcame me. I selected the mute button on my remote control, sitting once again in silence, remembering how we helplessly stared at the workers joined to their children—stared at those weary families in utter disbelief.

Between "Sixty Minutes," Big John and my last trip, it all added up. I fell asleep, thinking *Ants, ants and more ants. What a terrible thing to say.*

The 1998 Hajj

CHAPTER EIGHTEEN

I moved from Maryland and back to my small townhouse in Key West the following summer. The cold winters and high income taxes of Maryland made the small Florida island appealing once again. With all my travels, it took many months to settle down. I eventually managed to unpack and arrange things in between the long flight trips throughout the fall of 1997 and into the winter of 1998.

I received a phone call from crew scheduling late in the afternoon of February 21. Jotting down the details, I understood that a lack of seats on other carriers meant leaving early for my destination. This equated to roughly a three-day vacation in London before flying to Dubai, my favorite destination in the Persian Gulf. This news delighted me. I wanted the trip for several good reasons. First and foremost, I needed to land the MD-11 airplane several times before my landing currency requirements expired. Otherwise a midnight check ride awaited me in Atlanta's dreaded simulator.

This trip also presented a fine opportunity to shop for long overdue wedding gifts. A duty free port, Dubai has a lock on "a market's market." The gold in the sueks (Arab shopping bazaars) is sold strictly by weight at London market prices. Additionally, every conceivable spice, along with the finest of coffees, nuts, figs, and exotic gifts are found in the sueks. Garments of all qualities made from Egyptian cotton, fine linen or silk are literally at your fingertips as the merchants call out for your business. Even posh hotel shops are reasonably priced.

My last reason came from my longing for new horizons. I adapted to the international lifestyle over the years sponsored by my flying career and I needed to work every month to be happy. I'd been too long in Key West and I itched for a change, remembering the sights of foreign grounds, the lights and sounds of people tall and short, thin and round, meeting daily at my table. Good times were coming and I desired the taste of diversity once again. The most interesting people I ever met wore strange clothes and spoke with funny accents. Together, our lives always mixed into an adventure for me. In some ways, I still was chasing "trains" bound for distant lands.

The commuter flight to Miami was uneventful, although early enough to make a couple of round trips possible in case of any delay. Unfortunately, the launch to London evolved to a small flight from hell—courtesy of British Airways. In a row of three seats, I sat on one end; a dignified, thin black gentleman sat on the other, and a largely overweight individual who was not even close to being civilized sat in the middle. He telegraphed his Cuban origins and exuded a sense of being better than anyone else of color to the cabin's collective cognizance. He also displayed a great need to buddy-up to the white boy sitting to his immediate left—me.

Havana-man loved to talk and he leaned into half of my chair when speaking, unmindful of my simultaneous occupation of the already confined quarters. We sat in the last row of coach, so I also listened to a disparate symphony of galley carts pounding against the bulkhead behind me and to the hollow, metallic whooshing of adjacent vacuum lavatories. I could smell one or the other and sometimes both. Fortunately, my Cuban neighbor bathed before the flight. Unfortunately, the airline could not accommodate my desire to be reseated, as the flight was completely full. At least I had an aisle seat.

Somewhere over the Atlantic, he took my hint when I inserted earplugs, put on a headset and turned up the volume. *At least he has his back to me,* I thought.

I don't know what made me look up. Everyone was staring at Professor Cuba in rapt shock and social dismay. I removed my headset to discover that the ugly walrus sitting next to me was an overt, outspoken racist. He spouted his sewerage at the top of his voice, wailing at the well-dressed but humble black gentleman to his right. This expressionless black man sat still with a great effort of tolerance written across his face.

I had to stop this race-in-your-face bull.

"Sir, please lower your voice," I requested, gently tapping the Cuban's shoulder. "You are disturbing the other passengers who want to rest."

He spent the rest of the flight snoring away in his seat and a-half. I spent it with my hands curled around a glass of wine, while everyone else sat back happily relieved of the ugly situation.

London was very good to me. My small, but elegant hotel room displayed an outstanding feather bed with a dozen soft pillows within easy reach. After a double hot shower, I took a six-hour nap to wash the jetlag away, waking fully refreshed and prepared for an evening out. The concierge recommended a nice district with "good restaurants"—a relative term considering British restaurants—and lively company. In the first pub, I met two middle-aged couples and had a nice chat with them. I mentioned the movie *Titanic* and one of the ladies became quite uneasy. She knew a survivor of the disaster. The lucky passenger, as a newborn, was lowered into a lifeboat while she slept in a mail sack.

"They were racing then," she said, "The Captain drove the Titanic at breakneck speed. It was simply a foolish attitude exhibited by the Captain."

She then spoke of the class of people left behind.

"And what about those sent to their watery graves behind locked doors?"

I tried to assure her of the movie's accurate documentation of those dreadful events, but she said, "No, I will never go see that movie. It is not entertainment to me, not in the least!"

A new friend recommended another place, Henry's on Piccadilly, for *"an evening of spirits and roar."* It was quite the place sporting a long bar in front of a large, open area filled with tables and a small, younger crowd. There, I met two Finnish ladies and their friend from Yugoslavia. The Northern European Finns were the most beautiful young women: high cheekbones set off perfect rose complexions and their eyes were as clear and blue as any winter's day sky. After little internal debate, I determined to do this London clubbing thing for a living, despite the high price.

The four of us left Henry's and went about town in their car. I suspected they were not legal to drive in England for good reason. The driver disregarded all convention, driving wherever she pleased on either side of the street and the sidewalks to boot. My seatbelt secured, I sat like a petrified square peg while we chased up and down Piccadilly looking for, of all things, ice cream. We eventually found a shop rated as having "very good" ice cream. But the end did not justify the means, in this case, the exotic transportation. After a brief exchange, I separated from them and walked about eight blocks to my hotel—the way it should be with those three!

The next afternoon I flew a cargo hop out of London Heathrow to Dubai, United Arab Emirates, where I stayed at the Intercontinental Hotel. I pushed a few weights in the twenty-four hour fitness center before jogging along the Dubai River. An extension of the Persian Gulf, the river hosts a small armada of watercraft known as Arabian Dhows. Their unique, sloping design adds romantic charm to the city where spices and hospitality are traditional and unsurpassed.

In Dubai, business destinations include Iran and Iraq with legitimate trade and smuggling, a way of life for both watermen and the local merchants. Yet, even though they live in a separate country hundreds of miles away from the Iraqi border, they are concerned with their own safety from the bloody tyrant. The topic of Iraqi politics is not broached, although one merchant did bring it up.

"Where are you from?" he asked.

"America," I responded with some reluctance.

He kept this to himself, at least for a minute or two. Then he quietly said, "America and England each have two aircraft carriers in the Persian Gulf."

We both just rolled our eyes.

"What do you think of the situation?"

"I hope for a very peaceful solution. You can't go too far wrong with peace, or can you? What do you think of Saddam Hussein?"

The man carefully looked around for anyone who might be listening, then cocked his right index finger, indicating I should come closer.

"Hussein is a psycho," he whispered, chuckling nervously.

I only smiled and walked out, going through the Arab markets back to the hotel. Soon I would launch for England on my return trip and it would be a long enough day just to make it to London. I would layover in Frankfurt.

Dead-dog tired. That's how I felt upon arriving in Frankfurt, Germany. A combat nap on British Airways was my only reprieve from the day. I made it to the hotel via company arranged ground transportation only to find that Conditioned Air had failed to reserve my hotel room. Fortunately, they were not booked up. I appreciated my host's gracious hospitality; they handled the embarrassing situation with style and grace.

Although small and stark, my room remained warm and cozy, which I greatly appreciated. After cleaning up, I went downstairs to the hotel lounge for some good German wine. I couldn't help but notice the English bartender; he spoke with a British accent to the man sitting next to me.

I don't remember how our conversation began, but it truly is a small world. The gentleman next to me attended the University of Nebraska at Lincoln, my hometown and alma mater. He graduated three years after me so we went to UNL at the same time. We compared a few more notes and then spoke of—what else—Nebraska football! Life is strange. There I sat after a week of traveling, talking to a man who lived in London, who was in Frankfurt by chance, but previously lived in Lincoln, Nebraska, where I was born and raised. We were both taken aback.

His claim to fame was that he consistently traveled the farthest to attend the Husker football games. Although he lived in London, he traveled to five or six U.S. games annually, including three out of the last five Orange Bowls. His dedication could best be described as an addiction—an expensive addiction. We discussed teams of yesteryear, games of importance, Coach Osborne's career and his retirement. I remembered the new coach, my old head football coach of Lincoln Southeast High School: Frank Solich. Trivial as the conversation might seem, this gift of home felt pretty good after being overseas so much. As the evening came to a close, we dropped a few more names before calling it quits. Being up for twenty-four hours was enough for this happy captain.

At my hotel near the main train station in Frankfurt, I met the man who commanded our aircraft during the first half of the Hajj, the Muslim's annual pilgrimage to Mecca. Captain Foghorn, who wore his John Deere ball cap proudly, was a good-old-boy from the deep woods of the Carolinas. We hit it off pretty well over breakfast and eventually figured out we would be traveling together to Uthong, on the island of Peabough, Micronesia. We pronounced it "Oou-Pou-Pee-Doo."

Our trip to Micronesia was long but uneventful. The stopover in Tagana allowed us to change money and I cashed in a stack of various foreign currencies that I had collected over the years. The story of the day was the currency exchange rate. Since my last visit to this island nation, the tongay—Micronesia's currency—tumbled sixty-five percent in value. Stacks of paper money were given in return for my few bills, bills that were more of a minor nuisance than anything else in my flight bag.

Our connecting flight took us to Uthong and we traveled with all different types of people. Well-to-do were aboard as well as peasants, who represented the vast majority of the country. In the short span of an hour, we found these simple people to be the friendliest the Good Lord ever created. Even the captain of the airplane came back and greeted us.

At the small airport of Uthong, we deplaned down steps leading to the tarmac area. Across the way were six Micronesian Air Force A-4 Skyhawk aircraft: single pilot, single-engine bomber aircraft that the United States used extensively during the Vietnam conflict. Their swept-back, triangular shaped wings and fuselage were painted forest camouflage with greens and brown, and shaded under ragged canopies. We walked across the ramp to the terminal and into the dark baggage claim area. Retrieving our bags, we were required to have them screened by an x-ray machine and some were hand searched. The authorities looked for all sorts of contraband, including illegal drugs and weapons. Hajj pilots, however, were not subjected to the same degree of scrutiny, as were the Micronesian people.

We made our way out of the crowded terminal and found a hotel van waiting for us after our long journey. The driver greeted us with a broad smile and great enthusiasm, an attitude that felt genuine and sincere. He loaded our large bags into a small, rear compartment of the van, just barely closing the hatch before ushering us to our seats. As each door closed, the outer body emitted a distinctive hollow tin ring. The van itself was small, a narrow five-passenger vehicle that reminded me of a 1960s Volkswagen van, only smaller. It rode low on its suspension and its thin, cramped seating was not designed for long journeys.

It was a long twenty-five minute ride to the hotel, including two tollbooths for the short spurt down the big highway. Our van cast a long shadow with the setting sun behind us, and the narrow main road resembled a 1930s blacktop without paint or lights. Traveling over thirty miles per hour was a death-defying feat, but locals on small motorcycles overtook and passed us. We took it all in stride, sitting back and observing the chickens, goats and water buffalo that roamed the yards of rickety housing. Several of us made ugly comments about the lack of running water, the kids with bare feet playing in the makeshift barnyard, and a whole slew of other indignant remarks without regard to the driver's knowledge and understanding of our language.

It was early evening when we arrived at the hotel that sponsored a large banner covering the face of the overhang. It read: "Welcome Conditioned Air! You Are Family." Outside the van, the hotel manager welcomed us with a warm smile and an invitation to a party, while a half-dozen people collected our luggage and opened doors for us. It was a brand new hotel with white, polished coral lining an oversized entrance and meeting area. Everywhere, beautiful Micronesian women—guest services representatives, eagerly assisted us with the smallest detail. The hotel virtually discounted everything, but considering the disastrous currency crash, who needed a discount! The price of goods to the dollar was one-third normal value. To begin, everything literally started at sixty-five percent off. A day's wage for a railroad worker was one dollar. Still, many Conditioned Air pilots wanted even more, especially those who made the most money. Several captains wanted everything for free. I was embarrassed by their greed.

In the hotel lobby, while waiting for their keys at the check-in desk, several of these captains argued the point that the Micronesian economy would be ruined if we Americans gave out tips in dollars or the equivalent.

"People will come to expect it," one said, "and when the tongay finally comes back against the American dollar—*fat chance*—they will expect the same amount without regard to the reevaluation of the dollar in terms of the tongay. Under such circumstances we will be behind because of the currency swing in the other direction."

I kept my mouth shut about that one.

After checking into my room, I showered, changed clothes and went to the hotel lounge. There I bought several rounds for our group of ten. As I paid the amazing seventeen-dollar bill, one of our first officers assembled a group to go out for dinner at another hotel. He then enlisted pedicabs for a race to the restaurant. All told, eighteen of us took up these cyclists. We each paid them ten thousand tongay, instead of the normal two thousand for cab fare. To make things more interesting, we offered a grand prize of twenty thousand tongay or two days wages for the winner.

The race began. We rode down the street, laughing and shouting as they cycled their hearts out for six or eight blocks to another hotel and its restaurant. Coming in last, I never knew who won but that didn't matter. It was just good fun and a laugh.

The hotel consisted of little islands of four separate accommodations bundled together, connected by wooden footbridges illuminated by tiki lamps. The restaurant was a ship: and inside we sat upstairs at a long table overlooking the small, moonlit bay. The staff was slow due to the unexpected arrival of eighteen Americans, but we dined in foreign luxury, a slight breeze wafting across our bamboo table. Our hosts served their finest fish and a variety of garden vegetables from local markets. Our simple Micronesian meal appealed to our jaded palates. It was a beautiful, carefree time spent together in a foreign land and by evening's end we had forgotten our concerns of the day, our long travels, and the many trips to Saudi Arabia that lay ahead. For us, life in this far-off land was dream-like, a separate reality where our wants and cares dissipated in the warm night air. Upon leaving, we made our way down the restaurant captain's ladder and strolled the boardwalk, while admiring the quiet reflection of torchlight on calm water.

This calm and quiet world, however, exploded at the hotel's front door. There began a wild reality ride. As we attempted to leave the hotel, the entrance seemed blocked with every pedicab within fifty miles—a miracle of the cellular telephone! If I had thrown a stone, it would not hit the street. Seeing us, the drivers' fever for our business intensified. They pushed cabs into our paths, insisting that we sit down in their carriages. We each fended for ourselves by virtue of their sheer numbers. Separated from the group, I took the first pedicab I could, hoping to arrive safely back at our hotel. After climbing in one, my shower-shoe clad driver pushed away from the others and peddled down the most direct route to my hotel. Off we went, hastily down a four-lane, one-way road against heavy traffic! My driver must have thought it was yet another race that, against all odds of survival, he would win by taking this short cut. We swerved between oncoming buses, trucks and cars, while I screamed at the headlights rushing toward us. Perversely thankful that I sat in the very front of this light metal frame contraption, I knew death upon impact certainly would be instantaneous and I would never feel pain.

I survived intact, the first of our party to arrive back. Yet there, too, I was surrounded by a mob of local young men. I gave the driver a dollar but he wanted more. Perhaps he thought that he deserved it as we "won" the undeclared race back to the hotel. Five other cabs delivered guests from the restaurant and the crowd kept growing. This multiplying wolf pack concerned me. After all, we were on the dark, dusty streets of Peabough, Micronesia, at night. We were rich Americans surrounded by poor, out-of-work locals.

They wanted more money so I flipped my wallet open. A single dollar bill, my very last, was all I found. I gave it to my driver, immediately diverting the crowd's attention away from me. Everyone shined flashlights on that single dollar, thoroughly inspecting it, while standing on the dark street corner. The extra buck served as my distraction and I left for my nearby hotel, feeling a bit shaken by it all. Once inside, however, I laughed about it. After all, my pedicab driver made two days wages in ten minutes. That was pretty good by anyone's standard.

A leisurely breakfast the next morning turned into the usual union meeting of pilots, grazing on and on for hours. The upcoming company contract and what we should put on the table for our opener was the main course. Money always came up. Many felt we were significantly underpaid and falling further behind the industry pay scales in comparison with the major airlines. Others reiterated that we were a charter group, and as the old saying goes, we compared apples to oranges. Still, others disagreed with the fixed-base hourly rate for all in a particular seat position and wanted years of service to be accounted for in our compensation. I threw in my two cents worth and began to think of how all of this must sound to the hotel staff. I dispelled that thought, however, with the idea that no matter where these talks were held, we would always be foreigners talking about our lives and our jobs. It was a simple fact of life.

However, after breakfast, several of these "gentlemen" went beyond the call of duty. They stood up and stiffed the staff that waited on them.

"Breakfast is on the room, isn't that your understanding?" they asked, looking one another in the eyes.

"Oh yes, that is the word from crew scheduling."

"They don't tip here in Micronesia, do they?"

"No, only in America is tipping the custom."

They left the restaurant.

The contract with the hotel didn't provide anything for free. However, with a sixty-five percent price reduction, there was no need for such a deal. In reality, the three-dollar charge was paid by the guest; but they never asked the host, while the country worked for less than a dollar a day. Even after this conversation, they added insult to injury by neither paying their bill nor tipping these bankrupt people for their service. These captains even had the nerve to ask for the airline discount at lunch and dinner!

The next day, I inquired about a massage at the hotel fitness center located in the basement.

"We will send someone to your room in twenty minutes," they said. "The cost is 35,000 tongay. We can either put this on your room tab or you can pay directly to the woman."

The standard massage lasts an hour but longer ones were available, obviously for an extra couple of bucks.

I was only in my room about ten minutes when the knock came. A middle-aged woman stood on the threshold. She carried extra-large white terrycloth towels and a couple of bottles of oil. Using minimal English and sign language, I understood her request to burn incense.

"No," I said, shaking my head, "But I would like an hour and a-half long massage."

I pointed this out on my clock. However, the woman didn't understand a word of what I said. Still, I received a very good massage in an hour.

Prior to her arrival, I laid out 60,000 tongay instead of 35,000 in anticipation of the extra half-hour and a tip. I gave her the entire 60,000 tongay or ten dollars, 35,000 for the hour of work and 25,000 for the tip. I felt it would have been wrong to do otherwise, displaying or waving six days' wages in front of her. In the states, the same rubdown cost fifty or sixty dollars, so I didn't care if she earned a little extra because of a language barrier.

As one of life's barometers, I will always remember her reaction to my meager generosity. This forty-five year-old woman, who could be considered lucky enough to literally rub my bare ass in this new hotel, got down on her knees in front of me and kissed my hands.

"Thank you, thank you, thank you," she whimpered.

This extraordinary gesture of gratitude for my pocket change made me uncomfortable and not a little guilty for what I had.

After she departed, I showered and changed into my uniform for our first trip to the Kingdom of Saudi Arabia, or as we called it, "The Magic Kingdom." I packed a small suitcase for the trip. Our overnight would last some two and one-half days before we ferried an empty airplane back to Micronesia. I went down to the lobby a half-hour before our scheduled departure time to enjoy the company of my fellow crewmembers.

Our American flight attendant and four pilots loaded up the hotel shuttle van and departed for the airport for a half-hour drive. On the road headed out of town, we drove by several shrimp farms. A man and his young son threw mud onto the dikes, scooping it out of the pond with their bare hands. Both of them were naked and we laughed out loud. Someone made a rude comment about the barefoot children we saw playing with sticks in the dirt in front of their meager dwellings.

At the tollbooth, our van got caught in a Hajj traffic jam. Police cars with their blue lights and sirens screeching at full strength escorted busloads of pilgrims to the airport. Crowds of people, three to four deep, stood along the roadway, waving to the faithful and cheering them on. At the airport, the pilgrims located their luggage and placed it on carts to be taken through to the x-ray machine.

Amid the hustle and bustle of the crowds as I waited to get out of our small van, I awoke. Somewhere on the road to the airport that day I changed. I can't place the moment, but my emotions caught up with me and pulled down the thick velvet curtain that blinded me to the circumstance of my life. Maybe it was my remembering the massage lady on her knees, thanking me for a large tip. Or possibly the sight of a naked man and his young son clawing mud out of their shrimp farm water with bare hands and flinging it onto a homemade dike. Or, could it have been the children playing with sticks in the dirt, barefoot in front of shacks while the Hajjis drove through crowds upon crowds of well-wishers waving goodbye. Those who followed us in large buses were on their journey to Mecca to pray for personal forgiveness, one of the five pillars of Islam. Their journey was so important to society that the police escorted their motorcade with flashing lights and sirens. In a real sense, they were heroes to their people.

As a world resident, perhaps a combination of the week's past events added up and challenged me to take another look at the haves versus the current surroundings of people who occupy the world of have-nots. I remember passing through the dark airport hallways and thinking of life's treatment of these most wonderful, peaceful people. Many of us came to their country and rejected them. Our loud talk and our excruciating fiscal conservatism left me ashamed. Those who made the most money were both the loudest and cheapest people imaginable.

These same poor Micronesians worked and saved all their lives; and with the help of their government, purchased a travel package that included two round-trip tickets for the Muslim Hajj. For this religious journey, each pilgrim required two, full round trips to complete their required acts of worship. The first trip out brought the pilgrims to Jeddah where they processed into the country and were transported by bus to their campsite. The empty plane then ferried back to pick up more passengers. After the hiatus, the pilgrims required an empty airplane to fly into Jeddah to pick them up for their return trip to Micronesia.

All of this flying was highly profitable, flying eighteen hours a day, seven days a week for two five-week periods. Still, we stood beside these poor, impoverished, yet humble people, who had nothing but love and respect for God and their families; and we exhibited neither empathy nor compassion, or even respect. I felt we flew half way around the world, flaunting our "birthrights"—our being born into the first world instead of the third world, or even further down the ladder—to our hosts and our new neighbors. I stood waiting at the gate with my crew, a blank stare on my face, mired deep within my own thoughts and observations.

Everything suddenly hit me like a bucket of cold water. In the dark airport hallways, my emotions spiraled down, accepting these contrasting memories like the ugly tattoo they represented. I was neither better nor worse than any of my passengers, just born with more opportunities laid out in front of me. When I stepped out of the dreary "OooPooPeeDoo" airport, the MD-11 crouched there in front of me with its ears laid back, glistening white paint and polished aluminum shining bright. The wealth and modern technology it represented shattered my previous train of thoughts.

"This is my country's product, my country's ability," I said to myself. "This plane is made in America. My country. This represents all of my country. With three engines and a tail standing sixty feet tall, the damn thing flies."

For a brief moment, that impression summed up my feelings toward the United States of America. I relished in it.

Once on board and in the cockpit, sitting comfortably behind nine computer screens, I looked out my large window at the long lines of people walking towards the plane. As the Hajjis boarded the flight, I noticed most were in the twilight years of their lives. From what little money they made throughout their lives, each had saved enough to pay for this sacred journey to Mecca, to be with millions of other Muslims and pray for forgiveness of their sins. Many dressed in the finest of their traditional clothing. The women wore long dresses in bright colors; their men wore simple white suits and caps. Others dressed in the black burkas with veiled faces and their husbands wore the garments of humility, two terry cloth sections without so much as a stitch of thread.

They were promised entry into heaven if they died during the Hajj. Many *would* die while camping in the extreme heat of the Saudi desert. On average, Conditioned Air flew a half-dozen fewer flights (2000 fewer seats) during the second half of the Hajj, when the faithful returned to their homeland, than during the first half. This may be one reason why they received a hero's send-off from their people.

Looking at them, I thought of all of this and then excused myself, moving to the forward galley. I came apart, crying. The contrasts of cultures and values in life returned my lost perspective. By just walking out to the airplane, I let the dazzle of my rich, western world blind me to the brotherhood of man. I was guilty as sin of my own inhumanity, caught and reminded by each drumbeat of my heart.

A flight attendant helped put things in focus. She shored me up and glued me back together. After all, I had a plane to fly, she reminded me—safely. We were taking hundreds of people to their chosen site of worship. With that perspective, I went back to my duties, completed the preflight, and realized my participation in their journey with more insight in a very meaningful way.

After a long day of flying, we sat in the ivory-colored, polished coral hotel lobby of the Topaz Hotel, in Jeddah, Saudi Arabia. We visited with friends, wearing blue jeans and polo shirts, keeping to ourselves. The Arabs frequented the other side of the lobby, wearing their traditional white robes or "chandras" and checkered headscarves. As Americans, we place a large, personal space or territory between others and ourselves, tending to speak loudly without concern of being overheard. The Arabs have a much smaller space and speak almost in whispers, nearly touching whiskers. On top of that, Saudi Arabia is an extremely conservative country. News is censored and pictures in magazines are blacked out for exposing a woman in an immodest manner. Alcohol is strictly forbidden. Therefore, we enjoyed our late afternoon conversation over some strong coffee instead of beer, as would be the case in Micronesia.

From the elevators, I heard a distinctive accent speaking thick English. A very large, strong man joined us and we chatted until he took over the entire conversation. He was hilarious and initially fit in well with our American military pilot group. Truman called himself a "fat communist" despite his deep hatred for the Soviet empire and communism in general. Obviously as strong as three men, he referred to himself as a bastard. Of course, having lived in Berlin for four years, I was most interested in what this "communist" had to say.

Truman ordered "a strong Turkish coffee" from the waiter and signed it to his room. Lighting up a big cigar, he took a few puffs to ensure it burned properly, then touched his coffee to his lips and spouted out for the entire lobby to hear, "Gentlemen, this is better than sex!"

His proclamation echoed throughout the large chamber. The entire lobby could not help but hear and understand his outlandish swipe at both the local culture and the perceived American value of sex. Every one of us stopped, transfixed. When I turned to look at the others in the lobby, I saw every Arab and foreigner in the hotel lobby scrutinizing us. But Truman meant to bring up a point and so he followed through.

"You know, here I am with my big cigar, drinking a strong cup of coffee and talking with my buddies in a far-off land. It doesn't get any better than this, no not anywhere, not even in bed having sex with my lovely wife or one of your girlfriends."

Truman, the fat communist bastard from Romania, was just warming up.

"I remember my political officer. Yes, we really had political officers giving us the lectures, which we forced ourselves to sit through, take notes and recite back the bullshit the communist bastard wanted to hear from us. It was all a big game and we knew that, and we knew that he knew that we knew that. Who is right? The one that has the power is always right. They had the power because they had the guns and that is the end of the story."

"One day, my political officer calls me into his office with my boss. They never let anyone talk alone with anyone else, just because they were communist. So I went into his office where he asked me to close the door and sit down. I thought 'OK,' and I asked myself what might be the reason for this meeting. I just came back from getting married and I was in love with bells still ringing in my head. I knew nothing of the squadron for the past few weeks. So, I came in to the so-called meeting thinking something must be up, something important. Maybe there was some sort of news from NATO or something from the Kremlin." Truman paused to pat his mustache on one side.

"So in front of my commanding officer, my political officer spouts off from his open sewer. He asks me, 'Truman, there are nine million women in your country of Romania. Is this not correct?'"

"I said, 'yes sir,' not knowing where he might be going with all of this."

"'Then let me ask you a personal question, Mr. Truman,' he said."

"I replied, 'Yes sir, what is that?' and I leaned forward in my chair."

"'If there are nine million women in this stinking country of yours, why on earth did you have to marry a fucking Jew?'"

"So, I looked him right in the eye and I answered him without missing a beat. 'You want to know why out of nine million women I married a fucking Jew? Well. I will tell you why. Because I want to fuck the Jews!'"

"From that day forward, for some reason, I never got along with my political officer the same way as before. I am telling you the truth, I would not lie about a thing such as this, as close to me as the mother of my lovely daughter."

Everyone, man and woman, Arab and American was stunned. You could hear a pin drop. When I gained enough nerve to look around the hotel lobby, I saw the normally quiet Arabs shaking in their chandras, trying to hold back their laughter. Even the men dressed only in terry cloths, without so much as a stitch of thread in their garments, a symbol of humility before God—even they were smiling and shaking their heads, knowing full well that they had been 'had' by Colonel Truman. I will always remember how that moment, the laughter as precious as gold, no matter how politically oriented, bound everyone together in the lobby.

The Great Truman went on to tell many other stories of his flight training in the Romanian Air Force. His history included working with the Soviets against NATO and an interesting list of intelligence gathering circumstances.

In the middle of our conversation, or what I'll call an interrupted monologue, he mentioned his grandfather. Our conversation then became fascinating to me. At first there was nothing unusual about his grandfather except that he fought against Russia during World War II. During the aftermath, as a P.O.W., his grandfather rebuilt Russia for seven years before his release from captivity. Three years later, a midnight knock on the door took him by train to the Soviet Gulag where he was worked to death.

From that moment on, few people fascinated me more than Colonel Truman. Here sat a man who could tell stories about the Iron Curtain's hard side. Having lived in Berlin, I could not get enough of his history. His perspectives were uniquely East Bloc, but level in his own way.

He bored my colleagues and I apologized for their attitudes, saying, "They know nothing. Because they have not suffered, they know not what is good. They know nothing."

With this statement, which is a Russian saying, we started to bond in our initial relationship. I told him about my living in Berlin during the cold war and a few of my travels in communist countries and East Berlin—"The Picture Show" as the West Berliners called it. I shared some of my knowledge of the cruelty and depravation that went on, undocumented except in the souls and spirits of the millions of victims for the forty-five years following World War II, undocumented behind the devil's horizontal monolith: the Iron Curtain. It impressed him that a westerner possessed even my few limited facts. I continued with details of one more subject that truly cemented our relationship. I possessed knowledge of the battles of Russia where his grandfather fought against the communists.

After a brief pause, Truman changed subjects and shared the events that he believed were the four greatest crimes of World War II. In all respect to the victims, I did not agree, but I did not argue. However, when I thought about his perspective, it gave me enormous insight into the twentieth century and its problems.

The first on his list was the massacre of Polish officers by the Russians. This was accidentally discovered through an aerial photograph taken by an axis aircraft trying to jettison a bomb load. The Germans then tented the area and exhumed the remains of thousands of dead Poles. They even brought in the Red Cross for documentation, propaganda and humanitarian reasons.

The second crime was the Russian turncoats. Over a million Russian soldiers, whole armies, fought against their country out of hatred for Stalin.

The return of the Russian prisoners of war from Germany was the third crime. Russia executed all of these men in the belief that they collaborated, committing crimes against the fatherland. To Stalin, these men were living testimony against themselves.

The fourth was the Russian assault on Berlin.

History documents the Russians pushing recklessly into eastern Germany. Joseph Stalin himself gave their objective: to have the Soviet flag fly over the Reichstag on May Day, 1945. They did it. According to Colonel Truman and his books, the Russians paid dearly for this propaganda, losing two and one-half million soldiers during this, the final assault campaign against an arbitrary clock and a fortified German defense. In my own readings, I had never come across such a high figure, but after living in Berlin and touring the city, it was not hard for me to believe him.

He and I then discussed the war memorial, Treppetower Park in East Berlin, where ten thousand Russians were put to rest. It is the only place where the swastika is allowed in Germany, in a large bronze statue placed firmly under a conquering soldier's foot. There the trees grow with branches pointing unnaturally down. When the Russians were questioned as to why they did this unnatural thing to these trees, they answered, "It is unnatural for a country to lose twenty million solders in a war." Historians believe this number to be another inaccuracy. Most now agree that twenty-eight million Russians were lost in the war.

"As Americans, we celebrate the victory in a blind way. We are taught that we won the war in Europe. The actual facts, however, remain decidedly in favor of the unparalleled sacrifice by the Soviets. Four of five German soldiers fought on the Russian front, rather than against the Western Allies. As respectful as I can be toward the human cost of the

American sacrifice, our sacrifices were but a statistic, a grease mark on the highway of that generation's hell."

It was an interesting conversation, especially in a Saudi Arabian hotel lobby.

So there we sat in our hotel lobby in Jeddah, Saudi Arabia, eye to eye, heart to heart, obviously in pain. Remorse hung suspended between our imaginations, between the two of us for the memory of millions. Everyone could see our empathy with the suffering. World War II did not end in 1945 or in 1989, or as of yet. The most vilifying circumstance of the twentieth century, too large to be understood by any one man, again sang from the crypt of our memories and shone in our eyes.

"You are the second person I've known whose grandfather was taken to the Soviet Gulag and worked to death by the Russian communists," I said, military officer to military officer, pilot to pilot, eye to eye, in front of those who could not comprehend the significance. We held time in our hands at that moment, the both of us contemplative, and the Americans in the lobby were again quiet.

Later that month, I took a commercial flight from Uthong to Tagana and then on to Tokyo. I lay over for several days in Japan with one of our chartered crew. We had a couple of very nice dinners together and were able to watch the Oscars as a group. After being out for so long away from our home, we could taste being back in the States through the awards ceremonies.

Our flight to Los Angeles was routine enough until the final air traffic controller gave us the slam-dunk arrival. We were too high, too fast and too close to the airfield for our aircraft. I dropped the slats, the flaps and the landing gear early to compensate and stabilize the approach, only to have the auto throttles fight me all the way to the touchdown. After a ten-hour night flight, I did not need the aggravation; but somehow, I was able to put the aircraft on for a pretty good landing.

I caught a dawn launch on American Airlines headed east for Miami and then a commuter flight to my home in Key West. After recuperating from jet lag for the better part of a week, I went out that Friday night to The Blue Lagoon, a local neighborhood bar. Several sailors operated the establishment. They were aviation ordinance specialists who had back problems from lifting heavy bombs onto airplanes. We spoke for a while about the Navy and during our conversation a very pretty lady with short blonde hair stood behind me, catching my eye and twisting my rubberneck.

She was a tourist, taking a week off from the cold of northern Michigan. No surprise there, the town was full of snowbirds. She spoke of her career as a schoolteacher and I spoke of my experiences as a pilot flying the most recent Hajj. The fun began when she referred to her past, living in Romania, behind the Iron Curtain.

"Romania, where the people survived on garlic and lard. At the airport, we watched CIA transport aircraft bring in food for the American diplomats and their dependents. Believe it or not, the citizens were not allowed to drive from November until April. The streets were not lighted to save energy."

She spoke of the long, downtrodden faces, staring between the barred gates of the American food distribution centers. I could only imagine being so close and yet so far away.

I told her my many stories about living in Berlin and we spent a good deal of time comparing notes. I stared off for a minute. Thinking that she bored me, she excused herself to step away.

"No," I said, "You don't bore me at all. I was just thinking back on some of my experiences."

"Did you ever enjoy the rush of feeling rich and privileged while in these poor countries, driving while others must walk in the cold?" she asked. She dwelled on this, repeating her query several times.

Each time I replied in the same manner.

"No, not hardly. However, I do enjoy shopping at the bargain exchange rates. Mostly, I feel for the people. They have so little."

Shortly before parting, she said, "The happiest day of my life was when I stood in front of the Romanian leader, Nicolae Ceausescu, and his lovely wife Elena. With my own eyes, I saw that they were dead, filled full of bullet holes."

Aghast, I was taken aback. That was certainly unusual for a beautiful woman or anyone else to say in a bar to a complete stranger.

It was late, eleven-thirty at night, but right then I knew I had to make a phone call. Because of the Easter holiday, it would have to wait until Monday. For the life in me, I just had to ask Colonel Truman, "How do you spell Ceausescu?"

An African Child

CHAPTER NINETEEN

The flight to the African coast was a mixed bag. High altitude cruise kept most of the problems away from the crew and their corresponding air traffic controllers—if they can be called controllers. They consisted rather of rudimentary, flight-following personnel who update the position of the various sector aircraft from pilot reports. These position reports contain the aircraft's position by either named, five-letter intersections or a latitude and longitude reading, the time at the reported position, the altitude at that position followed by the next position, an estimated time at that position; and then, the following on position with the selective doorbell or telephone ringer for airplanes—the SelCal (select call) check.

I called into the microphone, "Dakar, Dakar, Conditioned Air 322 position. Dakar, Dakar, Conditioned Air 322 position on eight—nine—three—zero."

"Conditioned Air, Conditioned Air, this is Dakar, go ahead with your position."

"Dakar, Conditioned Air 322 position Andar, time zero, four, three, nine, flight level three seven zero, estimating Amdon, time zero, five, zero, seven, Axion next. SelCal check Golf, Hotel, Oscar, Lima."

"We finally got through to this guy."

"Woke him up I bet."

"Roger. Conditioned Air 322 reports Andar, zero, four, three, zero, flight level three, seven, zero, Amdon zero, five, zero, seven, next Axion. Report Axion on this frequency."

I replied, "Report Axion on this frequency, Conditioned Air 322 out."

"Well, once you got in touch with Dakar, he came in loud and clear."

"So we have that going for us!" I said.

The window of accuracy is plus or minus three minutes. The reporting pilot is the accounting agency for the report, because without radar, who really knows what took place, when or where? Collisions have taken place mid-flight because of bogus information or misunderstandings of these position reports.

The rudimentary controlling from these reports keeps aircraft at least fifteen minutes in a trail while on the same airway and separated by altitude at intersections. Aircraft traveling on headings from 001 degrees to 180 degrees are considered eastbound; and by convention, they fly at odd altitudes including flight levels 290, 330, 370 and 410. Aircraft flying on westerly headings fly at the other odd altitudes, 270, 310, 350, 390 and 430, if able. Contrarily, the ICAO conventional altitudes vary in the North Atlantic tracks between Europe and America where too many aircraft fill too few pieces of air space. There, one thousand feet of separation and unidirectional flight is required. Across the Pacific, they stray from convention, too, as everyone wants his bird in the jet stream, getting a free one hundred fifty mile-an-hour push from the wind.

However, common to all, is the primary regard for position reporting. Everyone complies with the requirement. Safety of flight dictates several other methods to control the madness of flight in the non-radar environment. For the continent of Africa, an African common frequency, 126.9 on the VHF radio, allows pilots to communicate with each other, "air-to-air," as it is called. The pilot broadcasts his position in the blind, using time estimate, direction of flight, altitude, track and destination for the other pilots to cross-reference on their charts and flight management system estimates. That is, if they are fortunate enough to have a flight management system. Most aircraft flying in Africa are quite tired, old forms of low-grade aluminum and not so fortunate. They are lucky to have windshield wipers, let alone a computerized anything.

A third method, an electronic means of obtaining at least a warning of bad things to come, came about from a project I flew on while serving in the Navy. I took a large, four-engine turboprop, the P-3 Orion aircraft, and dropped sonobuoys behind a glorified fishing boat in Monterey Bay, California. The Monterey Post Graduate School used the boat for various research projects. The new device located the transmission device by calibration of signal strength and change of relative bearing from the moving aircraft. We dropped about a dozen buoys one afternoon and even received kudos from the project manager for our accuracy. Surprisingly, he requested one drop to land within reach of his tape measure. That took some lack of forethought on his part since each buoy weighed forty pounds. Accuracy? Try a hole in your boat! We received many accolades from our precise drops at one hundred feet and two hundred knots. I thought of it as the Polish sport of javelin catching.

The project was a complete success and enabled the advancement of a Navy antisubmarine warfare program as well as the development of TCAS, or Terminal Collision Avoidance System. With an operable transponder in each aircraft, this system displayed the aircraft in its airspace box, or envelope, in terms of relative position and altitude; as well as calling out oral warnings and giving commands for vertical separation maneuvers. Currently, this technology is employed throughout the world, except in the poorer regions such as the continent of Africa. At our destination, the old Soviet aircraft that littered the tarmac may have a second radio for the air-to-air frequency, but forget about an operable western transponder!

The last method of obtaining separation between aircraft is a natural gift from the Almighty. We dubbed it the "Mark One Eye Ball"—see and avoid. This essentially perfect method for avoiding collisions in the terminal environment (pardon the pun) is almost useless for high altitudes. At high altitude, the equipment is moving so rapidly that an aircraft can overtake another plane from behind; or at such an angle so as to be descending from above, or ascending from below, and yet not be in line to detect the position lights, which once again assumes proper operation. It also assumes the pilot is not distracted by eating his lunch or tracking a rising hemline. After that, the complete degradation of the "see and avoid" method is in the hands of Mother Nature. Flying in the clouds completely obscures the vision of the entire crew. Imagine, as your wing tips disappear, closing on an object at 1000 miles an hour. See and avoid has limitations.

Flying at flight level three, seven, zero gave us plenty of time to plan and execute the approach to the Diamond City Airport. Our main concern was the weather and the use of the navigational aids, specifically the instrument landing system, or ILS. We briefed the approach in a standard company manner; but only the captain knew the airport from prior experience.

"John, while we have time, let's brief the approach and keep everyone reading from the same sheet of music," he said.

"Alright," said John, who now flew as the first officer but acted as the flying pilot and gave the brief.

"This will be the ILS to runway one five. The initial approach altitude is three thousand five hundred feet. The final approach course is one, five, one degrees. The final approach fix, Papa Alpha, is crossed at eighteen hundred seventy-five feet with a decision altitude of three hundred fifty feet. Missed approach is straight ahead until three thousand five hundred feet and then return to Papa Alpha and enter holding. Frequencies are one, eleven point five for the ILS and four, forty-five for Papa Alpha. We can back it all up with the VOR radio on one, fifteen point six. The needles should align and correspond because the station is on the field. Minimum sector altitude is twenty-four hundred feet. Any questions?"

We both responded, "No questions."

Our air traffic controller handed us off to the next sector and the female voice there gave us the initial let down to flight level two, five, zero. The weather radar indicated light showers. Nothing alarming. We entered the clouded sky without hesitation but the ride became quite rough.

We switched radio frequencies to arrival and continued the descent into the approach arena where we again switched radio frequencies and spoke to the approach control. She kept the arriving and departing aircraft separate by directing them to geographic intersections; but because her directions came without radar, the process of departures and arrivals was a slow one. Once again, accurate position reports and timing claimed the day. The fun began when she cleared us for the approach.

Our electronic map indicated our position accurately, but none of our navigation radio receivers concurred or even received a signal. While crossing over land, we flew under a broken layer of dark, cumulus clouds and concentrated on finding landmarks through the rain showers. If the captain could recognize one, he would feel confident as to where the airport would be in relation to our aircraft. We were flying low under the clouds in a two-hundred-foot long, one-hundred-forty-million-dollar airplane. Commuter pilots call it "running scud." Others call it "getting the job done." It is not a preferred method for navigating, but without confidence in the aircraft's inertial reference system, nothing else would do in a pinch. We descended to two thousand feet and then slipped under the ragged scud at seventeen hundred feet, just fifteen hundred feet above the ground. It was flying by Braille, still with no sight of the airport.

A hard right turn to the displayed airport position was our only option. We were now below our minimum sector altitude in a clear corridor used for approach, groping for the airport.

The landing checklist and tower control frequency completely occupied the captain.

"Gear?"

"Down and green," came John's response.

Tom sighted the gear position indicator lights and repeated, "Down and green. Spoilers are armed, auto brakes are minimum, and cabin crew is notified. Flaps?"

Before John's response, the captain radioed the control tower.

"Diamond tower, Conditioned Air 322 on final requesting clearance to land."

I picked up the approach plate and cleared us down to twelve hundred feet. The captain still had not acquired a reference point. We could not go lower.

"Boss, this isn't pretty," I said.

The copilot agreed and advanced the power, initiating a missed approach.

At that moment, we broke through the rain and saw the airport for the first time. The initial line-up came with confusion, as we were offset to the left.

Again we requested, "Diamond tower, Conditioned Air 322 requesting clearance to land on runway one, five."

We knew one runway would be occupied with a departing Soviet aircraft. A second Soviet freighter sat waiting for us downfield on a turnout, waiting so he could back track on the active runway to the tarmac. The landing clearance became the captain's primary concern. Mine became calling my observations out to the flying pilot, the rate of descent and the line up, concurring with his judgment and flying skills.

"Sinking eight hundred feet per minute, sinking one thousand, on center line, on air speed."

We rolled out and spotted the PAPI (precision approach path indication) lights, four lights that give either a red or a white glare depending on the elevation of the aircraft relative to their individual beams. Ideally, the PAPI displays two white lights and two red lights as the glide slope indication, positioning us directly on the three-degree glide path. This was the case. Our scud running had worked, in a wide body aircraft no less! Legal? What's legal in Africa in the first place, and where are you going to get a Federal Aviation Administration official in the middle of Africa in the second? In Washington D.C., maybe, but in Diamond City, not a chance!

The landing came soft and smooth.

"We cheated death again," was Captain Tom Talbot's response to the last ten minutes. We took a long roll out and turned around on the far pad. The Soviet aircraft back taxied once we passed his position.

Our clearance became, "Proceed on taxiway foxtrot, cross the inboard runway and follow the follow-me truck to parking."

We were quite happy to do exactly that. I immediately noticed the tenement, unfinished concrete block housing to our right, just past the tall cement wall that encircled the airport. Each of the houses had a corrugated tin roof held in place with large concrete blocks. Combined, the houses became the conventional, dirt-poor city of famine, refugees and disease. The flight attendants rang on the interphone and complained that the cockpit demonstrated an apparent lack of concern for their duties. We had not given them a landing time on the short, six-hour flight. If only they could see through our windows! Welcome to Diamond City, Mineland, Africa!

Guards stood next to the runways with their ever-present weapon of choice, the AK-47. The two taxiways remained clear of the armed guards. Once in our parking position, the interest of security became even more apparent.

We remained on the aircraft while the passengers disembarked. Guards surrounded us and they further cordoned off the plane with a red and white chain. Workers brought over large, portable floodlights for night illumination of the entire aircraft. Past the chain lay a vast sea of concrete, completed twenty or thirty years ago and since frozen in time. Fifty to seventy-five white airplanes were parked on the tarmac: all needed much more than just a bath. This is where old planes came to give their last breaths. The 727s were antiques, relics from the early 1960s. Four C-130 aircraft sat idle, yellowed with hydraulic fluid. Soviet aircraft made up the rest of the friendship fleet and each had the letters W.F.R. (World Food Relief) written on their oxidized white paint. Beyond them lay a large terminal building that was three stories high. It too showed many signs of neglect.

In the cabin, an Israeli-trained, South African gentleman gave us a thorough description of the political situation and our route of travel. He told of what would be expected of us during our time in and outside the hotel. We were to be escorted at all times by a multitude of guards armed with automatic rifles. We would travel through the city in a caravan with the armed guards and they expected our complete cooperation. Not one of us complained.

We proceeded to a van and were driven to immigration control. We came in through a small door where a man collected all of our passports. He disappeared for about two minutes, coming back with the necessary documentation that allowed us to enter the country—as if we were trying to break into Mineland from America! The short trip verified our existence in the country, but did little else. We stepped back into the van and thirteen of us drove a grand total of one hundred feet, getting off with all of our bags and belongings. Schlepping (dragging) your baggage, as we call it, is just part of the job. But for customs into Mineland, it became absurd. I thought, *What would an aircrew smuggle into such a place? Weapons into a war zone? Food?* Customs simply x-rayed our baggage and let us through without a hitch. The metal detector screeched at every pass, but the officials ignored it. *Why bother?*

Everyone packed themselves and their baggage back onto the van. It was ten o'clock in the morning and the crew had been up all night. Small talk came with little fanfare. We were beat. The van drove down the length of the building, turned right into an alley and circled up with the escorts. Our journey to the hotel began without incident. Fortunately, it also ended without incident.

The city of Diamonds came as no great shock to many of our crew. Several had seen much worse throughout the world. One Conditioned Air flight attendant told of flying the airlift out of there. The Europeans left their colony virtually overnight. Many took only what they could carry. Some carried a mere tablecloth full of possessions over their shoulder, as if they were hobos, when boarding the aircraft.

In between our conversations, an occasional beggar pressed against the window. It came with the territory. After my first glance at the east side of the airport, I knew the score. Civil wars plagued this African nation with disaster, wars supported by two powerful nations—the Soviet Union and America. Every day, refugees came out of their concrete shantytowns and filled the streets. They were everywhere. Obviously, the city catered to an unnatural number of poor, disheveled people out of work, out of housing, without schools, and all of them without a pound of flesh. The World Food Relief program airlifted food into distant cities, the sole means of support for these refugees and the millions of others scattered about the nation.

The wars left ten million land mines scattered throughout the fields. Heavy rains and floods pushed them to new locations, making their disposal all the more difficult. People huddled in the cities, fearing death and dismemberment, while the vast fertile lands of the diamond-rich country lay empty. In a cruel way, the United Nations spins its wheels in the muck of human calamity, the aftermath, the scrap heap left over from the superpower wars. The earth's natural resources were now seemingly supervised by an air force of old freighters far from the reaches of the common man, all in the name of humanity for the common man.

The irony of our flight was that we flew diamond executives and educated workers to and from America. Not only did America help bring about the destruction of Mineland, but American diamond companies and others worldwide loaned the government enormous sums of money to purchase the tools of the trade, the trade of war. Now that the battles subsided, these tools imprisoned the people, a catch twenty-two for most conflicts, especially in the land of the meek and the poor.

Their world was reduced to what lay immediately before them: supplies from the World Food Relief. The external forces that caused their country to be flooded with weapons, death and despair now collected cash and diamonds for those same evil goods and services. Ironically, the paybacks impoverished the nation even farther, robbing the people of badly needed monies that could be used for humanitarian efforts. I shook my head in disbelief of it all.

The structures in the city proper were also in a sorry state of disrepair. Every building contained empty sockets where windows once protected the people from the environment. The overcrowded streets were paved for the most part. But it didn't matter. Thick red dust was everywhere. It blanketed the city and its people. You could see it in their clothes and on their skin.

Our van took us by the American embassy. The ambassador's job came with many drawbacks, not the least of which was the never-ending parade of aftermath in a bad neighborhood. Humanity loitered aimlessly about, selling whatever, to buy whatever for themselves and their families. The embassy sat near a cemetery that looked as if it were the only thing in the city that someone attended. Its high, ornate, white walls were rather attractive. Someone reminded us that it was a final resting place, not a city park for the people. Being situated on a very high hill, it overlooked a large inland waterway: a tomb with a view. Ironically, across the water was a spit of land that reminded me of my home in the beautiful Florida Keys.

Our caravan traveled down the red switchbacks until we simply ran out of elevation. Here in the harbor area, life appeared to be a little better. Unlike the previous, congested adventure, late generation cars and trucks of all makes and models traveled in an orderly manner. The city on the lower side displayed planning. Buildings were occupied with businesses and people were dressed for work, many in a western manner. This small pocket of Diamond City contained our hotel, the last stop on our odyssey for the day.

The people of Mineland are known for their hospitality throughout Africa. They love to meet and greet, talk about everything or anything, dance and attend large social gatherings. Our hotel treated us with such warmth and gracious hospitality. We let our guard down and actually relaxed in the small lobby, eating their cakes and drinking coffee. The security agent checked us in and gave further briefings. Security would not allow us to leave the hotel for any reason.

When I inquired about an escort to do some shopping at the local market, they were polite but firm.

"Too close to Christmas and the holidays, but maybe next week when you return."

We had something to look forward to then. The art and batik were known to be the best of Africa.

My room key came with a repeated warning: "Never open the door for any person you do not know or a hotel employee you were not expecting." This, I thought, made good sense. I went up to the eleventh floor on one of four very small aluminum elevators. There I found the carpet and color schemes quite attractive—I thought a good sign that my stay would be a pleasant one. However, I opened my room door and changed my mind. Two narrow beds filled the small room with dank, green walls and fuzzy, worn-out carpet completed the decor. Fortunately, the cleaning staff kept everything spotless, something I could appreciate considering their dusty environment. Soap and shampoo sat in my bath; otherwise, the owners had ignored the facility since creation.

The window overlooked the plaza, a circular drive surrounding a small park, with two other buildings situated on the circle next to the harbor. I looked out but couldn't see the water from that vantage point, only an office building or two. At least these buildings were intact. My other window revealed the harbor with docks and cranes standing proud, proud of a day in the distant past. *Life in Mineland,* I thought.

Ten cranes sat idle at the pier, a port of call others chose to ignore. I imagined they longed for the future with the promise of work. Across the water lay that strip of land that reminded me of my home. Only here the water served not as recreation, but as a security barrier for the selected few. No freighters were present and the diamond dredgers, so vital to the recovery of the entire nation, were filling their holds far to the north in the open ocean. These were piers few Mineland people ever came to see. I wondered if they understood, or even knew, of the significance of their natural resource. Did the economic plan come as a blessing or as plunder of the people? I came here to provide transportation for companies that desired a direct connection to the United States and I felt relieved in not knowing the motivations of those who contracted for our service. *Was that a good thing?*

My speculation came from my window survey. A glimpse couldn't possibly reveal the black and the white, much less the finesse of the differences sitting before me. From my bathroom window, with my limited view of the small plaza, I again noticed the shiny automobiles, glistening in the sun, cleaned with self-respect, all parked in tidy rows. Organization found in the land of chaos, at the port with no business. I imagined what an attractive waterfront this might make with the right development and care. I turned my back to the street scene and viewed my dark room with new consideration.

One of the pluses of this hotel came in the form of its television. Someone had the forethought to connect fifty stations to the hotel. Movies were abundant and CNN International came through with its daily saga of horrific events. I settled onto my bed as CNN's program dealt with the cruel reality of African politics. An article came across concerning the assassination of President Laurent Kabila of the Congo, a nation near Mineland. My sense of immunity by distance, the "it-happened-over-there" security blanket quickly evaporated as the story named the culprit. The President's personal security guard, a man named Rashidi, took advantage of his situation and simply shot his way into African history. It did not take me long to realize that I was an African Government sponsored American, with a well-defined schedule. Factions could simply buy the scenario and embarrass the government at my expense. I remembered the chain around the aircraft. One weak link and the chain would be broken.

We were told not to stop for any reason while traveling. We were briefed about the security forces, briefed about the use of radios, briefed concerning our confinement to quarters, briefed about this, briefed about that and briefed about the other. Unfortunately, when comparing the relative ease of the assassination of a President to an airplane scenario, the idea of safety began to take on a whole new meaning. *Were the surroundings of heavy security just a porous window dressing?*

After watching the news, I slipped down to lunch on the sixth floor. It was a magnificent display of opulence with ten types of salads and five selections of fish and meats. Duck, lamb, lobster, exotic vegetable dishes and a dessert table that came fit for a king. Our company arranged this meal and extra pay in exchange for reducing our turnaround times. Whatever may be said about it, two extra hours in the dark of Mineland as compared to this luncheon and the choice became obvious. After gorging ourselves on the buffet, most of the crew departed for their rest. After lunch, I met two women hired by *Richman Magazine* to survey the economy and stability of Mineland. We spoke in the lobby and our minds began to race.

Which method of cooperation would return the dignity and the livelihood, stripped away by years of war? The city and country survived on the World Food Program and CARE packages. Which method would be best for these refugees? Could the industrialization of mineral resources be enough to restart an entire economy, for the redemption of an entire country? Could this occur fast enough to benefit the younger generation? Or are they flesh with no spirit, no desire and no love, reduced to the next CARE package? It was an interesting conversation.

The ride back to the airport came through the early evening hours. The people stood off the streets, gathering outside clubs and makeshift discos. The darkness gave me a bit of relief as no one could see into our van and the streets were no longer packed with vehicles. Our captain stood up in the van and gave a short, flight briefing consisting of the weather and time in route. It was my turn to fly, so I began my mental preparations on how I would organize the flight station.

A few moments later, the captain ended his brief with a security warning.

"Listen to your sixth sense. If something doesn't look right, if something is out of place, call the security personnel and have them check it out. Don't touch any foreign object regardless of its size or location. I'm sure Neal, with his military experience, can remember looking for trip wires on airplanes. I know I can, so use everything you have to keep us safe."

At the airport, we left the escort vehicles behind and proceeded through the customs and immigration screening. The x-ray machine staff was particularly attentive. We offloaded at the aircraft and I began my "trip wire patrol" along with the other copilot. He performed the outside preflight, while I went directly to the wheel wells with my flashlight. There I met a young man with a powerful, battery-operated searchlight. Together we went over every nook and cranny the four wheel wells had to offer. Grenade patrol, trip-wire scout—I had not done this since I left Djibouti, or was it Mogadishu? It wasn't any more fun now than it was back then. After all, just one person could make a difference and I needed to be the counter to that individual. Trip-wire patrol. Maybe it was Somalia. We traded fresh fruit to the Italians for wiring and stole parts from an abandoned Soviet aircraft to fix our P-3 and depart Mogadishu. I remember that one.

Our second trip to Africa came at an odd hour for us—the daylight hours. Our aircraft came in late due to a minor malfunction that sent the plane limping into Baltimore from over Bermuda. An oil-return line loosened up on the number three engine and this caused the loss of nearly all of the engine oil. Once tightened, the line caused the engine no other problems. The aircraft and original crew then flew on to the Azores, making a routine business day into a feat of endurance by comparison. Everyone gets their time in the barrel, with good luck and bad.

The plane arrived five hours late into the Azores. How were we to regain the lost schedule for this customer? Our crew was aware that, if we were able to return from Diamond City without utilizing the twelve-hour layover, we would be able to regain the hours lost by the oil problem. This was a problem with one of two variables.

First, we had to calculate if we had enough time to legally fly the trip. The flight times were less than six hours each way, but the block hours dictate the schedule. Every minute counted. We also figured we could make up at least ten, if not fifteen, minutes in the air by flying at Mach .85 rather than our more fuel efficient Mach .82.

The second problem became one of contacting all of the passengers, having them arrive at the airport four hours prior to their scheduled departure. No one ever heard of such a thing, but this is the business. Without their cooperation, we would run out of crew duty time. We were anxious to make the trip work, as the alternative would be to take a delay on three additional flights rather than just the one. An all-important telephone call to our operations department started the ball rolling. We were working with two important windows. Unknown to any of us, a third awaited us in Diamond City—one with plenty of authority and plenty of guns.

Our arrival came with the usual nuisance of an air traffic control system operating without a radar set. The woman sat in a room and timed the arrivals and departures, keeping each separate by timing each entering and exiting of her sector. This day, she kept us higher than normal for the entire approach. The solution came from deploying all of our high drag devices, including the landing gear, slats and speed brakes, creating a controlled drop into the African city. The clear sky and good visibility assisted us in our endeavor, although it still became an exciting landing. I don't know who taught our captain how to scoop out an MD-11 landing, but I have never seen it done better. As for our taxi to parking, I have never seen worse.

We were given instructions to the follow-me truck, a yellow and black checkered vehicle with rotating beacons. One simply follows it around the airport. This driver, however, must have thought something more of us, as VIPs or the like, as he tried to pull us into line with the red carpeted area of the tarmac. Knowing little about the size and turns of the MD-11, he nearly boxed us into a blind alleyway of aircraft and soft earth, with a Russian craft blocking the end. We stopped.

Another man frantically gave the driver directions with his orange batons. The scene to our left could be likened to clowns in a circus. However, trading paint with another aircraft would not be an entertaining event, especially in Mineland. Finally, the man with batons guided us through a 180-degree turn, to the opposite side of taxiway sierra and into a parking spot that we do not normally occupy. Our operations representative came across from our former position, leaving me to believe the team had been right the first time. We arrived at the airport safely and hoped our outbound passengers were ready to go. They were, but our departure would be delayed by the third time window. The President of Mineland was arriving shortly, complete with red carpet, a band and an overabundance of guns. The famous AK-47 Soviet assault rifles were everywhere. They wanted us off the plane.

We were taken to the arrivals building and told we must wait for the president who was coming from a funeral in the Congo. Security was especially strict, as this funeral was for President Kabila of the Congo, who was murdered by his own security guard in a double-cross. No one could stand next to the windows or watch the procession deplaning. We shuffled back and forth before several in the group spotted the duty-free shop that gave us an air-conditioned alcove. Having seen every price on every bottle at least twice over, I was bored and ventured upstairs to a supposed restaurant. The restaurant was closed. I ran into our own security service manager there, which was a pleasant surprise. That day, there was much to talk about.

We both awaited the arrival of the president. His 707 pulled onto the tarmac and taxied into the red-carpeted position of honor. The guard, observing our upstairs windows, which were actually two separate, double-pane windows with a walkway in between, motioned to us to back away from even the inner panes. This left us to our conversation, which was much more to my interest in the first place.

The Soviets backed the *BADBOYS* and gave great assistance through Cuba during the cold war. Many Mineland citizens were educated in Cuba and in the Soviet Union during that time. My country supported the series of wars against the Soviets and Cuba. The United States lost the effort against the BADBOYS and its government. In an ironic turn of history, the BADBOYS now did business with the United States and our companies. We now recognize them as the official regime and the *GOODBOYS* rebels as just that: rebels against a friendly government. What to make of the shift and its effect didn't concern me. How to bring hope for so many with so few resources, so few friends and so little money became my concern. I just had to know if this was possible and I asked my agent, Richard, just that question.

"In many respects, things have improved over the years. The revenues were working their way through the government's hands to pay off the arms debt. The United Nations food relief program kept the outlying country people alive with donations of food delivered primarily by older, Soviet cargo planes flying an average of four round trips a day to various cities and outlying villages. Efforts were underway to remove the nearly ten million land mines from the country's roads and fields. And, the rebel forces were no longer a factor impeding commerce into and out of the outlying regions," he explained.

However, I thought to myself as he spoke, *The country lived on donations and would continue to live on donations so long as the government's diamond revenue was used primarily to service war loans. This place is an inch away from being hopeless.*

Once again, we approached the windows out of curiosity. It's not every day that one witnesses an African Presidential arrival at the capital airport. We saw many people coming down the stairway. The old rule in politics followed the day. If you are going to be important, you have to look important. In Diamond City, this was no exception. From our distance of several hundred meters, we could not distinguish who was who. The band undoubtedly played, but we could not hear through the twin double panes. The President then made a small speech to his invited reception before departing for parts unknown. His security perimeter quickly disbanded and we were once again told to move away from the windows. Fortunately, these inside guards only carried radios, not guns. Had we stepped out on the ramp area, the guards outside would have shot us on sight.

An established government behaves in a civilized manner toward its people. However, up until recently, the "police" had unrestricted access to power. Life and death became their area of domain. If you drove around an officer directing traffic, accelerating through his miniature kingdom of power, an assault rifle settled the matter with a large number of high velocity rounds into your vehicle. If you were injured or worse, so be it! You failed to stop when he said "STOP!"

My security agent echoed more incidents of ruling by terror, ruling by the gun, and elaborated how he nearly died at the hands of the police.

"The police were breaking up a fight between rival youths. Gangland dispute, no doubt. The youth were in a crowded shopping area, and unfortunately, so was I. Trouble broke out and fists went into the air. The police arrived and ordered everyone onto the ground and the youths to stop fighting. All of the people, including the two gangs, complied with the directive; all but a few who got back up and began to fight again. The immediate response of the officers came in the form of violence accelerated to the extreme. They simply raised their rifles and murdered the boys at close range. Murder was sanctioned by the whim of those with unrestricted access to power and absolutely without regard for personal accountability or conscience."

I didn't feel comfortable asking why they stopped there and how the innocent shoppers, including my friend, were set free. I didn't bother the man. My curiosity and emotions seemed rather petty by comparison. Getting out alive was top priority. Ditch the rest.

Once the President departed, things quickly returned to "normal" at the airport. We were let out of our holding area and boarded a bus back to the airplane. Our passengers were nearby and the flight crew quickly fell into routine. I completed the engine and wheel well check before entering the aircraft. The captain pre-flighted the exterior of the aircraft, making sure all of the big pieces were still attached. He, too, cleared the wheel wells and obvious hiding places for explosives. None were found. Our security team remained loyal, much to my relief.

The following evening found us on our third flight to the dusty city. Our rotation between flying pilots was interrupted and I pulled the landing. The runway glistened from the night's heavy rain and made my full-flap landing a joy to behold. Even the operations representative commented on it and he wasn't even on the airplane.

However, once through immigration and customs, I noticed the disadvantage of the seasonal showers. All of the sidewalks in the neighborhood turned to mud. People stood around as usual, hawking their wares for anything to anybody, but there were fewer of them. Yet, when we reached the main arteries, the scene returned to normal. Nothing changes with the passing of only one week.

We did our best to ignore a child with part of his face removed, as he stood patiently next to our window, peering through the glass. He could close his mouth, but the open scar, the open hole from the injury, left half of his teeth on the right side of his face exposed. The wound started high on his cheekbone and ended where the corner of his mouth normally would be, forming a triangle. Quite possibly this was the work of an AK-47, just creasing the "lucky" victim. His eyes were filled with the dust, as he gave us an unfocused, distant stare. It is said that the eyes are the windows to the soul. In his own way, he begged us to look through his windows and into his life, into his misery-filled soul. However, at that moment we filled our windows with cold indifference and even a bit of laughter.

While seeing the child walk up and stare at us, I felt a surge in my gut, muscles tensed in a momentary reflexive grip, a defensive reflex that accompanied my own laughing in chorus with the others. In horror, I sensed my own insignificance, my own cruelty, defending myself from his dismay and shocking appearance with a quick, but punishing laugh at a child whose life, still in its youthful innocence, was worse than mere punishment. It was hell. I wished and I hoped that he didn't see me, but I knew that wasn't true.

No, I did not laugh, I told myself over and over again.

Yes, you did. Yes you did laugh and you felt it in your gut, didn't you Neal?

As the boy stared down at our tire tracks on the mud covered asphalt road, I thought, *They laughed too!"*

My internal debate continued. *A beggar stared for sympathy, exploiting his wounds for money, a carnival freak being rude to us. I lurched defensively; a strangled laugh, a weak one, squeezed through the thin smile that slid off my face.*

Neal, you laughed. You're just a person. You're only elevated by the bus seat under your ass, but not to him. You laughed Neal, and with your smile, the shocked little boy turned his face down and away, even as you stare at him now.

My manners won't allow that. I have better judgment than that; I know better than that, I told myself as I looked toward the front of the bus.

A moment later, I returned my eyes to the disfigured child only to find his still unfocused, dusty stare off somewhere under us to his left, teeth displayed through his war's kiss from death. As I stared into his distorted face, I hated myself for the little laugh, hastily coughed for the duration of a reflexive twitch, and my mind returned to the shock of it all.

That I could.

Did not.

Yes, you did.

I mocked this poor child. For what reason?

Exactly. For what reason?

How did I? Why did I?

I did not; he couldn't hear us. He couldn't see us.

Then why did he walk to your window in the first place? To gain your attention and sympathy, but what did you give him in return?

The bus moved forward as I recoiled from my thoughts and reflected stare. I had no answers for my silent, internal exchange. Deep within me I prayed, *Oh Jesus, forgive me for my own shame and spit me from Your mouth with disdain.*

My hotel room was on the 25th floor. I waited, seemingly forever, for just one of the three elevators that stopped at random floors, every random floor without being summoned. The southwest corner room came as a pleasant surprise. But little did I understand what surprises it would bestow upon me later in the afternoon. I peered out my two windows. One caught the view of multistory apartment buildings, corrugated tin roofs, and children playing on the flats as well as balconies. Laundry flew everywhere: the international flag of impoverishment. I thought of the many citizens of the world flying the colors of the poor.

The western window gave an all-together different impression of the harbor than my first visit to Diamond City. I counted twenty or more ships there. Several were at the previously empty bays with the silent cranes now working to unload containers of freight. I could see schools of fish breaking water, children swimming, and fishermen working the harvest of their trade. All the while, orange fluid curled its way down the bank and along the spacious motorway. Eventually, it joined up with two areas of dark sheen on the small bay's waters. I surmised it to be oil from the rusting bilge of the container ship unloading at the dock.

Going downstairs to the sixth floor for lunch, I discovered several paintings that fascinated me. The stretched cotton cloth came to life with interpretations of the continent's animals, fish and birds in fantastic color. I wanted to buy some batik and the quality of this art made me all the more anxious. Piano music erupted in the background and I spied one of our flight attendants as he began to sing a broken song with a voice made from crystal and brass. His song was a slow, blue jazz number. He combined heart-felt emotion with long, hanging notes from the black piano. Haunting and beautiful, it commanded my attention, but I stayed away from the grand piano so as not to disturb him. There, in a soft lobby chair, I closed my eyes, listening intently to the music, relaxing before lunch.

My hunger from the all-night flight came and went. When we sat down to eat—the highlight of the trip—everyone treated us with great courtesy and respect. Even so, my mind began to wander, wander back to the scenes outside my windows, the living quarters, the pollution, the children and the women from *Richman Magazine.*

We retired after lunch to our accommodations. My room's air conditioner had a difficult time keeping up with the sun coming in both the south and west windows and the humidity from the day's showers began its oppressive march through the room. I stripped to the buff, threw the bedspread onto the other single bed and lay on top of the clean sheets. I slept for two hours until the afternoon sun completely overpowered the room, waking me in a dead sweat. A thought came to mind while I fetched a bottle of spring water that I brought from the aircraft.

During childhood, my dog cooled himself during the hot Nebraska summers with our window air conditioner. Being on ground level, Tony found where the cool air from the air conditioner sank onto the living room floor. There he would lie, guarding his spot as if it were sent by heaven to cool his black, wooly body. Remembering this animal trick, I searched for the coldest spot in the room. There, in the entryway, I found a cool breeze and taking the bedspread, I covered the well-worn carpet. The aroma from the plumbing came in from one side, the noise from the outside hallway came from the other, and the sauna I sought to avoid was at my feet. The air conditioner sat directly above me and cooled my body. My dog would have been proud.

Then it hit me. SPLASH. I moved, but still: SPLAT...SPLASH. The drip pan from the cooling unit leaked water right on top of me. I curled around the hollow of my hip, hiding from the moist drops and slept in a naked sweat on the covered, concrete floor. When I awoke, I was angry.

I needed to shower. The hotel offered me little more than that. I noticed the privacy provided by the clouded bathroom windows. *Luxury at its finest. At least no one could see me lying on the floor, naked, trying to get some rest in the heat. That isn't the manner in which this pilot wants himself portrayed to the traveling public.*

What am I thinking? I asked myself, while preparing to shower. *I'm on the twenty-fifth floor of this hotel, above everyone and everything, as this is the tallest building on the harbor. No one can see into my room, my life or my shame. Should I even care? The natives are all beneath me. They don't fly on airplanes. The distance out my bedroom window, between the closest other human being and me, keeps them from peering into my life. Distance keeps me safe, safe from anyone except those invited through my door. I have the only key to that door. Why then do I bother myself with such trivial matters?*

Later that evening, my take-off was smooth. The winds were calm and the sky clear. It would be a good flight back to the Azores, although heavy crosswinds awaited our arrival. Between both airports lay five and one-half hours of droning on into the sunset and the blanket of darkness that followed. Although a spectacular sight, as it is every night at forty-one thousand feet, we spotted a unique and rather special reflection stimulating our conversation that airborne evening.

Clearly visible in the early evening sky, the international space station dominated the night with the brilliance of diamonds under hot lights.

"Captain, I have a friend whose brother flew the space shuttle for NASA," I mentioned.

"What's his name?"

"Horowitz."

"SCOTT HOROWITZ, YOU KNOW DOC HOROWITZ?"

I knew his sister Jennifer but not him. The captain, however, went through flight training in the United States Air Force with Doc Horowitz. Already possessing a Ph.D., he got his nickname for showing up in a room full of those with undergraduate degrees. Scott wanted to become an astronaut, and one day he appeared on television from the shuttle in space. That's how the captain knew Scott had achieved his dream of becoming an astronaut.

I told a couple of the Horowitz family stories that I knew from flying with his brother-in-law.

"There lay the school of hard knocks," I said. "Doc's brother-in-law is one of four surviving members of his eleven-member graduating class from naval flight training. Everyone else died in aviation accidents. When I met Tom in a P-3 squadron, he wanted to reinvigorate his aviation career. He was delighted to be there because of the aircraft's marvelous safety record. Engines were so plentiful that they weren't considered a safety of flight item. He also wanted to gain a release from the pain of his memories.

"Jenny, Horowitz' sister, served as an officer in the U.S. Army as a nurse, safely hidden in the heart of Berlin, Germany. Tom, her husband, flew for Pan Am at the time and I flew for Pan Am Express. The three of us lived in Berlin during the collapse of the Soviet Empire. Life became a gravy train for the two of them until Saddam Hussein invaded Kuwait. Late that fall, during the build-up of armed forces in Saudi Arabia, it became apparent that another full corps of American troops would be required to serve in the desert.

"Coincidently, the 7th Corps was shortly to depart Europe, part of a disengagement from the Cold War. My friend, Jenny, soon found herself on a plane bound for the Gulf. The first attempt at leaving Frankfurt failed as an engine caught fire and the C-141 returned for maintenance. The second ride ended in the Gulf region; they took two days just to thaw out from the bitter cold conditions inside the C-141.

"Jenny's duties brought her deep into Iraq, treating the American and Iraqi wounded as they came from the front. Her recall of the war completely astounded me: the workload, the lack of rest, the sand, the cold rain that no one ever expected, and the Iraqis losing at their own game of tank warfare, resulting in our complete victory over brutal oppressors."

One family, one group of dedicated Americans, shone as bright as the space station before our eyes. Their stories made the all-military cockpit feel a bit more united.

"If we only had their frequencies," the captain said, as we gazed at the space station that looked closer than the distant lights of ships at sea through our window. At two hundred and forty miles, it was closer than any other airport we could divert to and land. Somehow we felt closer to home.

The descent came soon enough and we headed directly to the intercept point for the ILS in Cape Verde. At the lower levels, the winds were quite strong and the aircraft appeared to be flying against a much stronger crosswind than registered on my screen. At four thousand feet, we entered a small cloudbank and the autopilot disengaged with a small rolling movement. The instrumentation was a hindrance at this point, as the flight director's cross bars were in opposition to the commands we gave it from the control panel. I fought to keep the wings level and called out several requests that were slow in execution.

The rough ride further complicated matters along with the localizer capture that sent the aircraft into a whole new hierarchy of logic, and the capture of the glide slope earlier than I anticipated. We bled off our airspeed with the extension of the landing gear, while we dirtied up the aircraft's wings with the slats and flaps. The runway was seen as a black hole on this arrival, and slowly we realized the aircraft presented the localizer bar far to the left of the correct course. Basic airmanship and teamwork fought against the ironclad will to believe the instruments—instruments that were wrong.

Fortunately, we were visual with the field; but at the bottom, our line-up came to the left of the centerline. Unfortunately, my corrections came later than my hope and the touchdown, while safe, didn't please anyone.

I licked my wounds while taxiing to the tarmac. When the mechanic found multiple faults in the electronic auto-monitoring squawk box, I joked about my effort and shifted blame to the inanimate objects I fly. I heard about the landing from several of the flight attendants. Their teasing and laughter hurt.

Enough already, I thought. *We missed a touchdown, but everything else was fine. If only you would look through my window.*

I bit my lip, but after ten minutes, I guess I still licked at an open wound that left a bitter taste in my mouth.

The 1990 Cruise

CHAPTER TWENTY

I experienced a critical turning point in my life during a cruise Donna and I took aboard a soviet ship shortly after the Berlin Wall fell. We planned a vacation to a world hidden to the West for many years; but our destination proved to be a voyage into history, one heretofore known only to its victims and perpetrators.

Donna came home with an advertisement from the Berlin Army Recreation Center shortly after the Berlin Wall went out of business. For the first time, we would be allowed to enter the Soviet Union and several other Eastern European nations without the burdensome restrictions imposed by the United States and the Communist Governments. This news was truly astonishing. Not only were they allowing active duty, American military personnel into their countries, the Soviets were advertising for their business in the U.S. Army Morale, Welfare and Recreation Services' fliers. On top of that, the Soviets hosted a two-week tour on their own cruise ship, the *Azerbayzhan*. Without a doubt, all else immediately took second place in Donna's life. She worked her butt off to provide us with this new adventure behind the freshly drawn Iron Curtain.

Donna and I flew on my airline to Bremen, West Germany, on Saturday for a day of sightseeing. We chose this city because it was near the cruise departure port of Bremerhaven and it was an excellent location for us to layover the night before our ship departed, giving us the chance to tour another city. However, we weren't as impressed with this German city as the Allies must have been during the Second World War. All that remained of the old city were the memories of the elderly. The Allied bombers razed everything else, and through years of hard work by the German survivors, the city was made new. We made the best of our walking tour, finding a small hotel and several pubs to explore. Due to strict German labor laws, most other shops were closed on Saturday afternoons.

On Sunday, we took a taxicab to Bremerhaven and boarded the beautiful Russian cruise liner, the *Azerbaydzhan*. The ship was named after a state in the former Soviet Union, which lay in the south of the country and north of Iran. We booked an interior, three-star room without a window. Donna said that we would never be in the room, so there was no reason to pay extra for a window we wouldn't use. She was right on that one! The room came with four bunk beds, all singles, so we booked it for ourselves, as we didn't want to share two weeks in a room with another couple. We were surprised that the private bath was so nicely furnished.

The ship's two dining rooms were large and beautifully decorated. With two extremely punctual and formal sittings for each meal, we set our watches from their schedule. Service was swift; the entire restaurant staff worked like slaves if you were friendly with them. We even befriended several of the waiters and waitresses.

Coming from Berlin, less than a year after the fall of the Berlin Wall, the temptation to speak openly with our hosts was far too great. This bothered their higher-ups and the political officers stopped them from talking with us. After the obvious change in atmosphere, we only spoke with the more senior, selected members of the crew.

The fall of the Berlin Wall came up in a conversation.

"It was good to see the walls of the world fall," the man whom we assumed to be the political officer said.

He brought up other problems such as the United States blockade of Cuba. This sounded good on the surface; but two weeks prior, Fidel Castro gave the same argument to Ted Turner during a long television interview I had the misfortune of watching. I kept quiet about the coincidence. While on board their ship, I saw no sense in further embarrassing or confronting the devout communists.

After sailing two days on the ship, we stopped at Visby, a little-known island off the coast of Sweden. The town was overcrowded with tourists. I wanted to return in the off-season, as this city was a major Baltic port for thousands of years. Over those millennia, the land—constantly rising from out of the sea—was active enough to change the harbor into a park. Visby proper was a true delight. The town had seventeen churches. Sixteen were in ruins, beautiful ruins of towering silver stone and dark green moss. We explored their ancient splendor. One church in particular had the roof restored and added the sound of monk chants on speakers hidden in the old quarters. Bent-over figures dressed as monks walked up and down the stairs, lending an authentic atmosphere.

The coast of Visby revealed a craggy waterline with tall cliffs and small fishing villages, while the inland countryside consisted of small farms and forests. We stopped at the local gallows, of all places! There, the doomed were given one last commanding look at island life and beauty. We thought this gift to the doomed generous, yet a bit odd, and even perverse. Another curious place was Visby's burial ground for ancient rulers. We viewed an arrangement of large stones, about thirty meters in length, forming the outline of a great ship. This was a gravesite for a king who lived in 1500 B.C. There were roughly three hundred of these memorials from past inhabitants. It was unexpected and we were delighted with our tour.

We traveled from there by ship to the city of Stockholm, Sweden, an overlooked and very attractive city. Stockholm is built on a cluster of twelve islands. Dependent on the sea for transportation and livelihood, the Swedes chose this site because of easy fortification, creating a difficult approach for any seagoing enemy. Over the centuries, it worked quite well for them.

During the morning hours, we enjoyed our own romantic hiking tour of the island city away from the organized and crowded ship tours. Donna and I took the "Under the Bridges" boat tour of the city that afternoon. Many beautiful and interesting sites and magnificent buildings were pointed out to us, albeit in German. I picked up on a few of them and Donna helped me out with the rest. The port of Stockholm must be one of the most beautiful harbors in the world. It reminded me of the boundary waters of Northern Minnesota, with craggy island shoreline and clear blue water everywhere. The land wasn't forested, but rather dotted with beautiful buildings. Downtown Stockholm stood with open water in the foreground, where stately old buildings interspersed with new architecture created a splendor and glamour rivaling any city in Europe.

Donna and I agreed that we would like to return.

"Two or three days should be sufficient for our next visit," I said, concerned with the street prices.

Stockholm is an interesting city except for one thing. Socialism costs the taxpayer a very heavy price. In 1990, a common magazine cost $4.50 so we only purchased one magazine plus a few postcards and a newspaper. We were glad to be touring by ship and not on our own at those prices!

The *Azerbaydzhan* took us further north into the Baltic, stopping in Helsinki, the capital of Finland. Although an old city much like Bremen, Helsinki is actually a new city because a fire destroyed most of the wooden structures in 1833. Exceptionally clean by anyone's standards, the city is quite pretty. We purchased a tour that lasted several hours, taking us to a suburb built after the war. It looked remarkable, like any other hilly, wooded European suburb, except much of it was built with poured concrete. The university and several parks and inlets were other points of interest. Donna and I had lunch in a Mexican restaurant, of all places, where we ordered tacos with reindeer meat. After realizing the Finns domesticate reindeer as we do cows, we decided to remember Helsinki through the purchase of Rudolph's hide to place in front of the fireplace.

We visited a farmer's market on our walk back to the ship. The most perfect, clean and polished vegetables we had ever laid eyes on were on display. Even the onions were skinned and shined. A peculiar snack food was popular at this market—green peas sold in the pod for immediate consumption. I purchased about a quart of these pea pods and we were on our merry way shopping around Helsinki.

Our ship departed late that afternoon for what I call the political education portion of our cruise, beginning across the great gulf between the east and west—Leningrad, Russia. This visit to the Communist Bloc can best be described as a continuous contrast between beautiful façade and cold, cruel reality.

When we arrived in Leningrad harbor, it was highly polluted, downright ugly, and most disappointing. However, once we made our way into the heart of the city, Leningrad was nothing less than spectacular. In fact, in all my travels, I can't recall a prettier city anywhere in the world. The communists spent a fortune restoring this "Venice of the North."

In cruel irony, hundreds of these buildings were as glorious as they were *empty*. As so often would be the case, while they demonstrated the magnificent grandeur of previous wealth, we found stark and inhuman contrasts in those rebuilt buildings. We kept in mind, that with all the unparalleled artistry and grandeur we saw in and about Leningrad, the average Soviet earned $35.00 per month. The country also experienced a severe housing shortage. If a Soviet had more than sixty-six square feet for each person in their apartment, then that person was not eligible for a new, larger apartment. With all the empty space in state-owned buildings, with all the space and splendor, the Soviets housed no offices, no families or citizens of this *worker's paradise* in these massive, real estate debacles. It reminded me of the 1930s, when Stalin locked up the food, thereby creating an illusionary, but deadly famine for millions of his own people. I could only wonder, *Why?* I did not dare to ask the question.

We were taken by bus to a city vista that overlooked the site of the October Revolution. Stately and formal buildings stood across a broad canal where many boats and hydrofoils scurried about the city on one of its many waterways. There at this plaza, a four-man band welcomed us playing American music—*patriotic* American music.

When we walked up to the square, "The Stars and Stripes Forever" was going like gangbusters. Next came "America the Beautiful" and finally "The Star Spangled Banner." I stood at attention through the American National Anthem at our first bus stop, my introduction to Leningrad, while overlooking the ship that started the Russian revolution, the *Aurora*. Five years prior, I flew the P-3 Orion aircraft against the Soviet Navy, and then I found myself standing at the sight of the Russian revolution while the Soviets played "The Star Spangled Banner." Totally surreal, this was beyond my imagination or comprehension. *What heresy,* I thought.

Back on the bus, we again toured the city for a bit, finally crossing the canal near the Hermitage, Leningrad's most famous museum. We stopped on the western side of the building, at Saint Isaac's Cathedral, for a quick foot tour of the outside of the church. The structure impressed us with granite columns stretching some sixty feet into the sky, interrupted only by the massive, ornate overhang. The Cathedral had four small domes, one on each corner, with one very large, gold dome in the center supported by a ring of granite pillars. Large bronze castings overshadowed every corner.

There, at Saint Isaac's Cathedral, the same little band previously playing its heart out greeted us once again, passing the hat wherever Western tourists were found. The band played mostly American music, and mustered a couple of Italian songs for our Italian friends. However, despite bus after bus of German tourists from our ship, absolutely no German music ever graced the city. We speculated that the history of World War II, with Germany's nine-hundred-day siege against this city and her inhabitants, ran deeper than the Cold War conflict against the Americans.

We boarded the bus and drove past several other churches and convents, all quite impressive. Again, all were empty museums under the communist dictatorships that considered them opiates for the people. We were told that a few were just beginning to hold services. Our schedule called for lunch back at the ship, but our tour guide asked if any of us held visas for the city. Donna and I had Soviet visas for Leningrad, so we declined the bus ride back. Instead, we departed the group at a city square where we headed into a few shops, looking for lunch and a bookstore. Here the fun really began!

One of our friends on the trip worked for the Army as an intelligence officer and spoke quite a bit of Russian. Together, we wandered about running into a line of people some two hundred yards long.

"Why are you standing in line," my friend asked.

"Cigarettes!"

The reply amazed all of us. The line didn't move, yet there they stood—half the day long for cigarettes. I thought that the smuggler's dream must be real American cigarettes, complete with seals from the United States.

We ducked into a poorly lit bread shop to look around. You needed a candle to find anything; but to Soviets, this was routine. We soon mastered the purchase of one loaf of bread at four cents a loaf and headed down the street. I must say that the bread was very good. We ate it for lunch as we meandered across town, snapping pictures and exploring for whatever window-shopping there was to do in the communist society—absolutely none.

We came across a large, artist market and decided to shop for anything that wasn't nailed down to the sidewalk. We were satisfied with just a few items, but there was so much to choose from that it made us forget that we were in the Soviet Union. There at the market, people sold just about anything and everything for a U.S. dollar. The German Mark was exchanged, but at a twenty-five percent higher exchange price than that of U.S. Dollars. Unfortunately, we came on the trip heavy with marks and light in dollars. There were other forms of currency. Blue jeans were accepted as payment by many traders, as were Nike tennis shoes and belts.

We purchased a hand-painted stack doll or two: hollow-nested, wood sculpted dolls that typically contained five dolls to the set ranging from two inches to eight inches high. Although they were of Lenin, Stalin, Khrushchev, Brezhnev and Gorbachev, they were quite colorful. We also purchased a nice watch, commemorating the 45th anniversary of the great naval victory over the Fascists. This Rolex knock-off came complete with a picture of a Soviet admiral on the wristband. All of this for the low, low price of twenty dollars.

I inquired about a book on five hundred years of French art. The young man would not take the book out of the brown paper bag and wanted to trade it for my shoes and possibly my belt. I said that I would look silly without any shoes and that I did not want my pants to fall down. I continued bargaining and finally purchased the book for around twenty German Marks. Just as soon as the man had my money, he thrust the book into my hands and lit out in a mad dash. Later, our tour guide overheard someone asking me about the book and she took a suspicious interest in me. I let the subject drop like a hot potato. When I subsequently found the same book for 120 German Marks, I understood her interest.

After this shopping excursion, we walked about a mile to the entrance of the Hermitage Museum and waited for our group to arrive from their lunch on the ship. Along the way, we were impressed with the buildings and the sense of order that seemed to prevail everywhere. We saw many young soldiers on the streets, perhaps patrolling; yet we were asked to change money on nearly every street corner. The only place protected from the sales, music, and money exchange was the Winter Palace, the Hermitage.

The Hermitage Museum is a series of five buildings that join one another over the course of two city blocks. It was designed by the architect B. Rastrelli, and built between 1754 and 1762 as the Winter Palace of Peter the Great. The building exterior dripped with art. Large, bronze casts in the most intricate detail stood atop each and every pillar. There were countless pillars. The building's colors, blue with white trim, complemented each other in the bright sunshine. However, the exterior couldn't compare with the real story, the interior, not just for what it possessed but for its caretakers as well.

We learned when once inside that the Hermitage contained over three million individual pieces of art spread out over countless displays and stored in warehouses for rotation. These works included many priceless works from the great masters. For example, one room contained nineteen Rembrandt paintings. Another wing contained two full rooms of Picassos, including a large selection from his famous blue period. An unfinished statue by Michelangelo graced a small, almost obscure hallway. A malachite bowl, made from one piece of stone at least two meters across, sat on an equally large pedestal, virtually unacknowledged by anyone without a guide.

Our tour guide was at her finest in this museum. She was a self-taught, art history student and she could talk for weeks, months and maybe even years about the content of the Hermitage. But it was not all about the displays. For her, the content merely paralleled the interior of the building itself. After all, this was the Winter Palace of the Russian Czar, Peter the Great. He lived the good life.

Exotic wood inlaid every floor, forming patterns and pictures that knocked our eyes out. Every wall had castings of family and religious figurines. Gold pillars supported the ceilings. Artists spent years painting or placing the ceilings that this Russian god, Peter the Great, strolled beneath. There is no comparison to the Hermitage in America.

While every room was different, and every decoration outlandish, believe it or not, almost every window was open. Yes, in a city heated by coal, the windows of this most extravagant museum stood open for ventilation. Only thin, sheer white curtains provided protection from the sunshine and pollution. The Soviets protected few, if any, paintings or sculptures with Plexiglas. They even allowed visitors to walk on the antique floors in street shoes; and if a person dared, they could touch almost any piece of art at will. However, we could only imagine what the Soviet-style penalties might be for someone who did actually touch or vandalize one of these rare treasures.

The next day in Leningrad, we traveled about forty minutes south of the city to visit Peter the Great's Summer Palace. Along the way, our guide showed us what must be the world's largest apartment complex. Stark white buildings, each fifteen stories high and a city block long, made up this goliath complex. There were hundreds of these ugly buildings that covered an area approximately five-miles long by three-miles wide. I couldn't tell one building from another. If that weren't enough, we were told that no building stood over fifteen stories high because by law, an elevator would be required.

Once at the Summer Palace, we found it to be in its final stages of reconstruction from the days of Nazi occupation. A few buildings were still off limits to tourists. The palace was grand and the backyard attractive. The Russian Czar built a canal lined with fountains for his arrival. A large pool that lay in front of the palace powered each of the fountains. Simple gravity provided the water pressure and the Russians took great pride in telling us about this achievement. A cascade stood at the palace, approximately eighty-feet high, with a series of fountains accentuating the grandest fountain of them all. Unfortunately, at the time of our visit, this main attraction was also under repair. We did encounter twelve smaller fountains scattered throughout the massive garden grounds.

The buildings of this palace were quite ornate, both inside and out. During World War II, they suffered terribly in the hands of the Nazi occupation force. The Nazis used the palace and its surrounding grounds as a stable and motor pool. We traveled with approximately four hundred Germans, many of them elderly. *What is going through their minds,* I wondered. I never entered the Summer Palace—it was too crowded for me; but Donna and her friends took the tour.

"Neal, there were still signs of damage to the ornate tiles and the tour guide took great pains in pointing out the senseless destruction to the timeless beauty found on the palace walls," she later told me. "And I saw many elderly, German gentlemen pointing to objects, doorways and the like, in a manner suggesting that they were recalling things familiar to them. I think they were here in the past, recalling their experiences during the war."

It must have been like completing a circle for them in their tour of life, fulfilling a journey before their death. We'll never know for sure. It did give a new and interesting perspective of those whom we traveled with, explaining at least one of the reasons why so many Germans, especially the elderly, chose this particular cruise.

Afterwards, we headed off to a sandwich stand for a bite of lunch. The girl who worked in the small wooden structure took her time about everything. When she received a customer, she gave them a long, drawn-out look from her dark, hollowed-out eyes. She had nothing prepared in advance. When a customer asked for a sandwich, she sliced the bread, just two slices at a time, and the meat and the cheese in the same way. She would wrap the sandwich, ever so slowly with paper, and bring it to the window at a snail's pace. Making change was equally as painful. Then she went on to the next customer in the very same manner.

At first I thought it was because she couldn't anticipate the daily crowds. But that made no sense. After all, this was a major tourist attraction with dozens of buses every day. Then the weight of her position in the Soviet system fell on me like a stack of bricks! This poor woman and these poor people under the communist government had every detail of life planned by the state. She got paid her wage with or without her input to the quality of the product. Whether she made one sandwich an hour or sixty, whether it be a really good sandwich, completely satisfying the customer, or a mediocre gut bomb, it didn't matter to her.

Her plight reminded me of the Alabama prison I flew formation flights high above nine years prior. The person I never wanted to meet, the one who resided far below my airplane, behind high concrete walls and double fences, threatened with blood and pain for daring to escape to freedom: that prisoner now stood in front of me—within a small shack, making sandwiches for the western tourist. She was a prisoner of the state, they all were: all of the Russians and everyone else who resided in the communist countries. We western tourists were free-flying spirits, able to come and go with our freedoms and lives—the things she could only dream about, yet never experience.

In my eyes, her plight was a dreadful full-circle, leading all the way back to the beginnings of my flying. I said nothing, keeping everything to myself. The internal, bitter poetry of our separate lives coming together by chance after the Berlin Wall fell left me no hunger for the sandwich she made me.

This was a terrible thing to see, especially contrasted with Peter the Great's Summer Palace as the backdrop for her experience. All of her motivation and natural zest for life had been removed by the Soviet system. The state owned everything and planned everything. She was a possession. The state owned her body and she lost her spirit. Unfortunately, these difficult lessons from the East Bloc were just the beginning of our schooling as we traveled from this city to our next destination.

The Soviet Union ruled Poland for over forty years after the extreme war, the total war of Europe. You knew you were in the Soviet East Bloc by just looking around at the old, gray factories and power plants. Huge coal piles stood outside old brick buildings and added another chapter to the story. You knew from a glimpse of Gdansk that you just stepped back fifty years in time.

Our tour guide in Gdansk was a chemistry professor who moonlighted as a tour guide. He learned the English language by listening to British radio stations and Radio Free Europe, as did so many others. Although quite knowledgeable and very bright, what he could show us was fairly limited.

There again in Gdansk, the apartment buildings were massive. One stood twelve stories tall and one kilometer long. Interestingly enough, nice single-family homes were under construction in the suburbs of Gdansk,

447

but were a rare occurrence. I saw some townhouses being built as we drove to the downtown district. Obviously, money from western relatives flowed into this country.

I liked Gdansk's downtown; it reminded me of Amsterdam. In fact, many Dutch settled in Poland some five hundred years ago. However, the city was reconstructed from absolute, complete destruction. Hitler started World War II in Gdansk and the German Navy shelled the town into oblivion. Anticipating the conflict, the people sunk many of the city's statues in lakes, resting them on the bottoms for safekeeping. To rebuild the city in its former glory, the survivors of the conflagration referred to old photographs, original plans and blueprints from a library, using these to return the city true to its old form.

We also learned about the interesting demographics of the region in the years preceding the war from our guide. Once, the Poles ruled much of Europe—as did the Austrians—the Germans—Napoleon—and the U.S.S.R. Poland didn't exist before World War I. But after the war, it popped back up in a small portion of its former territory. When Poland regrouped in the early 1920s, Gdansk was a border town and an important port city. The population was about 70% Polish vs. 30% German. That created a lot of hate and discontent because, as with all minorities in Europe, the Germans got the short end of every deal—housing, culture, jobs, voting blocks, *und so weiter* (and so on).

This set the stage for the great trumpet of propaganda. The night before Germany attacked, the Nazis used a couple of Germans in a Polish radio station as announcers, broadcasting inflammatory remarks, exploiting Germans and vowing not to take any more grief. In response, Hitler attacked Poland and for starters, liquidated the educated population.

We shifted gears in our conversation and asked our guide about Lech Walenssa, the famous leader of the anticommunist movement in Poland. Much to our surprise, our guide didn't think highly of Mr. Walenssa as a political leader.

"Walenssa believed that the workers should make the most money in the country," he said.

Our guide, a chemist after many years of schooling, realized that his profession was not included in Walenssa's definition of "workers."

In his further explanations, he said, "Mr. Walenssa's philosophy rewarded those who were the tradesman, the plumbers, the carpenters, the steel workers, and the like; while careers for the doctors, the engineers and the higher educated would be least rewarding."

We found this an interesting blend of the worker's paradise and capitalism.

We left our guide in Gdansk and traveled by bus out to the Polish shoreline where the shopping opened up a bit; but our driver cautioned us to only exchange our money in reputable venues such as banks. As a demonstration of what could happen to someone who changed money with people on the street, he held up a ten-thousand schlotti note, revealing that someone had pasted a cut out number five over the one.

Out of schlottis, Donna and I headed for the nearest bank next to the shoreline park. Entering the small bank building, we waited in line to exchange our dollars. Several people approached us to change money right there in the bank lobby. These people simply surrounded foreigners and bartered in front of the guards and tellers who could care less. Donna exchanged money with a lady who paid the highest rate for our dollars in the middle of the bank lobby. I thought it quite interesting for the Poles to black market in a bank and I laughed a bit at the situation.

The capitalization of the economy from its former, state controlled manner mainly consisted of flea markets and quick street bargaining. Once at the impromptu flea market, we saw a few nice things to buy, western items mostly: televisions, satellite dish antennas, even cans of German beer. After years of watching the Poles purchase these goods on the streets of Berlin, Donna and I knew that the goods they were reselling came from Polish tour buses visiting the closest western city for the East Bloc to access, West Berlin. The scene taught us another political lesson.

From all of the East Bloc, from Russia to Poland, our most politically incorrect stop on the cruise was a small state in what was still the Soviet Union, the country of Latvia. We came ashore in Riga and unknowingly began an aggressive political indoctrination, not from the Soviets, but from the local Latvian population. Our tour guide took us quickly through the city and deliberately out into the countryside. It was disappointing and featureless when compared to the city. However, when our tour guide told us her family's history, her generation's philosophy, and the Latvians' collective desire to tell all to their admired hope—America, the afternoon became fascinating. I found what she said so amazing that, when I returned to the ship, I wrote down a two-page outline to make good on our promise to her to tell this story.

In dramatic contrast to our previous tours, our tour guide spoke of many horrors while we were on the bus and also as we stood in front of a memorial to a poet. The Latvians honored this man for his struggle for truth in his art, and for so accurately reflecting his own feelings and convictions. I shook my head and thought to myself how we, too, as Americans, have honored such people. I thought of how much our forefathers had in common and I began to better understand the Latvian quest to be free from oppression. Simultaneously, I became disillusioned at how we Americans take our freedoms for granted.

Our tour guide, who shall necessarily remain nameless, started out by describing the "ECONOMIC BLOCKADE" of Latvia by the Soviets.

"It was a pain that will just have to be suffered," she said. "The real drive for Latvian independence is completely misunderstood by the West."

According to our guide, it all began slightly before the start of World War II, before 1938, when many Germans lived in Latvia. When the Third Reich was in its prewar heyday, the German population moved back to Germany to live within the borders of the German state. Coincidently, during that time, Germany signed a secret pact with the Soviet Union that gave the Baltic nations to the Russians. What followed in 1940 came by order of Joseph Stalin himself. The paranoid Soviet leader determined that if war broke out between Germany and the U.S.S.R, because of their past relationships, the Latvians would side with the Germans. Therefore, he speculated, it would be easier to get rid of these people than to have to deal with them later. In 1940, after the Soviets completed their annexation of Latvia, the genocide of the Latvian people by the Soviets began in earnest.

In classic Stalinist tradition, cloaked by the darkness of night, Soviet trains pulled into Riga and the educated, the leadership, and the middle class were given the midnight knock. In just one night, the Soviets forcibly removed two hundred thousand Latvians from their homes and sent them to the Soviet work camps, or Gulags, of Siberia—never to return. That is where our tour guide's grandfather, who was the mayor of Riga at the time, died after serving a remarkable two years in the cold of Siberia. He was remarkable because the average life span of forced labor in the Gulag was less than one year.

In an ironic way, the outbreak of the war actually helped the Latvian people. After the German invasion, the Soviets could not exercise any of their murderous madness on the Latvian people, at least not for another nine years. Unfortunately, the invasion became a good-news bad-news scenario: Latvia lost twenty percent of its population during the war.

After such a great European armed conflict, as an American, I wanted to believe that the lessons learned were enough to keep these atrocities from happening again. I was wrong. With Stalin's paranoia, that just wasn't the case. In 1949, Stalin again sent his trains and removed another large group of Latvians to his forced labor camps. Later, after Stalin's death, I wanted to hear, as an American whose family fought for the freedom of Europe, that those awful chapters in history closed. However, that too was not the case. The poor Latvian population suffered yet again. In 1959, the year the Soviet leader, Nikita Khrushchev, busied himself with a visit to Iowa cornfields and Disneyland, this same Nikita Khrushchev ordered yet another purge. The Soviets forced trainloads of Latvians from their surroundings and loved ones, sending them once more to the Siberian Gulags to be worked to death. In all, the Latvian people estimate that the Soviets killed seven hundred thousand Latvians in these mad purges.

According to our guide, this gruesome history with the Soviet Union provoked the Latvian drive for independence. Those remaining from older generations passed this information to their offspring by word of mouth.

"My grandmother told me all of this," the guide said. "She wanted me to know the truth about my grandfather and the suffering of the Latvian people."

Quite understandably, the Latvians wanted to remove the Soviets from their country while this window of opportunity existed. They were quite scared of history repeating itself, as the Latvians estimated that the Soviets liquidated forty percent of their entire population through these purges. They killed the Latvians to provide inexpensive labor for the Soviet empire and silence—the silence in which their political elite thrived.

Our guide went on to describe the Latvian population as being divided into two groups, the original Latvians and the Soviets. The Soviets exported their people to Latvia to work in the factories that the Soviet government built. Thus, the Soviets made up seventy percent of the population. The city of Riga represented the "west coast" of the Soviet empire. In terms of luxury, there lay the best of what the Soviets could offer their people. The Soviets took advantage of this by buying up everything they could and sending it back to relatives living in other regions of the U.S.S.R. For example, all of their furniture went east, leaving nothing to buy in terms of furniture with the Soviet Ruble. For other goods, the story remained much the same. There was nothing for the Latvians themselves to purchase.

Part of the Latvian solution to this problem lay in Latvia having its own currency. From former days, they had gold to back their currency. In fact, our guide said that it was already printed and waiting for them in England. Having their own currency would make it impossible for the Soviets to shop in Latvia, economically driving them home.

As one might expect, racism dominated this little country. Facial features revealed who was from which part of the world and that made all the difference. The Russians, with their high cheekbones, were passionately singled out. They knew it. From the Latvian point of view, the Soviets killed forty percent of the population and replaced them with nearly double that amount of Soviets to work in state dictated factories built on their soil, which they constantly polluted. The heavy pollution was another major sore point for these people and all of it was blamed on Moscow.

We asked the question, "What will you do if the Soviets leave?"

Our guide looked around to see if anyone could overhear our conversation.

"It is a very closely held secret amongst the young people, but I shall tell you," she said in a very quiet voice. "We want to tear down all of the Soviet factories that pollute our country and are not needed to support Latvia. We are a seaport and we intend to remain a seaport."

Donna and I saw real fear in her eyes.

She went on to explain Latvian nationalism and it made sense to us. Her plea to us was, "Do not let America turn a cold shoulder to our plight."

At this point, she was begging.

I explained the recent turn of events from the American point of view, that a great fear of ours is the internal destruction of law and order in the Soviet Union.

"The Soviet army is very large, very powerful, and it is backed by an enormous nuclear arsenal, most of which is pointed directly at the United States. Our attention is now divided between this and helping the Eastern Europeans out of their poverty stricken mess."

I asked her to be patient with us. She understood all of this and, in my opinion, she had a very open mind.

All of this conversation occurred beneath the granite gaze of a Latvian poet's statue. Unfortunately, it also was in earshot of an unsympathetic German informant: one who seemed to wander aimlessly about, but not unnoticed by me. On our cruise, he always showed up at the most interesting times without much to say, while keeping a curiously low profile. Later on, I put two and two together.

After our bus tour of the countryside, our guide gave us a foot tour of Riga. It is a most beautiful city and we were genuinely grateful for this generous display of friendship. By chance, Donna and I spotted a Monopoly game in one of the stores. Although the game was in Russian, we knew it would serve as both a gift, and ironically, an introduction to capitalism. Our guide had never seen the game before. We generously tipped her at the ship, and as it turned out, it was just the second day that it was legal for the Latvian people to possess hard currency.

Once back on the *Azerbaydzhan*, between the Germans and the Russians, I felt like I was living amongst murderers and I only wanted off the ship. Obviously, that wasn't going to happen anytime soon. So Donna and I went to dinner and had yet another unusual political experience. While waiting in line, a senior officer approached us and poured out his heart, talking about how crazy his country's leaders had been.

"Only recently had the Soviet people learned of their haunting past," he said.

In his anguish, much of which I didn't buy, he stated that, "No city in the Soviet Union was beautiful. Clouded with the past, how could it be?"

The officer kept repeating the insanity of Stalin and the wrongdoing of the Soviets in Europe. I tried to get a word in edgewise, but he just played me off while keeping Donna's attention. This little speech, as I saw it, went on for about ten minutes while we stood in the dinner line, of all places. After that, our newfound friend never spoke another word to us.

After dinner, I couldn't help but associate the earlier televised Castro speech and come to my own conclusions. I thought about the officer's statements and sided with our guide; her genuine speaking presence and sincerity had a powerful influence over me. I returned to our room to retrieve paper and a pen, and then spent the better part of the evening in the ship's library writing down our entire experience that day to honor her request.

In so doing, I wrote this last chapter—foremost as a letter for the Latvian people and more. Our guide was the first person I ever met whose grandfather had been worked to death in the Soviet Gulag, and she asked us to tell her life stories at our parties, of all places, so that we in the west might remember them.

After writing my cruise letter to friends, I felt compelled to expand the insight from the limits of our tour guide's point of view. Throughout my travels, I observed vast differences in lifestyles. Many of these lifestyles are centered in culture, while governments impose others over the free will of their people. In any case, whether created by birth defect, malnutrition, war or disease, oppression, religion, corruption or natural disaster, the eyes of those so afflicted always ask me to share their life stories with the rest of the world, so that we "in the west" might remember them.

Thus this book has been an effort to pay off the other special debt I spoke of in the beginning. In closing, I sincerely hope that we "in the west" will remember them, all of them. As we live our lives in freedom and affluence, may we remember the less fortunate.

Epilogue

One of my critics told me in November of 2003 that my effort to tell this story needed a stronger ending—that in the end, she felt there would be more stories, or at least a more defined finale than I had chosen.

"I don't want to lecture the reader," I remember saying quickly, never one to be shy about putting in my two cents.

Over the following months, however, I became convinced of the truth in her observation. Therefore, I write this epilogue from her desire for a conclusion on the human condition. Admittedly, a long essay on the human condition and my juxtaposition to the circumstances I encountered would have been a lot less work than these stories. However, I know without capturing the vital human elements, an essay could be viewed as simply an assignment or an argument, a far cry from a saga with an epilogue.

Therefore, I begin my ending with the most universal observation I made from half a lifetime of professional travel, personal journeys and living for at least five years outside the boundaries of the United States. Let me get right to the point. The largest and most damaging problem facing mankind today is the discrimination against and the degradation of women. It is the same as it has been for millennia; only now, in far greater numbers and with a genuine list of catastrophic consequences. It is created entirely by the attitudes of both genders. So let there be no finger pointing.

In college, I dated a woman whose mother told her that a man's education was more important than her own, as he would always earn more money. Yet there was no mention of what she would be able, or unable to do without a husband. This young woman helped me with my decision to join the Navy and enter flight school. She did so without a grudge, even though this was a career that, in 1981, was scarcely available to women due to gender discrimination by the Government of the United States of America and its uniformed services. Sorry, by reason of exclusion, there was very little flight pay for females.

Back in the 80s, women were banned from becoming direct combatants and aviation certainly qualified as direct combat. However, with their greater manual dexterity and instinctive group processing, why were they ever looked upon as being incapable of becoming highly skilled and successful mission oriented aviators, especially when interfacing with computer guided fly-by-wire "electric jets?" Fully half of America's finest were not allowed, or severely restricted, from participating in my chosen profession; and both sexes of America accepted that as the norm.

Other countries, too, have gender-based glass ceilings incorporated in society, some being lower than others. In Saudi Arabia, the government won't allow women to so much as drive a car. Even worse, they are entirely dependent upon their husbands. If their husband takes them before a holy man and says "I divorce you" three times, they are then divorced and the woman is left with nothing but what she is wearing at the time of the divorce. Therefore, under their black burkas, women wear as much gold as they possibly can because gold is a form of insurance, insurance that may be converted to currency in time of need.

Additionally, there are a multitude of nations where half of mankind is not allowed to speak freely, to vote, or to use their God-given minds in the advancement of medicine or agriculture; unless it is to feed and clothe the children they bore. All while their oppressors withhold contraceptive devices readily available, but for attitudes enforced by society, politics and religion. Women there aren't even allowed to participate in solving the problems of the very people who oppress them. Obviously, this form of discrimination degrades the entire population of the country, as males eliminate half of the intelligence of their society by decree.

As politically incorrect as my next statement may be judged, I will put it in print. Even today, as it has been throughout the ages, entire religions, faiths and social fabrics stand in the way of women's access to positions of personal achievement, financial success, leadership and power. Faiths, including Buddhism, Christianity, Judaism and Islam, all have males in leading positions. Abraham, Isaac, Jacob, Moses, Jesus, Matthew, Mark, Luke, John and Paul—to name a few from my religious teachings, were the conveyors of God's work. Women were kept in lesser roles as they are in many aspects of religions today. For example, the Catholic Church does not allow women to become priests. Rather, women who admirably volunteer their entire life to the church are subjugated as nuns. Men, by sole reason of their gender, are placed in a system of upward mobility.

Damage from the discrimination against and the degradation of women goes beyond mere religious, national or ethnic borders. The natural consequence of our behavior became the human population explosion and its associated problems. We are now forced to strip-mine the earth of its natural resources, create pollution, spread disease and turn a blind eye to hunger. Are women allowed to address these problems, along with their discrimination and degradation, as being an issue with men? NO! They may address only institutions and societies, and only when heard by men. Therefore, the potential for their abilities to be utilized for the good of the human race is drastically reduced, if not eliminated, by the preconceived notions and prejudices of both genders against women. It is as universal as it is true—as it is evil. For that we are all less fortunate.

The End

Captain Schupbach caught in one of life's full circles as he stands in front of the very first aircraft he flew on June 30, 1981. This picture was taken completely by coincidence and without prior knowledge of its significance.

ABOUT THE AUTHOR

Photograph by Lea Williamson, copyright© 2005

Author Neal Schupbach

Born in Lincoln, Nebraska, Neal Schupbach graduated in December of 1980 from the University of Nebraska with a degree in Life Sciences. He enlisted in the United States Navy during February of the following year and earned his commission at the Aviation Officer Candidate School in Pensacola, Florida.

In June of 1981 Ensign Schupbach entered flight training and received the "Wings of Gold" in May of 1982. Schupbach flew antisubmarine missions in the P-3C Orion aircraft against the Soviet nuclear submarine threat during the height of the Cold War. These missions took him to eastern Africa, Diego Garcia, the Philippines, Japan and Alaska. He departed the Navy after serving in Key West, Florida. His civilian travels found him in the occupied city of Berlin, Germany, from 1987 through 1991 where he experienced the fall of the Berlin Wall coupled with the disintegration of Communist rule in Europe. Since that time he has flown jumbo jets throughout Asia, the Persian Gulf and Third World locations. *Flying the Canyons of the Sky: Navigations of an Aviator's Soul* is his first book. Captain Schupbach currently resides in Tampa, Florida.

Military Service...

...is essentially unselfish service. It implies personal hardship, discomfort, inconvenience, financial loss, broken health and many other forms of sacrifice even unto the giving of life itself. So America's soldiers, sailors, marines and nurses are most honored of all the people.

May their service to the Nation in its hour of greatest trial serve to elicit the esteem of all patriotic citizens, and may their brilliant acts of devotion to Country serve as an everlasting inspiration to all loyal citizens of the Republic to place national welfare above individual selfishness or personal gain.

Samuel R. McKelvie
Governor, State of Nebraska
May 3rd 1921

When remembering the less fortunate, please give generously to our disabled American veterans. Thank you.

On-line orders http://www.flyingthecanyons.com

Postal orders: **Neal Schupbach**
                P.O. Box 130284
                Tampa, FL 33681-0284

FAX: 888-837-9079

Telephone orders: Call Toll Free: 888-837-9079
Have your VISA, MasterCard, (others) ready.

Please send ____ copies of *Flying The Canyons Of The Sky: Navigations* of *an Aviator's Soul* by Neal Schupbach to:

Print Name: _____
Company Name: _____
Address: _____
Apt Number: _____ City: _____
State: _____ Zip: _____ Telephone: _____
Fax: _____ Email: _____

Autographed COLLECTORS EDITION! ADD $5.00 US Currency
Privacy Policy: We never share your information—period!

Book Price: $21.95 USA $28.95 Canada
Sales Tax: Florida Residents please add $1.54 per book.

Shipping

1 Copy-2/3 Day Priority Mail	$4.95
Additional Book -2/3 Day Priority Mail	$3.50
1 Copy Regular Mail	$3.95
1 Copy Canada/Global US Currency	$8.00
Additional Copy Canada/Global US Currency	$4.00

Payment: ❑ Check ❑ Money Order (Payable to Neal Schupbach)
Canadian orders must be accompanied by postal money order in U.S. Funds. Call for other shipping if desired. ❑ Credit Card: ❑ VISA, ❑ MasterCard, ❑ AMEX, ❑ Discover

Card number: _____
Name on card: _____
Exp. date: ____ / ____

RAVE REVIEWS

"While reading the adventures of my young friend from long ago, I was reminded that freedom demands responsibility, whether one is a Navy pilot, political leader or ordinary citizen. In his enthusiastic and outspoken memoir, Neal Schupbach conveys the impact that historical events and heartbreaking realities made on one aviator's life. I can say without hesitation that I am very proud of the compassionate and wise man he has become."

Bob Kerrey, President, The New School

"Neal Schupbach is a true Renaissance man who recaptures the compelling journey from his early life in Nebraska to the fast paced life as a Navy pilot during the Cold War, eventually flying people and cargo around the world. His story is of a hardscrabble boyhood and how his life turns decisively upon the advice of a Viet Nam hero (who later represented Nebraska in the U.S. Senate). He weaves together an insider's view of the military, with a dose of politics and humor. Neal gives you a much deeper appreciation for our service men and women—their dedication to our country and their leaders. This hard-hitting book demands everyone assess his or her own humanity. As citizens, we should reach out to help our fellow man instead of turning a blind eye. I could not put the book down after being moved by his thought provoking vantage point, exploring how other cultures respond to Americans, and how the world treats human beings with gender bias and other inequities. Hats off to Schupbach for such a superb book."

John L. Bohanan, Jr., Delegate,
Member of the Maryland House of Delegates

"*Flying the Canyons of the Sky* is a must read for all aviation aficionados and seekers of political truth. Neal Schupbach's memoir allows the reader to vicariously experience his near maddening stress and fatigue as he struggles to perfect his art and live his passion. Schupbach takes us through death defying training scenarios and flight maneuvers, revealing the tremendous motivation and focus that is required to do the job and stay alive. The reader follows Neal through his successes as they lead him to work and travel abroad. He interfaces with citizens from political hot beds and war torn nations and vows to tell their stories. The dismal fate of many women in foreign lands is an obvious contrast to the freedoms enjoyed by women in the U.S. American women reading this memoir will know of the second-class status of women around the globe. They will thankfully recall the dedication of our military pilots to insuring the freedoms of all Americans. The book pays a well-deserved tribute to the dedication and selfless deeds of the U.S. military pilots."

Gisele Riscile,
M.D.

"Neal Schupbach uses his world travel, both as a military and commercial pilot, to open our eyes to hunger, prejudice and immorality. In a world torn apart by religion, politics, and greed, Neal shows us how to put all of that aside, and focus on what's really important. He travels to places most of us can only dream of seeing and in the remote communities of the world speaks with the poorest of poor. What emerges is an understanding of how similar we all are. But he doesn't stop there; Schupbach offers his simple solution to help a troubled world whose large problems have one thing in common. It's an uplifting story that shows there is hope for the human race, from someone who's *been there*. Far from the media's spotlight, Neal comes to a conclusion, an epiphany really, as to how to bring the human race closer together.

Paul Csibrik, B-767 Captain

"Beyond building memories, *Flying the Canyons of the Sky* constructs a window on a world very different from the one in which author Neal Schupbach grew up. Hints of that other world and the urge to know more haunted him even as a child, when he met the physically and mentally challenged children his mother taught, or accompanied her as she delivered meals to elderly shut-ins. A career as a naval aviator—and later as a commercial pilot— quenched his wanderlust as he crisscrossed the globe from Japan to Alaska, the East Germany to Micronesia, and Dubai to Dakar. Time and time again, he felt compelled to reassess the haves and have-nots of the world, questioning his own motives in the process. Riveting descriptions of life in Berlin before and after the collapse of the Wall, the terror and hardships endured by East Africans, the desperate lives of freedom-starved Eastern Europeans, and the abject poverty of Micronesians make this book much more than a travel memoir. It is a must read for any Westerner who ponders the human condition."

Andrea Cranford
Associate Executive Director for Communications
Editor, Nebraska Magazine
Nebraska Alumni Association

"This is a fine, well written, highly detailed book about the Navy's system of acquisition, training and deployment of aviation worldwide and air travel around the globe. The descriptions of life in other parts of the world are extensive and touching. For one who has not seen or experienced conditions as the author describes, this novel provides an outstanding look of life at the other extremes."

Jack A. Albright
Major General, U.S. Army (Ret)

"Flying the Canyons of the Sky is a candid, honest account of an aviator's career. Neal Schupbach takes the reader from his early years of wonder and a desire to fly, to the pinnacle of aviation as a captain for a world class airline, flying heavy equipment to the far reaches of the globe. His vivid memories as a Naval Aviator thrust the reader into the cockpit, experiencing firsthand the hazards of aviation, documenting how incredibly often career aviators find themselves in harms way. Additionally, readers enjoy many eyewitness accounts of world events, including Berlin, Germany before and after the fall of the Wall. Captain Schupbach's viewpoints and unique insights are exceptional, leaving the reader with many thoughts to ponder."

Carl Hendershot, MD80 Captain

"Neal Schupbach presents a provocative and often disturbing view of the realities of war, global power and international intrigue. The reader is compelled to follow Neal's journey around the world for a fascinating look at the places, events and people that have shaped not only his outlook on life, but also the complex world in which we live. Looking behind the scenes at his challenging life as a pilot adds adventure in every chapter. It is a great book and an unforgettable story."

Ed Rood
Philanthropist, Tampa, FL